Perpetration and Complicity under Nazism and Beyond

Perpetration and Complicity under Nazism and Beyond

Compromised Identities?

Edited by
Stephanie Bird, Mary Fulbrook, Stefanie Rauch and
Bastiaan Willems

BLOOMSBURY ACADEMIC
LONDON • NEW YORK • OXFORD • NEW DELHI • SYDNEY

BLOOMSBURY ACADEMIC
Bloomsbury Publishing Plc
50 Bedford Square, London, WC1B 3DP, UK
1385 Broadway, New York, NY 10018, USA
29 Earlsfort Terrace, Dublin 2, Ireland

BLOOMSBURY, BLOOMSBURY ACADEMIC and the Diana logo are trademarks of
Bloomsbury Publishing Plc

First published in Great Britain 2023
Paperback edition published in 2025

Copyright © Mary Fulbrook, Stephanie Bird, Stefanie Rauch and Bastiaan Willems, 2023

Mary Fulbrook, Stephanie Bird, Stefanie Rauch and Bastiaan Willems have asserted their right under the Copyright, Designs and Patents Act, 1988, to be identified as Editor of this work.

Cover image: Image owned by author Bastiaan Willems

Bloomsbury Publishing Plc does not have any control over, or responsibility for, any third-party websites referred to or in this book. All internet addresses given in this book were correct at the time of going to press. The author and publisher regret any inconvenience caused if addresses have changed or sites have ceased to exist, but can accept no responsibility for any such changes.

Every effort has been made to trace the copyright holders and obtain permission to reproduce the copyright material. Please do get in touch with any enquiries or any information relating to such material or the rights holder. We would be pleased to rectify any omissions in subsequent editions of this publication should they be drawn to our attention.

A catalogue record for this book is available from the British Library.

Library of Congress Cataloging-in-Publication Data

Names: Bird, Stephanie, editor. | Fulbrook, Mary, 1951- editor. | Willems, Bastiaan, editor. | Rauch, Stefanie (Historian), editor.
Title: Perpetration and complicity under Nazism and beyond : compromised identities? / edited by Mary Fulbrook, Stephanie Bird, Stephanie Rauch and Bastiaan Willems.
Other titles: Compromised identities?
Description: London; New York: Bloomsbury Academic, 2023. | Includes bibliographical references and index. | Summary: "An examination of perpetration and complicity under National Socialism and beyond which covers self-understandings, representations and narratives of involvement in collective violence both at the time and later"– Provided by publisher.
Identifiers: LCCN 2023015584 | ISBN 9781350327771 (hb) | ISBN 9781350327818 (pb) | ISBN 9781350327795 (ebook) | ISBN 9781350327788 (epdf)
Subjects: LCSH: Holocaust, Jewish (1939-1945)–Moral and ethical aspects. | National socialism. | World War, 1939-1945–Atrocities–Germany. | World War, 1939-1945–Collaborationists. | World War, 1939-1945–Occupied territories– Social conditions. | Responsibility. | Agent (Philosophy)
Classification: LCC D804.7.M67 P47 2023 | DDC 943.086–dc23/eng/20230419
LC record available at https://lccn.loc.gov/2023015584.

ISBN: HB: 978-1-3503-2777-1
PB: 978-1-3503-2781-8
ePDF: 978-1-3503-2778-8
eBook: 978-1-3503-2779-5

Typeset by Deanta Global Publishing Services, Chennai, India

To find out more about our authors and books visit www.bloomsbury.com and sign up for our newsletters.

Contents

List of Contributors	vii
Acknowledgements	xii

1. Introduction: 'Compromised Identities?' *Stephanie Bird, Mary Fulbrook, Stefanie Rauch and Bastiaan Willems* — 1

Part I Theorizing ambiguity, compromise and complexity

2. 'Compromised identities?', ageing perpetrators and compromising forgiveness *Stephanie Bird* — 21
3. Conformity, compliance and complicity: 'Ordinary people' and the Holocaust *Mary Fulbrook* — 35
4. Complicities, re-presented: Literary portrayals in totalitarianism and neoliberalism *Juliane Prade-Weiss* — 52
5. In search of the bystander: Some reflections on the 'social turn' in Holocaust studies and its ramifications *Christina Morina* — 67

Part II Confrontations with violence

6. Studying East European perpetrators: The case of Belarus *Leonid Rein* — 85
7. Compromising roles: German actresses in German-occupied Minsk *Anne-Lise Bobeldijk* — 99
8. Gender and transgressive violence in post-war accounts *Stefanie Rauch* — 113
9. Israeli national narratives, complicity and activism: Noam Chayut's *The Girl Who Stole My Holocaust* and Breaking the Silence *Nina Fischer* — 129

Part III Law, complicity and perpetration

10. The constitutive role of Nazi law: Constructing complicity in the Third Reich *Simon Lavis* — 145
11. Public execution in your community: The summary courts of 1945 Germany *Bastiaan Willems* — 159
12. Excess and normality: West German and Austrian media and Nazi crimes trials from the 1950s to the 1980s *Christoph Thonfeld* — 173

13 Pinochet's accomplices: Perpetration, civilian complicity and individual versus institutional culpability in domestic atrocity crime accountability *Francisco Bustos, Cath Collins and Francisco Ugás* 187

Part IV Framing the past

14 Perpetrator memory and the fascist exile in Argentina: A case study *Zoltán Kékesi* 205
15 Complicity versus cooperation: Zygmunt Bauman's *Modernity and the Holocaust* and Claude Lanzmann's *Shoah* and its outtakes *Sue Vice* 219
16 Challenging the museum visitor? Complicity and perpetration during and beyond the Second World War in contemporary museum exhibitions *Stephan Jaeger* 235
17 *Compromised identities? Reflections on perpetration and complicity under Nazi rule*: An exhibition *Stephanie Bird, Mary Fulbrook, Stefanie Rauch and Bastiaan Willems* 250
18 Conclusion *Stephanie Bird, Mary Fulbrook, Stefanie Rauch and Bastiaan Willems* 270

Index 277

Contributors

Stephanie Bird is Professor of German Studies at University College London. She has published on topics ranging from the interaction of fact and fiction in the biographical novel, the relationship of female and national identity and the representation and ethics of shame. In her most recent book, *Comedy and Trauma in Germany and Austria after 1945: The Inner Side of Mourning*, she analyses how a comic aesthetic interrogates the expectations and ethics of representing suffering and trauma. In it, she offers a critique of dominant paradigms, such as that of trauma and of victim identity. Her recent publications include 'Perpetrators in Literature' (2019) and 'Imre Kertész: Complicity and Comedy' (2022). She was Co-I on the AHRC-sponsored collaborative research project on 'Compromised Identities? Reflections on Perpetration and Identity under Nazism' and is currently working on a monograph on representations of perpetration and complicity under National Socialism in novels.

Anne-Lise Bobeldijk is a researcher and lecturer at Wageningen University and Research and the NIOD Institute for War, Holocaust and Genocide Studies. She specializes in the history and memory of the Holocaust and the Second World War in the (former) Soviet Union. Currently she is part of the NWA research project 'Heritages of Hunger', in which she researches the use of the memory of hunger in the Holodomor famine and the Leningrad Blockade. In 2022, Anne-Lise will defend her PhD thesis at the University of Amsterdam on the history and memory the German forced labour camp Maly Trostenets and mass grave Blagovshchina nearby Minsk, Belarus.

Francisco Bustos is Observatorio research associate and human rights lawyer at the firm Caucoto Associates, where he is an active litigator, highly experienced in accountability case claim-making in Chile and before the Inter-American Court. He holds a masters' in human rights from the Universidad Diego Portales.

Cath Collins is Professor of Transitional Justice, Ulster University, Northern Ireland and Director of the Transitional Justice Observatory, Universidad Diego Portales, Chile's leading academic centre on truth, justice and reparations for dictatorship-era crimes. Her relevant publications include the paper 'Transitional Justice from Within: Police, Forensic and Legal Actors Searching for Chile's Disappeared', *Journal of Human Rights Practice*, 2019 and the co-edited volume *Transitional Justice in Latin America* (2016, Routledge).

Nina Fischer works at the 'Religious Positioning' research hub at Goethe-University Frankfurt. Previously, she taught at the University of Edinburgh and ran the 'History & Memory' group at the University of Konstanz. She has held fellowships at IASH

Edinburgh, the Australian National University and the Hebrew University of Jerusalem. Nina is a cultural studies scholar whose research areas include Memory, Holocaust as well as Peace & Conflict Studies, focusing on Israel/Palestine. She is the author of *Memory Work: The Second Generation* (Palgrave, 2015), a study of Holocaust writing by children of survivors. Her most recent publications include: 'Entangled Suffering and Empathy: The Holocaust, the Nakba, and the Israeli-Palestinian Conflict in Susan Abulhawa's *Mornings in Jenin*' (*Memory Studies*, 2020) and 'Palestinian Non-Violent Resistance and the Apartheid Analogy: Framing Israeli Policy in the 1960s and 1970s' (*Interventions: International Journal of Postcolonial Studies*, 2020).

Mary Fulbrook, FBA, is Professor of German History at UCL and former Executive Dean of the UCL Faculty of Social and Historical Sciences; she also serves on a number of international academic advisory boards, including on Holocaust research and remembrance. A graduate of Cambridge and Harvard, she was founding Joint Editor of *German History*, and is the author or editor of some twenty-five books, including *Reckonings: Legacies of Nazi Persecution and the Quest for Justice* (OUP 2018), which won the 2019 Wolfson Prize, and the Fraenkel Prize-winning *A Small Town Near Auschwitz: Ordinary Nazis and the Holocaust* (OUP, 2012). Her previous books include *Dissonant Lives: Generations and Violence Through the German Dictatorships* (OUP, 2011) and studies of the GDR, questions of national identity after the Holocaust and theoretical issues in history. She directed the AHRC-sponsored collaborative research project on 'Compromised Identities? Reflections on Perpetration and Identity under Nazism'. Her most recent research has focused on *Bystander Society in Nazi Germany: Conformity, Complicity and the Holocaust* (OUP, 2023).

Stephan Jaeger is Professor of German Studies and Head of the Department of German and Slavic Studies at the University of Manitoba (Winnipeg, Canada). He researches on contemporary narratives, representations and memory of war and genocide in German and European museums, literature, film and historiography. He has published three monographs, most recently *The Second World War in the Twenty-First-Century Museum: From Memory, Narrative, and Experience to Experientiality* (De Gruyter, 2020) and nine co-edited books, most recently *Views of Violence: Representing the Second World War in German and European Museums and Memorials* (Berghahn 2019 with Jörg Echternkamp). He is the co-editor of the newly inaugurated book series *Museums and Narrative* (De Gruyter with Kerstin Barndt). Current research projects discuss immersion, empathy and experientiality in Holocaust and war exhibitions, with a particular focus on perpetration/collaboration and on the role of art in historical museums.

Zoltán Kékesi is a cultural historian with an interest in memory studies and a focus on Central and Eastern Europe. He has held an Alexander von Humboldt Senior Research Fellow at the Center for Research on Antisemitism, TU, Berlin, and is a Research Fellow at the UCL Institute of Advanced Studies. He holds masters' degrees in Hungarian and German literature and a PhD degree in comparative literature from ELTE, Budapest. He worked as a research fellow at the Center for Jewish History (NYC), the United States

Holocaust Memorial Museum (Washington, DC), the Yad Vashem International Institute for Holocaust Research (Jerusalem), the Leibniz Institute for the History and Culture of Eastern Europe (Leipzig) and the Institute for Advanced Study at CEU (Budapest). From 2009 to 2018 he was assistant professor at the Department for Art Theory and Curatorial Studies, University of Fine Arts, Budapest. He is the author of the book *Agents of Liberation: Holocaust Memory in Contemporary Art and Documentary Film* (2015).

Simon Lavis is Senior Lecturer in Law at The Open University. He completed his PhD thesis on the jurisprudential and historiographical representation of Nazi law at the University of Nottingham in 2015. His research focuses on the nexus between law, history and theory in relation to the Third Reich, including the historical and theoretical nature of Nazi law and its representation in academic discourse. His publications include 'Nazi Law as Non-law in Academic Discourse' in Stephen Skinner (ed.), *Ideology and Criminal Law: Fascist, National Socialist and Authoritarian Regimes* (Hart, 2019), and he is co-editor of *States of Exceptions: Law, Theory, History Recent* (Routledge, 2020). He is a qualified solicitor in England and Wales (currently non-practising).

Christina Morina is Professor of Contemporary History at the University of Bielefeld. Her research focuses on major themes in nineteenth- and twentieth-century German and European history, especially the history of Nazi Germany, political and memory cultures in Germany since 1945 and the history of Marxism. She received her PhD from the University of Maryland in 2007. Her dissertation was published as *Legacies of Stalingrad: Remembering the Eastern Front War in Germany since 1945* (Cambridge University Press 2011, paperback 2013). In 2017, she published her second book, *Die Erfindung des Marxismus. Wie eine Idee die Welt eroberte* (Siedler). She is co-editor of *Probing the Limits of Categorization. The Bystander in Holocaust History* (Berghahn, 2018, with Krijn Thijs, paperback 2020), co-author of *Zur rechten Zeit. Wider die Rückkehr das Nationalismus* (Ullstein, 2019, with N. Frei, F. Maubach, M. Tändler) and co-editor of *Das 20. Jahrhundert erzählen. Zeiterfahrung und Zeitforschung im geteilten Deutschland* (Wallstein, 2016, with Franka Maubach).

Juliane Prade-Weiss is Professor of Comparative Literature at the Ludwig-Maximilians-Universität in Munich. From 2007 to 2019 she was Assistant Professor of Comparative Literature at Goethe-University Frankfurt, where she earned her doctorate. During 2017–19 she was a DFG research fellow at Yale University to complete her habilitation, published as *Language of Ruin and Consumption: On Lamenting and Complaining* (Bloomsbury, 2020). From 2019 to 2020 she was an EU Marie-Curie fellow at Vienna University working on a project titled 'Complicity: A Crisis of Participation in Testimonies of Totalitarianism in Contemporary German-language Literatures'. She is currently working on the cultural memory and transgenerational transmission of discourses justifying and denying acts of mass violence in Central and Eastern Europe.

Stefanie Rauch is Head of Collections at the Wiener Holocaust Library and Honorary Research Fellow at the UCL Institute of Advanced Studies, where she was previously a Research Associate. Her research which was funded by the AHRC and the Pears Foundation focuses on the impact of the Second World War, National Socialism and the Holocaust on individual biographies, society and culture. Her recent publications include *Rethinking Holocaust Film Reception: A British Case Study* (Lexington Books/ Rowman & Littlefield, 2021) and 'Good Bets, Bad Bets, and Dark Horses: Allied Intelligence Officers' Encounters with German Civilians, 1944-45' (in *Central European History* 53:1, 2020), winner of the Society for Military History Vandervort Prize 2021.

Leonid Rein is a researcher at International Institute for Holocaust Research, Yad Vashem. He received his PhD degree from Haifa University (Israel). His most recent publications are: *The Kings and the Pawns: Collaboration in Byelorussia during World War II* (New York 2011), an article 'Entre mépris et génocide: soldats allemands et Juifs d'Europe de l'Est pendant les deux guerres mondiales' in a collection titled *En territoir ennemi 1914-1949: Expériences d'occupation, transfers, héritages*, edited by James Connoly, Emmanuel Debuyne, Élise Julien and Matthias Meiralaen (Villeneuve d'Ascq, 2018); chapters on 'Belarusian Auxiliary Police' and (co-authored with Oleg Romanko) 'The Belarusian Home Guard' in *The Waffen-SS: A European History*, edited by Jochen Böhler and Robert Gerwarth (Oxford, 2017); a chapter on 'The Radicalization of Anti-Jewish Policies in Nazi-Occupied Belarus', in *Nazi Policy on the Eastern Front, 1941: Total War, Genocide & Radicalization*, edited by Alex J. Kay, Jeff Rutherford and David Stahel (Rochester NY 2012).

Christoph Thonfeld is a historian and has done research and/or taught at Bremen University, Hagen University and Trier University (all in Germany), at Cheng Chi University and National Taiwan Normal University (both in Taiwan/ROC) and at University College London (UK). Currently, he is head of the research department at Dachau Concentration Camp memorial site in Germany. His main areas of interest are twentieth-century German and European history, especially the Nazi era and its aftermath (Nazi crime trials and pertinent media coverage, remembrance and commemoration), Oral History and Memory Studies. His key publications are: *Normalisierung des Außergewöhnlichen. Der Wandel der Erinnerungskultur des Zweiten Weltkriegs und des Holocaust in Deutschland 1990-2010* (Taipei 2015); *Rehabilitierte Erinnerungen? Individuelle Erfahrungsverarbeitungen und kollektive Repräsentationen von NS-Zwangsarbeit im internationalen Vergleich* (Essen 2014) and *Sozialkontrolle und Eigensinn. Denunziation am Beispiel Thüringens 1933-1949* (Cologne/ Weimar/ Vienna 2003).

Francisco Ugás is Observatorio research associate and human rights lawyer at the firm Caucoto Associates, where he is an active litigator, highly experienced in accountability case claim-making in Chile and before the Inter-American Court. He holds a double masters in law from Spain's Universidad Carlos III, and formerly headed Chile's principal state agency concerned with criminal prosecution and administrative and symbolic reparations for dictatorship-era human rights violations.

Sue Vice is Professor of English Literature at the University of Sheffield, where she teaches and writes on contemporary literature, film and Holocaust Studies. Her recent publications include the co-edited volume *Representing Perpetrators in Holocaust Literature and Film*, with Jenni Adams (2013), *Textual Deceptions: False Memoirs and Literary Hoaxes in the Contemporary Era* (2014), *Barry Hines:'Kes', 'Threads' and Beyond*, with David Forrest (2017) and *Claude Lanzmann's 'Shoah' Outtakes: Holocaust Rescue and Resistance* (2021).

Bastiaan Willems is Lecturer in the History of War in 20th Century Europe at Lancaster University. Previously, he was a Research Fellow at the UCL Institute of Advanced Studies and Leverhulme Abroad Postdoctoral Fellow at the Ludwig-Maximilians-Universität in Munich. His research examines violence and forced migration during the Third Reich and its immediate aftermath. He currently analyses the impact of German intra-ethnic violence on the German late-war society and on policies and discourse in the first years of the Federal Republic of Germany. He recently published *Violence in Defeat: The Wehrmacht on German Soil, 1944-145* (Cambridge University Press: 2021).

Acknowledgements

This book reflects in part discussions arising from an interdisciplinary research project based at UCL and generously funded by the UK Arts and Humanities Research Council on 'Compromised Identities? Reflections on Perpetration and Complicity under Nazism', on which the four editors of this volume collaborated. Christoph Thonfeld was also a central and valuable member of the AHRC research team before taking up his current position at Dachau Concentration Camp Memorial Site. We are very grateful to the AHRC for its funding for this project, and to UCL and in particular the Institute of Advanced Studies for hosting the project and related events. We would also like to thank the Pears Foundation for its generous support of our work, which allowed us to make the project exhibition into the multimedia online exhibition it has become. We would like here to express posthumous appreciation for filmmaker Luke Holland, for his dedicated pursuit of interviews with those who had been closely involved in or witnesses to the Holocaust. Special thanks are owed to Graham Riach for his advice in making the exhibition films, his willingness to pick up his camera and travel across Europe and for making the filming process so rewarding, and to Dan Edmonds for his indefatigable efforts to liaise with partners and bring our project to wider audiences, ensuring maximum impact even under Covid conditions. The academic research project was supported throughout by our advisory committee, who offered critical and constructive feedback from the outset: Kjell Anderson, Susanne Knittel, Andy Pearce, Paul Salmons, Dorothee Wierling and Michael Wildt. Finally, we would like to express our thanks to Catherine Stokes of the IAS for so ably and warmly facilitating our work, and to the many colleagues and students who participated in stimulating discussions relating to perpetration and complicity.

Stephanie Bird
Mary Fulbrook
Stefanie Rauch
Bastiaan Willems

August 2022.

1

Introduction

'Compromised Identities?'

Stephanie Bird, Mary Fulbrook, Stefanie Rauch and Bastiaan Willems

What is often called a 'difficult past' can be approached in many different ways, both individually and collectively, and in different contexts over time. Often, the focus is on the violence itself, or on later representations; here, however, we want to explore some of the entangled inner connections through the lens of what we have, with a question mark, termed 'compromised identities'. This notion is intended to bring together present and past in ways that sensitize us to the continuing significance of self-understandings, justifications and emotions, as well as attributions by others, within changing historical circumstances; and it explicitly thematizes, too, the roles of later scholars and audiences (in the broadest sense), by drawing attention also to modes of representation and response by others, including ourselves. This concept invites reflection on who is evaluating what or whom, and in what contexts over time.

Questions around agency, identity and a sense of responsibility for violence lie at the heart of this inquiry. The concepts of perpetration and complicity surface in a variety of ways – if only implicitly – in the chapters that follow, and need to be addressed directly at the outset.

Questions of perpetration, complicity and 'compromised identities'

We readily think of 'perpetrators' as those directly involved in physical violence: giving the orders, pulling the trigger, killing innocent victims. But under Nazi rule, millions more became involved in processes of discrimination and persecution. How could so many become complicit in systemic violence, or more actively involved in perpetration – and how did they justify their behaviours and continue to think of themselves as 'good people', at the time or later? How can we best analyse their roles and self-representations, as well as the ways in which others have portrayed them? And what can we learn from incidents of collective violence in other contexts?

Historical research on Nazi crimes initially tended to concentrate on the active ends of the spectrum: high-level policy makers; front-line killers in the concentration camps, extermination squads, SS units and police battalions. Since the later twentieth century, a wider range of professionals involved in planning, initiating and implementing Nazi policies, alongside regional and local bureaucrats and functionaries, as well as grass roots interactions, have increasingly come under the spotlight.[1] Research has expanded to focus on the significance of context rather than individual biography or ideology, with a widespread emphasis on the 'ordinariness' of people involved; there have also been attempts to set these studies in a wider comparative context.[2] The complex histories of societies under German occupation have also developed, exploring for example the complicity of victimized Poles who nevertheless assisted the Nazis in 'hunting' Jews, or ambivalent collaboration in Vichy France.[3] Both in Holocaust historiography and in comparative genocide studies, the focus is increasingly on social processes rather than on individuals assumed to have a stable identity as 'perpetrators'.[4]

Discussions about the meaning and scope of complicity have been largely held in response to authoritarian regimes where human rights violations, systematic violence and genocide are evident. The challenge of how to understand complicity has at its core the awareness that individual agency cannot be separated from the social processes, power structures and legal and other discourses that constitute that individual as a subject. In response to the Holocaust, Karl Jaspers developed four notions of guilt, demonstrating both the inseparability of complicity from the notion of guilt and the need to name wider forms of culpability: criminal guilt, political guilt, moral guilt and metaphysical guilt.[5] Hannah Arendt recognized the danger that metaphysical guilt in particular might result in guilt being de-politicized, but she too insisted on the responsibility that people have by virtue of being social beings: 'This vicarious responsibility for things we have not done, this taking upon ourselves the consequences for things we are entirely innocent of, is the price we pay for the fact that we live our lives not by ourselves but among our fellow men'.[6] The philosophical impetus to account for 'the manifold forms of human community',[7] is also at the heart of Mark Sanders's exploration of complicity in relation to South African apartheid. Pointing to the Latin etymology of complicity, with its meanings of folding and intertwining, Sanders argues that humans are 'folded-together' with others as human beings, a recognition of complicity with others that enables the individual 'to assume responsibility for what is done in one's name'.[8] Complicity is therefore not in opposition to responsibility but its precondition: '[i]n the absence of an *acknowledgment* of complicity in a wider sense of foldedness with the other, whether welcomed or not, there would have been no opposition to apartheid'. Nevertheless, this existential 'project of human folded-together-ness' can be undermined by the specific complicity of holding a particular loyalty, of belonging to a particular party or cause, when 'the actors in question ultimately accept responsibility only in front of their own'. As a result, 'any profession of responsibility – be it in the name of justice, resistance to injustice, or merely in the cause of solidarity – entertains the possibility of *doing* injustice'.[9]

These vital and thought-provoking explorations of complicity point further to the ethical complications signalled by the term. Yet as Stephen Clingman states, if we accept Jacques Derrida's assertion that '[e]ven if all forms of complicity are not equivalent, they are *irreducible*', then to the extent that they are irreducible, they are also equivalent: 'All roads lead to complicity, in such a version, and what this means is a certain reconciliation with (if not short-cut to) the irreducible, and the preclusion of any history in an analytical or sequential sense'.[10] Clingman's observation that this may become a problem is worth heeding, for the concern with complicity has increasingly shifted into emphasizing the structural and universal. Paraphrasing Arendt's criticism of collective guilt, narratives of dictatorship in which if all are complicit, no-one is complicit, have assumed new application in relation to neoliberal networks of racialized capitalism, data capture and climate change. The possibility of agency, understood ideally as individual liability of a free and rational actor, has been further eroded by the heightened awareness that merely by existing we contribute to and maintain structures of historical and contemporary harm. In Michael Rothberg's attempt to further refine the complex terrain of contemporary responsibility for historical harm and complicity in structures that are rooted in and perpetuate those harms, the 'implicated subject' is ascribed almost ontological status. Not only do 'structures of power produce implicated subjects as a necessary effect', but 'most subjects find themselves enmeshed in histories and structures of violence they may not realize they inhabit and help prop up'.[11] Yet, in response to Rothberg's emphasis on 'the "impurities" that characterize all identities',[12] Juliane Prade-Weiss advocates embracing these impurities, as well as the ambiguity of conceptual traditions, as 'the field *in* which to work rather than a contaminated starting ground', and as a constructive starting point for thinking further about complicity, 'functioning participation and relationality'.[13]

'Compromised identities?' Why the question mark?

The impurity of all identities, yet the desire to be or become pure, is at the core of the question that this volume asks about compromised identities. The notion of 'compromised identities' challenges us to think about contentious questions relating to empathy and complicity. The volume does not seek to offer a novel definition of complicity but rather to move towards a more dynamic, relational and situational understanding of complicity over time and depending on place, identity and belonging. Inevitably, this involves scrutinizing the categories of perpetrator, bystander and victim, groupings that are associated with moral evaluations as well as judgements of responsibility and guilt. Using 'compromised identities?' as a heuristic device facilitates the work of critical enquiry into complicity by stepping back from categories that are often *a priori* laden with judgement. Indeed, this heuristic framework is interesting at many levels. We seek to understand how contemporaries viewed their behaviours and sought to live with a compromised past under later, very different circumstances. We also seek to understand how these behaviours are perceived as compromised (or not) in cultural representations, in the courts and among historians and cultural critics. It is an old adage that to explain is not to excuse, and to understand is not to exculpate. But understanding is also not intrinsically an a-moral or exculpatory position. Indeed, the extent to which the focus of analysis affects judgements of responsibility is one of the layers of 'compromised identity' that we explore, namely, the critic's position in relation to his or her subject. In our view, laying bare strategies of self-exculpation is in itself a contribution to fostering heightened moral sensitivity and intelligent, informed awareness among those addressing issues of collective violence, both past and present. 'Compromised identities' offers a vantage point for developing critical, interdisciplinary perspectives on the Nazi period, its representation and the moral judgements imposed on its interpretation in a later present. For this reason, we emphasize the question mark in 'Compromised Identities?'

Compromise has positive connotations in many situations and is generally seen as necessary to the successful completion of any negotiation, be it political, institutional or personal. Conversely, compromising in relation to moral values is often judged to be a sign of weakness, a character flaw that reflects on the identity of the individual as whole. The evaluation of compromise is thus dependent on context and the norms through which the context is understood. These norms are contingent and are socially produced through narratives that change over time. Individuals and societies understand themselves and create identities through the narratives they tell, narratives that evolve under changing circumstances and through social interaction. As Ernesto Verdeja succinctly argues, identity is shaped through group membership, with individuals both constituted and constrained by their context.[14] An 'uncompromised identity' could thus be understood as one in which there is full alignment between the individual's identity and the social narrative or belief system within which they are operating, as well as later perceptions of this. This alignment can be maintained over time, either because there is no challenge to the narratives, or because the individual adapts to the shifting hegemonic narrative. Most obviously, values of decency, honesty, 'the good' in whatever form (*Volksgemeinschaft*, father, mother, citizen, worker), may continue to be espoused, but with variations and qualifications: for example, the content of the work may be altered but changes can still be encapsulated in continuing notions such as 'German quality work'.[15] Such adaptations need not take the form of active support or radical ideological commitment; people may accept what organizational sociologists term an expanded 'zone of indifference', referring to the range of tasks that exist within organizations and to which members cannot say no without challenging their membership.[16] An individual who is by law suddenly deemed to be 'Aryan' and who subsequently experiences material improvement does not have to change much in their own eyes, in what Welzer describes as the 'normative power of fact'.[17]

However, even while people are to some degree constituted by changing norms, they are not necessarily at their mercy. People's actions or inaction contribute to the process of attitudes and values becoming consolidated as norms, even before they become internalized. Stefan Kühl points to the importance of a 'fictional' antisemitic consensus under Nazism, an un-tested assumption that others agreed with antisemitism and which therefore put the onus on those who protested against antisemitism to have to justify themselves.[18] This and any fictional consensus is reinforced by silence and further strengthened through 'false enforcement': to demonstrate their sincerity, an individual is required to publicly demonstrate conformity to a norm that privately they do not agree with, such that the norm and its moral underpinnings prevail.[19] It is the reference to norms and values that enables individuals to feel uncompromised in their view of themselves as good people. Some members of the newly defined

Volksgemeinschaft experienced dictatorship as enhancing their sense of personal freedom or empowerment; this was variously enabled or condoned by the state and by widespread real or perceived public support. Bodies that might have questioned such consensus, such as the judiciary, universities and churches, confirmed the moral privileging of the *Volksgemeinschaft*, knowing full well 'that the Nazi state was hard-edged and brutal'.[20] There were also large swathes of the population who could later argue that their interaction with the community the Nazis were trying to create had been extremely limited. Especially in rural areas, where many people still did not have a radio, did not visit cinemas and where the population density was too limited to warrant a Party office, the regime struggled to get its message across. People in these areas did not have much cause to subscribe to the Nazi vision of their own accord, and subsequently had little reason to feel compromised (unless, of course, they were caught up more directly in Nazi violence in some way, particularly during the war).[21] That is not to say, however, that they opposed the *Volksgemeinschaft* in any meaningful way. Many communities were centred around traditional values, and the Nazi promise to uphold these values ensured that they had little reason to question the policies the regime implemented. Even less so when considering the often cyclical reasoning applied by those who witness violence, theorized as 'just world hypothesis' by behavioural scientists Melvin J. Lerner and Carolyn H. Simmons: in order to explain people's inaction in the face of brutal acts in front of them, many choose to assert that 'people get what they deserve'[22] rather than question the status quo – an idea that is particularly pervasive in societies that adhere to the idea of 'providence', as was the case with Nazi Germany.[23]

It is easy to see how in a context which combines a discourse of ethical continuity with the promise and moral affirmation of personal fulfilment through community, individuals have plenty of scope for feeling that their sense of self has not been compromised; a perception that is reinforced if questioning is discouraged by the threat of punishment. Furthermore, it is simplistic to think only of 'a' compromised identity, since individuals have multiple points of reference for their identity, such as religion, class, or region. Their sense of identity, and the value systems attached, can also change according to circumstance. As Kjell Anderson argues, 'the decision to perpetrate, like all decisions, is made not in terms of absolute values, but rather according to the ranking of values'.[24] Thus not only does continuity in the method of decision-making lend itself to a sense of uncompromised identity, but the ranking of values means that a person's course of action need not rely on jettisoning certain core values at the expense of others. On the contrary, values are relegated in the light of other considerations that are esteemed in many non-dictatorial contexts, such as the welfare of one's own family, doing a good job or obeying the law. Indeed, in post-war West Germany, individuals and institutions involved in perpetration had their view of themselves condoned through the values promoted by the Cold War. The myth of the 'clean' Wehrmacht was accepted by the American military not least because of a shared attitude towards the threat of the Bolshevik, and Slavic, enemy.[25] Similarly, the Allies' definition of Austria as the first victim of the Nazis was eagerly propagated by Austria's political elites, including on the left of the political spectrum. A person's sense of who they are can therefore be perfectly coherent and plausibly rationalized to themselves and others. Furthermore, such rationalization is aided by the fact that people can move in and out of complicity or perpetration and they can be perpetrators in one situation and victims in another, or even both concurrently. This allows for a considerable range of narrative possibilities for sustaining and indeed believing in oneself as a good person.

Moreover, even when confronted with evidence that challenges or counters someone's preconceived notions (such as literature examining the criminality of the Nazi regime, and the different roles ordinary Germans played in it) beliefs are not that easy to dislodge. This behaviour, the incapability and unwillingness to alter one's world view in the face of new information, is known as 'belief perseverance'. When there is a risk of cognitive dissonance, people have a variety of possible strategies: they may avoid interaction with contradictory information, or preconceptions may prevent them from accurately judging (or believing the truth of) new information.[26] At its most extreme, the presence of conflicting information might even force people to push back so forcefully against it that they grow even stronger in their convictions.[27]

Norms may be sustained within relatively enclosed communities, reinforcing the specific world view that legitimizes behaviours that would otherwise be seen as transgressive. Members of German occupation society who were complicit in Nazi violence in wartime Warsaw or Minsk, for example, were readily able to interpret their acts at the time – including robbery, rape and murder – as the legitimate behaviour of 'overlords' against those they viewed as 'inferior' and subjugated people; later, they were still able to frame mass murders in terms of supposedly 'justified' acts of 'retaliation' or appropriate ways of treating 'resistance' and those who allegedly supported 'partisans'.[28] Such self-justifications might become even stronger in the face of post-war critiques of former actions and norms – particularly of course when facing legal investigations, but also when challenged by members of the family (e.g. their children, as they came to maturity in the later 1960s) or wider society. So challenges may serve to reinforce rather than undermine legitimatory discourses in certain circles without any sense of having been compromised.

Maintaining the sense that one has not compromised one's identity need neither be seamless nor passive, with challenges to the narrative of the good self having both internal and external provenance. Internally, sustaining one's sense of an uncompromised identity is fundamentally undermined by the recognition that one's behaviour has violated standards or values by which one evaluates oneself (often resulting in a sense of shame rather than guilt). Carrying out violent acts of perpetration, the negative impact of the resulting cognitive dissonance can be such that people will change their attitudes to match the behaviour, even going so far as to repeat that behaviour as a further retrospective justification.[29] Achieving and then maintaining a positive self-image becomes particularly difficult when the political and moral context changes following a period of state-condoned violence or genocide, when different values and expectations are used to judge violent or complicit behaviour. Cognitive dissonance is effectively re-imposed from the outside when a person's identity is deemed compromised and when they are accused of being perpetrators or complicit with perpetration when they do not see themselves in that way: the 'reestablishment of the self, after the moral restructuring that enables acts of atrocity, can be traumatic'.[30]

Or not: such trauma can be avoided by drawing on various strategies to insist that the self was never fundamentally restructured in the first place. After 1945 narratives emerged that safeguarded individual identity and that further evolved in response to fresh challenges. Most blatant were forms of denial: the quick shift from Germans admitting knowledge of mass murder of Jews before April 1945 to never having known what was happening;[31] 'All of a sudden no one was a Nazi!';[32] people claimed internal opposition to the Nazis all along. Individuals emphasized their lack of agency and denied responsibility: they were following orders; members of the Wehrmacht had sworn an oath; they only acted out of fear of Nazi terror. From the 1950s the quick emergence of a victim narrative was socially condoned by blaming a small Nazi elite for the evils that had been visited upon the Germans; in their own eyes, they were the main victims.[33] Individual narratives were legitimized by reference to the wider group, be that through specific social meetings of former SS members or army veterans after the war or through hegemonic social narratives that colluded with the exculpating division between evil Nazis (the perpetrators) and good Germans (innocent or victims).

The notion of 'compromise' is thus a productive one, offering as it does a double meaning depending on context and positioning. In democracies we tend to value the reaching of compromise, the willingness to compromise for a common goal. In response to authoritarian states, however, we often condemn the readiness to compromise – whether for a common goal or individual interests – as moral bankruptcy. From the Nazi perspective, uncompromising behaviour was valued too, particularly with regard to fighting the regime's political and racialized enemies, at home and abroad, and in its conquest for eastward expansion. That is not to say that Nazi leaders never compromised – sometimes even in the interest of being 'uncompromising'. As Nathan Stolzfus has argued, compromises were made on a number of important public issues, such as the mobilization of women into the workforce, the role of religion within German society, and at least the scale, character and visibility of the T-4 'euthanasia' programme. Given Hitler's concern with maintaining his own charisma and popularity, occasional apparent 'concessions' to popular opinion help to explain the regime's mass appeal.[34] The regime both instilled a sense of obligation towards the *Volksgemeinschaft* and yet left Germans some room to weigh the needs and demands of the community of which they were a part. Encouraging them to renegotiate their moralities in the light of changing circumstances deliberately left space for personal agency, in this way tying individual Germans more closely to the Nazi project through personal compromises.

The notion of a compromised identity is thus often one that is imposed from the outside. Yet it is evident that the aspiration to an uncompromised identity is prized only in relation to values that are held to be good or moral. The belief system that sustained the refusal by Jehovah's Witnesses to give allegiance to the National Socialists also sustains the rejection of blood transfusion even in the case of minors.[35] An uncompromised identity is lauded as a marker of integrity, honesty and virtue in a moral context that advocates those very virtues. It is a state aspired to by individuals, since self-worth is inseparable from the approbation of others. When it relates to those involved in or complicit with atrocity, the reality that many feel uncompromised is judged by others as dissimulation, self-deceit and further immorality. In contrast, the signs of a person's willingness to admit to wrongdoing and that they betrayed their own fundamental values, is positively evaluated in as far as it resonates with the ethical framework of others.

Past and present: The shapes of complicity and perpetration over time

While the notion of complicity has received increasing theoretical attention, there is much that remains to be addressed in relation to those living with a system of persisting collective violence, including under Nazi rule. Just as perpetrators do not think of themselves in those terms, so too those who are not directly engaged in violence do not tend to think of themselves as complicit even when acting to sustain a system of violence. A person who is legally complicit is deemed to carry individual liability for aiding, abetting or benefitting from a crime, and doing so knowingly. Yet this focus on agency and intentionality, which makes it difficult enough to demonstrate a connection between an accomplice and a perpetrator at the individual level, also makes the term contentious when crimes 'are committed in the context of ongoing violence involving many actors at different levels of state hierarchy'.[36] This description most immediately fits state-condoned violence carried out under dictatorships, where the constraints on agency are apparent. Compulsory participation in crimes may undermine the notion of individual liability, and refusal to comply may move the individual into the terrain of resistance. Coercion, real or perceived, constraining people to commit crimes, rightly makes the notion of complicity inappropriate – a point, however, that plays into the self-exculpatory narratives of defendants at war crimes trials as well as members of the wider population under authoritarian systems. But even under dictatorships, the relationships between coercion and choice are complex and variable. Debates about whether or how far the National Socialist state was a 'consensual dictatorship' (*Konsensdiktatur*) inevitably raise questions about how we understand willing participation in complex social and political structures, especially when participation was rewarded for members included in the 'people's community' (*Volksgemeinschaft*), while failure to comply attracted penalties of varying degrees of severity. If involvement in the in-group, such as the Nazi 'people's community', brings tangible benefits such as material well-being, career advancement and familial security, then considering forms of complicity becomes relevant insofar as persecution of out-groups is not merely known about but actively supported in some way.

This volume addresses the complex relationships between people's behaviours and self-understandings through and beyond periods of collective violence from a variety of disciplinary perspectives. Contributors explore the compromises that individuals, states and societies enter into both during and after such violence; case studies highlight patterns of complicity and involvement in perpetration, and analyse how people's stories evolve under changing circumstances and through social interaction, using varying strategies of justification, denial and rationalization. Chapters also address the ways in which contemporary responses and scholarly practices may be affected by engagement with perpetrator representations.

Stephanie Bird and Juliane Prade-Weiss interrogate literature's ability to confront compromise and complicity. Bird's contribution explores what is understood by a compromised identity and how the notion is useful in understanding critical anxiety around empathizing with a perpetrator's perspective in fictional representations. It considers how the notions of compromise or being uncompromising become morally and emotionally invested to sustain a positive sense of identity, including at the level of critical engagement with perpetration and its representations. Concerns around compromise and identity are particularly crystallized in relation to forgiveness and perpetration. In its inevitable interaction with justice, forgiveness may be seen as compromising the demand for justice, and vice versa, even while they can both be restorative of people's identities. Taking Vlademir Jankélévitch's insistence on forgiveness as an absolute act as a starting point, the chapter analyses how texts figure compromise and identity in relation to the competing demands of justice and forgiveness. By focusing on texts that have an ageing perpetrator at their centre, it considers how vulnerability and the empathy it elicits easily sentimentalizes the relationship of compromise and identity. Finally, it suggests that serial melodrama as a form may lend itself to the complex exploration of compromised identities not least through its dramatization of Jankélévitch's insistence that there is 'no last word!'

Prade-Weiss considers recent portrayals of complicity in literature in light of increased interest in political participation and entanglements in neoliberal wrongdoing. The notion of compromised identity takes the form of examining the role of literary criticism, the literary critic and the literary text in relation to complicity, understood as a marker of complex relationality. She argues that literary criticism contributes to understanding the 'meaning' of events by analysing the justificatory discourses that establish the narratives and modes of understanding by which violent events are subsequently discussed. The critic herself participates in constructing and mediating this framework and cannot assume a position of non-involvement, which would undermine the events being described as continued matters of concern into the present. Literary criticism can make a productive contribution to understanding the relationality of complicity both because of its focus on language as a model of individual participation in a communal structure and because of the reader's 'suspension of disbelief' which can be understood as a form of complicity. By analysing two examples of documentary fiction, Radka Denemarková's *Money from Hitler* and Elfriede Jelinek's play *Rechnitz (The Extermination Angel)*, she points to the importance of exposing the ways in which justificatory discourses that locate complicity in mass violence in the past are also effective in concealing the compromising complicities of involvement in neoliberal wrongdoing in the present.

These issues are particularly acute in relation to bystanding. Raul Hilberg's classic triad of 'perpetrators, victims, bystanders' presents essentially moral categories of evaluation; but this remains problematic as far as his extraordinarily broad category of 'bystanders' is concerned. This ill-defined concept is however also again becoming the subject of attention.[37] The choices of action in one direction or another by members of the wider population – those who are initially neither direct perpetrators nor immediate victims of violence – may potentially tip the balance of historical outcomes, depending on degrees of passivity or more active involvement on one side or another. This is a theme that runs through several chapters and is addressed most explicitly by Mary Fulbrook, Christina Morina and Leonid Rein. To what extent is the possibility of passivity and retreat a privileged position open only to citizens of an aggressor country, such as Nazi Germany, and not to the subjugated citizens of occupied and annexed territories?

Empathy is a key issue here. The limitations of empathy can already be observed during the Nazi dictatorship, as communities and identities shifted, and as people increasingly learned to look away when witnessing acts of violence against Jews and other social outsiders. Fulbrook's work explores how those who were at first 'bystanders' become caught up in policies of persecution, crucially affecting historical outcomes. She argues that it is important to understand degrees of dissonance between inner views and outer behaviours, and to trace the ways in which it was possible to be functionally complicit while varying in subjective perceptions of and attitudes towards such complicity. She explores the shifts from conformity and compliance into ever-greater complicity in Nazi Germany during the peacetime years, as a process of 're-segregation' took place in which changing social relations and everyday practices were as important as official policies. Structural changes and the mobilization of a nation at war then turned huge numbers of people into more active accomplices in an inherently racist national mission. Moreover, in wartime there was a fatal conjunction of factors: German initiatives, coordinated both centrally and regionally; local movements hoping to benefit from cooperation with the occupiers; the active compliance of some members of the local population; and the impotence of others who remained passively on the side-lines. The chapter thus raises wider questions around conformity and compliance within a system premised on exclusionary violence. Fulbrook argues that structural and social dynamics as well as cultural frameworks of interpretation are key to understanding how those who were initially bystanders to violence eventually choose to act in one way or another once it becomes no longer possible to remain 'neutral'.[38]

Morina considers how the understanding of so-called bystanders, a term which she sees as a heuristic device rather than a fixed category, can be further developed. She argues that a concise understanding of the motivations and perceptions of bystanding is still lacking. Although statistics point to the importance of bystanders' actions or inactions for the Holocaust and ego-documents show the variety of bystanding behaviours, in her view no systematic bridge between these macro and micro levels exists. Bystanding is a relational position involving a wide spectrum of behaviour which in some way reproduces the positions of victims and perpetrators, be this engaging in harassment of those who are stigmatized or offering gestures of empathy. She raises the important question of what drives the current work around bystanding in different national contexts. In this way, her chapter explores the compromised positions of the so-called 'bystanders' as a way of understanding their subjectivities, agency (perceived and actual) and the dynamics of systemic violence. She also warns of a compromising ('problematic') 'sense of identification' of scholars who empathize with bystanders, reflecting on her own positioning as a German scholar from a non-persecuted family and how this affects her research.

The issue of bystanding further points to significant differences within European societies. Raul Hilberg argued that effectively all who remained citizens of Nazi

Germany were more or less by definition complicit in the racist regime; indeed, he suggests, in Nazi Germany 'the difference between perpetrators and bystanders was least pronounced; in fact it was not supposed to exist'.[39] Passivity, in effect, meant implicitly condoning and indeed actively complying with Nazi racism in ways that necessarily furthered persecution and facilitated the eventual policies of extermination. The chapter by Rein takes this further by exploring the responses of people in Nazi-occupied Belorussia. This case might suggest that there was little alternative for people to variously facilitating, or benefitting from, the Nazi-instigated persecution and mass murder of the Jews. The very nature of the German occupation and killing programme in the East makes the notion of bystanding redundant in these contexts, since whole populations were drawn into, and offered themselves for, the violence at their doorstep and the opportunities it entailed. Rein also addresses the problems of confronting perpetration and complicity in the context of a lack of accessible or available sources, thus compromising the scope and quality of knowledge production about Belorussia under Nazi occupation. This severely limits evaluations of the extent to which local perpetrators of the Holocaust felt themselves to be compromised and how far they were seen to have been compromised by the situation in which they were acting. Rein notes that widespread involvement of local perpetrators indicates that they did not feel compromised by their actions. In political discourse in contemporary Belarus both President Lukashenko's loyalists and the opposition compare the other side to Nazi occupiers and their local accomplices. This suggests that perpetration and complicity with atrocities and mass murder are used as abstract markers of or shorthand for moral compromise, but in a way that entrenches political identities as uncompromised.[40]

This in turn alerts us again to the degree to which notions of compromise are often imposed from the outside. In the Belorussian context, 'compromised identities' would be a matter of the external imposition of later views, rather than self-perceptions either during the period of German occupation or subsequently. The papers by Stefanie Rauch, Zoltán Kékesi and Nina Fischer suggest the interplay between different systems of values: internal, local community and (changing) authorities. Compromises from one perspective may not be from another; and may not affect a person's sense of either personal or collective identity.

Rauch's chapter explores the ways in which former members of the Wehrmacht spoke about acts of extreme violence against women after the war and how they framed their narratives to maintain a positive self-identity. She analyses two accounts of extreme violence against female combatants, exposing the strategies of justification that the men use to protect their image of themselves in tense interactions with different audiences. The men draw on discourses of protective masculinity, comradeship and the demands of combat, as well as the trope of the 'fanatical' fighting woman, to relate their actions, differentiating their behaviour from the killing of helpless civilians. Indeed, their apparent candour in talking about their violence is itself a mechanism for constructing themselves as 'decent'. Such narratives of violence are influenced by the audience to which they are directed and also change over time so as to continue to project an uncompromised identity in a context of changed cultural expectations.

Fischer analyses the conversion narrative of IDF veteran Noam Chayut, whose memoir examines his own complicity in Israel's 'crimes in the Occupied Territories' following his confrontation with a Palestinian girl. This confrontation made him fundamentally re-examine his coherent and affirmatory sense of self, which rested on a seamless continuum between his individual identity and Israeli national identity. Chayut's memoir traces his shift away from this unified, uncompromised identity. It involves his fundamental re-evaluation of the dominant narrative of Israeli national identity based on Jewish victimhood, with the Holocaust as the most radical example of the permanent threat to Jews. His experience of being viewed as a perpetrator leads him to consider his own and his nation's identity as compromised and he writes his memoir as a political intervention: political activism offers a new path for being uncompromised.

By contrast, the chapter by Kékesi indicates how stable identities can be maintained throughout life. It examines the post-war career in interwar Hungary and post-war Argentina of the Hungarian journalist György Oláh, who, along with other pro-fascist intellectuals in Argentina, re-formulated the past to reclaim respectability and moral authority after the war. Oláh viewed the destructive forces of massification, materialism and technological progress, of which Marxism and psychoanalysis were symptoms, as what compromised European-Christian civilizations. His call to émigré intellectuals to lead a post-war renewal of Christian civilization helped entrench a sense of moral superiority and purpose. Kékesi's discussion of Oláh confirms the ways in which perpetrators may construct a stable identity across time and one that is not only not felt to be compromised, but that is grounded in the moral belief that their actions continue to be justified within the framework of European, white Christian civilization. It is we ourselves or other later audiences who would see him as having been and still being in some way compromised – he felt the need to flee but not because of any recognition of wrongdoing or illicit complicity on his part. He did not experience an inner sense of compromised identity, but rather it was externally imposed by the post-fascist world (and then quite at home in Latin American dictatorships). If exile constituted a compromise for Oláh, he fashioned it into an uncompromising vision for the future, by projecting racist and colonial ideas onto Argentina in the context of the Cold War.

The notion of compromise is especially acute in relation to the courtrooms, where the absolute demands and expectations of justice meet the limitations of the law, its actors and representation amid shifting political and cultural circumstances. Simon Lavis, Christoph Thonfeld, Bastiaan Willems and Francisco Bustos, Cath Collins and Francisco Úgas explore the compromises of justice and the legal process – justice as compromise – from a variety of geographic and temporal perspectives.

Lavis begins with the Nazi legal system, exploring how Nazi law and legal institutions contributed to the construction of normative decision-making and complicit behaviour in the Third Reich among those ordinary Germans who became implicated in violence. In doing so, he makes the arguments that law had a significant role in constructing complicity in the Holocaust and that it is important for researchers to uncover this role in order to understand the relationship between law and state violence, past and present. This is in contrast to the dominant historical and jurisprudential interpretation of Nazi 'law' as one of unlawfulness, barbarity; a state of non-law. While this has now been challenged on a number of fronts, a strong current of this paradigm endures, particularly when it comes to explaining the role of law in the Holocaust. Additionally, while the use of individual laws prior to the Holocaust to persecute those considered undesirable by the Nazi leadership has been examined, the concomitant use of law, legality and legal institutions to contribute to fostering a National Socialist identity and to implicate German society in Nazi violence is less well-studied, notwithstanding the growth of a considerable body of 'consent' literature in Nazi historiography.

Willems considers two aspects of the legal process: intra-ethnic executions of alleged 'defeatists' following summary courts-martial during the final year of the Second World War and the prosecution of these killings shortly after the end of the war in West Germany. The chapter contrasts the uncompromising mindsets underpinning the violence with the ways in which actors presented themselves as mere witnesses to avoid sentencing and the perception of having been compromised. The prosecutions themselves were compromised by this shift in roles assigned to actors, and the need to prove base motives. Such narratives were vital in consolidating the developing exculpatory myth of Germans as victims of a small group of perpetrators and in exonerating the wider community of complicity in crimes. Painful questions regarding wartime complicity were quashed by the need to establish an uncompromised identity.

Thonfeld's chapter examines compromises in the way in which law and media have responded to Nazi trials, charting changes in perceptions of perpetration and how representations of Nazi perpetrators were negotiated within post-war media and society. By examining the shifting media responses from the 1950s to the 1980s, Thonfeld shows how the media helped fashion the broad sense that perpetration was limited to the few and that the interest in understanding perpetration and the motives of perpetrators remained largely historical. In the 1950s and 1960s the media contributed to sensationalizing the crimes of the few while normalizing the crimes of those who were not brought to trial and omitting to examine the culpability of the wider society. Although in the 1970s social attitudes shifted to a more abstract interest in perpetrators' motives, the media discourse continued to normalize most perpetrators despite shifting representations. Concerns with how the individual perpetrator could function within a dictatorship and with the educational value of reporting trials did not fundamentally question the separation of a smaller group of morally compromised perpetrators from the majority of perpetrators who were compromised by circumstance and whose identity as a decent person therefore went unchallenged.

The chapters by Willems and Thonfeld have highlighted the compromises of the criminal justice system for redressing past crimes. Bustos, Collins and Ugás discuss a different approach in Chile where the law's domestic arena is used to prosecute past atrocities. The justice system in Chile has an individualizing dynamic at work in relation to the defendants and those that bring a case, usually relatives or survivors rather than state prosecutors. Even when relatives' associations have been admitted, the group may be treated as a collection of individuals at verdict stage, often without explanation. And even when collective responsibility is implied by findings of liability against the state, the understanding of accountability remains atomized through reference to events, victims and perpetrators. So a version of identity is being upheld that relies on a narrow focus of proving individual agency in doing harm (and being harmed) that does not do justice to the nature of collective and systemic violence. The focus on individual culpability means that state institutions and the Armed Forces can uphold their view of themselves by using a 'rotten apple' defence. Similarly, a collective solution to the convictions imposed by courts under the dictatorship, which would recognize the courts' own responsibility in historic injustice, has not been implemented. The use of domestic or civil courts opens up possibilities (and aligns with truth-telling, reparation and reform dimensions of transitional justice) but limits the scope of justice meted out. This is also linked to the uneven process of confronting the past in Chile and the complicity of wide sections of state and society.

The representation of compromise, perpetration and complicity poses significant challenges, not least in the realms of public history. The chapters by Sue Vice and Stephan Jaeger consider the compromises entailed in developing narratives about complicity in different contexts.

Vice's chapter considers the notion of compromised identities in relation to Zygmunt Bauman's and Claude Lanzmann's treatment of victims' cooperation in the Holocaust. Vice contrasts Bauman's characterization of complicity, the process whereby the subject is trapped by his gradual commitment to actions, as though being sucked into a bog, with that of cooperation. This was the process which put victims in the position of making 'rational calculations' about survival that resulted in them betraying their moral duty. By portraying the victims as subject to the same abstract workings of modernity as their murderers, Bauman suggests that they have compromised their moral identity. Lanzmann likewise views the victims as entrapped in a system from which they could not escape but eschews any generalized moral evaluation. Both Bauman and Lanzmann explore the cases of Willy Just and Rezsö Kasztner. Bauman finds in Shoah evidence for his argument about the process of instrumental reason in the cooperation of the Jewish Councils at the expense of moral considerations. However, Lanzmann's Shoah outtakes refuse such a definitive reading of rational obedience both through their filmic language and through their status as outtakes. He thus seems to suggest that there is no scope for considering victims' cooperation in terms of compromised identity because the system caused them to choose.

Jaeger explores different approaches to exhibitions that deal with perpetration and complicity and select cases, and the compromises involved in their curation. Distinguishing between the concepts of empathy, experientiality and agonism, he considers how these displays reinforce feelings of moral compromise or lack of compromise. Jaeger argues that even good, reflexive exhibitions tend to reinforce dichotomies of right and wrong and impose a master narrative that may restrict experientiality. A balance between analysis and emotional responses in the visitor is key if the exhibition is to challenge the visitor's subject position. Those that are too analytical allow the visitor to maintain a safe distance and those that are too emotional facilitate simplification of the complex causes and positions of perpetration and complicity. Rather, a balance must be achieved between empowering visitors to consider different viewpoints and scenarios, to empathize with different choices and to empathize with victims. Such empowerment must be presented within a moral framework founded in inclusion and justice. Exhibitions that achieve this balance will enable visitors to relate cognitively, emotionally and ethically to the complexity of complicity and perpetration and reflect on their own position.

Finally, the editors of this book jointly contribute a chapter reflecting on a research-based exhibition we have developed, *Compromised Identities? Reflections on Perpetration and Complicity under Nazi Rule*.[41] This exhibition seeks to highlight, probe and stimulate reflections on the complexity of involvement in perpetration and complicity under Nazi rule, and perceptions, representations and responses both at the time and later, while also indicating the continuing relevance of these questions today. The website includes not only text and images but also a collection of short films, including discussion of key themes and extracts of interviews with people involved in or in close proximity to Nazi crimes, as well as primary sources and guides for further study. It is aimed both at a general public, including those who have little or no prior knowledge, as well as professionals and educators. The editors' chapter seeks to situate their approach in the wider context of other exhibitions in this field, highlighting challenges around the use, for example, of graphic images, and the potential benefits and risks of 'giving perpetrators a voice' without adequate contextualization from external vantage points. Given the intrinsically emotive character of the subject matter, we chose to adopt a specifically cognitive, analytic approach to the material, while raising open questions with which visitors can engage critically in an informed manner.

We conclude with brief reflections on the wider significance of these discussions. The approach developed in this book aims to transform our understanding of the character and personal legacies of perpetration and complicity in systems of collective violence over time. Taken together, then, the following chapters examine the ways in which people who were involved in or witnesses to state-sponsored crimes talked about, silenced or variously negotiated accounts of their roles, often constructing retrospective accounts of having been merely an 'innocent bystander'. We analyse how individual identities come under pressure when circumstances and value systems change, and how self-representations develop over time. We explore how public discourses – political, cultural, journalistic and judicial – address state-sponsored violence and interrogate or contribute to exculpatory strategies at a personal level. Public images often helped to demonize 'excess perpetrators' as unlike 'ordinary people', while others suggested the significance of 'just following orders'; private self-understandings and exculpatory strategies were affected by such images. Contributions analyse entanglement in collective violence under Nazism and beyond, and later reflections on such experiences. Drawing on the notion of 'compromised identities?' as a point of departure, the contributors explore historical subjectivities under changing circumstances.

In doing so, the volume illuminates both the dynamics of widespread involvement in collective violence and the complexities of dealing with its aftermath, whether in courts of law, in public representations, or in the privacy of the family. It extends the field beyond narrow definitions of 'perpetrators' and across the 1945 divide. Through interdisciplinary exploration, it systematically situates individual self-understandings among those 'on the perpetrator side' within changing political, social and historical contexts. This includes (often multiple, sometimes conflicting) organizational, institutional and professional affiliations, networks and cultures, in which individuals are situated and within which they locate themselves or rally against, such as the legal profession, journalism or the army. Where contributions take a biographical approach, these are individualizing only insofar as that they consider constraints alongside scope for agency and fulfilment, but in the context of institutions and organizations, some of which, notably the military, mobilize millions of people. We cannot understand collective violence without the organizational and institutional contexts, frameworks and expectations in which it is carried out and justified; but neither can we comprehend this structural dimension without understanding the perceptions and self-understandings of the individuals shaping, negotiating and confronting it. The volume therefore also explores ways in which people performed new roles or capitulated to new pressures and demands, in the process transforming social relations and having effects that often bore little relationship to motives; the extent to which people felt they were compromising previously held values, and ways in which they justified complicity with violent practices; strategies to legitimize what was later seen as a 'compromised past'; and attempts to avoid compromising views of themselves as being a 'good' person across time, despite significant changes in worldview and political and moral frameworks. Contributions analyse changing notions of what it meant to be a 'perpetrator' and how post-war conceptions of justice were variously compromised in order to integrate key groups or sustain dominant narratives. In these ways, the book clarifies key issues raised by individual participation in a system of state-sanctioned collective violence, developing an analytic framework that will be of broader relevance.

Notes

1 Cf. for example, Donald Bloxham, *The Final Solution. A Genocide* (Oxford: Oxford University Press, 2009); Christian Gerlach, *The Extermination of the European Jews* (Cambridge: Cambridge University Press, 2016); Dan Stone (ed.), *The Historiography of the Holocaust* (Basingstoke: Palgrave Macmillan, 2004).
2 For example, Christopher Browning, *Ordinary Men* (London: Harper Perennial, 1998); Olaf Jensen and Claus-Christian Szejnmann (eds), *Ordinary People as Mass Murderers* (Basingstoke: Palgrave Macmillan, 2008); Stefan Kühl, *Ganz normale Organisationen* (Berlin: Suhrkamp, 2014); and cf. Scott Straus and Robert Lyons, *Intimate Enemy: Images and Voices of the Rwandan Genocide* (New York: Princeton University Press, 2006), 24.
3 See for example Jan Gross, *Neighbors: The Destruction of the Jewish Community in Jedwabne, Poland, 1941* (Princeton: Princeton University Press, 2003); Anthony Polonski and Joanna Michlic (eds), *The Neighbors Respond: The Controversy over the Jedwabne Massacre in Poland* (Princeton: Princeton University Press, 2003); Jan Grabowski, *Hunt for the Jews. Betrayal and Murder in German-Occupied Poland* (Bloomington and Indianapolis: Indiana University Press, 2013); Michael Marrus and Robert Paxton, *Vichy France and the Jews*, 2nd ed. (Stanford: Stanford University Press, 2019; French orig. 1981); Julian Jackson, *France: The Dark Years 1940–44* (Oxford: Oxford University Press, 2001).
4 Cf. for example, Lee Ann Fujii, *Killing Neighbors. Webs of Violence in Rwanda* (Ithaca: Cornell University Press, 2009), 11–14, 188; Adam Jones (ed.), *New Directions in Genocide Research* (New York: Routledge, 2012); Scott Straus, *The Order of Genocide: Race, Power, and War in Rwanda* (Ithaca: Cornell University Press, 2006).

5 Karl Jaspers, *Die Schuldfrage* (Heidelberg: Lambert Schneider, 1946).
6 Hannah Arendt, *Responsibility and Judgment*, ed. Jerome Kohn (New York: Schocken Books, 2003), 158.
7 Ibid.
8 Mark Sanders, *Complicities: The Intellectual and Apartheid* (Durham and London: Duke University Press, 2002), 4.
9 Ibid., 11, 8.
10 Stephen Clingman, 'On Ethical Grounds', *Law and Literature* 17, no. 2 (2005): 282.
11 Michael Rothberg, *The Implicated Subject: Beyond Victims and Perpetrators* (Stanford: Stanford University Press, 2019), 35, 49.
12 Ibid., 20-1.
13 Juliane Prade-Weiss, 'Guilt-tripping the "Implicated Subject": Widening Rothberg's Concept of Implication in Reading Herta Müller's *The Hunger Angel*', *Journal of Perpetrator Research* 3, no. 1 (2020): 11.
14 Ernesto Verdeja, 'Moral Bystanders and Mass Violence', in *New Directions in Genocide Research*, ed. Adam Jones (New York: Routledge, 2012), Ch. 9, 153-68.
15 Alf Lüdtke, 'People Working: Everyday Life and German Fascism', *History Workshop Journal* 50, no. 1 (2000): 84.
16 Kühl, *Ganz normale Organisationen*, 92.
17 Harald Welzer, 'On Killing and Morality: How Normal People Become Mass Murderers', in *Ordinary People as Mass Murderers. Perpetrators in Comparative Perspectives*, ed. Olaf Jensen and Claus-Christian W. Szejnmann (Basingstoke: Palgrave Macmillan, 2008), 172.
18 Kühl, *Ganz normale Organisationen*, 101-4.
19 Froukje Demant, 'The Many Shades of by Standing: On Social Dilemmas and Passive Participation', in *Probing the Limits of Categorization. The Bystander in Holocaust History*, ed. Christina Morina and Krijn Thijs (New York and Oxford: Berghahn, 2019), 94.
20 Robert P. Ericksen, *Complicity in the Holocaust. Churches and Universities in Nazi Germany* (Cambridge: Cambridge University Press, 2012), 1, fn. 1. See also pp. 230-1.
21 See, for example: Jill Stephenson, 'The Volksgemeinschaft and the Problems of Permeability: The Persistence of Traditional Attitudes in Württemberg Villages', *German History* 34, no. 1 (2016): 49-69; Bastiaan Willems, *Violence in Defeat. The Wehrmacht on German Soil, 1944-1945* (Cambridge: Cambridge University Press, 2021), 29-30.
22 See Melvin J. Lerner, *The Belief in a Just World: A Fundamental Delusion. Perspectives in Social Psychology* (New York: Plenum Press, 1980), 149.
23 See Rainer Bucher, *Hitler's Theology: A Study in Political Religion* (London: Continuum, 2011), Ch. 4: '"Providence": Hitler's Theology of History', 49-57.
24 Kjell Anderson, *Perpetrating Genocide. A Criminological Account* (London and New York: Routledge, 2018), 142.
25 Esther-Julia Howell, *Von den Besiegten lernen? Die kriegsgeschichtliche Kooperation der U.S. Armee und der ehemaligen Wehrmachtselite 1945-1961* (Berlin: de Gruyter, 2016), 302.
26 See Leon Festinger, *A theory of cognitive dissonance* (Stanford: Stanford University Press, 1957); Roy F. Baumeister and Kathleen D. Vohs (eds), *Encyclopedia of Social Psychology 1* (Thousand Oaks: Sage, 2007), s.v. Belief Perseverance.
27 Briony Swire-Thompson, Joseph DeGutis and David Lazer, 'Searching for the backfire effect: Measurement and design considerations', *Journal of Applied Research in Memory and Cognition* 9, no. 3 (2020): 286-99. http://dx.doi.org/10.1016/j.jarmac.2020.06.006.

28 See on these two cases Stephan Lehnstaedt, *Occupation in the East. The Daily Lives of German Occupiers in Warsaw and Minsk, 1939–1944* (New York and Oxford: Berghahn, 2019; trans. Martin Dean).
29 Leonard S. Newman, 'What is a "Social-Psychological" Account of Perpetrator Behaviour? The Person Versus the Situation in Goldhagen's *Hitler's Willing Executioners*', in *Understanding Genocide: The Social Psychology of the Holocaust*, ed. Leonard S. Newman and Ralph Erber (Oxford: Oxford University Press, 2002), 50–3.
30 Anderson, *Perpetrating Genocide*, 208.
31 Stefanie Rauch, 'Good Bets, Bad Bets and Dark Horses: Allied Intelligence Officers' Encounters with German Civilians, 1944–45', *Central European History* 53, no 1 (2020): 120–45. This denial could take on what would be comic proportions, were it not for the fact that the denial was eagerly believed. Karl Wolff, Himmler's adjutant, was present at mass shootings and saw reports relating to 'Aktion Reinhard'. But he denied being 'conscious of being made use of, even remotely, in the possible perpetration of any inhumanity'. NARA RG498-UD308-1379, Department of Defense, European Command, Intelligence Division, Intelligence and Interrogation Records, 1945-1947, Report No: WCIU/LDC/1436(a)-APS-HC: Voluntary statement by PW LD 1470 formerly General Karl Wolff, Subject: Low Pressure and Low Temperature Experiments in Concentration Camps, 5 December 1947, p.7.
32 Hertha von Gebhardt, quoted in Nicholas Stargardt, *The German War. A Nation under Arms, 1939–45* (London: The Bodley Head, 2015), 543.
33 Stargardt, *The German War*, 548.
34 Nathan Stoltzfus, *Hitler's Compromises. Coercion and Consensus in Nazi Germany* (New Haven: Yale University Press, 2016), 5–6; see also Ian Kershaw, *The 'Hitler Myth'. Image and Reality in the Third Reich* (Oxford: Oxford University Press, 1987).
35 See Adelaide Conti, Emanuele Capasso et al., 'Blood Transfusion in Children: The Refusal of Jehovah's Witness Parents', *Open Med (Wars)* 13 (2018): 101–4; Juliet Guichon and Ian Mitchell, 'Medical Emergencies in Children of Orthodox Jehovah's Witness Families: Three Recent Legal Cases, Ethical Issues and Proposals for Management', *Paediatric Child Health* 11, no. 10 (2006): 655–8.
36 Marina Aksenova, 'Complicity in International Criminal Law', *Oxford Bibliographies*. https://www.oxfordbibliographies.com/view/document/obo-9780199796953/obo-9780199796953-0152.xml (Accessed 21 March 2022).
37 Raul Hilberg, *Perpetrators Victims Bystanders* (New York: Aaron Asher Books, 1992); Christina Morina and Krijn Thijs (eds), *Probing the Limits of Categorization. The Bystander in Holocaust History* (New York and Oxford: Berghahn, 2019).
38 This approach is explored in greater detail in Mary Fulbrook, *Bystander Society: Conformity and Complicity in Nazi Germany and the Holocaust* (Oxford: Oxford University Press, 2023).
39 Raul Hilberg, *Perpetrators Victims Bystanders. The Jewish Catastrophe 1933–1945* (New York: HarperCollins, 1993), 196.
40 It is notable too how in the context of his aggressive invasion of Ukraine in 2022 Russian President Vladimir Putin has resorted to this discourse, accusing the Ukrainians of being 'Nazis'.
41 See https://compromised-identities.org/. We are very grateful to the AHRC and the Pears Foundation for their financial support for this project. Crucial to the development of this exhibition was also Christoph Thonfeld, who was at the time a part of the AHRC research team. Originally designed as a travelling exhibition, the physical panels had to be transformed rapidly into a web-based version due to the constraints imposed by the coronavirus pandemic from March 2020.

Part I

Theorizing ambiguity, compromise and complexity

2

'Compromised identities?', ageing perpetrators and compromising forgiveness

Stephanie Bird

In Borislav Pekić's novel *How to Quiet a Vampire* (1977), the ex-SS officer Konrad Rutkowski writes twenty-six letters and two postscripts to his brother-in-law in which he offers an apparently candid confession of how he was forced into making compromises with a regime that he loathed.[1] He is writing from the Croatian town of D in 1965, where he is taking a holiday with his wife. But he entered the town for the first time in the summer of 1943 as a Gestapo interrogator, a history about which his wife knows nothing. Rutkowski sees compromise as being at the heart of his identity and refers freely and critically to his 'soul's pathetic adaptability to compromise' (95). He recognizes the fact that by developing 'an unusual, basically compromising attitude toward the past', he has ensured that the twenty years since the end of the war have been the most successful in his life (278) Rutkowski's open acknowledgement of his compromises, his apparent willingness to be critical of his behaviour and the seemingly candid confession that he makes, give the impression of a man who is attempting an honest assessment of his role in violent occupation and torture. He thus admits to hating himself for being opposed to the 'demonic spirit' of National Socialism, on planning to take action against it, but in the end only 'serv[ing] as its slave' (44).

Yet his self-criticism is at the same time turned into support for a narrative of resistance. Rutkowski dignifies his behaviour by describing it as a case study for the clash of the Spirit and Reality: entering the war was a compromise between being unable to avoid it (Reality) and making it 'more bearable in [his] sphere of activity'(Spirit); slapping the prisoner Adam was a compromise between a serious beating (Reality) and not wanting to harm an inviolable human being (Spirit); and beating up the worker was a compromise between murdering him and only wanting to slap him. Rutkowski presents each example of compromise as a 'contribution to the humanization of reality' (359). So even though his colleague, the enthusiastic Nazi Rotkopf, also beat the worker, in Rotkopf's case it was senseless torture because 'the beating wasn't an expression of an effort to humanize the war'. In contrast, because Rutkowski's motive was to save the worker from death, the fact that he subsequently died from his injuries anyway is of no significance for Rutkowski's argument: 'That was an error in dosage, not in the motive. I did what I could. You can't expect the impossible, not even from an intellectual'. The exaggerated and even comically excessive escalation of his position makes Rutkowski's reasoning appear ludicrous, self-exonerating and arrogant. For all the insight into his actions in D that Rutkowski offers, his critical emphasis on compromise is intertwined both with self-deception and willed deception to justify himself. He is adept at casting compromise as resistance. By admitting to a compromised identity and his failure not to stand up more to the Nazis, Rutkowski seeks to lend credibility to his confession as authentic. At the same time, he advocates for compromise as a virtue. Pekić thus exposes just how malleable the notion of compromise is in constructing positive narratives of identity.

The malleability or refusal of compromise is central to this article, which explores the relationship of compromise, or the lack of it, to identity in the fictional representation of ageing perpetrators. It considers how the notions of compromise or being uncompromising become morally and emotionally invested to sustain a positive sense of identity. Concerns around compromise and identity are particularly crystalized in relation to forgiveness and perpetration. In its inevitable interaction with justice, forgiveness may be seen as compromising the demand for justice, and vice versa, even while they can both be restorative of peoples' identities. I first point to how the notion of a compromised identity is useful in understanding critical anxiety around empathizing with a perpetrator's perspective in fictional representations. Taking Vlademir Jankélévitch's insistence on forgiveness as an absolute act as a starting point, I analyse how texts figure compromise and identity in relation to the competing demands of justice and forgiveness. By focusing on texts that have an ageing perpetrator at their centre, I consider how vulnerability and the empathy it elicits easily sentimentalizes the relationship of compromise and identity. Finally, I suggest that serial melodrama as a form may lend itself to the complex exploration of compromised identities not least through its dramatization of Jankélévitch's insistence that there is 'no last word!'

Uncompromising empathy

Fiction is full of any variety of compromised identities. Through its ability to explore identity using multiple perspectives, competing voices and the play of empathy, fiction can ask probing questions about responses to perpetration and complicity, because it is not in service of an argument. Given the nature of fiction as non-serious discourse, with no obligation to heed a demand for congruity,[2] it is interesting to see how far the representation of perpetrators who show no signs of a compromised identity, evokes anxiety and even censure. Obvious examples include Jorge Luis Borges's 'ideal Nazi', Otto Dietrich zur Linde, who feels no guilt and does not wish to be pardoned for his involvement in torture and murder since Nazism 'is intrinsically a *moral* act'; George Steiner's Hitler in *The Portage to San Cristóbal of A. H.* (1979), who offers a powerful self-defence; and Max Aue, the Nazi protagonist in Jonathan Littell's *The Kindly Ones* (2006), who tells us that he is no worse than his readers.[3] Each author defended his freedom as a writer in the face of criticism, criticism that is imbued with concern about emotional and moral contamination: we might be persuaded by the perpetrator's position or seduced into empathizing with their plight. This then raises the unsettling possibility that the reader becomes complicit with an exculpatory narrative, lending credibility to the moral context within which the perpetrator affirms himself.[4] This fear of complicity is alleviated when the reader is confronted either with a victim whose identity is not compromised or with a perpetrator whose identity is and who recognizes that it is, through signs of remorse, guilt or trauma. Or anxiety is alleviated if the reader can be assured that the text is inviting a critical position, through alienation devices, language or self-reflexive moments. The critic is then comforted by their own uncompromised identity. Juliane Prade-Weiss points to the critic's own desire to 'strive for a position of critique that is untouched by the complicities and involvements of which others are accused', as though the critic could be uninvolved.[5]

Pekić is acutely aware of the desire for such redemptive avenues and disavows them all. Rutkowski plays the game of confession turning acknowledgement of his compromised identity into a virtue. His attempt to battle the logic of torture and interrogation fails because he is unable to use the tools of reason (as he sees them) against itself. This culminates in his embrace of reason's necessary converse – non-reason in the garb of the supernatural vampire umbrella. The reader is forced to look to the editor's erudite and reasonable analysis for an explanation of what is happening. Yet gradually the editor's humanism itself becomes contaminated by the material he is working on. He increasingly assumes Rutkowski's outlook and himself becomes enthralled by the circularity of so-called logical thinking and the necessary existence of the malevolent umbrella. And in a final twist, the editor, sitting in London with the umbrella carefully chained up in the basement, is called Borislav Pekić. So writing about the world of perpetration exposes layers of evasion in which writing itself is suspect and even the author cannot evade complicity. Pekić plays with our desire for redemption and epistemological closure and points only to a desolate ethical domain which has been reduced to the horrifying alternative of reasoned, logical violence or supernatural violence.

Yet perhaps the uncompromising and stark conclusion, that literature is 'yet another apparition in the system of apparitions in which we are imprisoned without hope', makes it easier to disengage from questions of perpetration and complicity.[6] The lack of empathy generated in Pekić's novel for any of the characters, compounded by the forbidding discussions of logic, sustains an impression that perpetration is a distant event; even more so complicity. It is precisely empathy for perpetrators, however, that is often viewed with suspicion, as a mark of complicity and betraying the assumption, reflected in the very use of the word complicity, that this would be a bad thing anyway. For Shlomo Neuman, David Grossman's narrator in *See Under: Love* (1986), the question of empathy with a perpetrator is far from settled. He finds Neigel, the commander of the death camp, strange, very different from himself: 'And yet, my responsibility as a writer, and my curiosity: Where will Neigel burst forth for me? Is it possible to bridge the gap between us for the sake of art?' And later, Neigel confronts Neuman for his negligence, asking whether it is true 'that writers are supposed to enter all the way into their characters?'[7]

The distrust of empathy in relation to perpetrators is the obverse of casting the capacity for empathy as ethically valuable, as an affect that structures the encounter with the other in recognition of their shared humanity and therefore necessarily positive. In this understanding, the person who shows empathy becomes a more virtuous person, and the person who is empathized with is humanized. Similarly, the perpetrator who reveals himself to be capable of empathy, becomes a more ethical person. The work of historians and those working on collective violence has long demonstrated the limits of this view, since empathy, like other emotions, can be channelled to cause just as much harm as good. Following Fritz Breithaupt's definition of empathy as 'the coexperience of another's situation', which encompasses cognitive processes as well as emotions, it is evident that empathy can forge bonds for members of an in-group that sustain the values of that group and facilitate violence against others.[8] Without empathy for those who perpetrate violence we perhaps shore ourselves up in our in-group. We sustain our easy identification with victims and carefully guard society's 'tacit agreement' whereby the executioners are found guilty for deeds the world did nothing to prevent but where their guilt serves to redeem others.[9]

The mistrust of empathy for perpetrators rests on the fear that it will relativize the seriousness of the atrocity or offer ideological justification; empathy heralds moral compromise. The constellation of identity, empathy and compromise becomes particularly acute in relation to questions of forgiveness and justice.

Forgiving compromise?

There is no scope for compromise when it comes to forgiveness in the work of philosopher Vladimir Jankélévitch. Forgiveness for him is not the product of 'virtuous parrots', doled out regularly so that the 'flabbiness of forgiveness' has become a daily spectacle.[10] In his book, *Forgiveness* of 1967, Jankélévitch describes forgiveness as an absolute, an instantaneous event, a miracle or instance of grace that exists outside the law and its discourses: 'simply the idea of a right of forgiveness destroys forgiveness' (9–10). It cannot be instrumentalized for another purpose, be that as the product of an individual willing spiritual improvement for herself nor a response to the 'apostles of reconciliation' (53). Nor can forgiveness be a product of knowledge in the immediate sense of 'to understand is to forgive', since this would mean that there is no other forgiveness than knowledge. Even if intellection can 'imply a real communication with the offender and a real transfiguration of the offended person' (68), this remains in the realm of excusing and not forgiving. This is a crucial distinction, since for Jankélévitch forgiveness operates in the realm of the inexcusable. The excuse along with the love of what is lovable 'represent the order of justice', whereas forgiveness and the unmotivated love of the enemy represent the 'paradoxical order of charity' (94). In a further step, he also insists that forgiveness has no reasons and does not need to justify itself. Jankélévitch's discussion of forgiveness seeks to describe a moment of grace that is ineffable and which is, of its nature, outside language (117).

Nevertheless, despite the need for grace and forgiveness to be rendered unconditionally to be what they are, Jankélévitch remains troubled by the relationship to remorse. For in his conclusion he points to the need for 'desperate remorse' on the part of the criminal, without which forgiveness remains meaningless: 'Forgiveness is not aimed at contented people with clear consciences [. . .]. When the guilty person is fat, well nourished, prosperous, and takes advantage of the economic miracle, then forgiveness is a sinister joke' (157). The tension between forgiveness needing to be unconditional and the demand for remorse is addressed in part through Jankélévitch's conceptualization of both as types of despair. The efficacy of forgiveness and remorse lies in the 'perfect innocence' of the despairing person, by which he means that any redemptive outcome cannot be part of the motivation. The remorse of the guilty person is a monologue, a stagnating ontological condition since the past cannot be undone. Forgiveness is a dialogue, 'in itself a liberating act' that 'posits the foundations of a new era' (122). Nevertheless, the tension remains in his work between the ethical ideal of a forgiveness that 'forgives everyone for everything for all times' (157), deriving its very point from the incomprehensibility of evil, and the fury for the 'swine and their sows' (157) who do not recognize their crimes even to ask for forgiveness in the first place. With strong parallels to his polemical essay, 'Should We Pardon Them?', he decries the haste with which criminals have been excused. Such haste renders forgiveness impossible. He also, however, points to the pride of the man who refuses to forgive, a position that shows he has decided 'a priori that he is above sin' (161).

The tension in his work is not resolved.[11] Indeed, Jankélévitch sets up two absolutes in opposition, neither of which can be compromised by the other: love, with which forgiveness is aligned and the unforgivable, which demands the memory of the crimes and justice. The synthesis of the two is impossible: 'Fortunately, the last word is always the penultimate word' (162). He offers a powerful riposte to St Paul's 'where misdeed flows, grace overflows': 'where grace overflows, evil overflows in response' (164–5). So 'No! there is no last word' (163).

'Should We Pardon Them?' was published in 1971 and in it Jankélévitch develops the themes that he first articulated in a letter to Le Monde and his article 'L'Imprescriptible' in 1965. He wrote in opposition to an official pardon of Germany by France and in response to the debates around statutory limitations for Nazi war crimes. These pressures to forget by contemporaries who have 'had enough' of Auschwitz make forgiveness impossible.[12] In 1969, Simon Wiesenthal published *The Sunflower* in France, a text which in its content refuses flabby forgiveness and in its form keeps open the question of whether to forgive. In it, Wiesenthal recounts an episode that occurred when he was in Janowska concentration camp engaged as a slave labourer. He, as a Jew, is summoned by a young SS man on his deathbed, who asks him for forgiveness for his participation in murder. Wiesenthal remains silent. He again remains silent when he meets the man's mother after the war and so does not shatter her idealized belief that her son was inherently good. The memoir ends with the closing request to the reader: 'ask yourself the crucial question, "What would I have done?"'.[13] Wiesenthal in part writes in response to the '[world's] demand' to forgive, forget and remain silent. But he also writes because he feels this 'profound moral question' (97) emotionally and intellectually. Wiesenthal, who was committed to bringing to trial those involved in perpetration, is still asking a question about forgiveness and its place: the 'crux of the matter is', he says, 'the question of forgiveness' (97), which 'is an act of volition' (98). Following his question, *The Sunflower* also includes responses from participants invited to respond, which in the most recent edition number fifty-three.[14] The responses are diverse: some are more academic, others more personal; some are more theological, others more political; some are distant in tone, others emotional; some are clear in their view and others do not attempt to resolve the question. The responses are presented alphabetically and no answer is prioritized, leaving the text to function as 'a powerful resistance machine to the world's demand for closure and normalization'.[15] No, there is no last word.

In Jankélévitch's and Wiesenthal's case, the refusal of a last word remains uncompromising and for that reason uncontroversial. For Jankélévitch, forgiveness belongs to the order of the miraculous and therefore barely possible. Wiesenthal did not forgive the SS man and his reputation as someone in pursuit of 'justice not vengeance' is the context within which his question about individual behaviour is asked. However, Steiner's refusal of a last word in *The Portage to San Cristóbal of A. H.*, published in 1979, did provoke controversy, despite the fairly clear rejection of forgiveness and the novel's concern with justice. The novel depicts a group of Jewish men, who find the aged Hitler in the Amazon jungle with the aim of bringing him back to face justice. Finally, realizing that the key national players of the Second World War are planning to lay claim to Hitler for their own purposes, they themselves hold a trial at which Hitler speaks in his own defence. The novel ends abruptly and ambivalently with the indigenous boy Teku's cry of 'Proved' drowned by descending helicopters. Steiner uses character to explore different responses to justice, focusing particularly on its relationship to identity and how it is instrumentalized. Emmanuel Lieber is a man whose identity is determined by the search for Hitler and whose insistence on justice is not diminished with years. Elie Barach is an orthodox rabbi for whom justice ultimately rests with God, and the young Isaac Amsel is driven by the desire for revenge for the murder of his father. Gideon Benasseraf voices greater scepticism. He recognizes that each of them has their own motives for finding Hitler and that these motives reinforce their sense of identity. He dismisses Isaac's desire for revenge, seeing it as a self-affirming fantasy that draws on the tropes of action films and also feeds Isaac's plan to make a luridly embellished movie of their successful mission. For Benasseraf, revenge is futile, for it is impossible to get even. He points to the influence of the figure of Hitler in defining Jewish identity, saying that 'To be a Jew is to keep Hitler alive' (65). For this reason, he posits that in Isaac's film Hitler's and Lieber's face will 'become as one' (66) in the final frame.

Benasseraf's motive for pursuing Hitler is complex and disturbing. He is wary of an attempt by Jews to bring Hitler to justice and hang him since this would allow history to 'draw a line' and 'forget even faster' (63). He suggests that Hitler should be left at the first town for 'them' to do what they will: 'He's theirs' (64). Benasseraf's view that justice is political and ideological is borne out by the self-serving concerns of the governments racing to get to Hitler first, so that they can determine what justice looks like to suit them. What led Benasseraf to seek out Lieber was his confrontation with his own fantasy of the future, experienced with the precision of a memory: he sits opposite an admiring woman in a Parisian café for lunch, a glowing review of his book on modern French poetry on the table, moving on to sex in their dark hotel room. In contrast to the increasingly blurred memories of his horrifically murdered family, the 'future tense' is becoming more dominant, diminishing his hatred and substituting it with 'Hope as cliché' (69). Benasseraf's interior monologue is bracketed between two references to forgiveness, which as Margaret Burton writes, is Steiner's oblique question of whether survivors can forgive.[16] Benasseraf cannot and the question of forgiveness does not even arise for the others. But nor can Benasseraf live with forgetting or with a clichéd future or with the conviction that justice offers resolution. Steiner has been criticized for the views articulated by Benasseraf, with critical concern that the author 'perceives the Shoah as a test limit judging the authenticity of an individual and as a crucible which should have purified the victim'.[17] Aligning Benasseraf with Steiner in this way overlooks the character's function as representing one in a range of views. The fact that it is he who succumbs to fever points to the impossibility of his position, one in which he denies himself a future, cannot recall the past and recognizes the impossibility of achieving justice in the present.

In an afterword written for the 1999 edition, Steiner defends his lack of an answer to the 'unthinkable paradoxes' (174) articulated mainly by Hitler, including the question of the relationship of the Holocaust to other mass state killings (under Stalin and Mao, for example). Steiner admits to his growing distrust of people who confidently do have answers. In the novel, the absolutes of forgiveness and justice are both negated. Forgiveness is not posited as an option for the survivors and justice is compromised; by the political exploitation of nation states, because no justice can rectify the past and because the survivors' identities continue to be formed in relation to perpetrators. Crucially too, Steiner's work marks a shift in authority in terms of who it is asking about forgiveness and justice. Jankélévitch and Wiesenthal pose the question; they assume the moral authority to do so and see it as their prerogative as Jewish (resistance member and survivor). In the novel, the authority of the survivors is dispersed and weakened in the interaction with other voices. They face an inevitable confrontation with justice that is flawed and politicized and which, to comply with the demands of justice, requires Hitler's defence to be heard. The novel dramatizes the disturbing reality and emotional impact of 'no last word'.

The crack of age

Jankélévitch, Wiesenthal and Steiner were responding to pressures to forgive and forget and the commensurate lack of appetite for bringing perpetrators to trial. Since the millennium, however, the increasing age of the perpetrators has been key for focusing attention once again on bringing them to justice. In 2002, the Simon Wiesenthal Center launched 'Operation Last Chance', citing the increasing age of both perpetrators and survivors as urgent reasons for finding ex-Nazis who had evaded justice. The trial of 91-year-old John Demjanjuk in 2011 gave further impetus for prosecutions, since it was the first trial at which a defendant was convicted of being an accessory to murder on the basis of being a camp guard rather than on evidence of being involved in the murder of a specific prisoner. Yet the age of those involved in National Socialist violence brings more risks than their imminent death. As Lieber warns in *The Portage* when he hears that the old Hitler has been found: 'Do not let him speak freely. You will hear the crack of age in his voice. He is old'. If Hitler speaks, those who hear will 'grow uncertain [...] and no longer believe what he did' (45).

The crack in the voice and lines in the face are forceful reminders that perpetration occurred, almost, before living memory. The perceived vulnerability of age and proximity to death can evoke strong empathy. Margaret Renkl writes that 'some creatures are so manifestly vulnerable that they inspire a near universal tenderness [...]. In the presence of vulnerability most of us instinctively stop what we are doing and try to help'.[18] She gives examples of a lost child and a person near death. In fact, Renkl is writing about the case of Karl Friedrich Berger, who was deported from the United States and flown back to Frankfurt on 20 February 2021. He had served as a prison guard at a Neuengamme sub-camp and the US court found that his actions 'constituted assistance in Nazi-sponsored persecution'.[19] In this context, Renkl is evoking the transgression of those who remain indifferent 'or worse', such as Berger in his role as guard. Unfortunately, her sentimental universalizing belies the reality that vulnerability can inhibit empathy and fuel rejection and aggression.[20] Nevertheless, in proposing that the natural response to vulnerability is the desire to help and by casting the failure to react in this way as a moral lapse, Renkl unintentionally condones the need to 'try to help' perpetrators who appear weakened by age.

Two novels that explore the implications of the vulnerability of age in relation to the tension between justice and forgiveness are Michael Lavigne's *Not Me* (2005) and Jodi Picoult's *The Storyteller* (2012).[21] Both can be understood as fictional re-workings of Wiesenthal's *The Sunflower* with the added dimensions of age and a lifetime of remorse on the part of the perpetrators. Lavigne's novel explores Wiesenthal's themes and Picoult is explicit that her novel developed from wondering what would happen if the dying SS man's request were made decades later. In *Not Me*, Heshel Rosenheim is dying of Alzheimer's in a care home, and gives his son Michael his memoir to read. It emerges that Heshel Rosenheim is the assumed name of ex-SS officer Heinrich Mueller, a keen Nazi and anti-Semite, who was accountant at Bergen-Belsen and Majdanek. He disguises himself as Jewish to evade justice, but after participating in the Israeli War of Independence and loving and losing his Jewish lover, he moves to the United States where he becomes a devout Jew. In *The Storyteller*, the kind Josef Weber admits to Sage Singer that he is Reiner Hartmann, the former vicious SS *Schutzhaftlagerführer* in charge of Appel at Auschwitz. He asks her to help him to die, a fate he feels he deserves, and asks her to forgive him. She informs the FBI of his identity and agrees to get a full confession from him by wearing a wire-tap. But, unbeknown to the FBI, Sage finally decides to help him die by baking him a bread roll containing monkshood. However, she tells him that she will never forgive him. Only after his death does it emerge that Weber was not Reiner Hartmann but his more educated brother, SS *Hauptscharführer* Franz Hartmann, in charge of Kanada in Auschwitz and much less cruel. Indeed, and softening up the reader for the flabby forgiveness to follow, Weber/Franz was always opposed to the Nazis and on occasion tried to protect Jews.

In both novels, the former SS men have lived exemplary lives since the war, full of remorse and paying penance in the form of good deeds. They are loved and respected by their community, a positive relationship dependent on maintaining the lie about their identity. Rosenheim does so until, as Sue Vice puts it, his 'dementia confirms the possibility of leaving the past definitively behind',[22] and Weber until his wife dies and he no longer has her to see the good in him to counter his self-loathing (117). They thus avoid criminal and common justice, instead choosing to see themselves as recipients of divine justice. Rosenheim interprets the death of his eighteen-year-old daughter as punishment for his sins, which triggers his confession. Weber wants to die but cannot, which he sees as 'God's joke': he has twice survived cancer, a car crash, a broken hip and a suicide attempt (54).

Picoult's figures represent different positions drawn directly from Wiesenthal: Leo, the FBI agent, pursues justice; Mary the ex-nun, who echoes the views of Eva Fleischner in the responses to *The Sunflower*, is the enlightened Christian who argues that forgiveness is necessary for personal liberation from hate; Minka is the survivor who cannot forgive the SS man who saved her but who believes that hating all Germans makes her no better than the murderers; and Sage is the Wiesenthal figure who is objectified by the perpetrator as 'a Jew' in order to pacify his guilt. In *Not Me*, Israel Rosenheim, the real Heshel Rosenheim's son, serves the purpose of the representative Jew who may be able to offer forgiveness. Wiesenthal's silence in the face of the SS man's mother is transformed into Lily Rosenheim's silence about her husband's past, and then Michael's silence about his father's; all silences that sustain a narrative of a good person. In *The Storyteller*, a new silence is generated by Sage's final lie. The question at the end of Wiesenthal's text is answered in both these novels through figuring compassionate empathy as a path to individual maturity and in turn as a signifier of moral value. Both novels treat justice, confession and forgiveness as solely private concerns, that test the moral maturity of the main protagonist. Both Michael and Sage are embroiled in their own identity crisis that is resolved through their redemptive interaction with the former perpetrator. It is this governing redemptive trajectory that renders the treatment of the themes sentimental.

In *Not Me*, Michael has not recovered from his divorce and is struggling to assume emotional responsibility for his son. His immaturity is signalled by his investment in his identity as a 'funny person' (44) and his need to joke about everything. His father's revelation is finally something he cannot joke about. He is overwhelmed by emotion at his father's death, emotion that is assigned moral value in the text through the enlightenment it confers: 'suddenly I understood' (279). Michael realizes that his father found and helped the original Heshel Rosenheim's son, Israel, who, after reading Mueller/Rosenheim's confession, decided not to expose him. Indeed, Israel left the journals for Michael, so that he might say Kaddish for his father. The fact that Mueller/Rosenheim 'may have been a monster' is washed away by 'tears of love' in the face of his father's 'emaciated' and 'only barely human' body: 'I would not be his judge. I would be his son' (281). Michael is liberated to feel more profoundly and as a result to become more morally mature and responsible. The privileging of emotion and positive empathy as arbiter of moral value is also central to Israel's change of heart and the forgiveness it implies. His name also points to the ability of the Jewish nation to make the shift from seeking justice to generating hope. Redemption and emotional maturity are achieved by privileging love and a hint of forgiveness. Justice becomes the enemy of the future good. Michael's mother Lily, the only person to whom Mueller told his secret after they married, also decided not to report him after seeing him fervently praying in the synagogue.

Even more sentimental is the redemption-all-round at the end of *The Storyteller*. Here, Sage refuses to forgive Weber but sees herself elevated above 'the monster' by showing compassion and helping him die. When in the big reveal she realizes that she has helped the nicer Weber, she whispers her apology: 'Maybe it is the forgiveness Franz had been seeking. And maybe it's just the forgiveness *I* need, for killing the wrong man' (527). Forgiveness bursts through after all and even the old Nazi becomes a better person by taking the sins of his brother upon himself. As with Lavigne's protagonist, Sage attains a new emotional and moral maturity by showing compassion to Weber. She has spent years hiding from the world after a car crash that left her with scars on her face and killed her mother. Now she can finally accept her mother's pardon for her moment of inattention while driving, regain self-esteem and find love with Leo, the FBI agent. The novel's ending unambiguously reinstates compassion and forgiveness at the cost of justice. Sage even describes Leo as living 'within the narrow boundaries of right and wrong, of justice and deceit'. As in Lavigne's novel, the optimism of liberating redemption has greater moral value than the perpetuation of secrets and lies. We are invited to agree with Sage's convenient re-definition of her lies as a necessary fiction because redemption demands it.

Not Me and *The Storyteller* repeat Wiesenthal's questions but are intent on a last word. They both endorse empathy as a guide to moral resolution at the diegetic level and seek to mobilize the reader's empathy to validate forgiveness.

Soap opera

The drama of justice and forgiveness, bound up in questions of identity and intense and often profound pain, lends itself to racy plot twists and emotional gestures. The public appetite for feeling the drama but being satisfied by a resolution of comforting forgiveness is clear from *The Storyteller*'s rapid ascent to the top of the *New York Times* bestseller list and the marketing of both novels for book clubs. The interest in drama and forgiveness is not, however, limited to fiction. In July 2015, the 94-year-old Oskar Gröning, 'the book-keeper of Auschwitz', was found guilty of being accessory to the murder of at least 300,000 Jews and sentenced to four years' imprisonment. It was a well-publicized case, all the more so when Eva Moses Kor, a survivor of Mengele's twin experiments, was embraced and kissed by Gröning when she approached him to thank him for testifying. In 2020, aged 93, Bruno Dey was convicted of 5,232 counts of accessory to murder at Stutthof and given a two-year suspended prison sentence. During his trial, Peter Loth, a co-plaintiff and child survivor of Stutthof, asked Dey whether he would forgive Loth for the hatred that he had felt for the Germans. Loth then announced to the court that he forgave Dey and embraced him. This event was widely reported, but nowhere near as widely as the subsequent twist: Peter Loth, it transpired following a *Spiegel* investigation, was not a survivor and once his status was questioned, he withdrew from the trial.

Loth's individual investment in receiving and bestowing forgiveness, inseparable from his lifelong '[search] for his true identity', mirrors a wider fascination with forgiveness.[23] Much of the reporting of this event, and of Kor's interaction with

Gröning, betrays the appetite for forgiveness as a redemptive gesture. Not surprisingly, such events attract considerable positive interest in Germany, with *Die Welt* describing Loth's 'ergreifende Geste' ('moving gesture') and the *Hamburger Morgenpost* hailing the 'ergreifender Moment' ('moving moment') as one that stirred the onlookers in court, though it offered no evidence of this. In the UK the *Daily Mail* encouraged big emotions with big letters: 'Holocaust survivor HUGS Nazi death camp guard'.[24] Interestingly, ZDF referred to Loth as a 'mutiger Zeuge' ('brave witness'), a value judgement that by singling him out makes other witnesses seem somehow lacking in courage when they testified to the atrocities that they had witnessed and survived.[25] ZDF's failure of judgement, although it acquires a comic dimension courtesy of the *Spiegel* exposé, rests on their quick assumption that, even if Loth had been a survivor, his dramatic gesture of forgiveness was courageous. His demonstrative staging of 'a morally weighty act' raises questions about the complex emotional needs that forgiveness is felt to serve.

The coverage of Kor's embrace by Gröning also reflects the heightened fascination with forgiveness. The embrace was much more widely reported than the testimony of other survivors at the trial, alongside references to Kor's previous gesture of forgiving 'all the Nazis' in her name alone. Although it is clear from the film's footage and from what Kor said afterwards that Gröning pulled her into an embrace, much of the reporting implied that it was a mutual gesture or that she embraced him, suggesting a desire that it should be so. However, the emphasis on Kor's forgiveness was not always positive. *The Times of Israel* implied Kor was the active agent to add weight to the critical response of her forty-nine co-plaintiffs who were angered by her very public statements.[26] Their criticism of Kor was also reported in leading German papers. The *Süddeutsche Zeitung* pointed to the plaintiffs' objection to Kor's reiteration on German television that instead of trials of former SS officers, they should be urged to share their stories publically. In contrast, the other plaintiffs insisted on the importance of trials to ensure justice was done for those who were murdered.[27] Similarly, *Die ZEIT* had a headline about the International Auschwitz Committee's criticism of Kor and how the public gesture turned the trial into a 'personality show and soap opera'. This not only harmed the integrity of the other plaintiffs, it also ran the risk of German society misunderstanding Kor's gesture as a 'moral acquittal'.[28]

That the relationship of justice and forgiveness should take on such dramatic form at a public trial demonstrates how the desire for one is felt to compromise the integrity of the other. The potential for drama is heightened by the awareness of time running out, be that for justice to be done or forgiveness to be granted. The emotional investment in the debate is further affected by the constellation of age, frailty and the actors' proximity to death, all of which draw attention to the ever-growing temporal distance of the crimes. Indeed, the judiciary itself is very much part of the drama, with Operation Last Chance also offering them, as a professional body, the opportunity to compensate for their compromising complicity with National Socialism and their post-war contribution to the failure of justice. It is, from this point of view, not surprising that a trial should assume elements of a soap opera, for the desire for justice or forgiveness is so intimately linked to confirming or restoring identity. But perhaps we should be less dismissive of soap opera, or, to put it more kindly, to serial melodrama, as an appropriate form for the drama to assume. Jankélévitch's association of remorse with tragedy, as an ontological condition stemming from freedom, suggests the potential for tragic representation of perpetrators.[29] However, the redemptive spark of tragedy would determine the outcome, for which, following Jankélévitch, there can be no guarantee. Furthermore, as the Old Boy ruminates in Kertész's *Fiasco*, unlike tragic murderers like Richard III, who vow to do evil, totalitarian regimes claim to be working for the common good. There is no place for tragic individuals, or tragic representation, in response to mass murder. If Ilse Koch cannot be thought of as 'a great sinner worthy of Dostoievsky's pen' because she epitomized a moral order rather than opposing it, then these ancient juvenile prison guards even less so.[30]

Melodrama, as Peter Brooks argues, is not a debased form of tragedy but a response to the loss of the sacred and the moral certainties it guaranteed. Melodrama seeks moral meaning in the world, with the battles between good and evil played out at a personal level. Consequently, ethics is associated with emotional states, and played out with an intensity of feeling that often offends social norms. This is one reason for melodrama's poor reputation, but as Brooks points out, melodrama need not lack subtlety. In Henry James, for example, evil may mean 'denying to someone the means to free realization of his (or [. . .] her) full potential as a moral being'.[31] In serial melodrama, the 'uncovering, demonstrating, and making operative the essential moral universe in a post-sacred era' does not demand an ending and its form resists resolution.[32] Despite the required closure of a verdict making trials more obviously akin to theatre, entertaining a shift from theatre to the story-telling of serial melodrama allows us to understand trials as an ongoing and serial engagement with the ongoing social process of public secrets becoming public contests. In this form too, Picoult's protagonist Sage would not hoodwink the FBI with monkshood, but the results of the post-mortem would lead to a new trial in which her crisis of justice and forgiveness would be scrutinized. The very conventions of serial melodrama demand the exploration of how people move in and out of complicity and perpetration in a changing social context, how they construct their narratives in relation to those changes and how we empathize with those narratives in the knowledge of what has gone before. And if the end does have to come, a *Sopranos* cut to black is one way of refusing the last word.

Notes

1 Borislav Pekić, *How to Quiet a Vampire. A Sotie*, trans. Stephen M. Dickey and Bogdan Rakić (Evanston: Northwestern University Press, 2005).
2 Michael Mulkay, *On Humor: Its Nature and Its Place in Modern Society* (Cambridge: Polity, 1988), 37.
3 Jorge Luis Borges, '*Deutsches Requiem*', in *The Aleph*, trans. Andrew Hurley (London: Penguin, 2000 [1949]), 65; George Steiner, *The Portage to San Cristóbal of A.H.* (Chicago: University of Chicago Press, 1999 [1979]); Jonathan Littell, *The Kindly Ones*, trans. Charlotte Mandell (London: Vintage, 2010).
4 See Erin McGlothlin, 'Empathetic Identification and the Mind of the Holocaust Perpetrator in Fiction: A Proposed Taxonomy of Response', *Narrative* 24, no. 3 (2016): 251–76.

5 Juliane Prade-Weiss, 'Guilt-tripping the "Implicated Subject": Widening Rothberg's Concept of Implication in Reading Herta Müller's *The Hunger Angel*', *Journal of Perpetrator Research* 3, no. 3 (2020): 55.
6 Borislav Pekić, quoted in Olga Nedeljković, '"The Destruction of Reality, or the Myth of Man" in Borislav Pekić's Essay-Manifesto: "The Myth of Literature and the Myth of Reality"', *Serbian Studies Research* 1, no. 1 (2010): 69–101.
7 David Grossman, *See Under: Love*, trans. Betsy Rosenberg (London: Vintage, 1999), 252 and 280.
8 Fritz Breithaupt, *The Dark Side of Empathy*, trans. Andrew B. B. Hamilton (Ithaca and London: Cornell University Press, 2019), 10.
9 Imre Kertész, *Fiasco*, trans. Tim Wilkinson (New York: Melville, 2011 [1988]), 305.
10 Vladimir Jankélévitch, *Forgiveness*, trans. Andrew Kelley (Chicago: Chicago University Press, 2005), 4 and 3.
11 Aaron Looney discusses Derrida's criticism that Jankélévitch reduces forgiveness to an exchange with remorse. Looney contextualizes the vexed relationship of conditionality or unconditionality within the Abrahamic traditions, all of which debate the 'logic of conditionality and the logic of unconditionality'. He argues that Jankélévitch and Derrida are both concerned about reducing forgiveness to 'an exchange, a meritorious affair, or an economic activity, and both principally agree that the gratuity of forgiveness precludes conditions, including repentance'. Both 'recognize the necessity of negotiating the aporia of the gift of forgiveness between the order of knowledge, acknowledgment, and rationality, on the one hand, and love, charity, and grace, on the other'. See *Vladimir Jankélévitch: The Time of Forgiveness* (New York: Fordham University Press, 2015), 210–11.
12 Vlademir Jankélévitch, 'Should We Pardon Them?', trans. Ann Hobart, *Critical Inquiry* 22, no. 3 (1996): 552.
13 Simon Wiesenthal, *The Sunflower. On the Possibilities and Limits of Forgiveness*, trans. H. A. Pichler (New York: Schocken Books, 1998), 98.
14 The first American edition of 1976 contained ten responses. The revised and expanded edition of 1997 included thirty-two new responses, including three translated from the 1981 German edition (by Jean Améry, Cardinal König and Albert Speer). The paperback edition of 1998 was expanded with seven further contributions.
15 Peter Banki, *The Forgiveness to Come. The Holocaust and the Hyper-Ethical* (New York: Fordham University Press, 2017), 46.
16 Margaret Burton, 'From Polarity to Moral Ambiguity: Language in *The Portage to San Cristóbal of A. H.*', *Studies in American Jewish Literature* 22 (1981): 114.
17 Ibid., 115.
18 Margaret Renkl, 'Of Nazis, Crimes and Punishment', *New York Times. International Edition*, 9 March 2021: 10.
19 The US Department of Justice, 'WWII Nazi Concentration Camp Guard Removed to Germany', Saturday, 20 February 2021. https://www.justice.gov/opa/pr/wwii-nazi-concentration-camp-guard-removed-germany (Accessed 29 March 2021).
20 At a personal level, violence is more likely if there is a 'weak victim to attack', just as there are institutionalized forms of attacking the weak. Indeed, a key pattern of adult violence involves 'the situationally strong ganging up on the weak and fearful'. Randall Collins, *Violence. A Micro-Sociological Theory* (Princeton and Oxford: Princeton University Press, 2008), 9 and 26.
21 Michael Lavigne, *Not Me* (New York: Random House, 2005). Jodi Picoult, *The Storyteller* (London: Hodder & Stoughton, 2013).

22 Sue Vice, 'Memory Thieves? Representing Dementia in Holocaust Literature', *English Language Notes* 57, no. 2 (2019): 121.
23 'The Concentration Camp Victim Who Never Was', *Spiegel International*, 14 January 2020. https://www.spiegel.de/international/germany/the-concentration-camp-victim-who-never-was-a-a7c50dd3-773f-4697-b9c0-e40618a62e9e (Accessed 18 April 2021).
24 '"Ich werde ihm vergeben" – KZ-Insasse umarmt einstigen SS-Wachmann', *Die Welt online*, 12 November 2019. https://www.welt.de/vermischtes/article203435808/Stutthof-Prozess-Zeuge-umarmt-einstigen-KZ-Wachmann.html; 'SS-Prozess in Hamburg. Emotionale Szene rührt Beobachter im Gericht', *Hamburger Morgenpost*, 12 November 2019. https://www.mopo.de/hamburg/ss-prozess-in-hamburg-emotionale-szene-ruehrt-beobachter-im-gericht-33453232; 'Holocaust survivor HUGS Nazi death camp guard', *Mail Online*, 12 November 2019. https://www.dailymail.co.uk/news/article-7706095/Holocaust-survivor-HUGS-Nazi-concentration-camp-guard-93-trial-accessory-murder.html. All accessed 30 March 2021.
25 '"Ich werde ihm vergeben". Zeuge umarmt ehemaligen KZ-Wächter', *ZDFheute*, 12 November 2019. https://www.zdf.de/nachrichten/heute/stutthof-prozess-in-hamburg-zeuge-umarmt-ehemaligen-kz-waechter-100.html (Accessed 30 March 2021).
26 'Survivor Who Embraced Auschwitz "Accountant" Slammed for Urging end to Trials', *The Times of Israel*, 27 April 2015. https://www.timesofisrael.com/survivor-criticized-for-urging-end-to-trials-of-ss-officers/ (Accessed 30 March 2021).
27 'Versöhnungsgeste im Auschwitz-Prozess sorgt für Protest', *Süddeutsche Zeitung*, 27 April 2015. https://www.sueddeutsche.de/panorama/prozesse-versoehnungsgeste-im-auschwitz-prozess-sorgt-fuer-protest-dpa.urn-newsml-dpa-com-20090101-150427-99-10953 (Accessed 30 March 2021).
28 'Auschwitz-Komitee kritisiert Vergebungsgeste von Eva Kor', *Die ZEIT*, 27 April 2015. https://www.zeit.de/gesellschaft/zeitgeschehen/2015-04/auschwitz-prozess-eva-kor-versoehnung-kritik (Accessed 30 March 2021).
29 Looney, *Time of Forgiveness*, 240–1.
30 Kertész, *Fiasco*, 49.
31 Peter Brooks, *The Melodramatic Imagination: Balzac, Henry James, Melodrama, and the Mode of Excess* (New Haven: Yale University Press, 1976), 169.
32 Ibid., 15.

3

Conformity, compliance and complicity
'Ordinary people' and the Holocaust

Mary Fulbrook

The Nazi mass murder of European Jews, Roma, the mentally and physically disabled and innumerable other victims, was only possible with the active assistance or at least passive acquiescence of millions of 'ordinary people' across Nazi-dominated Europe. Who were those 'ordinary people' who witnessed but were unwilling – or unable – to act against mass murder on an unprecedented scale, or who even became in some way complicit in the process of perpetration? To what extent was passivity rooted in partial consent or agreement with the persecution of minorities, or rather in subjugation and fear of the persecutors? Victim experiences have increasingly come to the fore, with the explosion of research on the Holocaust since the later twentieth century.[1] And alongside a continued focus on Nazi decision-making and policy formation, the immediate perpetrators of mass murder have also increasingly been the subject of intensive research, with heated debates about the relative significance of ideological socialization, brutalization in warfare and the implications of peer group pressure in mobilizing members of police battalions and Wehrmacht soldiers to work alongside the dedicated SS extermination squads or Einsatzgruppen in killing civilians.[2] The ways in which activists in territories occupied by or allied with Germany played a role as collaborators and auxiliaries have also increasingly been subjected to detailed and comparative analysis.[3] Yet the responses of those who initially stood on the side-lines of Nazi violence – often termed 'bystanders' – remain to date somewhat out of focus.

The responses of members of surrounding societies could be all important to the survival chances of victims. In a situation of all-engulfing violence, people who could at first be considered 'innocent bystanders' inevitably became caught up in war and genocide; and their evolving responses could crucially affect historical outcomes. Understanding the circumstances and ways in which people in surrounding societies choose to act, or fail to act – or even change direction on the spur of the moment – is vital if we are to comprehend how mass murder on the scale of the Holocaust was possible. This issue is particularly relevant to understanding the roles of citizens of the Third Reich, the prime instigator and organizer of the Holocaust. Controversies over the involvement of 'ordinary Germans', in what has variously been characterized as a 'consensual dictatorship', a 'perpetrator society' or a 'regime of terror' held together by force and fear, show little sign of resolution. Whichever way the historical research seems to point, questions arise about the extent of complicity and the veracity of later self-justifications among people included in the Nazi 'national community'.

Moreover, debates about the Third Reich, as the initiator of war and genocide, are rarely linked to discussions about the societies over which it held sway during the war. The nature of surrounding societies could make a significant difference to victims' experiences and chances of survival. The contrasts between survival rates of Jews, ranging from more than 95 per cent in Denmark or 75 per cent in France to around 25 per cent in the Netherlands and a mere 5 per cent in Lithuania, are rooted in more than just the distinction between western European countries from which Jews were deported and eastern European countries in which Jews were killed. Geopolitical locations and shifting considerations across the stages of the war clearly shaped Nazi strategies and differing regional policies; but the wider social context also affected the extent to which Germans were able to control particular areas and put into effect repressive, exploitative and murderous policies. From the victims' perspective, the wider environment affected chances of obtaining food, shelter, medical assistance, means of escape or hiding, including 'going under' in plain sight through the adoption of false identities.

While there have long been challenges to heroic resistance narratives in western European countries, research on complicity and collaboration in eastern Europe only developed significantly after the collapse of communism and remains hampered by the relative inaccessibility of some archival materials.[4] Systematic comparisons between eastern and western Europe, and among eastern Europe societies within fluctuating borders, require further development. European-wide comparisons undoubtedly raise major challenges around area expertise: any overview must always be open to revision in light of emergent language-specific historiographies and sources. But there are also other, often extraneous, factors affecting comparisons. On occasion, there seems to be a moral hesitancy about bringing conquerors and conquered into the same universe of comparison, as though to delineate the contributing complicity of others might somehow reduce the burden of German culpability. There is also a (well-founded) fear that highlighting how eastern Europeans were victims of both Stalinism and Nazism might be misused to exonerate nationalist heroes from complicity in Nazi antisemitism, as evident in controversies in Poland, Lithuania and Latvia. In the crossfire of contemporary identity politics, the field is complicated by an underlying ethno-nationalism: the reputation, even the supposed 'honour', of 'the nation' is held to be at stake.[5] There are also individual sensitivities, where people are still affected by the consequences of the massacres and social upheavals of the Nazi era.

At the heart of all these controversies lies the issue of compromised identities, whether individual or collective, which are seen to be tainted by varying degrees of historical culpability. How then can we best understand gradations of guilt and complicity in different circumstances? Can the wider 'Aryan' population of Nazi Germany really be described as a 'perpetrator society', essentially rephrasing the outmoded 1945 claims about 'collective guilt' or that 'all Germans are bad Germans'? Or can we reach a more differentiated understanding of constraints, pressures, potential for acting in different ways, even as we also explore how people were themselves changed by living through a period of immense terror and pressure for conformity? We need right at the outset to take seriously Kurt Tucholsky's comment – made in a despairing letter written in exile, shortly before his death in December 1935, to Arnold Zweig, also in exile – that 'a country is not only that which it does – it is also that which it is prepared to stomach, to put up with'.[6] But Tucholsky's characteristically sharp insight does not in fact go far enough, in two respects: we need, first, to explore further how specific political conditions and historical circumstances affected social perceptions and interpersonal relations over time, with implications both for *what* people are prepared to 'put up with' and against *whom*; and secondly, and importantly, we need to go beyond the assumption of a uniform 'land', 'nation' or homogeneous 'society', to understand in a more differentiated fashion *who* precisely, and under what conditions, is more or less likely to 'put up with' – or alternatively to stand up and speak out against – injustice and violence against which others.

The passivity of bystanders can make a crucial difference to the course of persecution. We therefore need a differentiated approach to analysing the diversity of responses in persisting systems of collective violence; an approach that can disentangle the small steps, over time, that make ever-greater numbers of people more likely to remain silent in face of violence against selected groups of 'others'.

Theoretical approaches: The problem of bystanders

The general field of forces is often summarized, following Raul Hilberg, in terms of three nouns: 'perpetrators, victims and bystanders'.[7] A great deal of attention has rightly focused on the first two: those directly responsible for ordering or executing acts of violence and their immediate victims. Yet despite the significance of the third and extremely broad element in this triad, there is little agreement on the scope or even the value of what proves to be an extremely slippery concept.[8]

Social psychologists have much to offer in terms of understanding individual responses within small group contexts in a broader environment where certain behaviours are not officially condoned.[9] But the situation is very different when violence is state-sanctioned or it is the authorities themselves who are instigating collective violence. Moreover, individuals are not in some sense historical 'givens' or fixed personalities, but are constantly changing, affected by their times. People living within a persisting system of collective violence – whether for a matter of days, weeks or years – are themselves changed by the circumstances in which they make their lives. Social relations and cultural perceptions begin to shift, with significant implications for attitudes and action. Those who are initially simply witnesses to violence by chance coincidence of time and place – happening to be 'present' at both the time and the scene of the crime, so to speak – become themselves more deeply involved in the dynamics of systemic or state-sanctioned violence over an extended period of time. Their progressive involvement on one side or another is not readily captured in the notion of 'bystanders'.

Simply coining a concept such as the 'implicated subject' as an 'umbrella category' that is so capacious as to be effectively meaningless does little to further historical analysis of key distinctions.[10] Rather than simply rejecting Hilberg's somewhat unsatisfactory triad of nouns, suggesting fixed identities, it may be helpful to explore further the possibility of a more differentiated approach to understanding changing roles, behaviours and attitudes in relation to collective violence.

There are clear benefits in taking a 'social process approach' to understanding the ways in which people may variously become involved in acts of perpetration at certain times.[11] Even so, this too can seem on occasion a little evasive. A social process approach may be good for understanding the social dynamics of changing configurations of violence over a period of time, but there is still some value in identifying precisely who did what to whom in particular moments of crime. The 'perpetrators' who instigate, organize or engage in violence, and the direct 'victims' of crimes, are in principle identifiable, despite the undoubted complexities of the real world. So we might want to retain those two nouns, at least for the moment of the criminal act. But to (re)assert this does not solve the wider problem of understanding the field of forces or social contexts within which the direct actors are operating. 'Bystanding' is intrinsically a temporally unstable, relational concept, with 'bystanders' defined purely in terms of initial location on the periphery of violent situations; yet it is nevertheless their changing perceptions and actions that may eventually make a significant difference to outcomes. And here, time operates in the opposite direction from that explored in 'social process' approaches. While people may *become* perpetrators over time, people inevitably *cease to be* 'innocent bystanders' the longer the violence lasts. Even by remaining passive, they do not remain neutral; passivity in effect condones violence, and in this way facilitates it.

So we need to ask: under what conditions do people come either to side with initiators and perpetrators of violence, or to extend sympathy and even assistance towards victims? There are a range of ways of exploring this question, with respect both to short-term situations – momentary incidents of violence – and to shifts in the character of social relations and political conditions over longer periods of time.

It is not easy to interpret bystander responses when captured, for example, in the fleeting instant of a photograph: passers-by watching impassively as Jews are taunted, attacked, marched along the street by persecutors; audiences laughing as old men are subjected to rituals of humiliation such as having their beards cut off or being forced to scrub the pavement on their knees; onlookers curiously taking photographs at public hangings or mass shootings. Do apparently eager facial expressions as captured on photographs – often the only traces we have, decades later – signal genuine approval, or nervous alignment with what are perceived to be dominant views? Are enthusiastic gestures – hysterically smiling heads forwards, arms outstretched in the Hitler greeting – just momentary effects of crowd behaviour? Are such expressions in effect masks, habitual 'public faces' readily donned under dictatorial conditions; or do they reflect genuine emotions, only expressed once approval of violence against 'outsiders' was legitimized? Is squinting, or looking away, a sign of discomfort at witnessing the subjugation of others, or merely a momentary attempt to avoid blinding sunlight in the eyes? Does a downcast head signal disapproval of what was going on, or simply distraction at registering a blistered heel or rumbling stomach? Clearly, images of 'bystander' responses at particular moments – whether visual or verbal, as captured in equally snapshot reports on popular opinion – need to be supplemented by a range of other materials to explore internalities as well as external expressions, and to trace changing responses over time.

Exploring changing subjectivities over a longer period of time raises further questions. At what point, when inhabiting a persisting system of collective violence, does outward conformity become internalized and effectively normalized, as invidious categories and values are repeatedly expressed and enacted in everyday behaviours? At what point, or in what ways, do conformity and compliance cross the threshold into more active complicity? In what ways do individual situations and motives for action (or inaction) make a difference to later evaluations of passive or apparently complicit behaviour? Do professed motives – acting out of fear, or for 'good' reasons, rather than in service of 'bad' ideals or for 'selfish' personal ends – help to justify behaviours; and if so, how far can we believe which stories and forms of self-exoneration, produced under changed circumstances and for different audiences (including the self)? How, in short, do people's norms and values, as well as their perhaps mistaken perceptions of the situation, play a role in later analyses of actions and consequences? And, bearing these questions in mind, can we develop relevant distinctions between different degrees or forms of complicity?

The legal definition of complicity relates to 'aiding and abetting' a criminal act, providing assistance to those committing a crime or benefitting from such an act; and the definition of what constitutes a 'crime' varies with jurisdiction. But for historical assessment of degrees of involvement in both systemic violence and specific incidents, we need a wider conceptual framework. In particular, we need to develop ways of understanding both subjective perceptions and outward behaviours, which may often be somewhat at odds with one another.[12]

Patterns of involvement: A framework for analysis

The following analytic framework may be useful in assessing ways in which it is possible to be, for example, functionally complicit through roles and behaviours while varying in subjective perceptions of and attitudes towards such complicity. A sense of unease at the moral compromises entailed might affect a person's sense of identity, but personal morality may also be in conflict with commitment to a wider collective identity (as for example, membership of a group, a religious community, a nation). There are multiple ways in which living in a persisting system of collective violence intrinsically entails compromised identities, and also multiple ways in which individuals can seek to alleviate their own sense of discomfort at registering a degree of dissonance, in one way or another, by variously adjusting their perceptions, attitudes or actions according to circumstances.

It is important to note that the following categories are intended solely for analytic purposes: individuals might occupy or move between several positions. Combining subjectivities and behaviours, this framework is intended to help us understand the roles people play, the fields of forces they inhabit, and their perceptions and evaluations of the situation. It starts from the premise that in a system of persisting collective violence the 'neutrality' of 'innocent bystanders' is only momentarily an option, if at all, and that people are continually faced with pressures to move in a variety of directions.

1. Conformity

Life in a dictatorship based on terror inevitably entails high levels of conformity. From the moment Hitler was appointed Chancellor of Germany on 30 January 1933, people who were not necessarily Nazi enthusiasts rapidly 'fell into line'. Outward conformity was rooted partly in genuine enthusiasm for the new order, the national 'saviour' who would supposedly restore law and order to the streets, and make Germany great again. Conformity was partly a matter of simply going along with the crowd. But conformity was also based in justified apprehension, in light of the early and vicious crackdown on left-wing opponents of Nazism. One of the odder phenomena of the early Third Reich was that of what were jokingly called 'beef-steak Nazis' – brown on the outside, red on the inside – who donned Nazi uniforms to try to bury their communist or socialist past. There is a huge literature on support for Nazism; rather less on the ambivalent combination of outward conformity and inner misgivings.[13]

But what is more puzzling are the ways in which, over the early months of the regime, many citizens went well beyond what was formally required of them. They not only mouthed the slogans and raised their arms in the Hitler salute in public but also conformed to Nazi precepts in what might be thought of as 'private spaces'. Particularly notable in the memoirs of Germans excluded from the 'national community' on grounds of 'race' are stories of how formerly close friends and acquaintances rapidly dropped all contact with 'non-Aryan' fellow-citizens. Breaking of friendships was, for example, one of the most painful memories of the period after 1933 in autobiographical essays written on the brink of war under the title 'My Life in Germany before and after 1933' – essays penned at a time when the worse that was still to come was not yet known about, and before knowledge of camps and gas chambers overshadowed all the agonies of persecution in everyday life that had taken place in the peacetime years.[14]

2. Compliance

Conformity and compliance are related to slightly different kinds of awareness and pressure to align with dominant views or practices. Conformity may be the result of informal pressures, not always made explicit, and of which people may not be consciously aware even as they come to behave in similar ways to others. Compliance is related to more clearly expressed and registered requirements: people find that in certain settings they have to comply with particular demands and regulations, requests and expectations. Non-compliance generally entails sanctions of varying degrees of severity, or potentially disagreeable consequences (as when an electrical device or plug that does not comply with safety regulations sparks a fire).

Ambivalent conformity can readily be turned into regularized compliance – and even what might be called pre-emptive over-compliance. People may come to believe that compliance is not only unavoidable but also morally right: in the interests of the wider community with which they identify, furthering collective aims which they share, and so on. This is particularly the case where a sense of a 'national community' is being energetically propagated, with the assertion of a return to national greatness being eagerly accepted by large numbers of people. With increasing Nazi control of the media, law, cultural institutions, education and socialization, it required strong commitment to alternative or prior belief systems to hold out against falling in with new hegemonic discourses and practices.

With the Law for the Restoration of a Professional Civil Service in April 1933, many Germans were surprised to discover that colleagues, acquaintances or even they themselves, had the odd Jewish grandparent of whom they had perhaps not previously been aware. Moreover, it was not only the areas of state employment covered by the law, but also many other businesses and leisure associations that now excluded people with 'non-Aryan' ancestry. Whether or not individuals were personally affected, this – and further legislation, a few months later, on compulsory sterilization of the supposedly hereditarily diseased – instantly highlighted the salience of 'race' and the notion of a 'healthy national community' as principles structuring exclusion and inclusion.

The 1935 Nuremberg Laws (while somewhat ameliorating the status of 'quarter-Jews', but too late to mitigate individual experiences of social decline since 1933) served both to normalize racialized perceptions of difference, and to foster both physical and social segregation of 'Aryans' and 'non-Aryans'. As a consequence of practical measures, enforceable in law, there was growing distance between shifting communities of empathy, with an impact not only on those ousted as Jews, but also on 'Aryans'. Many became increasingly indifferent to the fates of people with whom they were losing contact. Loss of contact meant they could more readily ignore the distress of those who had been stigmatized, marginalized, ousted from the new 'national community'. But others felt powerless, resigning themselves to going along with things. Growing *indifference*, alongside learned *ignorance*, and an increasing sense of *impotence* as it was ever more clear that the regime was firmly entrenched and far from transitory, variously contributed to *inaction* in the face of state-sanctioned violence against Jews and other victims of the Nazi regime.

Although compliance among older Germans was often still a matter of public performance accompanied by inner reservations, it was increasingly rooted in Nazi convictions among members of younger generations, brought up in an already racialized view of the world. And many adults were enthusiastic about the return to full employment and assertions of national pride in the mid-1930s. But this was not always the case.

'Constrained compliance' relates to the effectively powerless participation of those who feel forced by circumstances to comply. Through following regulations in a system of collective violence, people may be sustaining persecution without necessarily wanting to. Uncomfortable in their roles, yet unable to see safe means of opting out, they may seek ways of alleviating their own distress, even if only through occasional expressions of sympathy towards victims. They feel they have to go along with things, fearing the greater risks of other courses of action. A sense of apathy rooted in awareness of impotence may underlie this path of least resistance.

3. *Varieties of complicity*

There are varying forms of complicity with a persisting system of collective violence. Two in particular may be highlighted: active facilitation of the regime's persecutory aims; and benefitting from the persecution of others. These may, similarly, be further subdivided according to degrees of agency and willingness to be involved.

'*Willing facilitation*' refers to playing an identifiable role in making systemic violence possible, and hence being, in effect, *complicit*. People may later claim they had merely worked as 'cogs in the machine', and should not be held responsible for the overall outcomes to which their own small part had contributed, but without them the system could not have functioned. This category would encompass, for example, innumerable German civil servants and collaborators in territories under Nazi rule.

'*Unwilling facilitation*' is a variant of this to be more thoroughly explored, as in the cases, for example, of Germans called up for Reich Labour Service who found themselves working in a concentration camp, or in a sanatorium where people with mental and physical disabilities were being killed, or eastern Europeans who were 'requisitioned' by the invading Germans to assist in providing materials and labour for killing operations. Some may have come to terms with their new roles and begun to behave accordingly, adopting and to some extent internalizing the rules and discourses of the organizations or contexts in which they now worked, and trying to persuade themselves that what they were doing had some justification; others may have found it far more difficult to accept, yet considered it impossible to get away unscathed (although many more later, wrongly, used such claims in attempts at self-justification). These cases might be better covered by the notion of 'constrained compliance', since despite constraints and misgivings they also actively contributed to the furtherance of the regime's persecutory and murderous policies.

'*Wittingly benefitting*' relates to knowingly improving one's own situation at the expense of the persecuted, whether through accruing privileges, possessions, housing, enhanced opportunities or employment prospects. To ease any discomfort in their construction of an 'unselfish self', people may find justifications for their improved situation, perhaps in terms of supposed benefits to the wider community with which they identify, rather than just themselves personally. This is closely related to ideologically tinged perceptions and '*acquired indifference*' to the suffering of the victims, which can be justified by supposedly higher priorities concerning one's own community. Benefitting at the expense of others can take place ad hoc, through individual initiative – seizing the property of murdered Jews – or be systematically organized, as in the unequal distribution of food through ration cards for different categories of people.

Again, there is a variant. '*Wilfully blinkered benefitting*' refers to 'turning a blind eye'. People may be fleetingly aware of the morally tainted nature of their benefits, but do not want to register this fully; they may rapidly suppress uncomfortable thoughts and find it easier to live with compromises if they ignore disquieting aspects; they may find it easier to say they 'didn't know' – for example, combatting a sense of contamination if forced to recognize they are wearing a fur coat from a murdered Jew. There are specific social conditions that can foster a capacity to 'turn a blind eye', or to engage in '*learned ignorance*'. (Of course, some may benefit while genuinely being entirely unaware of the tainted nature of the goods or privileges they enjoy, as in the case of young children at the time, or later generations ignorant of the source of their family's wealth. This I would exclude from any useful notion of complicity, although others take a different view.[15])

4. *Principled retreat and refusal*

Basic conformity and compliance can be combined with behaviours that do not always further the aims of the regime. The famed 'inner emigration' was probably overstated after 1945 by people who had at the time engaged in compromises from which they later sought to distance themselves, claiming they had 'always been against it'. In the case of those who stayed within the system, a degree of everyday conformity and compliance was essentially for personal survival. It is extraordinarily difficult to live within a system built on an ideology and practices of exclusionary violence without having to make compromises and becoming in the process tainted, particularly in the eyes of people who may live under far less challenging circumstances and yet want to hold them to higher standards. But again, there are variations.

This category encompasses those who *retreat* from engagement as far as practicable: people who, insofar as they had any leeway for choice (far more so in some social positions than others), endeavoured neither to benefit from nor to further the persecution of those ousted from the 'national community'; or who, while not themselves subject to persecution, decided to leave Germany because they were unwilling to engage in the compromises required of them. Whether inner dissent combined with outward conformity should be garnished with the label 'opposition' is questionable, however much of a relief it might be for family members to find that a relative really had been 'always against it'.[16]

More significantly, *principled refusal* might lead into momentary or more persistent attempts at *resistance and rescue*, actively seeking to mitigate the adverse effects of persecution on victims. This might still entail engaging in compromises. For example, having to use the language of the regime to appeal to authorities on behalf of victims may simultaneously serve to reinforce the apparent validity of the regime's language. Janus-faced tightrope walking is of the essence of survival in a dictatorship while simultaneously seeking to subvert it or mitigate its consequences. Yet despite inevitable compromises, such behaviour is intended to work *against* rather than *for* the regime's ends. Depending on circumstances, there may be only very limited possibilities for acts of rescue or resistance, but even small actions or simple gestures of support and sympathy might make a huge difference to individual fates.

The possibility for principled refusal and retreat varies significantly according to social standing as well as national, regional and local conditions. Perceived risks often massively outweigh the benefits or impulse to engage in refusal and retreat, let alone acts of resistance or rescue. Under Nazi rule, there were far greater penalties to face in some areas than others; networks of social support or fear of denunciation varied with community solidarity, and degrees of dependence on mutual goodwill and neighbourly relations shifted significantly, not only during but also after the war.

Challenges to 'neutrality' in peace and war

In a persisting system of collective violence, it is not possible to remain 'neutral' for any length of time. Even in the years up to 1937, large numbers of 'Aryan' Germans had become complicit in the persecution of 'non-Aryan' compatriots and others excluded from the Nazi 'national community'. But not every Reich citizen was complicit. That the population of the by-now-expanded Reich was deeply divided was evident in polarized responses to 'Kristallnacht' in November 1938.[17] This was not, despite attempts at the time (and rather more surprisingly also recently) to label it as such, a 'pogrom' in the sense of a spontaneous popular outburst of violence, as Goebbels sought to portray it: the arson attacks on synagogues, the smashing up of Jewish homes and businesses, and the mass arrests and incarceration of adult male Jews, were clearly initiated and orchestrated from above. Yet many members of the wider population, particularly young people, participated in the violence, benefitted from looting and assisted in the humiliation of victims. Nazi activists encountered little by way of public resistance, whatever the widespread mutterings of shame. People who disapproved tended to look on passively, and only offered help to individuals in private, where risks were lower. Many 'Aryans' felt discomfited by the violence and extended personal sympathy to victims, despite simultaneously engaging in compromises through continued behavioural compliance. Non-Jewish Germans were, in effect, becoming ever more complicit by playing roles that furthered the goals of the Nazi regime, while at the same time assuaging their sense of unease by being kind to individual victims along the way. This dissonance and related sense of compromise was at the heart of subsequent discomfort about an 'unmasterable past'.

At this time, it was far from clear where exactly Nazi policies would lead. But by the late 1930s, within the Reich a 'bystander society' had developed in which the fates of those designated no longer part of one's own community of empathy could more easily be ignored. What do I mean by a 'bystander society'?[18] It is one in which, first, there are fewer emotional or other connections between different groups or communities, such that it is easier for more people to ignore the fates of those now seen as 'others', to look away or 'turn a blind eye' to violence against them; secondly, in which conditions and perceptions have changed or been sufficiently manipulated as to ensure that people will variously believe, or act as though they believed, invidious discourses about 'others', and will fail to challenge prejudices and stereotypes; and finally, in which degrees of repression and control are such that those who are still unable or unwilling to accept the dominant norms feel essentially impotent, powerless to affect the wider situation in any effective way that would make it worth taking the associated risks. 'Bystanding' – passively observing or ignoring rather than intervening on behalf of victims – is in this way promoted and sustained by specific social, ideological and political conditions. While the position of being an 'innocent bystander' can only be momentary, the socio-political circumstances that secure widespread passivity and conformity – essentially permitting violence to continue – persist and may become ever more firmly entrenched over a lengthy period of time. This is the transformation that took place in Nazi Germany in the peacetime years from 1933 (including Austria from 1938) – and with infinitely more fatal consequences in the circumstances of an aggressive and ultimately genocidal war from 1939 to 1945.

As conditions changed in wartime, priority was given to the supposed 'national interest' of the 'people's community' which with 'Aryans' were enjoined to identify. The 'Final Solution' as it emerged in late summer 1941 was not predetermined. The sequential transitions – from provoking emigration and terrorizing Jews (Kristallnacht, November 1938; Poland, September 1939 onwards); through killing adult male Jews seen as a potential security threat on the eastern front (June–July 1941); to killing Jewish women, children, the sick and the elderly, whose labour could not be exploited (from mid-August 1941 onwards); banning emigration and deporting Jews to the east (from October 1941 in the Reich, 1942 from elsewhere); to the European-wide coordination of the 'final solution' of total extermination – were shaped by changing circumstances. Considerations related to the course of the war, conceptions of military necessity, the politics of food and hunger and the need for labour power. There were continual adjustments to methods and timing, with negotiations between centre and periphery, and competing demands, even as policies of persecution, exploitation and murder all tended in the genocidal direction set by Hitler. And everywhere, the implementation of exterminatory policies was affected by local political configurations and the character of surrounding societies.

How did widespread conformity and compliance among 'ordinary people' shift into complicity and perpetration – or, by contrast, into isolated attempts at retreat, refusal and even rescue? Once mobilized for war, and particularly with the unleashing of the 'Holocaust by bullets' in summer 1941, Reich citizens became ever more deeply involved in the persecution and mass murder of civilians. Increasing numbers of direct perpetrators, mobilized within organizations specifically designed for violence the SS, Einsatzgruppen, members of police battalions and Wehrmacht soldiers – were increasingly implicated in the escalating mass murder of civilians along the eastern front. With the growth of the Nazi empire, the mushrooming structures of administration, the expansion of the system of concentration and labour camps, alongside resettlement and 'Germanization' policies, and the exploitation of foreign forced labour, many more civilians were brought into the machinery of persecution. This was a structural change of enormous proportions. Mobilization of a nation at war effectively turned huge numbers of people into facilitators and accomplices in an inherently racist national mission.

It is arguable whether, for most of the Reich citizens involved on the ground, antisemitism was a prior motivational force – as it was for Nazi leaders and ideologues – or whether ideological frameworks of interpretation served rather to provide a reservoir of post-hoc justifications for violence that transgressed all previous moral boundaries, helping to regulate otherwise uncomfortable emotions. As mass murder became increasingly a matter of public knowledge, so there were inevitably also reactions of shock and distress, particularly at the murder of women and children – a point explicitly acknowledged by Himmler in his infamous Posen speeches of October 1943. Yet most Reich citizens managed in some way to ignore what many tried to dismiss as 'excesses', and continued to support the 'national community' at war.[19] Preoccupied with personal survival, protection of the homeland and anticipatory anxiety or devastating grief about the fate of loved ones, most simply turned a blind eye to morally uncomfortable compromises on the perpetrator side. Deception about the destinations and fates of those who were not part of their own community of empathy was easier for the deceivers as well as the deceived.

When drawn into facilitating deportations, ghettoization and mass murder, subjugated members of defeated populations did not have quite the same repertoire of justifications on which to draw; they also had limited options and resources, and questions of power were crucial. In western European states, there were degrees of leeway to support, subvert or amend Nazi policies, depending on political circumstances, which significantly affected Jewish survival chances.[20] In eastern Europe, despite the more repressive German policies and drastic aims for the region, many locals nevertheless cooperated in the vain hope of promoting nationalist interests, or to vent antisemitic spleen, or to benefit in other ways, as was evident in the particularly virulent slaughter of Jews by some Lithuanians and Latvians in the six months following the German invasion, or the collaboration of Poles in the killing of 'neighbours' or participation in the 'hunt for the Jews'.[21] Many ordinary eastern Europeans were, however, simply 'requisitioned' for tasks that were essential to the Nazi-initiated and organized murder of their former schoolfriends, workmates and neighbours: providing materials to build fences around ghettos, shovels and labour power to dig death pits, carts and trucks to transport Jews to their deaths and to bring back their clothing and possessions. Locals were often still deeply troubled, decades later, by having witnessed or been forced to participate in killing 'actions', organized by Germans but only possible with local assistance.[22] Simply trying to survive through a combination of constrained compliance and a degree of blinkered benefitting – not thinking too hard about why a newly acquired blouse was bloodstained – while suppressing painful emotions, was all that was possible for the majority of impoverished eastern Europeans under Nazi rule.

Once the war was over, stories everywhere changed. And as individuals concentrated on building up their lives again, states and societies were reshaped in altered circumstances. From spring 1945, Germans who had facilitated, benefitted from, or been compliant with Nazi persecution began to claim they had 'known nothing about it', even when millions had helped to make 'it' possible. Narrow legal definitions of culpability made it easier to use the notion of perpetration primarily in relation to intentional and brutal physical violence. Shades of complicity could slide by more easily, and more readily be made compatible with new normative frameworks. Particularly when personal discomfort at compliance with the system had been ameliorated by small gestures of sympathy towards individual victims, it was possible to construct a sense of self that had 'always been against it', even despite having also sustained the regime. Among those who had actively facilitated Nazi rule, the less immediately visible consequences of policies such as expropriation of property, reduction of rations, forcing people into cramped and unhygienic housing conditions, exploitation of labour, expulsion and 'resettlement' – administrative practices contributing to death at a distance, as it were – did not seem to have unduly troubled the consciences of those responsible. Former civilian bureaucrats, employers or participants in Germanization, generally betrayed little sense of personal responsibility for the wider consequences of individual actions. Accounts by facilitators and beneficiaries often shifted the blame onto local auxiliaries who carried out direct acts of physical violence, or people portrayed as the 'real Nazis' (the SS, police, Gestapo, certain 'fanatical' members of the NSDAP), while often also still betraying racist sentiments decades after the events in question.[23] Meanwhile, eastern Europeans who had hoped that cooperation with the Germans would lead to national independence soon found their hopes further dashed by inclusion in the expanding Soviet empire in the Cold War. While they could hardly even try to claim they 'knew nothing about it', they found other ways of silencing, re-narrating or whitewashing a compromised past, further distorted in various ways by new official narratives under communist rule, and further adapted eventually in post-communist national colours.

Conclusions: Compromised identities and complicity

This analysis highlights the significance both of systems of power and repression and of interpretive frameworks for self-constructions, perceptions of others and justifications of action or inaction at different times. Historical situations are always more complex than can be captured in any typology. But the analytic framework suggested here attempts to highlight the possibility of complex combinations and changes over time, under changing circumstances. In particular, the significance within different categories of acquired indifference, learned ignorance and a sense of impotence, may help us understand the continuing unease of people who were initially neither direct perpetrators nor immediate targets of persecution but yet, over time, in a variety of ways became increasingly compromised by living within a system of collective violence.

Within the Third Reich, the racialization of identity and the radicalization of violence led to a definitive parting of the ways. Out of initial bystanders grew accomplices and perpetrators, as well as those who, by continuing to comply, effectively acquiesced in and furthered the violence. Very few were in a position to take the risk of resistance or rescue attempts, and many paid for dissenting remarks or defeatism with their liberty, even their lives.

Were those who did not approve, yet continued to conform and comply – perhaps through a sense of sheer powerlessness – in an attempt to muddle through also, in effect, in some sense complicit? Something does not feel quite right about such a claim. Not all Germans were bad Germans: this was not simply a 'perpetrator society', and blanket descriptions without adequate differentiation do not help very much.[24] Rather, I suggest, we need to enhance our understanding of perpetration and victimhood by exploring in greater depth the emergent structures and situational dynamics of a 'bystander society' in which people are more likely to withdraw and try not to be involved, as well as the processes leading individuals progressively into either greater complicity through facilitation and even acts of perpetration, or, alternatively, into modes of retreat, rescue or resistance. Cultural, social and political circumstances are absolutely central to any evaluation of individual responses. The analysis of the types of 'surrounding societies' that make collective violence more or less possible, in terms of the likelihood of passivity or inactivity in different quarters, needs to complement – not displace – analyses of forms of mobilization and involvement in acts of perpetration.

Understanding the significance of widespread conformity, popular compliance with a hostile environment and evolving complicity serves to contextualize, not replace, the analysis of culpability. Crucially, it helps us to understand the conditions under which perpetrators are able to pursue their deadly goals more effectively, and the extent to which, by contrast, victims may be able to develop viable strategies for survival.

In exploring questions around the conditions fostering widespread passivity, a more extensive and detailed comparative analysis would be necessary than could be even intimated here. This would include exploring not only the differing character of lived relations between Jews and gentiles over time, and the varieties and degrees of antisemitism in different regions, but also the specific historical circumstances in which antisemitic myths and ideologies can become salient and reservoirs of stereotypes and prejudices drawn upon. Important too are shifting 'communities of empathy', which make it easier for people to feel indifferent to the fates of others, as well as notions of civic activism, and the borders of what is sometimes called the 'universe of obligation'.[25] These relate in complex ways to conceptions of personal and collective identity, and distinctions between 'self' and 'other'. Emotional, social and cultural connections, the nature and extent of personal ties across different communities, as well as moral frameworks for understanding and acting in the world, all affect the choices people will make when confronted with systemic violence.

But equally important – perhaps more so in terms of the consequences – are changing structures of power and repression, and the unequal distribution of resources and opportunities for action. Perceptions of wider conditions inform feelings of powerlessness to affect the course of events in any way that would make the risks of action on behalf of others seem worthwhile. Expectations and aspirations for possible futures also play a significant role in people's decisions under challenging circumstances. For some individuals, commitment to political, moral or religious ideals may be so powerful as to override considerations of personal risk; at the extreme, a life is only worth living if it is deemed a worthy life, and there are compromises that cannot be contemplated if one is to be able to 'live with oneself' afterwards. These are matters of individual character and belief, however, informed and shaped by social environment, culture and circumstances. Approaches focusing on individual perceptions, social relations and cultural understandings serve to complement analyses of the historical circumstances of action, the institutional and organizational structures within which people act and prevalent discourses about, for example, the social context or collective aspirations for the future.

Such a comparative approach would need to be developed more extensively and on a broader European canvas, with detailed in-depth probing as well as wider comparisons and exploration of interconnections. It is all the more important, then, that historians develop conceptual frameworks and empirical analyses that will allow ideologically charged 'national' narratives and self-justificatory personal accounts to be critically evaluated. The Holocaust was a European phenomenon, and all who lived through this period were in some way affected. We need to understand the diverse ways in which people became involved and caught up in the enveloping tragedy, and how those who could not remain 'innocent bystanders' in this all-encompassing period of systemic violence also, by their actions and inaction, came to play a crucial historical role.

Notes

1. For the call for an 'integrated' history of the Holocaust, incorporating the voices of victims alongside the policies and practices of perpetrators, see Saul Friedländer, *Nazi Germany and the Jews 1939–1945. The Years of Extermination* (London: Weidenfeld and Nicolson, 2007).
2. See for example the path-breaking work by Christopher Browning, *Ordinary Men. Reserve Police Battalion 101 and the Final Solution in Poland* (New York: HarperCollins, 1992), and recent responses in Thomas Pegelow Kaplan, Jürgen Matthäus and Mark Hornburg (eds), *Beyond 'Ordinary Men'. Christopher R. Browning and Holocaust Historiography* (Paderborn: Brill, Ferdinand Schöningh, 2019). See also, for example: Alex Kay, *The Making of an SS Killer: The Life of Colonel Alfred Filbert, 1905–1990* (Cambridge: Cambridge University Press, 2016); Thomas Kuehne, *Belonging and Genocide: Hitler's Community, 1918–1945* (New Haven: Yale University Press, 2010); Ben Shepherd, *Hitler's Soldiers. The German Army in the Third Reich* (New Haven: Yale University Press, 2016); Edward B. Westermann, *Hitler's Police Battalions: Enforcing Racial War in the East* (Lawrence: University Press of Kansas, 2005).
3. See for example: Waitman Wade Beorn, *The Holocaust in Eastern Europe. At the Epicenter of the Final Solution* (London: Bloomsbury, 2018); Peter Black, Bela Rasky and Marianne Windsperger (eds), *Collaboration in the Holocaust and World War II in Eastern Europe* (Vienna, Hamburg: New Academic Press, 2019); Martin Dean, *Collaboration in the Holocaust: Crimes of the Local Police in Belorussia and Ukraine 1941–44* (Houndmills: Macmillan, USHMM, 2000); David Gaunt, Paul Levine and Laura Palosuo (eds), *Collaboration and Resistance during the Holocaust. Belarus, Estonia, Latvia, Lithuania* (Bern: Peter Lang, 2004).
4. See for example Leonid Rein, 'Studying East European Perpetrators: The Case of Belarus', Ch. 6, below.
5. As in the 2021 judgment in the legal case against Jan Grabowski and Barbara Engelking. See also Mary Fulbrook, 'Complicity and the Holocaust in Eastern Europe', *Jewish Historical Studies* 53 (2021): 115–35.
6. The letter of 15 December 1935 is reprinted in Kurt Tucholsky, *Gesamtausgabe. Texte und Briefe*, 22 vols, ed. Antje Bonitz, Dirk Grathoff, Michael Hepp and Gerhard Kraiker (Reinbek: Rowohlt Verlag, 1996ff). My translation of the original German is taken from web version of the letter at http://www.sudelblog.de/?p=186.
7. Raul Hilberg, *Perpetrators Victims Bystanders: The Jewish Catastrophe, 1933–1945* (New York: Aaron Asher, 1992).
8. See further Mary Fulbrook, 'Bystanders: Catchall Concept, Alluring Alibi, or Crucial Clue?', in *Probing the Limits of Categorization: The Bystander in Holocaust History*, ed. Christina Morina and Krijn Thijs (New York: Berghahn, 2018).
9. Cf. Catherine Sanderson, *The Bystander Effect: The Psychology of Courage and Inaction* (London: William Collins, 2020).
10. Michael Rothberg, *The Implicated Subject. Beyond Victims and Perpetrators* (Stanford: Stanford University Press, 2019), 1, 20. Rothberg's definition shifts uneasily, from 'a figure to think with and through' (199) to real people in '"transmission belts" of domination' who should be held 'accountable in both moral and political registers' (200). Key distinctions sometimes dissolve entirely, as when Rothberg claims that 'implication comes in diverse forms: it describes beneficiaries and descendants, accomplices and perpetrators, and it can even attach to people who have had

shattering experiences of trauma or victimization and are thus situated within "complex implication'" (200).
11 See for example Andrea Löw and Frank Bajohr (eds), *The Holocaust and European Societies: Social Processes and Social Dynamics* (London: Palgrave Macmillan, 2016).
12 For the notion of 'history from within', see further Mary Fulbrook, *Dissonant Lives: Generations and Violence through the German Dictatorships* (Oxford: Oxford University Press, 2011, 2017).
13 See for example Robert Gellately, *Hitler's True Believers. How Ordinary People became Nazis* (Oxford: Oxford University Press, 2020) and Robert Gellately, *Backing Hitler* (Oxford: Oxford University Press, 2001); contrast Richard J. Evans, 'Coercion and Consent in Nazi Germany', *Proceedings of the British Academy* 151 (2007): 53–81; see also, for differing approaches, Michael Wildt, *Hitler's Volksgemeinschaft and the Dynamics of Racial Exclusion. Violence against Jews in Provincial Germany, 1919–1939*, trans. Bernard Heise (New York and Oxford: Berghahn, 2012); or Janosch Steuwer, *'Ein Drittes Reich, wie ich es auffasse': Politik, Gesellschaft und privates Leben in Tagebüchern 1933–1939* (Göttingen: Wallstein, 2017).
14 Archival collection in the Harvard Houghton Library (HHL) of essays under the title 'My Life in in Germany before and after 1933'. See also Mary Fulbrook, 'Private Lives, Public Faces: On the Social Self in Nazi Germany', in *Private Life and Privacy in Nazi Germany*, ed. Elizabeth Harvey, Johannes Hürter, Maiken Umbach and Andreas Wirsching (Cambridge: Cambridge University Press, 2019), 55–80; and Fulbrook, *Bystander Society: Conformity and Complicity in Nazi Germany and the Holocaust* (Oxford: Oxford University Press, 2023).
15 Cf., for example, Götz Aly, *Hitlers Volksstaat: Raub, Rassenkrieg und nationaler Sozialismus* (Frankfurt am Main: S. Fischer, 2005), or Bernhard Schlink, *Guilt about the Past* (Beautiful Books, 2009).
16 Cf., for example, Friedrich Kellner, *My Opposition: The Diary of Friedrich Kellner - A German against the Third Reich* (Cambridge: Cambridge University Press, 2018).
17 Cf. Alan Steinweis, *Kristallnacht 1938* (Cambridge, MA: Harvard University Press, 2009); Wolfgang Benz, *Gewalt im November 1938. Die 'Reichskristallnacht'. Initial zum Holocaust* (Berlin: Metropol, 2018); Wolf Gruner and Steven Ross (eds), *New Perspectives on Kristallnacht: After 80 Years, the Nazi Pogrom in Global Comparison* (West Lafayette, IN.: Purdue University Press, 2019).
18 See further Fulbrook, *Bystander Society*.
19 Cf. Nicholas Stargardt, *The German War: A Nation under Arms*, (London: Bodley Head, 2015).
20 See for example: Pim Griffioen and Ron Zeller, *Persecution and Deportation of the Jews in the Netherlands, France and Belgium, 1940–1945, in a Comparative Perspective* (Amsterdam: Mémorial de la Shoah, Paris, July 2013, EHRI; updated 2018); Julian Jackson, *France: The Dark Years 1940–44* (Oxford: Oxford University Press, 2001); Bo Lidegaard, *Countrymen: How Denmark's Jews Escaped the* Nazis (London: Atlantic Books, 2013); Jacques Sémelin, *The Survival of the Jews in France, 1940–44*, trans. Cynthia Schoch and Natasha Lehrer (London: Hurst and Co., 2018; French orig. 2013); Jonathan Steinberg, *All or Nothing. The Axis and the Holocaust 1941–1943* (London: Routledge, 1990).
21 See, for example: Christoph Dieckmann, *Deutsche Besatzungspolitik in Litauen 1941–1944*, 2nd ed. (Göttingen: Wallstein Verlag, 2016); Katrin Reichelt, *Lettland unter deutscher Besatzung 1941–1944. Der lettische Anteil am Holocaust* (Berlin: Metropol-Verlag, 2011); Rūta Vanagaitė and Efraim Zuroff, *Our People. Discovering*

Lithuania's Hidden Holocaust (London: Rowman and Littlefield, 2016; English transl. 2020). On Poland, pathbreaking texts include: Jan Grabowski, *Hunt for the Jews. Betrayal and Murder in German-Occupied Poland* (Bloomington and Indianapolis: Indiana University Press, 2013); and Jan Gross, *Neighbors: The Destruction of the Jewish Community in Jedwabne, Poland* (Princeton: Princeton University Press, 2001).
22 Father Patrick Desbois, *In Broad Daylight: The Secret Procedures behind the Holocaust by Bullets*, trans. Hilary Reyl and Calvert Barksdale (New York: Arcade Publishing, 2018).
23 Cf. also Mary Fulbrook, *A Small Town Near Auschwitz: Ordinary Nazis and the Holocaust* (Oxford: Oxford University Press, 2012); and Fulbrook, *Reckonings: Legacies of Nazi Persecution and the Quest for Justice* (Oxford: Oxford University Press, 2018).
24 Cf. Frank Bajohr and Andrea Löw, 'Beyond the "Bystander": Social Processes and Social Dynamics in European Societies as Context for the Holocaust', in Löw and Bajohr (eds), *The Holocaust and European Societies*, 3–14.
25 Helen Fein, *Genocide: A Sociological Perspective* (London: Sage, 1993), 36–44. Fein's 'universe of obligation', based on 'Durkheim's notion of rules and the domain of the collective conscience' (36), differs in certain respects from my conception of 'communities of empathy'; there is insufficient space here to expand on this.

4

Complicities, re-presented

Literary portrayals in totalitarianism and neoliberalism

Juliane Prade-Weiss

During the past fifteen years, literatures from Central and Eastern Europe have been marked by a boom of documentary fiction portraying involvement in twentieth-century mass violence and totalitarianisms. Texts such as Radka Denemarková's *Peníze od Hitlera* (2006; Money from Hitler, 2009), Elfriede Jelinek's *Rechnitz (Der Würgeengel)* (2008; Rechnitz [The Extermination Angel] 2015) and Maria Stepanova's *Памяти памяти* (2019; In Memory of Memory, 2021) portray complicity with Nazi occupation, Stalinist terror or other forms of mass violence among contemporaries and descendants. Since understanding the past serves requirements of the present, this boom prompts the question: why the interest in past complicities now? One hypothesis is that the texts address convergences between, on the one hand, involvement in past acts of mass violence and, on the other hand, current forms of participation in humanitarian, political, ecological or other wrongdoing in neoliberalism. While these issues differ in many respects, they are, still, related in structural and historical terms. Structurally, both present the challenge of forming a nuanced notion of participation, the idea and promise at the heart of democracy that is highly valued yet poorly conceptualized. Historically, both issues are related since justifications of past involvement have established the terminology, narratives and heuristics with which acts of mass violence are subsequently discussed by inscribing them into cultural traditions. They thus also form the framework for negotiating current problematic types of involvement. This convergence is of particular interest in view of the global crisis of political participation, which is currently undermined by an often unwilling but inevitable participation in detrimental economic structures that can be linked to the increasing delegitimization of democracy and the retreat to identitarian ideologies.

Documentary fiction is especially relevant for this issue because texts portraying historical events in fictional plot or dialogue give accounts of acts of mass violence that evade conventional historiographic means. While the conflation of fact and fiction is prone to raise ethical concerns,[1] non-factual accounts, or those that are not verifiable beyond doubt, are seminal in forming reconstructive narratives and a collective memory of mass killings.² Fictional portrayals of historical instances of problematic involvement thus work within the ambivalent stance of complicity as they perform those practices and speech acts that bring about and justify mass violence. Documentary fiction is, therefore, a useful medium for understanding how the representation of violence relates to its replication and transmission.

The chapter will proceed in four steps: first, I outline what I mean by justificatory discourses and why 'justificationalism'³ needs to be considered; second, I explore how the notion of complicity relates to them; third, I look at the role of language in an ethnopolitical paradigm; and fourth, I focus on complicity in the transmission of terms.

Justificatory discourses

In an article on 'ethnic cleansing' in former Yugoslavia, Jacques Sémelin notes that it is disputed whether 'atrocities have a meaning [. . .] we do not know enough about mass crimes'.⁴ Literary criticism may contribute to understanding the 'meaning' of events of mass violence by focusing on the justificatory discourses surrounding them. Mass violence, it has been acknowledged, has an understudied linguistic dimension. 'Nationalist discourses, myths and rumours' have repeatedly proven to be 'conducive to violence'.⁵ These narratives are unlikely to vanish after acts of mass violence have been committed, but contribute to the subsequent interpretation of the events through justificatory discourses. Such discourses, including legal legitimizations, moral vindications downplaying or screen memories, bestow meaning onto the events from the perspective of perpetrators and accomplices.⁶ While they may be perceived as mere pretexts to manifest material or strategic interests, they nevertheless establish the terminology, narratives and heuristics through which acts of mass violence are subsequently discussed. Justifications of mass violence that are negotiated in, for instance, juridical discourses, historiographical narratives and literary texts, give a culturally specific, often identificatory meaning, to acts that from a critical perspective are mostly either deemed senseless, or comprehended in economic or sociopolitical terms. Acts of mass violence do create socio-economic and political realities that are inhabited by surviving victims, perpetrators, accomplices and their descendants. It is due to justificatory discourses that acts of mass violence do not remain single, seemingly exorbitant events, but shape the linguistic and heuristic framework for their subsequent evaluation. This means that they are not strictly past, but last.

Even the common evocation that mass violence is irrational bestows a meaning on it. Christian Gerlach notes that the 'claim that the deed was irrational, so that by tendency it cannot be explained or perhaps even told, existing beyond the limits of representation, or falling out of history', serves the purpose of constructing unique 'national or ethnic identities'.⁷ By way of a moral judgement, the claim refutes a causal explanation in favour of an argumentative purpose. This is unsurprising as historical understanding serves the purposes of the respective present. Still, such embeddedness marks a complication, namely the uneasy stance of the analyst who tries to understand the willingness to commit and, especially, contribute to mass violence by aiding, abetting, ignoring and taking part in other forms of enabling that are summarized as complicity.

Why uneasy? Because any critical analysis participates in forming the heritage of mass violence. Analyses cannot but discuss and thus repeat terminologies, narratives and distinctions employed to incite mass violence and thus contribute to the transgenerational transmission of justificatory discourses even in criticizing them. Viktor Klemperer's analysis of National Socialist idiom testifies to such transmission by mimetic participation. He not only points out the unsettling terminological continuity of notions of 'cleansing' in the concept 'Entnazifizierung' (denazification),[8] but also himself performs (whether consciously or unwillingly) the idiom of *Gleichschaltung*, designed to leave no room for an outside stance or voice, when he speaks of Nazism as 'a rampant degeneration of German flesh'.[9]

Literary and cultural studies analyses of both participation in mass violence and current instances of complicity with wrongdoing are often structured by rhetoric that seeks to safeguard an analytical position untouched by problematic involvement. Essential as it is to distinguish between historical analysis and moral or juridical judgement, the insistence on non-involvement itself constitutes an instance of complicity by ignoring the complexity of many different types of involvement – in globalized markets, security politics and ecological destruction, as well as of forced involvement in mass violence. Making victims complicit in violence committed against them is a crucial strategy in executing mass violence, as Primo Lévi's notion of the 'grey zone' highlights.[10] Nevertheless, readings of documentary fiction are often marked by a rhetoric of analytical non-involvement. Quite a few critiques of supposedly 'complicit texts'[11] display, as Rothberg notes, 'narcissism [. . .] that keeps the privileged subject at the center of analysis'[12] as untouched judge of the involvement of others by failing to reflect on the issue of mimetic participation. As Susanne Knittel points out, the insistence on analytical non-involvement produces the detrimental effect of rendering 'perpetrators and their actions into inert matters of fact' instead of 'matters of concern'.[13] Yet only the latter perspective requires, and allows for, understanding 'how' something 'came to be *acceptable as* legitimate'[14] due to justificatory discourses.

One seminal element of complacent approaches to problematic involvement and their justification is spatiotemporal distancing. Literary portrays of complicity with mass violence or totalitarianism and the persistence of suffering have often been discussed in terms of identity discourses, as pertaining to specific others, but not in relation to a general structure or a problematic transmission of complicity. The part 'Ethnization of Language' of this chapter focuses on documentary fiction that discusses the logic of distinctions based on national languages, which still inform current European memory politics. A second seminal element of complacent approaches to problematic involvement, especially in mass violence, is an identificatory reception that assumes the position of a victim witness. As Sanyal notes, this 'conflates survival and spectatorship',[15] thereby 'muting any sense of the subject's political agency and responsibility'.[16] The part 'Tragedy and Audience Complicity' of this chapter focuses on the complicity of audiences. This, however, requires acknowledging that complicity is an ambivalent charge.

Complicity

As a legal term, complicity describes aiding or abetting a crime. Yet complicity poses a challenge to the law as it undermines the juridical principles of individual accountability and autonomous action: dependent on the actions of a principal wrongdoer, the accomplice is still autonomous insofar as aiding or tolerating wrongdoing makes a difference.[17] Accountability is based on individual intentionality, which gives rise to a particular difficulty in current corporate and international law. Corporate and state complicity with human rights infringement and environmental damage often evades sanction, because corporations and states are not understood to have intentions. This, paradoxically, renders them actors without intent.[18] Complicity marks the limits of legal discourse by pointing beyond the law's methodological individualism to fundamental structures of social relationality. This connectedness is exploited in the totalitarian strategy of lessening the individual's sense of guilt while, at the same time, undermining individual action and personal accountability – a process outlined in Hannah Arendt's maxim, 'Where all are guilty, nobody is'.[19] Where complicity is distributed throughout the population,[20] there is no one to be responsible to, no one to judge (or to forgive).[21] The analytical difficulty is that declaring everyone guilty is tantamount to labelling wrongdoing inevitable; it is to drop the differentiation between moral choices, just as they were aborted under totalitarianism. Twentieth-century European totalitarianism might be regarded as symptomatic of, rather than contrasting to, neoliberal (Post-)Modernity in that both have rendered participation and complicity 'a matter of course' rather than a subject of decision.[22] What makes complicity a currently ubiquitous phenomenon might be the coexistence of a far-reaching desire for civic participation of individuals in mass-based societies on the one hand, and the lack of sophisticated political concepts of participation on the other; concepts that would allow the relationality of the so-called Modern individual to be negotiated.

To move beyond methodological individualism, recent legal research proposes the evaluation of the causal contribution to wrongdoing independent of intent,[23] or notions such as 'shared responsibility'[24] and a 'participatory conception of collective action'.[25] What participation means, however, is a second challenge posed when thinking about complicity beyond its status in legal thought. For despite its popularity in political philosophy and popular parlance, participation as a concept is not defined by Leibnitz, Kant, Fichte, or by Schelling, Hegel, Nietzsche or other authors of classical Modern thought.[26] Participation is left mostly to economics, as the idea of shareholders, and the complexity of agency is left to the law, where it is understood as complicity, as a crime. Yet while the law is highly political, it is not based on a strong concept of relationality.

Understanding participation is where literary criticism with its focus on language can make a decisive contribution. Assessments of historical involvement in wrongdoing rely on reconstructive narratives,[27] and conceptual analyses of involvement are based on hypothetical scenarios.[28] The structure of these narratives, the relation between fictional, documentary, and prescriptive legal speech, is hardly reflected upon. Yet the medium of language is, in fact, a good model for approaching the complication of complicity, understood as individually responsible participation in a communal structure. Responsible individual speakers cannot but use preformed phonetic, semantic and syntactic structures. The relational aspect of human action that poses a problem to legal thought is the focus of literary criticism, which analyses language as the principal medium of human interaction. Reading is based on participation as texts speak to implicit readers. Literary language is a genuine means for comprehending problematic involvement as it relies on the participation of audiences, be it the voice and imagination of the reader or the gaze of the spectator. Fiction, moreover, depends on the audience's suspension of disbelief,[29] which mirrors the media studies notion that audiences are complicit in media discourses if they uncritically accept representational claims.[30] The notion of complicity is useful not because it provides clarity (it does not), but because it marks problematic participation, enmeshment and degrees of responsibility that may evade straightforward legal culpability.[31]

Complicity is an ambivalent charge as it is hardly functional within a legalistic framework and is too general outside one. Complicity can, however, be analytically productive if used not as a charge but as a marker for complexity. One such usage has been proposed by Mark Sanders in analysing the role of intellectuals in South African apartheid. He distinguishes 'acting-in-complicity', which can be legally and ethically judged, from an underlying 'responsibility-in-complicity', a connectedness with other beings that explains why even silence or inactivity may affect the lives of others.[32] In the following, I take responsibility literally, to mean how analyses of discourses justifying mass violence *respond* to their critical role in transmission.

What is critical about documentary fiction is that it encompasses two interlinked aspects of mimetic participation: representation and reception. Artistic representation of complicity with wrongdoing is significant as it runs the risk of replicating past violence by turning the suffering of victims into a spectacle.[33] This issue can be clarified by looking into the structure of the reception of artworks, which relies on reader (or viewer) identification, affect and empathy.[34] This emotional investment is the basis for raising public awareness of the suffering of victims, yet it may also elicit emotional complicity with perpetrators, which Wayne Booth calls 'the most tragic false identification of the reader'.[35] This is certainly 'false' in a moral sense, still, it is one of several ways of reading that may be induced by the artistic representation. And even if a text fosters such problematic empathy,[36] it does not necessarily align the reader with the perpetrators' moral outlook, but might confer upon the reader the task of working through an ethically complex situation towards a desirable moral judgement.[37] The point is that literature differs eminently from juridical discourse in that the authorial intent is not decisive for the reception history of a text. What matters is the complex relation between identificatory options offered by the text and the readers' various ways of adopting them which might differ or deviate drastically from original contexts and purposes. In documentary fiction, this relational openness is decisive, since its purpose is neither solely to convey facts, nor to form juridical decisions. Rather, it confronts audiences intellectually and emotionally with situations that have led to mass violence and totalitarianism, and with discourses that seek to justify the involvement in both. Documentary fiction relies on the audiences' mimetic participation to reflect on instances of historical participation in mass violence and totalitarianism.

I shall outline this by taking a brief look at two literary texts. The first one, Denemarková's *Money from Hitler*, discusses how ethnopolitical violence is based on the distinction between presumed national languages while pointing out that languages are interwoven. The second one, Jelinek's *Rechnitz (The Extermination Angel)*, focuses on complicity in the transmission of justificatory discourses and explores the implications of the term 'tragedy' and how it is used both to condemn and to downplay mass violence. What Anja Tippner writes on Denemarková's text holds true for both: 'Pointing backward and forward at the same time', they 'perform acts of witnessing on both levels – the historical and the contemporary'.[38]

'Ethnization'[39] of Language

Recent portrayals of complicity with mass violence and totalitarianisms in Central and Eastern European literatures differ from the negotiation of collaboration with the Nazi regime in Western literature in their positionality. They are concerned not with a distinct historical period but with what Stepanova calls '*a traumatic enfilade*'[40]: like a suite of rooms, 'a suite of traumas' leads 'from war to revolution, to famine and mass persecution, and on to new wars, new persecutions',[41] thus creating the point of view of the observer who cannot claim to look back at a distanced past but speaks from within an ongoing transmission of justifications of violence.

Denemarková's novel *Money from Hitler* presents such an involved portrayal of complicity with mass violence and totalitarianisms in the hybrid form of documentary fiction. While the characters are fictional, the flyleaf states: 'All these stories [events] happened'.[42] The story is inspired by the life of Eliška Fábryová, whose father was murdered in Auschwitz, and who was designated as German after the war despite her Czechoslovak citizenship.[43] In Czech, the text is subtitled 'A summer mosaic', as it portrays several traumatic returns of the Jewish protagonist to her parents' estate in the summers of 1945 and 2005. Deported to the Theresienstadt Ghetto by the Nazi regime, she finds, upon returning home, not only that the estate is now occupied by Czech inhabitants, but also that in terms of the newly issued Beneš decrees, she is considered a collaborator with the National Socialist occupation of Czechoslovakia. The novel's title, *Money from Hitler*, evokes a colloquial Czech term for reparations paid by the Western German Adenauer government, and, more importantly in Denemarková, the ongoing transmission of profit gained by perpetration.[44] Yet the text outlines that the common wording *Money from Hitler* may also serve to voice a resentment that conflates the roles of victim and profiteer of the Nazi rule. This becomes most obvious is the novel's central theme, the ethnization of language.

In May 1945, Czechoslovak president Evard Beneš issued the first of a series of decrees concerning the legal status and expulsion of ethnic Germans, Hungarians and other groups. Commonly denoted by the shorthand Beneš decrees, they were approved in the Potsdam Agreement and largely implemented. Their aim was to establish 'demographic homogeneity' as a means both to prevent atrocity and to promote socio-economic modernization. Therefore all ethnic Germans and Hungarians were to be expelled from Czechoslovakia.[45] Denemarková's text outlines how language is fed into the ethnopolitical paradigm to tell Czechoslovakians apart. Yet people often speak many languages (Czech and Slovak, for instance). The decisive criterion is, therefore, the language spoken behind closed doors, which in the protagonist's family had been German, according to the neighbours' testimony.[46] 'And whoever spoke German is gu-guilty, that much is clear'.[47] The character who delivers this verdict stutters, a poetical strategy to point out that language resists any claim to purity and mastery. Nevertheless, based on the reasoning voiced in the verdict, descendants of German-speaking Czechoslovakian citizen victims of the Shoah are still denied Czech citizenship.[48] With the Beneš decrees, Denemarková suggests, national identities are redefined on the basis of the assumption that there is one primordial native language which determines ethnicity and political convictions. The ethnization of language produces absurdly conflated, compromised identities, such as with the protagonist's brother: 'A dead Jewish Sudet[en German] with nowhere to resettle'.[49] In a post-war scenario, this designation is absurd because it was the Sudeten German Party and other, in part paramilitary, organizations in Czechoslovakia that pressed for the ethnization of languages, the annexation of the realm they claimed as Sudentenland by Nazi Germany in 1938 and the implementation of its genocidal politics. The Beneš decrees appear as a continuation of a pre-established ethnopolitical paradigm. Denemarková portrays this enfilade in terms of contagion: 'They were tainted [infected] with the Nazi mange without even realizing it. Tainted [infected] with hell, by whose laws (who can speak of justice here?) the Nazis should have been punished'.[50] The post-war claim to linguistically constructed ethnic purity is compromised[51] as it seems infected by the very National Socialist politics that had started the war.

But Denemarková's text does not stop at outlining how national ideologies of purity are compromised historically as they adopt violent means of implementation. It also expounds the view that ideologies based on the idea of national languages are structurally compromised. They are both 'subject to [. . .] compromise',[52] as subject of negotiation in social discourses and, therefore, 'exposed to [. . .] discredit',[53] and to the accusation of impurity. One of the passages pointing this out is when a woman complicit in killing the protagonist's brother upon his return from the concentration camp confesses: 'All the time [*Imrvére*]. My whole life. I have participated in it'.[54] 'Imrvére' is a colloquial Czech Germanism, echoing the word 'immerwährend' (perpetual). While the accomplice speaks of her participation in acts of violence, her speech mimetically participates in the other whom the violence was supposed to eradicate, pointing out that natural languages are interwoven, despite all claims to purity. This interwovenness is the structural reason why it takes violence to establish the paradigm of national languages and purity. But it also points out what Kutz calls the 'hidden promise of complicity', namely 'the conception of community upon which it draws: a world where individuals shape their lives with others'.[55] This, however, requires overcoming the comfortable assumption that the critic of complicities with mass violence and totalitarianisms is positioned outside the enfilade, somewhere else than in an ongoing transmission of justificatory terms, narratives and heuristics.

In the narrated present of 2005, the transmission of justifications of mass violence is still ongoing when the protagonist's efforts at establishing a memorial for her murdered father on the family estate tie in with the present inhabitants' fear of restitution claims[56]:

It is fascinating that the shadow of suspicion, the implication of duplicitous theft, should fall on me, the robbed, after all these decades. Those who remember are dying off. The legend of the invasion of the grasping old witch is awakened.[57]

Post-communist fears of being impoverished are negotiated in the established ethnopolitical distinctions based on language, which effects a switch of the position of victim and perpetrator. One of the residents is quoted as saying, with reference to the Jewish protagonist, 'that she's not gonna have a fascist […] kicking her out of her house'.[58] Post-communist neoliberalism is manifested in the protagonist's lawyer. While supposedly representing her aim of memorialization, he seeks restitution not out of a sense of restorative justice, but due to his own 'participatory intention'[59]: 'He is looking forward to falling on fat prey'.[60] As during the Nazi occupation and with the implementation of the Beneš decrees, the ethnopolitical paradigm based on language provides the vocabulary and heuristics for articulating conflicts over very different issues, notably possession. This, however, does not mean that ethnopolitical justifications of mass violence can be dismissed as a mere pretext for purely material interests. Denemarková's text outlines that while material interests provide the occasion and the need for the transmission of the ethnopolitical vocabulary of violence, it is the distinctions suggested in this vocabulary, and the history of enmity it serves to narrate, that *create* cleavages by concealing present conflicts, interests and involvements.

Tragedy and audience complicity

Jelinek's play *Rechnitz (The Extermination Angel)* provides further insights into the transmission of justifications of complicity with mass violence and totalitarianisms: first, because dramatic texts correspond structurally to the law, where complicity appears as a complication, since both plays and the law 'consider the role agents play in reproducing, and hence becoming complicit in, […] wrongdoings'.[61] Second, because Jelinek's choice of genre appears as a commentary on a pervasive element in discourses of mass violence. In condemnations, justifications, historiography and popular parlance, acts of mass violence are often called 'tragedies'. This is problematic because by casting mass violence in terms of tragedy, human action is submitted to superior divine power in an unchangeable (because scripted) course of events. The notion of events as 'tragedy' implies that actors are unable to avert doom. Yet this is only true on the intradiegetic level, on the level of the plot. What is missing is that someone wrote the tragic plot. With this metadiegetic level in mind, the reference to tragedy implies that someone orchestrated events in such a way that people had no way to evade terror, no choice but to comply. And if we believe Aristotle that tragedy aims at catharsis, purification from the politically detrimental affects of misery and fear,[62] then considering mass violence as tragic elicits a problematic relief. Theodor Adorno notes in 1962 that 'by turning suffering into images', it is 'thrown to the consumption of a world'.[63] This effect has been studied in German mass media representations of the Shoah, which have created a 'collective memory' by way of 'identification with the past', but at the price of permitting audiences and readers to 'consume this disconnected past as exotic alterity and even as sentimental entertainment'.[64] Consoling or hedonistic readings evoke instances of past complicities in order to appease the sense that all is not quite well, even after the demise of Nazi and Soviet terror; they draw attention to how much worse things have been and grant distancing. Yet even the display of traumatic memories in shocking rather than consoling images poses the same problem, as recent criticism holds:

> trauma is placed in a marketplace [. . .], being revalued in each transaction according to the logic of supply and demand. Victim and witness; witness and reporter; reporter and audience; producer and consumer: all these parties bargain to suit their different interests.[65]

Lacking in this list is the role of the accomplice in memorialization and commodification, a figure that is the focus of Jelinek's *Rechnitz*. Jelinek's text portrays the transmission of local knowledge about a 1945 massacre near the Austrian town of Rechnitz, close to the Hungarian border. A few days before the arrival of the Red Army, at a dinner party hosted by Margit von Batthyány, daughter of Heinrich Thyssen, at the local castle, 180–200 Hungarian Jews were shot by party guests. Most of the victims' bodies have not been found to this day, and suspected perpetrators have evaded prosecution. The 1994 documentary *Totschweigen (Wall of Silence)*[66] portrays an unsuccessful campaign to recover the bodies as well as the locals' reports on the event. A local hunter points out one of the many assumed sites of the massacre and the mass grave, and comments on it: 'We are on the site, I would say, where the tragedy approximately happened'.[67] Pointing upward, he later concludes: 'If this turns out not to be the place, and it is not found, one should more or less leave the affair to the Almighty and finally, I would almost say, be quiet'.[68] This illustrates what it means for perpetrators, accomplices and descendants to call mass violence a tragedy: it means *not* calling it murder, casting it as the enactment of a superior force (so that no one is a responsible actor with intent) and implying that the victims were guilty of some hubris punished by their 'tragic fate' (which is not only the logic of Attic tragedy but also a key element of antisemitism). Referencing the film, Jelinek's play desists from giving a clear account of the massacre itself and thus responds radically to the question of whether the representation of past violence should become a source of entertainment or consolation for the spectator. This issue is by no means detached from understanding historical massacring which is, as Sémelin puts it, 'the most spectacular practice which those in power have at their disposal to assert their ascendancy'.[69] Massacres are designed to be watched. In order not to assume a position in this order of violence, not to confirm the logic of massacre by way of mimetic participation, Jelinek focuses on the local testimonies, on the cruelty and denial that is not past but still passed on by a multitude of voices that seem to testify to events while claiming their personal non-involvement:

> As a messenger I would of course have liked to provide you with evidence in the form of a report, but that would have made me a witness, not a messenger, and possibly liable for prosecution, just because I might also have seen what others saw;

with an emphasis on also, because there were also others present [. . .], including people who were more highly regarded than you?[70]

The German text links seeing ('sehen') to the respectable ('angesehen') status of the many inactive witnesses.[71] Exploring what follows from seeing and witnessing, *Rechnitz* establishes a poetical distinction akin to the terminological distinction drawn by Sanders.[72] On the one hand, 'responsibility-in-complicity', or how the text responds to violence, takes the form of not portraying it as source of amusement and, on the other hand, 'acting-in-complicity' is staged by actors. Complicity lies in the way they fulfill their role as messenger. Their aim is not to reveal what happened out of plain sight as in tragic or Biblical messengers but to prevent clarity while also enjoying the importance of the role of the messenger. This requires not telling anything while also talking all the time, indicating just enough to make clear that there is a secret to uncover:

> I could also tell you where it will not be easy to find those bodies, no, nothing will be easy to find, but I say nothing, otherwise it would be too easy a find and much too easy a finale.[73]

Focusing on messengers rather than historical events, Jelinek's poetics of anonymous voices 'performs', as one critic writes with reference to earlier plays by Jelinek, 'those complicit practices and ways of thinking that bring about cultural politics of exclusionary and annihilating violence'.[74] Jelinek's focus on the transmission of justificatory discourses, however, also reflects on the distancing implied in the gesture of finding others complicit in mass violence and totalitarianism – a distancing that the documentary film allows. For it is easy to dismiss the pictured gentleman as an old Nazi, to feel morally and intellectually superior to him. The distancing effect of this moral high ground is fundamental to Eva Menasse's novel *Dunkelblum* (2021), which is based on the Rechnitz massacre without spelling out the name.[75] While, in Denemarková, a first-person narrator interferes with the third-person perspective to highlight the difficulties of giving an objective portrayal,[76] the narrative positions in Menasse's text are clear-cut, with a third-person omniscient narrator singling out a few good characters from among many parodically bad ones. Jelinek's text impedes such complacent pleasure by questioning the role of the audience in the portrayal of justificatory discourse. Why watch, or read – in short: consume – the reproduction of this desolate speech of repression and denial? To create distance, one of the text's voices suggests: 'We transfer good and evil to where we are not. That's how it's done, it's called outsourcing'.[77] The identification of perpetrators and accomplices creates the good conscience of not being guilty oneself, the consolation of knowing who is and it also allows the campaign to recover the massacre's victims to turn into a narrative of suspense.

To highlight the role of the spectator, Jelinek references a Greek tragedy, Euripides' *Bacchae*, which relies heavily on messengers to convey the gruesome plot on stage: people being torn apart and eaten alive by the hands and mouths of women frenzied by Dionysus, god of theatre. Dionysus elicits an interesting confession from his antagonist eager to catch sight of these women:

DIONYSUS: Ah! Do you wish to see them sitting together on the mountains?
PENTHEUS: Very much so, and would give an enormous weight of gold to do so.
D: Why have you fallen into a great passion [lust: ἔρως] for this?
P: It would give me pain to see them drunk.
D: And yet you would enjoy seeing things that are bitter to you?
P: To be sure, sitting in silence under the firs.[78]

Pentheus wants to see, not despite, but because of being disgusted by the sight. In Euripides, it thus seems that if tragedy achieves catharsis (which is not clear), then it is by way of voyeurism, the lust of looking at violence from a supposed distance. In Jelinek, documentary fiction is not a genre of moral purification, but one of contamination. She desists from staging the massacre to draw attention to the audience's participation in violence, a participation that Sigmund Freud sees inscribed in the staging of victimization: tragedy seems to provide spectators with the position of an uninvolved, distanced beholder but their gaze and pleasure – the purpose of the spectacle – makes them complicit in the violence.[79] Jelinek's play highlights the lust that drives participation in the audience, the messengers and the party guests who appear to have committed a massacre for entertainment. This lust is pointed out by one of the messengers, who adopts the charge of complicity for the discourse of repression:

> I know you are mesmerized by stories of those horrible times, you are not interested in anything else, I can see that, and by staring at the horrible crimes this country committed, you once again make Germany the navel of the universe![80]

This quotation emphasizes how the charge of complicity by no means produces clarity. Rather, its unsettling volatility lends itself to very different agendas, marking the way in which complacent ascriptions of perpetrator roles work to conceal different forms of involvement. The point of Jelinek's documentary play is thus not least the ambivalence of its genre: documentary fiction draws attention for the suffering of victims, to the issue of participatory violence, and to complicity in the transmission of justificatory discourses, by making the audience participate in this very complicity.

Analysing mimetic participation in documentary fiction helps us better understand two aspects of justifications of involvement in mass violence and totalitarianisms that have, so far, been left largely to the arts to explore: first, the dynamics that shape transgenerational transmission; second, the role of emotions such as the lust in power and perpetration that tends to be passed over when the industrialized and bureaucratic character of modern perpetration is highlighted. Both aspects evade a legalistic discourse yet mark the position of the individual in relation to preformed organizational and discursive structures. Why the interest in past complicities now? Recent Central and Eastern European literary texts point out that declaring problematic involvement in mass violence and totalitarianism *past*, such as in memorializing them as a 'tragic past', functions as an efficient way of concealing the historical transmission of their respective justificatory discourses. It also hides the adoption of such discourses in very different contexts in the interest of repressing and denying current involvement in neoliberal wrongdoing.

Notes

1. James Young, *Writing and Rewriting the Holocaust: Narrative and the Consequences of Interpretation* (Bloomington: Indiana University Press, 1990), 52–60.
2. Robert Stockhammer, *Ruanda. Über einen anderen Genozid schreiben* (Frankfurt am Main: Suhrkamp, 2005), 79–81.
3. Stefan Ihrig, *Justifying Genocide: Germany and the Armenians from Bismarck to Hitler* (Cambridge, MA: Harvard University Press, 2016), 12.
4. Jacques Sémelin, 'Analysis of a Mass Crime: Ethnic Cleansing in the Former Yugoslavia, 1991–1999', in *The Specter of Genocide: Mass Murder in Historical Perspective*, ed. Robert Gellately and Ben Kiernan (Cambridge: Cambridge University Press, 2003), 370.
5. Jonathan Leader Maynard, 'Preventing Mass Atrocities: Ideological Strategies and Interventions', *Politics and Governance* 3, no. 3 (2015): 71.
6. Max Silverman, 'Screen Memory', in *The Routledge Companion to Literature and Trauma*, ed. Colin Davis and Hanna Meretoja (London: Routledge, 2020), 121–30.
7. Christian Gerlach, *Extremely Violent Societies: Mass Violence in the Twentieth-Century World* (Cambridge: Cambridge University Press, 2010), 258–9.
8. Viktor Klemperer, *LTI: Notizbuch eines Philologen* (Ditzingen: Reclam 2010), 9–10.
9. Viktor Klemperer, *The Language of the Third Reich*, trans. Martin Brady (London: Bloomsbury, 2013), 57; cf. *LTI*, 68–9: 'eine wuchernde Entartung deutschen Fleisches'.
10. Primo Lévi, *The Drowned and the Saved*, trans. M. F. Moore, in *The Complete Works of Primo Levi*, ed. Ann Goldstein, 3 vols. (New York: Liveright, 2015), III:2414–5.
11. Ivan Stacy, *The Complicit Text: Failures of Witnessing in Postwar Fiction* (Lanham: Lexington, 2021).
12. Michael Rothberg, *The Implicated Subject: Beyond Victims and Perpetrators* (Stanford: Stanford University Press, 2019), 19.
13. Susanne Knittel, 'Memory and Repetition: Reenactment as an Affirmative Critical Practice', *New German Critique* 137, no. 46.2 (2019): 178.
14. Ibid., 179.
15. Debarati Sanyal, *Memory and Complicity: Migrations of Holocaust Remembrance* (New York: Fordham University Press, 2015), 8.
16. Ibid., 12.
17. Pierre-Marie Dupuy, 'Introduction', in Vladyslav Lanovoy, *Complicity and its Limits in the Law of International Responsibility* (Oxford: Bloomsbury, 2016), vii.
18. Ibid., viii.
19. Hannah Arendt, *Responsibility and Judgement*, ed. Jerome Kohn (New York: Schocken, 2003), 147.
20. Hannah Arendt, *Origins of Totalitarianism* (San Diego: Harcourt Brace & Co, 1979), 408.
21. Hannah Arendt, *The Human Condition*, 2nd ed. (Chicago: University of Chicago Press, 1998), §33.
22. Arendt, *Responsibility and Judgement*, 154.
23. Chiara Lepora and Robert Goodin, *On Complicity and Compromise* (Oxford: Oxford University Press, 2013), 5–10.
24. Vladyslav Lanovoy, *Complicity and its Limits in the Law of International Responsibility* (Oxford: Bloomsbury, 2016), 11.
25. Christopher Kutz, *Complicity: Ethics and Law for a Collective Age* (Cambridge: Cambridge University Press, 2000), 11.

26 Juliane Prade-Weiss, 'Guilt-tripping the "Implicated Subject": Widening Rothberg's Concept of Implication in Reading Herta Müller's *The Hunger Angel*', *Journal of Perpetrator Research* 3, no. 1 (2020): 9–11.
27 Lepora and Goodin, *On Complicity and Compromise*, 13.
28 Gregory Mellema, *Complicity and Moral Accountability* (Notre Dame: University of Notre Dame Press, 2013).
29 Samuel Coleridge, *Biographia Literaria*, ed. Adam Roberts (Edinburgh: Edinburgh University Press, 2015), II:208.
30 Roger Silverstone, 'Complicity and Collusion in the Mediation of Everyday Life', *New Literary History* 33 (2002): 775.
31 Paul Reynolds, 'Complicity as Political Rhetoric: Some Ethical and Political Reflections', in *Exploring Complicity: Concept, Cases and Critique*, ed. Afxentis Afxentiou, Robin Dunford, and Michel Neu (London: Rowman & Littlefield, 2017), 35–52.
32 Mark Sanders, *Complicities: The Intellectual and Apartheid* (Durham: Duke University Press, 2002), 8–11.
33 Sanyal, *Memory and Complicity*, 113.
34 Erin McGlothlin, 'Empathic Identification and the Mind of the Holocaust Perpetrator in Fiction: A Proposed Taxonomy of Response', *Narrative* 24, no. 3 (2016): 251.
35 Wayne Booth, *The Rhetoric of Fiction*, 2nd ed. (Chicago: University of Chicago Press, 1983), 389.
36 Eric Leake, 'Humanizing the Inhumane: The Value of Difficult Empathy', in *Rethinking Empathy Through Literature*, ed. Meghan Marie Hammond and Sue J. Kim (London: Routledge, 2014), 177.
37 McGlothlin, 'Empathic Identification and the Mind of the Holocaust Perpetrator in Fiction', 255; 264–5.
38 Anja Tippner, 'Postcatastrophic Entanglement? Contemporary Czech Writers Remember the Holocaust and Post-War Ethnic Cleaning', *Memory Studies* 14, no. 1 (2021): 85.
39 Gerlach, *Extremely Violent Societies*, 255.
40 Maria Stepanova, *Памяти памяти. Романс* (Moscow: Novoe istadel'stvo, 2019), 74: 'травматическя анфилаба' (my translation).
41 Maria Stepanova, *In Memory of Memory: A Romance*, trans. Sasha Dugale (New York: New Directions 2021), 83.
42 Radka Denemarková, *Money from Hitler*, trans. A. Oakland (Toronto: Women's Press, 2009), cf. *Peníze od Hitler (Letní mozaika)* (Brno: Host, 2006): 'Všechny ty příběhy se staly'.
43 Wolfgang Schwarz, 'Money from Hitler', in *Handbook of Polish, Czech, and Slovak Holocaust Fiction*, ed. Elsa-Maria Hiemer et al. [EBOOK] (Berlin: deGruyter, 2021).
44 Denemarková, *Peníze od Hitler (Letní mozaika)*, 225: 'Vždyť to jsou vlastně peníze of Hitlera'. (What that is, [. . .], is money from Hitler. Denemarková, *Money from Hitler*, 237.)
45 Dirk Moses, *The Problems of Genocide: Permanent Security and the Language of Transgression* (Cambridge: Cambridge University Press, 2021), 338–63.
46 Denemarková, *Peníze od Hitler (Letní mozaika)*, 34.
47 Denemarková, *Money from Hitler*, 44; cf. *Peníze od Hitler (Letní mozaika)*, 50: 'A kdo brblal německy, tak je vi-vinej, to je snad jasný'.
48 https://www.deutschlandfunk.de/wunsch-nach-einem-eu-pass-warum-in-tschechien-die-benes.795.de.html?dram:article_id=493908 (Accessed 8 December 2021).

49 Denemarková, *Money from Hitler*, 174. In Czech, 'Sudet[en]' is an individual noun without reference to the denominator 'German'. Denemarková, *Peníze od Hitler (Letní mosaika)*, 169: 'Mrtvej židovskej sudeťák, kterýho nešlo nikam vodsunouť.
50 Denemarková, *Money from Hitler*, 81, my brackets. Cf. *Peníze od Hitler (Letní mosaika)*, 85: 'nakazili se nacistickou prašivinou, aniž by si toho vědomi. Nakazili se peklem, za jenož zřízení měli být po právu – protože spravedlivě nelze – potrestání'.
51 OED, '*compromised*, adj., d'.
52 Ibid., '*compromised*, adj., b'.
53 Ibid., '*compromised*, adj., c'.
54 Denemarková, *Peníze od Hitler (Letní mosaika)*, 151: 'Imrvére. Celej život. Dyť já se na tom podílela'. My translation; cf. *Money from Hitler*, 154.
55 Kutz, *Complicity*, 259.
56 Jan Kuklík, 'Restitution of Jewish Property in the Czech Republic', *Loyola of Los Angeles International and Comparative Law Review* 41, no. 3 (2018): 583–606.
57 Denemarková, *Money from Hitler*, 90; cf. *Peníze od Hitler (Letní mosaika)*, 92: 'Je fascinující, jak se za ta desetiletí podezíravý stín podvodné krádeže neslyšně přesunul na mě. Na okradenou. Pamětníci vymírají. Legenda o vpádu hamižné báby ožívá'.
58 Denemarková, *Money from Hitler*, 186; cf. *Peníze od Hitler (Letní mosaika)*, 179: 'že ji přece nějaká fašistka [...] nebude vykopávat z domu'.
59 Kutz, *Complicity*, 67.
60 Denemarková, *Money from Hitler*, 91; cf. *Peníze od Hitler (Letní mosaika)*, 93: 'Těší se na brzký a tučný příděl z kořisti'.
61 Reynolds, 'Complicity as Political Rhetoric'.
62 Aristotle, *Poetics* 1449b, 24–30.
63 Theodor Adorno, 'Commitment', in *Aesthetics and Politics*, trans. Ronald Taylor (London: Verso, 1977), 189.
64 Bernhard Giesen, 'The Trauma of Perpetrators', in *Cultural Trauma and Collective Identity*, ed. Jeffrey C. Alexander et al. (Berkeley: University of California Press, 2004), 142.
65 Terri Tomsky, 'From Sarajevo to 9/11: Travelling Memory and the Trauma Economy', *Parallax* 17, no. 4 (2011): 58.
66 Lukas Stepanik, Roy Dames, and Dieter Reifarth (producers) & Margareta Heinrich and Eduard Erne (directors), *Totschweigen (Wall of Silence)* [FILM] (Austria: HOANZL, 1994).
67 Ibid., 1:02:45; my translation: 'Also wir befinden uns, würde ich sagen, auf dem Platz, wo sich die Tragik in etwa zugetragen hat'.
68 Ibid., 1:03:33; my translation: 'Wenn's jetzt da nicht ist, und nicht gefunden wird, dann sollte man die Sache mehr oder minder dem Höheren überlassen und endlich, möchte ist fast sagen, Ruhe geben'.
69 Jacques Sémelin, *Purify and Destroy. The Political Uses of Massacre and Genocide* (London: Hurst and Company, 2013), 6.
70 Trans. courtesy of S. Bird as the official translation of this passage deviates immensely from the German wording; cf. Elfriede Jelinek, *Rechnitz (The Extermination Angel)*, trans. Gita Honegger, in *Three Plays* (London: Seagull, 2019), 179.
71 Elfriede Jelinek, *Rechnitz (Der Würgeengel)* (Reinbek: Rowohlt, 2009), 185: 'Ich als Bote hätte Ihnen selbstverständlich gern einen Beweis in Gestalt eines Zeugnisses gegeben, aber dadurch wäre ich ja Zeuge geworden, nicht Bote, und hätte mich womöglich selber strafbar gemacht, weil ich sowas auch nur mit angesehen hätte, wobei die Betonung auf mit liegt, denn es waren auch andre da, [...] und zwar Leute, die angesehener waren als Sie!'

72 Sanders, *Complicities*, 8–11; cf. note 41.
73 Jelinek, *Rechnitz (The Extermination Angel)*, 115–6; cf. *Rechnitz (Der Würgeengel)*, 112: 'ich könnte Ihnen noch sagen, wo kein leichtes Finden dieser Leichen sein wird, kein leichtes Finden wird das sein, aber ich sage nichts, sonst wäre es ja ein leichtes Finden und ein viel zu leichtes Finale'.
74 Michaela Grobbel, 'Haunted by History: Ghosts and "Ghosting" in Elfriede Jelinek's "Stecken, Stab und Stangl"', in *Elfriede Jelinek: Writing Woman, Nation, and Identity: A Critical Anthology*, ed. Matthias Piccolruaz Konzett and Margarete Lamb-Faffelberger (Vancouver: Fairleigh Dickinson University Press, 2007), 142.
75 Eva Menasse, *Dunkelblum. Roman* (Cologne: Kiepenheuer & Witsch, 2021).
76 Schwarz, '*Money from Hitler*'.
77 Jelinek, *Rechnitz (The Extermination Angel)*, 97; cf. *Rechnitz (Der Würgeengel)*, 91: 'Wir lagern Gut und Böse aus, dorthin, wo wir nicht sind. So gehört es sich, das nennt man Outsourcing . . .'
78 Euripides, *Bacchae*. Edited with an Introduction, Translation & Commentary by Richard Seaford (Oxford: Oxbow, 2015), lines 810–814.
79 Sigmund Freud, *Totem and Taboo*. In *The Standard Edition of the Complete Psychological Works of Sigmund Freud*, ed. James Strachey. 24 Vols, Vol 13 (New York: Vintage, 1999), 155.
80 Jelinek, *Rechnitz (The Extermination Angel)*, 88; cf. *Rechnitz (Der Würgeengel)*, 82: 'Ich weiß ja, daß Sie von der Geschichte dieser schrecklichen Zeit geradezu hypnotisiert sind, Sie interessieren sich für gar nichts anderes mehr, das sehe ich, und indem Sie auf das Entsetzliche starren, das dieses Land verbrochen hat, machen Sie Deutschland wieder zum Nabel der Welt.'

5

In search of the bystander

Some reflections on the 'social turn' in Holocaust studies and its ramifications

Christina Morina

In memoriam Evelien Gans (1951-2018)

Introduction

The systematic persecution and murder of the Jews between 1933 and 1945 was a crime of historic proportions. It was not just the result of the actions of the Nazi regime and a few hundred thousand perpetrators but of a complex social process engulfing the Jewish communities of eighteen European countries.[1] For decades after the war, historians had focused on the Nazi perpetrators and the bureaucracy of killing; since the 1990s, the victims' perspectives and the social cultural contexts in which their persecution unfolded have come into view as well as the myriad ways in which accomplices profited from it.[2] It was also long assumed that millions of non-Jewish contemporaries 'saw or heard something of the event' that later became known as the Holocaust.[3] Dozens of studies conducted since have provided abundant evidence indicating that, by 1942/43 at the latest, it was 'amply clear' to millions of ordinary Europeans 'that the Jews were destined for complete extermination'.[4] Today, there is largely a consensus that the (in)actions of numerous 'onlookers, the curious, and the passers-by' were an 'indispensable component'[5] in the dynamics of persecution – certainly in Nazi Germany, but also in the allied and occupied countries across Europe (where this scholarly consensus is often controversial).

Thus, historians have come a long way. The *social turn* in Holocaust Studies has produced an extremely complex picture of a system and movement of genocidal violence that was driven by factors way outside and beyond the political, military and ideological spheres. At the same time, we still lack a clear and concise understanding of the conditions and consequences of bystanding in the Holocaust as crucial aspects related to current attitudes and reactions 'still remain partly unclear' and 'elusive'.[6] In the current literature, there exists a curious blend of clear sense and profound uncertainty in our understanding of bystanding in the Holocaust (and, likewise, in other state-sanctioned contexts of violence). This chapter addresses this paradoxical state of the art by raising two sets of questions highlighting some of the historiographical, methodological and ethical challenges laying ahead.

First, in light of the extensive scholarship on the German and occupied societies' widespread knowledge of and responses to the persecution of the Jews, what remains unknown, left to be explored? What can a bystander, or better: *bystanding* approach add to our knowledge about the Holocaust as social process? Can the concept of the bystander really serve as 'crucial clue'[7] to a full(er) understanding of the causes and dynamics of systemic, state-sanctioned and genocidal violence? Secondly, what are the historiographical, narrative and ethical consequences of applying the bystander concept to the study of the majority populations' role in the Holocaust? Does it entail a shift of focus (away) from the currently dominant (if 'integrated') victims' perspective to the perspective of the non-Jewish majority populations or do our historical narratives simply become more inclusive, more comprehensive? Would such a shift deepen or challenge the foundations of Friedländer's project of an 'integrative and an integrated history'[8]? Both sets of questions cannot be addressed here in a comprehensive way; rather this chapter seeks to carve out ways to address them in future research. The second set of questions also leads to some personal thoughts that I believe are relevant and worthy of reflection in the wider context of our scholarly work and public engagements.

What is left to be learned?

The Holocaust was a complex social process engulfing Jewish communities of across Europe. Millions of bystanders – in the broadest definition, those non-Jewish contemporaries across Germany and Europe without a formal proactive role in the persecution – observed, witnessed, knew or assumed something about the systematic persecution of Jewish fellow-citizens. It was the result of a 'dynamic interaction between state and society'.[9] With the remarkable surge in research on victims' experiences and the social–cultural contexts in which their persecution unfolded, the myriad ways in which ordinary people reacted to and profited from it have come into view.[10] Yet, often vague notions of 'knowledge' (due not least to the complex nature of the question as such) speak to a lack of analytical precision and complicate rather than clarify the issue, as the controversy on Dutch bystanders has highlighted (discussed further below).[11] Studies on German society under Nazism talk of 'the German people', the 'local population' or the 'contemporaries', and identify collective attitudes ranging from 'indifference', 'tacit acquiescence or varying degrees of compliance', to an 'anti-Jewish consensus', resulting in 'passive complicity'.[12] Scrutinizing the '*Volksgemeinschaft*' as a locally unfolding 'social practice' (with the laden term serving as a kind of 'door opener'[13]), as well as the integrative power of 'visions of community' overall, has proven essential in understanding the dynamics of exclusion and violence.[14]

Still, after decades of Holocaust scholarship first focusing on the perpetrator side and more recently on the victims' perspective, the overall role, specific (in)actions and experiences of non-Jewish populations, as relating to and beyond the German context, remain to be explored systematically. This is evident not least from metaphors used to describe their role. Hilberg writes, for example, that local bystanders across Europe formed a 'human wall around the Jews entrapped in laws and ghettos'[15]; and Friedländer contends that the 'flames that the Nazi leader set alight and fanned burned as widely and intensely as they did' only because the widespread antisemitism provided a 'dense underbrush of ideological and cultural elements [..] ready to catch fire'.[16]

In fact, we lack a concise understanding of the motivations, perceptions and experiences – the 'inner world'[17] – of the often (anonymously) mentioned bystanding individuals or groups – and thus find it hard to systematically capture and narrate their actions and inactions and assess their specific role in the Holocaust. Research, above all on Nazi Germany, suggests that bystanders' micro-gestures of aversion or aggression (as well as occasional gestures of micro-help) played a role more crucial and concrete than has been acknowledged thus far. We know that '[a]ctions of Nazi groups often attracted the participation of large crowds of non-Nazis, though we know little about them'.[18] According to a survey carried out half a century after the war among survivors, 30 per cent of German Jewish men and 11 per cent of women reported that they had been beaten by German civilians – more than those who said they were beaten by officials.[19] And of 4,660 acts of violence known to have occurred between 1930 and 1938 against Jewish persons, institutions and businesses, 3,205 or circa 70 per cent were committed by 'unknown' individuals.[20] As the remaining 30 per cent comprised members of the SS, SA, HJ and DAF, most of these individuals may well have been persons we (perhaps wrongly) consider 'bystanders'.

In contrast to these abstract statistics, evidence from ego-documents, diaries in particular, offers concrete insights into the history of bystanding, yet still remain to be explored systematically.[21] From the days of the Nazi seizure of power and its ramifications in the German provinces in 1933 to the most brutal 'node[s] of acutely concentrated violence'[22] in occupied Eastern Europe, ego-documents illustrate not only the centrality and remarkable amount of detail and explicit as well as implicit reflections on this violence, but also an extreme *variety* of bystanding contexts and behaviours – and thus the historiographical challenges involved.[23] Therefore, in contexts of systemic and even genocidal violence, contemporaneous subjective documentation such as diaries, letters, drawings, memoirs, post-war testimony and oral history provide a superb source base to explore a population's 'availability for mobilization'[24] and thus specific 'interaction between individuals and the greater historical forces'[25] – bridging the divide between the micro and the macro levels.

Diaries in particular, 'the first literary response to catastrophe',[26] have proven crucial in reconstructing individual as well as communal responses to Nazism. They vividly document how Jewish men, women and children attempted to make sense of and reacted to the unprecedented onslaught on their civil and human rights.[27] Likewise, non-Jewish diaries have been examined to reconstruct peoples' self-perceptions as well as interpretations of their time and 'world' in general.[28] Yet, the only substantial analysis of a larger sample of bystander diaries focuses on discerning how Germans responded to Nazism as a personal 'challenge' (*Herausforderung*), how they positioned themselves, oscillating between 'coercion' (*Zwang*) and 'consent' (*Zustimmung*), in various ways and thus helped create 'the dynamics that made National Socialist domination into what it became in the 1930s'.[29] Steuwer's account largely leaves open how these diaries reflect the writers' subject position as bystanders to and in the persecution of Jews.

As we have come to appreciate diaries' unique 'quality of temporal proximity',[30] these texts can therefore not only be read as ego-documents but also as reflections of and evidence for broader societal developments. Yet, a systematic study of how persecution and violence against Jews are documented in bystander diaries, even well-known ones, has not been conducted.[31] Their particular value stems from the fact that they are time-spanning ego-documents, often running over months and years and thus, indeed, reflecting the Holocaust as a *process*, a mass crime unfolding *over time*. An analysis of a larger samples of diaries, both Jewish *and* non-Jewish, paired with other relevant sources, promises a clearer understanding of the people behind the above-mentioned numbers, their perceptions, motivations and (in)actions in response to the unfolding dynamics of violence. Not, of course, in a literal sense aiming to 'identify' the unnamed individuals in specific bystanding contexts, but using specific instances detailed in ego-documents, both Jewish and non-Jewish, as vantage points to explore the subjective dimension of bystanding; to read them as mutually relating reflections of one another. Thus, we would not only gain a more comprehensive grasp of the manifestations of bystanding in Jewish and non-Jewish diaries and of the specific *semantic responses* to the persecution (was there a *language of complicity* among bystanders and a *language for bystanding* among victims?) but also be able to assess the overall relevance of bystanding in the Holocaust itself.

Such an analysis needs to be grounded in a nuanced bystander concept. Bystanders or bystanding should not be understood as a fixed category but as a *heuristic device* to explore the gigantic social landscape in which the Holocaust unfolded as a result of millions of individual and collective acts of neglect – and as many ways of involvement. Bystanders did not play a proactive or formal part in the creation and implementation of the persecution measures and actual acts of torture and killing. Groups or individuals can only become bystanders to both temporally and spatially proximate and thus perceivable circumstances, in which psychological or physical harm is inflicted on fellow human beings. Being a bystander – or rather *bystanding* – is not a static mode of existence but a dynamic, relational and context-driven subjective position. People are never bystanders or bystanding *per se*, the role individuals play both in specific situations and over time, can vary significantly. They rather *become* bystanders, exhibiting various behaviours in and towards conflict situations – as a result of which they often became active participants. Bystanding thus captures a wide spectrum of behaviours ranging from, for example, tolerating or engaging in stigmatizing talk, shunning and harassing in everyday contexts, to observing the deportation, torture and murder of other human beings, but also words or gestures of empathy and solidarity.[32] Bystanders are involved – or 'implicated' – because 'their actions and inactions help produce and reproduce the positions of victims and perpetrators'.[33] That means we should *not* consider an entire non-Jewish population as bystanders; not everyone of the 'others' (or 'third parties', '*Dritte*'[34]) has 'seen or heard something of the event'; and neither should we count the numerous profiteers and accomplices as bystanders, because their actions involved much more than 'seeing or hearing something'. If defined in such a way, the concept of the bystander proves, in fact, much less vague and fuzzy than is often argued.

Having said that, the number of potentially bystanding people in a society marked by conflict is crucial for the level of violence that is allowed to emerge and develop. If a majority of the population 'for a wide range of reasons, [tends] to err on the side of not intervening on behalf of the direct targets of persecution'[35] – resulting in the 'avoidable impairment of fundamental human needs'[36] – violence becomes systemic and we might speak of a 'bystander society'.[37] Still, how this notion can be applied to Nazi Germany is debatable. There, persecution and violence against Jews and other targeted groups was the result of a 'dynamic interaction between state and society'[38] to a greater degree than in any other of the allied or occupied countries. Nowhere else in the world was the government *itself* driving a policy based on a 'redemptive anti-semitism', fusing 'murderous rage' with an 'idealistic' goal – an 'Aryan' *Volksgemeinschaft*.[39]

Thus, people are not bystanders (or perpetrators) per se; their behaviour depends heavily on social context and situational dynamics.[40] Virtually every (adult) person in any society has some measure of 'the ability to harm' – psychologically and physically – fellow human-beings.[41] This power is potentially fatal to targeted individuals in a system in which stigmatization – which is 'entirely contingent on access to social, economic, and political power that allows identification of differentness, construction of stereotypes, separation of labelled persons into distinct categories, and full execution of disapproval, rejection, exclusion, and discrimination' – becomes a dominant political, 'legal' and moral norm.[42] Bystanders' decision to use or relinquish this ability is thus a crucial factor in the dynamics of systemic violence. In context of the Holocaust as a transnationally unfolding genocide, it is essential to differentiate the degree to which such systematic impairment and ultimately denial of human needs is embraced and promoted by the government (or occupation authorities); or whether, as in Nazi Germany, it came to be its very raison d'être and, concurrently, a widely shared social practice entailing the 'self-empowerment' of the racially 'fit' and the exclusion of all those defined as 'unfit'.[43] Identifying people's leeway, and the leeway they *believed* they had, as well as the *conditions* which furthered or hindered such perceptions of agency, should be our concern – what they did and why, and not what ('we' believe/ imagine) they should have done. The variety of options, the room for manoeuver and thus the degree of agency was much greater and wider in the early years of the Nazi regime within Germany than subsequently in the occupied territories, particularly after the outbreak of the war. That is why bystander history perhaps has the most to teach about the *transition* of liberal into repressive societies. The extreme violence engulfing these territories created in many places a dynamic that has led some to claim that here, the concept of bystanding becomes plainly useless.[44]

Of great value and fundamental importance is a widening of our theoretical framework and a stronger interdisciplinary orientation. Social-psychological research describes the 'bystander effect' as an anthropological given. Numerous studies have shown that the more people are present in a conflict situation, the less likely are individual bystanders to intervene on behalf of a victim.[45] The way people react also depends on their (previous) relationship to the victim. Their individual 'universes of obligation',[46] the interpersonal, familial and communal networks of emotional and material connections, matter greatly. They widen and narrow under changing conditions – and precisely the interior and exterior 'landscapes' reflected in diaries offer valuable and often detailed insights into these networks and conditions.[47] In particular, as scholars continue to debate the relevance of antisemitism as primary cause of the Holocaust,[48] a more thorough exploration of the affective and emotional layers in Jew-hatred – next to perceptions and semantics – promises a more complete conception of the peculiar ferocity and pervasiveness of modern, ultimately genocidal, antisemitism.[49]

It might therefore be useful to identify and differentiate between perceptions, emotions and behaviour in our conceptual thinking and in the analysis of our sources. According to Social Identity Theory, these three dimensions are influenced by humans' basic propensity to 'rapidly and with minimal effort' distinguish between 'we' and 'they', ingroup and outgroup; and, conversely, such distinctions influence perception, emotions and behaviour.[50] Integrating these insights into the analysis might not only provide a fresh approach to the study of the (nexus between) 'knowledge' and (in) action of the majority populations in the Holocaust. Such interdisciplinary work and differentiation also guards against overly simplistic or moralistic interpretations. Overall, such a shift of focus to the perceptions, motivations, rationalizations and experiences of non-Jewish populations leads to a history of bystanding 'from within',[51] to a clearer understanding of the involvement of the non-Jewish majority population(s) in the Holocaust – a more precise understanding of that metaphorical 'human wall'.

Thinking through the 'bystander perspective'

How is the growing interest in bystanders and bystanding (re)shaping the field of Holocaust studies? What does the apparent shift, overall, towards the perspective of the majority population, as *'Erfahrungsgeschichte'* or 'new social history of National Socialism',[52] indicate? It would certainly be worth exploring the reasons for the astounding willingness to widen the perspective beyond the perpetrators and collaborators since the 1990s – beyond the obvious ones such as the opening of the Eastern European archives, the thaw of the (more or less) 'frozen pasts' (Tony Judt) across the continent after the end of the Cold War and the ensuing 'memory boom'. What scholarly, cultural–intellectual and generational–biographical factors have contributed to the remarkable transition from the *Mitläufer*-discourse via the critical *Volksgemeinschaft*-scholarship to the most recent focus on the 'history of the experience' of the '*Mehrheitsgesellschaft*'? A shift that partly stems from the notion that, concerning the pivotal year 1933, 'there are still less-known terrains and even white spots'. In particular, 'the history of experience of the contemporaries [*Mitlebenden*] – namely those contemporaries who were neither among the political actors nor the prominent victims', in other words 'the history of experience of the great majority of the German people'.[53] How have (historiographical and public) views of German society during the Nazi period – and of the ensuing mass crimes – changed as historians explore the self-perceptions, 'hopes' ('individualist') aspirations and 'dissonances' among ordinary Germans?[54] Or of French society, for which the notion of 'social reactivity' has been introduced 'to highlight why it is necessary to view the "bystander" no longer merely as a historical actor whose actions were potentially harmful but as one whose actions and inactions in many instances could and did have a positive effect on the victims of persecution?'[55] Or of Dutch society, where a self-critical consensus on the passivity and complicity of non-Jews in the persecution of their Jewish fellow-citizens is being replaced by a more 'empathetic' view of the contemporaries' behaviour, resulting in the verdict that 'if a behavior that was normal at the time – such as accommodation – outrages us today, then our comprehension seems obviously deficient'.[56] What drives these inquiries and narratives, respectively, and in what ways are they shaped by the national and transnational scholarly networks and political–cultural landscapes in which they are formulated?

These questions should be addressed for two reasons. First, the surge in interest in the history of the majority populations is as much due to the last survivors vanishing as to the (inter-)generational and (memory) political dynamics shaping Holocaust and genocide scholarship. Secondly, that historians write about the Holocaust from a bystander perspective (implicitly or explicitly) raises epistemological, methodological and ethical questions still to be addressed; their work can become problematic if a sense of *identification* is driving this new 'empathy', or rather productive if a sense of *implication* is being negotiated, openly and critically.

During my time at the German Studies Institute Amsterdam (DIA) a heated debate erupted among Dutch historians about the 'myth of the guilty bystander'. In 2012, Leiden historian Bart van der Boom published a book titled *'We knew nothing of their fate'. Ordinary Dutchmen and the Holocaust* (*'Wij weten niets van hun lot'. Gewone Nederlanders en de Holocaust*). It was based on the analysis of around 160 Jewish and non-Jewish wartime diaries, and, with that comparative approach (critics say 'levelling' approach[57]), feeding a revisionist narrative in which everyone was 'a little bit a victim',[58] it still remains a singular work. Van der Boom argued that due to *both* groups' hazy 'knowledge' about the genocidal intentions of the Nazis, Dutch Jews and non-Jews alike grossly underestimated the threat. Tragically lacking a proper sense of urgency, Jews – understandably so, Van der Boom contends – decided far too rarely to go into hiding and non-Jews decided far too often to remain passive.[59]

In the course of the debate that ensued after the book received the most prestigious history book award in the Netherlands, and in which I actively participated,[60] I was confronted for the first time not with my being German, but with my being the granddaughter of a non-Jewish family that had lived through the Nazi period. For the controversy not only circled around conceptual and methodological issues but very personal questions relating to the 'background' of its major protagonists – there was a strong sense that *Zeiterfahrung* – even that of historians' parents and grandparents – and *Zeiterforschung* were intricately linked.[61] Talking to Evelien Gans and Remco Ensel, the most vocal critics of Van der Boom (who declined to speak publicly about the role his ancestors had played during the occupation) over a long dinner one night, I was asked in a friendly but emphatic way what my family's part had been, and asked to consider the privileged position I enjoyed as a result.

Until then, I had considered my family as belonging neither to the victims nor to the perpetrators – although both my grandfathers had served in the *Wehrmacht*. Even as the historian I had become, studying the history and memory of the war, I had never considered myself consciously as 'implicated'. Now it became clear that in theory I had thought and read much about the ramifications of the war for surviving individuals and their interrupted and destroyed family histories. But I had never *really* thought through what that entailed for those survivors and their children, or for me personally. The postcolonial thinking that informed Evelien's and Remco's inquiries has since become much more prevalent, although current debates on the relationship between (Germany's) colonial and genocidal mass crimes indicate that this conversation has only just begun – among German historians not much less than among the general public, and the severe historiographical, political and memory political consequences of the increasing entanglement of both discourses remain yet to be determined.[62]

These inquiries, however, were not primarily aimed at uncovering a 'Nazi background' or the ways in which I might still be profiting from being a non-Jewish German (as is recently debated perhaps more openly and contentiously than ever before[63]) but at confronting still more fundamental, seemingly inconspicuous truths. However, that was not something we discussed right away; rather it led me to think more deliberately about my family background and how it related to my interest in bystanding and the Holocaust. I likely come from a typical 'bystander' family, nothing more, but also nothing less – a condition that was still profoundly tangible fifty, sixty years later, as *both* my grandmothers would, not often but occasionally, utter acid anti-Jewish prejudices, let's say, in a conversation about my doctoral advisor or a missing great-grandparent-entry in one of the family trees my village grandmother had to fill in as a school girl ('There were no Jews in our family!'). And the only Jewish people I knew personally when I was a child (growing up in the GDR) was the couple living next to my city grandparents. The man was an Auschwitz survivor with a tattooed number on his arm, but the most talked-about aspect of their existence was the fact that they were clearly 'privileged' as they owned a telephone.

The unease and unpreparedness my Dutch colleagues encountered when confronting me back in 2013 suggest that I was clearly wired as a member of 'my' majority society, in which, in spite of all the education and commemoration, awareness of the long-term effects of Nazism's enormous *societal* basis remains remarkably low. In a recent study, 45 per cent of respondents agreed partially or fully with the statement that the 'German people had no responsibility for the crimes of National Socialism', 68 per cent claimed that their ancestors had either been victims (36%) or rescuers (32%); asked what they believe *they* would have done, 65 per cent saw themselves as rescuers; and asked about different aspects of Nazi history, respondents said what they knew least about was 'daily life and the attitudes of the population towards Nazism'.[64]

There is always, of course, tension between public and academic history, memory and historiography, but the intellectual, political and ethical challenges ahead – in the German context and beyond[65] – are not only linked to the much-debated changing citizenry and the question of how immigrant communities relate to the Nazi past, but also to the still insufficient awareness of the social – and from a bystander perspective: *interpersonal* – processes which enable and sustain contexts of systemic discrimination, persecution and violence. That is why public history institutions that specialize in entwining larger historical developments with individual perspectives are of such fundamental importance. For example, exhibitions at Buchenwald Memorial – as is well known, a camp that was *not* a primary site of the Holocaust but rather a prison, forced-labour-, torture- and killing-complex in the heart of Germany – strenuously 'interweave the view into the camp with the view into German society'.[66] And the still singular USHMM's special exhibition *Some were Neighbors* (2013) with its focus on the (in)actions of non-Jewish bystanders – neighbours, friends, colleagues, acquaintances, local administrators and communities – seems to trigger in visitors particularly perceptive insights into genocide as a human possibility.[67]

Thus, a bystander perspective on Holocaust history (and education), can offer valuable impulses for a continued, twenty-first-century-fit historiographical as well as public reckoning with the persecution and mass murder of the European Jews. Moreover, it seems to be more than a purely scholarly undertaking to seek to understand 'ordinary' bystanders not by 'empathizing'[68] with them (which is neither the task nor the essence of historical understanding[69]), but by differentiating the perceptions, emotions and behaviours connected to the subject position and state of mind my grandparents attained in their youth and retained (as well as its present-day (re)incarnations). Working with sociological and social-psychological insights and not only with the methodological tool-kit of the historian, might not only render more precise historical knowledge but also help scholars to adequately address and (self-)critically engage with such personal and cultural biases, regardless of our actual, inescapable 'background'.

Identifying the social and interpersonal relevance of bystanding, historically and in terms of its long-term ramifications, is very much a task still ahead of 'us' – the '*Mehrheitsgesellschaft*', of which even chancellors and presidents speak routinely these days, reinforcing in Germans a comfortable sense of having learned – or, rather, internalized – the right lessons.[70] In light of the rising stream of interventions not only from the conservative and far right but also liberal corners of the republic, questioning the very premises on which Germany's political and memory culture has rested in the last decades, one might ask how much of that sense is really justified.

Ultimately, a comprehensive understanding of bystanding in the Holocaust can break new ground in our ongoing efforts to learn how systemic hatred, violence and genocide can become the worst possible outcomes of clearly discernible, interwoven social and interpersonal processes, to which every individual contributes in some way. History, as Ernst Cassirer once wrote, 'is not knowledge of external facts or events; it is a form of self-knowledge'.[71]

Notes

1 David Bankier and Israel Gutman (eds), *Nazi Europe and the Final Solution* (New York: Berghahn, 2009); Frank Bajohr and Andrea Löw (eds), *The Holocaust and European Societies: Social Processes and Social Dynamics* (London: Palgrave Macmillan UK, 2016); Christian Gerlach, *The Extermination of the European Jews* (Cambridge:

Cambridge University Press, 2016); Saul Friedländer, *Nazi Germany and the Jews*, vol. 1: *The Years of Persecution 1933–1939*; vol. 2: *The Years of Extermination 1939–1945* (New York: HarperCollins, 1997/2007); I reference only selectively from the vast literature. For a comprehensive review, see Christina Morina, 'Bystanders, Collaboration and Complicity', in *The Cambridge History of the Holocaust*, vol. 2, ed. Mary Fulbrook and Jürgen Matthäus (Cambridge: Cambridge University Press, forthcoming). Many of the considerations outlined relate to the research project 'Bystanding and the Holocaust in Europe. Experiences, Ramifications, Representations, 1933 to the present' on Jewish and non-Jewish diaries from six European countries conducted at the University of Bielefeld (2021–2025).

2 Frank Bajohr, 'The "Folk Community" and the persecution of the Jews: German society under National Socialist dictatorship, 1933–1945', *Holocaust and Genocide Studies* 20, no. 2 (2006): 183–206; Gerald D. Feldman and Wolfgang Seibel (eds), *Networks of Nazi Persecution: Bureaucracy, Business, and the Organization of the Holocaust* (New York: Berghahn, 2006); Jan Grabowski, *Hunt for the Jews: Betrayal and Murder in German-occupied Poland* (Bloomington: Indiana University Press, 2013).

3 Raul Hilberg, *Perpetrators Victims Bystanders: The Jewish Catastrophe, 1933–1945* (New York: Aaron Asher Books, 1992), xi.

4 Friedländer, *Years of Extermination*, xxii.

5 Michael Wildt, *Hitler's Volksgemeinschaft and the Dynamics of Racial Exclusion: Violence Against Jews in Provincial Germany, 1919–1939* (New York: Berghahn, 2012), 2.

6 Friedländer, *Years of Extermination*, xxii.

7 Mary Fulbrook, 'Catchall Concept, alluring alibi, or Crucial Clue?', in *Probing the Limits of Categorization: The Bystander in Holocaust History*, ed. Christina Morina and Krijn Thijs (New York: Berghahn, 2018), 15–35.

8 Friedländer, *Years of Extermination*, xv, xxv.

9 Bajohr, 'The "Folk Community" and the Persecution of the Jews', 183.

10 Frank Bajohr, *Aryanisation in Hamburg: The Economic Exclusion of Jews and the Confiscation of their Property in Nazi Germany* (New York and Oxford: Berghahn, 2002); Elisabeth Harvey, *Women and the Nazi Germanization of the 'East': Agents and Witnesses* (New Haven: Yale University Press, 2003); Feldman and Seibel, *Networks of Nazi Persecution*; Grabowski, *Hunt for the Jews*; Friedländer, *Years of Persecution*; Friedländer, *Years of Extermination*.

11 Christina Morina, 'The "Bystander" in Recent Dutch Historiography', *German History* 32, no. 1 (2014): 101–11; Krijn Thijs, 'Ordinary, Ignorant, and Noninvolved? The Figure of the Bystander in Dutch Research and Controversy', in Morina and Thijs, *Probing the Limits of Categorization*, 247–65.

12 Peter Longerich, *'Davon haben wir nichts gewusst!': Die Deutschen und die Judenverfolgung 1933–1945* (München: Siedler, 2006); Ian Kershaw, *Hitler, the Germans, and the 'Final Solution'* (New Haven: Yale University Press, 2008); Friedländer, *Years of Persecution*, 4; Frank Bajohr and Dieter Pohl, *Massenmord und schlechtes Gewissen: Die deutsche Bevölkerung, die NS-Führung und der Holocaust* (Frankfurt/Main: Fischer, 2008); Otto Dov Kulka and Aron Rodrigue, 'The German Population and the Jews in the Third Reich. Recent Publication and Trends in Research on German Society and the "Jewish Question"', in *The Nazi Holocaust: Public Opinion and Relations to the Jews in Nazi Europe: Part 5; Vol. 1*, ed. Michael R. Marrus (Berlin: De Gruyter, 2011), 46–60.

13 Janosch Steuwer, 'Was meint und nützt das Sprechen von der "Volksgemeinschaft"? Neuere Literatur zur Gesellschaftsgeschichte des Nationalsozialismus', *Archiv für Sozialgeschichte* 53 (2013): 534.

14 Wildt, *Hitler's Volksgemeinschaft and the Dynamics of Racial Exclusion*; Martina Steber and Bernhard Gotto (eds), *Visions of Community in Nazi Germany: Social Engineering and Private Lives* (Oxford: Oxford University Press, 2014); Janosch Steuwer, *'Ein Drittes Reich, wie ich es auffasse': Politik, Gesellschaft und privates Leben in Tagebüchern 1933–1939* (Göttingen: Wallstein, 2017).
15 Raul Hilberg, *The Destruction of the European Jews* (New Haven and London: Yale University Press, 1961).
16 Friedländer, *Years of Extermination*, xix.
17 Jie-Hyun Lim, review of *Volksgemeinschaft als Selbstermächtigung. Gewalt gegen Juden in der deutschen Provinz 1919 bis 1939*, by Michael Wildt, *International Review of Social History* 53, no. 2 (2008): 327.
18 Gerlach, *Extermination of European Jews*, 44; Wildt, *Hitler's Volksgemeinschaft and the Dynamics of Racial Exclusion*.
19 Eric. A. Johnson and Karl-Heinz Reuband, *What we Knew: Terror, Mass Murder and everyday Life in Nazi Germany* (London: John Murray, 2005), 277–80.
20 Jana Fritsche and Christoph Kreutzmüller, 'Eine Topographie der Gewalt. Übergriffe auf Jüdinnen und Juden im Deutschen Reich 1930–1938', *Zeitschrift für Geschichtswissenschaft* 68, no. 6 (2020): 493–517.
21 On perpetrator depictions in Jewish diaries, cf. Amy Simon, *'Surrounded by the Hunter on All Sides': Jewish Perceptions of Perpetrators in the Nazi Ghettos* (PhD Dissertation Indiana University, 2015); Mark Roseman, *The Barbarians from our 'Kulturkreis': German-Jewish Perceptions of Nazi Perpetrators* (Göttingen: Wallstein, 2017); on bystander depictions, cf. Barbara Engelking, '"We are Completely Dependent on Them . . .". Relations between the Helpers and the Hiding as Exemplified by Fela Fischbein's Diary', *Holocaust. Studies and Materials* 2 (2010): 128–56; Christina Morina, 'The Imperative to Act: Jews, Neighbors, and the Dynamics of Persecution in Nazi Germany, 1933–1945', in Morina and Thijs, *Probing the Limits*, 148–67. Friedländer's work has transformed how we think and write about the Holocaust, particularly because of his use of diaries. Yet, his pioneering work, interweaving diary passages into his narrative as 'lightning flashes' (Friedländer, *Years of Extermination*, xv, xxv), can be said to 'perform' diaries rather than analyse them systematically. See Wulf Kansteiner, 'Success, Truth, and Modernism in Holocaust Historiography: Reading Saul Friedländer 35 Years after the Publication of Metahistory', *History and Theory* 48, no. 2 (2009): 25. The 15-volume-edition *Die Verfolgung und Ermordung der der europäischen Juden durch das nationalsozialistische Deutschland 1933–1945* (2008–2021) underlines (and facilitates) the need for more systematic, comparative and transnational studies; diaries make up for an average of 10 per cent of the documents, about a third of which were written by non-Jews.
22 Fulbrook, 'Catchall Concept, alluring alibi, or Crucial Clue?', 23.
23 By way of example for the spectrum alluded to, one might point to the diary of Karl Kurz J., Deutsches Tagebucharchiv Emmendingen, Tagebuch/Erinnerungen Karl Kurz J., 1933–1938 (written in 1941), 3969, 1R, entries 11–12 March 1933, detailing the responses of 'ordinary' townspeople to a local pogrom; to Etty Hillesum's diary from the occupied Netherlands, for example, the entry of 4 July 1942 recounting a random encounter with a Dutchman at a pharmacy who – without a German in sight – protested her being there because she was Jewish; see Etty Hillesum and J. G. Gaarlandt, *An Interrupted Life: The Diaries, 1941–1943, and Letters from Westerbork* (New York: Henry Holt, 1996), 160f.; to the diary of Zygmunt Klukowski, a Polish doctor describing how he was caught 'looking on' as Jews were harassed by German soldiers across from his apartment in August of 1940, cf. the entry for 14 August 1940 in *Tagebuch aus den*

Jahren der Okkupation 1939–1944, ed. Zygmunt Klukowski, Christine Glauning, and Ewelina Wanke (Berlin: Metropol, 2017), 216f.; and to an incident that took place in Kiev in the days following the Babi Yar massacre in September of 1941, where nine elderly Jewish survivors were starving to death in front of the former synagogue under the eyes of the local population (and patrolling Germans threatening to kill anyone who dared to offer them food); one passer-by approached a soldier with the suggestion to shoot the last two men, which he did. Cf. Karel Berkhoff, *Harvest of Despair: Life and Death in Ukraine under Nazi Rule* (Cambridge: Belknap Press, 2004), 77.

24 Mary Fulbrook, *Dissonant Lives: Generations and Violence Through the German Dictatorships* (Oxford: Oxford University Press, 2011), 170f.

25 Victoria Barnett, *Bystanders: Conscience and Complicity During the Holocaust* (Westport: Praeger, 2000), 32.

26 Amos Goldberg, 'Jews' Diaries and Chronicles', in *The Oxford Handbook of Holocaust Studies*, ed. Peter Hayes and John K. Roth (Oxford: Oxford University Press, 2010), 410.

27 Alexandra Garbarini, *Numbered Days: Diaries and the Holocaust* (New Haven: Yale University Press, 2006); Friedländer, *Years of Persecution*; Friedländer, *Years of Extermination*; Dominique Schröder, *'Niemand ist fähig das alles in Worten auszudrücken': Tagebuchschreiben in nationalsozialistischen Konzentrationslagern 1939–1945* (Göttingen: Wallstein, 2020).

28 Steuwer, *'Ein Drittes Reich, wie ich es auffasse'*; Janosch Steuwer and Rüdiger Graf (eds), *Selbstreflexionen und Weltdeutungen: Tagebücher in der Geschichte und der Geschichtsschreibung des 20. Jahrhunderts* (Göttingen: Wallstein, 2015).

29 Steuwer, *'Ein Drittes Reich, wie ich es auffasse'*, 548.

30 Michael Wildt, 'Self-Reassurance in Troubled Times: German Diaries during the Upheavals of 1933', in *Everyday Life in Mass Dictatorship: Collusion and Evasion*, ed. Alf Lüdtke (Basingstoke: Palgrave Macmillan, 2016), 58. See further: Frank Bajohr, Beate Meyer, and Joachim Szodrzynski (eds), *Bedrohung, Hoffnung, Skepsis: Vier Tagebücher des Jahres 1933* (Göttingen: Wallstein, 2013), 10.

31 Friedrich Kellner, *Vernebelt, verdunkelt sind alle Hirne: Tagebücher 1939–1945*, 2 vols. (Göttingen, Wallstein, 2011); Klukowski, *Tagebuch aus den Jahren der Okkupation*.

32 Jacques Sémelin, *Survival of the Jews in France, 1940–44* (Oxford: Oxford University Press, 2019).

33 Michael Rothberg, *The Implicated Subject: Beyond Victims and Perpetrators* (Stanford: Stanford University Press, 2019), 1.

34 That is the term – next to onlookers (*Zuschauer*) – under which the VEJ-editors subsumed the '"Aryan" majority'; cf. Gruner (ed.), *Die Verfolgung und Ermordung*, 35; Susanne Heim, 'Bald sprechen nur noch die Quellen', *Die ZEIT*, 22 April 2021, 17.

35 Mary Fulbrook, 'Private Lives, Public Faces', in *Private Life and Privacy in Nazi Germany*, ed. Elisabeth Harvey, Johannes Hürter and Maiken Umbach (Cambridge: Cambridge University Press, 2019), 55–80, 61.

36 Johan Galtung, 'Kulturelle Gewalt', *Der Bürger im Staat* 43, no. 2 (1993): 106–12; cited from Kathleen Ho, 'Structural Violence as a Human Rights Violation', *Essex Human Rights Review* 4, no. 2 (2007): 3.

37 Fulbrook, 'Private Lives, Public Faces', 59f.

38 Bajohr, 'The "Folk Community" and the Persecution of the Jews', 183.

39 Friedländer, *Years of Persecution*, 3.

40 Harald Welzer, 'On Killing and Morality: How Normal People Become Mass Murderers', in *Ordinary People as Mass Murderers: Perpetrators in Comparative*

Perspectives, ed. Olaf Jensen and Claus-Christian W. Szejnmann (Basingstoke: Palgrave Macmillan, 2014), 165–81.
41 Heinrich Popitz, *Phenomena of Power: Authority, Domination, and Violence* (New York: Columbia University Press, 2017), 26; Martina Kessel, *Gewalt und Gelächter: "Deutschsein" 1914–1945* (Stuttgart: Franz Steiner, 2019).
42 Bruce G. Link and Jo C. Phelan, 'Conceptualizing Stigma', *Annual Review of Sociology* 27, no. 1 (2001): 367.
43 Wildt, *Hitler's Volksgemeinschaft and the Dynamics of Racial Exclusion*, 278.
44 Grabowski, *Hunt for the Jews*.
45 Peter Fischer et al., 'The Bystander-Effect: A Meta-Analytic Review on Bystander Intervention in Dangerous and Non-Dangerous Emergencies', *Psychological Bulletin* 137, no. 4 (2011): 517–37.
46 Helen Fein, *Accounting for Genocide: National Responses and Jewish Victimization During the Holocaust* (Chicago: University of Chicago Press, 1979), 4.
47 Alain Girard, *Le Journal Intime* (Paris: Presses Universitaires de France, 1963), xvi, here cited from David Patterson, 'Through the Eyes of Those Who Were There (Review Essay)', *Holocaust and Genocide Studies* 18, no. 2 (2004): 276; Garbarini, *Numbered Days*; Andrea Löw, *Juden im Getto Litzmannstadt: Lebensbedingungen, Selbstwahrnehmung, Verhalten* (Göttingen: Wallstein, 2006).
48 Friedländer, *Years of Persecution*; Friedländer, *Years of Extermination*; Jürgen Matthäus, 'Holocaust als angewandter Antisemitismus? Potential und Grenzen eines Erklärungsfaktors', in *Der Holocaust: Ergebnisse und neue Fragen der Forschung*, ed. Frank Bajohr and Andrea Löw (Frankfurt/Main: Fischer, 2015), 102–23.
49 Remco Ensel and Evelien Gans, 'The Dutch Bystander as Non-Jew and Implicated Subject', in Morina and Thijs, *Probing the Limits*, 107–30; Stefanie Schüler-Springorum and Jan Süselbeck (eds), *Emotionen und Antisemitismus: Geschichte – Literatur – Theorie* (Göttingen: Wallstein, 2021).
50 Jennifer A. Richeson and Samuel R. Sommers, 'Toward a Social Psychology of Race and Race Relations for the Twenty-First Century', *Annual Review of Psychology* 67 (2016): 439–63.
51 Fulbrook, *Dissonant Lives*, 2.
52 Norbert Frei, *1945 und wir: Das Dritte Reich im Bewußtsein der Deutschen* (Munich: Beck, 2005), 107–28; Michael Wildt, '"Volksgemeinschaft" – eine Zwischenbilanz', in *'Volksgemeinschaf' als soziale Praxis: Neue Forschungen zur NS-Gesellschaft vor Ort*, ed. Dietmar von Reeken and Malte Thießen (Paderborn: Ferdinand Schöningh, 2013), 369.
53 Andreas Wirsching, 'Die deutsche "Mehrheitsgesellschaft" und die Etablierung des NS-Regimes im Jahre 1933', in *Das Jahr 1933: Die nationalsozialistische Machteroberung und die deutsche Gesellschaft*, ed. Andreas Wirsching (Göttingen: Wallstein, 2009), 10, 23. In his view, such an approach demonstrates the 'double stranglehold of German society'. Ibid., 23.
54 Fulbrook, *Dissonant Lives*; Moritz Föllmer, 'The Subjective Dimension of Nazism', *The Historical Journal* 56, no. 4 (2013): 1107–132; Bajohr et al., *Bedrohung, Hoffnung, Skepsis*; Steuwer, *'Ein Drittes Reich, wie ich es auffasse'*.
55 Jacques Sémelin, ''The Notion of Social Reactivity: The French Case, 1942–1944', in Morina and Thijs, *Probing the Limits*, 225.
56 Bart van der Boom, *'Wij weten niets van hun lot': Gewone Nederlanders en de Holocaust* (Amsterdam: Boom, 2012), 428.
57 Evelien Gans and Remco Ensel, 'De inzet van joden als "controlegroep". Bart van der Boom en de Holocaust', *Tijdschrift voor geschiedenis* 126, no. 3 (2013): 388–96.

58 Evelien Gans, 'Iedereen een beetje slachtoffer, iedereen een beetje dader', *De Groene Amsterdammer*, 27 January 2010.
59 For an English synthesis, see Bart van der Boom, 'Ordinary Dutchmen and the Holocaust. A Summary of Findings', in *The Persecution of the Jews in the Netherlands, 1940–1945: New Perspectives*, ed. Bart van der Boom and Peter Romijn (Amsterdam: Vossiuspers, 2012), 29–54.
60 Morina, 'The "Bystander" in Recent Dutch Historiography'; 'The Imperative to Act'.
61 See Thijs, 'Ordinary, Ignorant, and Noninvolved?'. On the nexus between biography and historiography, see Franka Maubach and Christina Morina (eds), *Das 20. Jahrhundert erzählen: Zeiterfahrung und Zeiterforschung im geteilten Deutschland* (Göttingen: Wallstein Verlag, 2016).
62 As recently illustrated by the debate around the German edition of Michael Rothberg's *Multidirectional Memory*, see Katharina Stengel, *Rezension zu: Rothberg, Michael: Multidirektionale Erinnerung. Holocaustgedenken im Zeitalter der Dekolonisierung. Berlin 2021*, in: *H-Soz-Kult*, 11 May 2021, www.hsozkult.de/publicationreview/id/reb-95854 (Accessed 15 January 2022).
63 Cf. Michael Rothberg and Hanno Hauenstein, 'Nazi-Hintergrund, NS-Erbe und materielle Kontinuität: Das Schweigen brechen', *Berliner Zeitung*, 10 April 2021; Patrick Bahners, 'Genozid durch Gentrifizierung', *Frankfurter Allgemeine Zeitung*, 3 March 2021.
64 Michael Papendick et al., *Multidimensionaler Erinnerungsmonitor (MEMO) III/2020 - Fokusbericht* (IKG Bielefeld, 2020), 11, 7. Cf. Michael Papendick, Jonas Rees and Andreas Zick, 'Unknowing, Indifferent, or Committed: Relations between Age and Assessments of the German Population's Involvement and Inaction during the Time of National Socialism', *Asian Journal of Social Psychology* (2021): 9.
65 Claudio Fogu, Wulf Kansteiner and Todd Presner (eds), *Probing the Ethics of Holocaust Culture* (Cambridge, MA: Harvard University Press, 2016); David M. Seymour and Mercedes M. Camino (eds), *The Holocaust in the Twenty-First Century: Contesting/Contested Memories* (London: Routledge, 2017); Stuart Foster, Andy Pearce and Alice Pettigrew (eds), *Holocaust Education: Contemporary Challenges and Controversies* (London: UCL Press, 2020).
66 Volkhard Knigge et al. (eds), *Buchenwald. Ausgrenzung und Gewalt 1937 bis 1945. Begleitband zur Dauerausstellung in der Gedenkstätte Buchenwald* (Göttingen: Wallstein, 2016), 7.
67 Cf. the impressive anecdotal evidence from guest books in Susan Bachrach, '"Bystanders" in Exhibitions at the United States Holocaust Memorial Museum', in Morina and Thijs, *Probing the Limits*, 326–8.
68 Van der Boom means by that: 'Instead of judging them [the bystanders] – according to *our* standards – we should try to understand them from inside out, from *their* perception of the event and *their* thoughts about right and wrong. [..] This should instigate in us curiosity and empathy, not sacred indignation [*Verontwaardiging*]'. Van der Boom, '*Wij weten niets van hun lot*', 428. The last remark seems to be a direct reference to Friedländer's sense of 'disbelief' as a 'quasivisceral reaction', cf. Friedländer, *Years of Extermination*, xxvi.
69 Hans-Georg Gadamer, *Wahrheit und Methode: Grundzüge einer philosophischen Hermeneutik*, 2nd ed. (Tübingen: Mohr, 1965), 285–90; but rather delineating the 'horizon' of past experiences.

70 Neither bystanding nor '*Volksgemeinschaft*' might be proper, satisfying analytical terms; they both can serve as heuristic devices but surely we should try to find still different, more precise terms, cf. Steuwer, 'Was meint und nützt das Sprechen von der "Volksgemeinschaft"?', 534.
71 Ernst Cassirer, *An Essay on Man: An Introduction to a Philosophy of Human Culture* (New Haven: Yale University Press, 1944), 206.

Part II

Confrontations with violence

6

Studying East European perpetrators

The case of Belarus

Leonid Rein

Introduction

On 28 February 1947, a bespectacled man sat before the Soviet NKVD investigator. His name was David Egof; he was an ethnic German, a schoolteacher, who during the German occupation in Belarus had served as mayor of the small town of Zembin about 80 km to the northeast of Minsk, and later as commander of the auxiliary police in the city of Borisov, a district seat. In both these capacities, Egof actively participated in the mass murder of Jews. In his interrogation, Egof described in detail the massacres of the Jews of Zembin and Borisov, and his active role in them. Since the Soviet authorities were interested in portraying local collaborators with the Germans as morally debased people who had nothing to do with ordinary Soviet citizens, Egof depicted the massacre of Borisov Jews as a drunken orgy of violence perpetrated by local auxiliary policemen.[1] Later on, in the 1960s, Egof's testimony underwent certain doctoring when the sinister role played in the massacre of the Borisov Jews by the district chief of Borisov, Stanislav Stankevich, who at that time worked at the anti-Soviet Radio Liberty, was stressed more vigorously.

Five-and-a half years before Egof was interrogated by Soviet security organs, in October 1941, two officials from the Reich's Ministry for the Occupied Eastern Territories, Eugen von Engelhardt, a Latvian German, regarded as an expert on Belarus, and a young jurist from the department for Lithuania and Belarus, were on an information-gathering trip through the occupied Soviet territories. On their way to Smolensk, the two stopped for the night in a locality near lake Naroch, in north-western Belarus. The next morning the two took advantage of beautiful weather to walk to the lake. On their way to Naroch Lake they came across a small village where one of the local peasants volunteered to serve as a guide for the two Germans, who both spoke fluent Russian and were able to converse freely with him. At one point the three came to the edge of the forest, where the peasant pointed to an almost indiscernible mound in the ground, saying joyfully 'Our Jews are lying over there'. Then the peasant proceeded to tell the two Germans how the residents of the surrounding villages herded 'their'

Jews to this place, who were then shot by either Lithuanian or Belarusian policemen (the peasant did not know their exact identity). The peasant also complained about the 'damages' local inhabitants had suffered from the Jews. Afterwards the trio continued on their way to the lake.[2]

The Holocaust in the territories that up to 1991 were part of the Soviet Union differed markedly from the Holocaust in western and central Europe. First of all, it was a 'Holocaust by bullets'[3] perpetrated in an archaic way by rifles and machine guns, in or near the places where Jewish victims lived, with perpetrators directly facing their victims. Local auxiliary policemen, who during the murder operations drove the Jews out of the houses, herded them to the sites of murder, and in more than one case pulled the trigger of the gun in mass shootings, knew their victims well from before the war. At the same time, as shown in the example above and in countless other cases, the circle of those who were privy to the whole annihilation process and in many cases took part in it was broad indeed. Here the boundaries between the categories of perpetrators and bystanders were blurred to non-existent.[4]

The study of local perpetrators of the Holocaust in Belarus, not unlike other former Soviet territories, represents an enormous challenge for historians, both from a qualitative and quantitative point of view. The very definition of the category of perpetration here is not an easy task. As I will show, there were a great variety of forms of involvement of the local non-Jewish population in the Holocaust in Belarusian territory, beyond direct participation in the massacres. The question that I try to tackle is how far the local perpetrators of the Holocaust in Belarus felt themselves compromised in their actions, and how far they were regarded as compromised by people in their surroundings.

The challenging nature of Belarussian sources

To this day the theme of local complicity in the Holocaust in Belarus remains heavily under-researched. During the Soviet period, Belarus was portrayed as a 'partisan republic', the country whose population allegedly rose as one man to resist German invaders. The Nazi collaborators, if mentioned at all in this narrative, were characteristically designated by the term *politsai* (distorted German word *Polizei*), implying that they were elements alien to Soviet Belarusian society, existing somewhere on its margins. These people usually drew the attention of Soviet security organs and not of historians. Some of the former collaborators who left Belarus for the west in 1944 and were caught in the crossfire of the Cold War became subjects of Soviet propagandists, being portrayed as lackeys of imperialist masters hostile to the Soviet Union.[5]

The treatment of the very theme of the Holocaust in Soviet Belarus, like in the rest of the Soviet Union, was quite ambiguous too. It would be wrong to maintain that Soviet authorities were completely silent on, let alone denied, the Holocaust. Several publications in the 1960s and 1970s explicitly mentioned the persecution and murder of the Jews.[6] The trend hereby was not denial of the Holocaust per se, but rather denial of the uniqueness of Jewish suffering and 'drowning' this suffering in the general suffering of the Soviet people. In Belarus this was easier to do as three years of German occupation left this country in ruins and with a death count ranging between one and two million people.[7] The issue of local collaboration in the Holocaust did not fit into this narrative of universal suffering and universal resistance and was banned from public discourse to the judicial realm.

Being banned to the judicial sphere, the perception of the topic of collaboration generally, and collaboration in the Holocaust in particular, did not become less ambiguous. Even though in Soviet Union generally judicial proceedings against Nazi criminals were introduced much earlier than in the West, local perpetrators of the Nazi crimes were not prosecuted systematically. There were not many people who, like David Egof, occupied some sort of prominent position during the German occupation of Belarusian territory, did not retreat with the Germans and were apprehended quite early on by Soviet security organs. When the Soviet Army liberated/reconquered Belarus in 1944, only a minority of local collaborators chose to leave Belarus with the Germans.[8] It must be remembered that, already during the war, the Soviet approach towards local Nazi collaborators changed from hostility and outright executions to inducing them to desert to the partisans, promising a pardon to those who had joined the ranks of collaborators 'by mistake'.[9] After the Soviets retook Belarusian territory, all the able-bodied men they encountered here, including former auxiliary policemen, were recruited to the Red Army and sent to fight the same Germans with whom they had collaborated just a year previously. After the end of war these people, including those who had been heavily involved in persecution and extermination of Jews, returned to their homes, many as decorated war veterans eager to continue their lives and not at all eager to speak about more sinister aspects of their wartime activities. Actually, only a minority of them were subsequently recognized, often by Jewish survivors as their former tormentors, and brought to justice. Since the materials of the proceedings against such people are still largely unavailable for foreign researchers, it is impossible to say even approximately how many Belarusians who participated in the mass murder of Belarusian Jews were put on trial. At the same time, the general pattern of judicial proceedings against local collaborators was the same throughout the Soviet Union. In contrast to western judicial practices, these proceedings did not aim to prove the defendant's innocence, but rather to implicate him in the crimes. Thus they did not aim to reconstruct an objective course of events, but rather to adjust these events and the actions of the persons under investigation to a preset Soviet agenda. The Holocaust as such did figure in many of these proceedings and, as was shown in case of Egof, the massacres of Jews were often described in all their grisly details. Still, the persecution and murder of Jews was not regarded by Soviet investigators as a point in itself, but rather as part of a complex of crimes committed by the accused against Soviet people, and therefore treated together with crimes against Soviet war prisoners, partisans and non-Jewish civilians. While in trials conducted right after the war the murder of Jews was mentioned explicitly, later on when the Soviet agenda was set on downplaying the uniqueness of Jewish suffering, mention of the Holocaust was substituted by a generic term 'crimes against peaceful Soviet citizens'.

After the conclusion of judicial proceedings, their records were locked in the archives of the Committee for State Security (the dreaded KGB), far from the eyes of the general public and largely inaccessible to historians. These records are kept in such a state to this day. Contrary to the situation in neighbouring Lithuania and Ukraine, where the archives of the former KGB, where materials of judicial proceedings against former Soviet collaborators were stored, were opened for researchers some time ago,[10] this is not the case in Belarus. During the relative liberalization following the fall of the Soviet Union, Belarusian archives, including the KGB's archives, were opened briefly for the researchers, only to be shut tightly again in the mid-1990s. Needless to say, such a situation does not make research into the topic any easier.

Most of the available information about Belarusian Holocaust perpetrators comes either from official Soviet sources, such as the aforementioned materials of judicial proceedings, or from testimonies of Holocaust survivors, or from the official documents of German perpetrators. In these sources the perpetrators operate as a body without a distinct face, or even if we encounter individual perpetrators their modus operandi is adapted to the official narrative and official agendas. It is very difficult or impossible to say something about their motives in taking active part in the persecution and annihilation of people who often only recently were their neighbours, schoolmates, working colleagues, friends or even relatives. Speaking of compromised identities, it is almost impossible to say something about whether they indeed felt themselves as being compromised, or how they generally perceived their activities. Such insights can usually be gained from ego-documents such as letters and diaries. Unfortunately, none of these are available for researchers. In a predominantly rural country such as Belarus in the first half of the twentieth century, the auxiliary policemen most directly involved in the execution of the Final Solution were recruited mainly from among village populations,[11] which normally did not engage in belles-lettres writing. The only documents that can be regarded as ego-documents were memoirs published by a few of the former Nazi collaborators who left Belarus with the Germans and after the war settled in the west. In these memoirs they naturally do not mention either the Holocaust or Jews at all, concentrating on their alleged efforts to lay the foundations for the future Belarusian State under the difficult conditions of German occupation.[12]

The fact that makes research on the local perpetration of the Holocaust in Belarus even more difficult is the politization of the topic of the Second World War generally and of the Holocaust in particular in recent years, following the August 2020 presidential elections in Belarus and the protests that erupted in their wake. Both President Lukashenko's loyalists and protesters compare the other side to Nazi occupiers and their local accomplices, freely using and abusing the theme of the Holocaust and local complicity in it.[13] This certainly does not facilitate objective historical analyses.

Historical background

In a country such as Belarus the Holocaust destroyed centuries-old Jewish communities and disrupted the social fabric created over the years. It is impossible to grasp the involvement of broad sections of the Belarusian non-Jewish population in the persecution and annihilation of their former neighbours without casting at least a brief glance at inter-ethnic relations formed here over many generations.

For centuries, the relations between Jews and their non-Jewish neighbours here were more of cohabitation than true coexistence.[14] Between the late eighteenth and the early twentieth-century Belarusian territory was part of the Russian Empire in which Jews had a status of a discriminated and persecuted minority. On the local level Jews and non-Jews lived largely in parallel realities with little contact to each other. This territory was not bypassed by the national awakening in the early twentieth century; however Belarusian nationalism was too weak to be radicalized and, in a country where Jews represented a clear majority in urban centres, was inclusive rather than exclusive.[15] To be sure, the Belarusian population was not free of anti-semitism. However anti-semitism here was of an archaic nature: it reflected old Christian anti-Jewish prejudices as much as the antagonism of the rural population towards town-dwellers.[16] In the early twentieth century there were some changes in a fabric of Jewish/non-Jewish relations in Belarus. Between 1921 and 1939 Belarusian territory was divided between Poland and the Soviet Union. While in Polish Belarus the relations between Jews and Belarusians remained largely unchanged, with an amendment in that both became discriminated minorities in the Polish State, in the Soviet part of Belarus the centuries-old (uneasy) cohabitation between Jews and their non-Jewish neighbours gave way to true coexistence, at least formally: Soviet Belarusian Jews officially gained equal rights and could work and study with, and even marry, non-Jews.[17] This does not mean, however, that anti-semitism in that part of the country disappeared; it just acquired new elements. The fact that Jews, traditionally urban dwellers active for generations in the economic sphere, were better adapted for the modernization processes introduced by the Soviet regime, called forth envy and ire on part of their non-Jewish neighbours. Jews started to be regarded as the main profiteers of Soviet rule, being much better off both socially and materially than the rest of the population. Being traditional scapegoats in the Russian Empire, Jews now too were quickly to blame for all the wrongdoings of Soviet rule.[18]

The annexation of Polish Belarus by the Soviet Union in 1939, presented by Soviet propaganda as the 'Reunion of Belarus' and as the liberation of Belarusians from the Polish yoke, brought new tensions in interethnic relations. In a situation in which Poles were regarded by Soviet authorities as enemies, while Belarusians did not possess necessary skills, the new regime was compelled to rely, to a significant degree, on Jews in managing the newly annexed territory. At the same time, for many Jews themselves who had lost their source of income as a result of the Soviet nationalization of the economy, government service became about the only available employment. This of course made them Soviet collaborators in the eyes of Poles and Belarusians. The latter, moreover, initially believed Soviet slogans of liberation and saw themselves cheated in their hopes of occupying privileged positions under the new rule.[19] Adding to all this the fact that the Podlasie region, which the Soviets annexed in 1939, was traditionally a hotbed of Polish ultra-nationalism and ultra-Montanism, and a true witch cauldron was created here on the eve of the German invasion with anti-Jewish animosities boiling, ready to burst out at any moment. Such a moment arrived on 22 June 1941, when German troops crossed the Soviet border. Today many know about the place called Jedwabne[20]; however, not many are aware that this place, as well as numerous other places in the area in which in the first days and weeks of the German invasion into the Soviet Union gentiles turned against their Jewish neighbours, were within the borders of Soviet Belarus as of 22 June 1941.[21]

Multiple complicities

As was shown many decades ago by Raul Hilberg, the Holocaust was not only the mass murder of the Jews. Rather, mass murder was but a culmination of a multi-stage process that started with disenfranchising, dispossessing and dehumanizing Jews.[22] In occupied Belarus too, we can see all these stages even though, as mentioned above, here the transition between stages was much quicker, and in many cases some stages were skipped altogether. And we can see here the involvement of the local population in all stages. This involvement proceeded on two levels: on an organized level, in the framework of auxiliary institutions created by the German occupiers; and also on a popular level. It is impossible to define even approximately the scope of this involvement. While we know more or less the size of the local administrative institutions that played an important role in what we call the preparatory stages of the Holocaust, and of local auxiliary police which participated actively in mass-murder itself,[23] we cannot say how many ordinary Belarusians were involved in this process.

The very character of this involvement is also not always clear, while here once again we need to differentiate between organized complicity and popular involvement. Based on the preserved records of the auxiliary administrative institutions themselves, and on the records of German occupying authorities, we can reconstruct more or less precisely the role of these institutions in the Holocaust. The institutions of local self-administration in Belarus were formed by German authorities at the very early stages of the occupation and were allowed to exist only up to district (pre-war Soviet *raion*) level.[24] Even though the activities of these institutions were controlled by Germans, it does not mean they played merely a subordinate role in the persecution and annihilation of the Jewish population in the territories for which they were responsible. People who manned this administration, especially at the levels below the district, were usually natives of the area they had to manage and were familiar with the local Jewish community. City and town mayors knew which city or town neighbourhoods were the poorest and most desolate, thus most 'suited' for the establishment of ghettos. Once established, ghettos were placed under the control of local administrations. In many places, such as Minsk, special departments for Jewish affairs were created in local city and town councils which had to regulate the supply of food and medicine to the ghettos and to allocate work to ghetto inmates. Among the responsibilities of local mayors was also hermetically sealing off the ghettos, preventing any contact of ghetto inmates with the outside world, and controlling the ghettoized Jews through wearing distinctive marks.[25] Actually, the complicity of local administrative institutions and of the persons who manned these institutions in the Holocaust stretched all the way to participation in, and even initiatives for, the physical annihilation of the Jewish population in the territories they controlled. Thus for example, the infamous *Einsatzgruppen* of security police and SD reported already in September 1941 that 'collective farms' chairmen and village elders' were coming 'from a distance of 40-50 km in order to ask that their communities be cleansed of Bolshevist and Jewish elements'.[26]

Also well known is the role played by local auxiliary police in the Holocaust. Like self-administration, local auxiliary police forces started to be formed at the very beginning of German occupation of Belarusian territory. Associated with massacres of the Jewish population, the auxiliary police forces were in fact actively involved in all stages of the Holocaust in German-occupied Belarus. Even before the mass extermination of the Jews started, local auxiliary policemen were enforcing the orders about compulsory wearing of distinct signs by the Jews, overseeing resettlement of the Jews into the ghettos, securing the property left behind by Jews who had been moved into ghettos, guarding ghetto perimeters and ruthlessly chasing down any Jews trying to avoid ghettoization. During the murder operations they collected Jewish victims from their homes, brought them to gathering points and from there took them to the murder sites. At the murder sites themselves local policemen cordoned off the area where the murders took place to prevent locals from seeing what was going on, brought Jews to the shooting pits or ravines and sometimes also pulled the triggers of their guns.[27] In his interrogation quoted at the opening of this chapter, David Egof depicted the extremely brutal conduct of the local policemen at the murder of Borisov Jews in late 1941. Even though we may suppose that Egof told the Soviet interrogator what the latter wanted to hear, there are plenty of other testimonies, corroborating the fact that the behaviour of the auxiliary policemen far exceeded the mere fulfilment of their duty. Already in the course of collecting Jews for murder, those victims who in the eyes of policemen did not go fast enough or were lagging behind were brutally beaten and abused.[28] While drunk, the commander of the Nesviž police, named Senko, told the inhabitants of the village of Snov about his participation in the massacre of Baranovichi Jews in June 1942, and how during this massacre he personally threw Jews off second- and third-floor balconies or out of windows.[29]

While German perpetrators sometimes had scruples about murdering women and children, such scruples rarely came to the fore on the part of local auxiliary policemen. On the contrary, in most cases they eagerly participated in the massacres, perceiving them as a sort of entertainment.[30] It is not easy to determine in each individual case the motives for such behaviour. Certainly, the general perverted reality created by the German occupation, the reality in which murder became a routine job and brutality displayed while fulfilling murderous tasks amounted to excellence in performing the job, which brought in first-rate material rewards, contributed to this.[31] In individual cases, Jewish property certainly provided a major incentive for eager participation in the massacres. Local auxiliary policemen were the first to take possession of property left by the murdered. After taking Jews to the murder sites they entered the ghettos in search of hidden people, and used this opportunity to lay their hands upon belongings left in abandoned Jewish houses and apartments. According to the post-war Soviet interrogation of the former chief of Korsakovichi rural community, auxiliary policemen who in late 1941 left the village of Korsakovichi to take part in a massacre of Jews of Borisov returned to their home village loaded with 'watches and other items that they had obtained as a reward, from the property of the shot Jews'.[32] According to the guidelines of the head of civilian administration in Belarus, Wilhelm Kube, local policemen and their families were also entitled to the better apartments vacated by the Jews.³³ It can be at least assumed that besides greed, violent anti-semitism, enjoyment of the feeling of superiority over other human beings, or sheer sadism, also contributed greatly to the conduct of local policemen in mass murder operations.

When speaking about outright collaboration in the Holocaust, it is worth mentioning that it occurred not only in deed but in word as well. During the German occupation of Belarus a whole media network in Belarusian language was created to propagate German occupation policies to the local inhabitants in their native language. People working in the media, mostly natives, also explained to their fellow countrymen in Belarusian language the necessity of getting rid of the Jews. Thus, for example, the articles published in the largest Belarusian language newspaper appearing under the German occupation, *Belaruskaia Hazeta*, contained direct incitement to genocide.³⁴

On a popular level, local complicity in the Holocaust assumed various forms, not all of which can be determined clearly. Two forms that should be mentioned here are denunciations and taking possession of Jewish property. We must remember that German units and institutions entrusted with carrying out the Final Solution in the Soviet territories operated in unfamiliar terrain. Especially in eastern Belarus, which was part of the Soviet Union before 1939, Jews were integrated in society and even visually could not be told apart from non-Jews. In this situation, these units depended much upon the assistance of the local non-Jewish population. For this purpose, German security police set up the whole row of 'information offices' to which Belarusian residents were asked to submit information about the whereabouts of Jews and communists.³⁵ Denunciations of Jews were quite widespread, especially in the early stages of the German occupation, though it is difficult to evaluate even approximately the scope of this phenomenon, given the fact that at least part of these denunciations were anonymous. The motives for denunciations varied widely, ranging from pure anti-semitism all the way to settling past scores for bad school grades or unrequited love.³⁶ These denunciations also testified to progressive social disintegration under the occupation, while even family ties did not necessarily serve as protection for Jews. We know from various sources about multiple cases of Jews being denounced to occupying authorities by their non-Jewish spouses or in-laws. For example, in Minsk, a non-Jewish woman, upon seeing her Jewish husband – who had fled from the embattled Soviet military unit – gave him away with the cry 'Catch the Yid!'.³⁷

An even more widespread form of complicity in the Holocaust on Belarusian territory, the scope of which is also impossible to define even approximately, was appropriation of Jewish property. Germans themselves noticed with disdain in their reports the 'local population's lust for robbery'.³⁸ At the same time, the occupying authorities eagerly promoted a centuries-old stereotype of 'fabulous Jewish wealth', allegedly accumulated by the exploitation of the non-Jewish population. Thus according to the *Einsatzgruppen* monthly reports in March 1942, for example, immediately after the mass murders of Jews in Minsk, Vileyka and Baranovichi, the Germans organized for the local non-Jewish population 'inspections' of the houses of those killed, during which the local non-Jews were supposed to draw the conclusion that 'the Jews still possessed large stores of food products, while their own supply situation was extraordinarily bad'.³⁹ Moreover, releasing part of the belongings of the murdered Jews to the local population was regarded by the occupying authorities as a cheap way to solve economic problems which arose under the occupation, and to enhance their popularity among the locals in a situation where occupation policies of exploitation and terror led to widespread resistance.

At the same time, the eagerness on the part of the local population to take the possessions of the murdered Jews cannot be understood without also taking into consideration the economic situation created under Soviet rule, with a total lack of the most basic wares and difficult living conditions. Many of the non-Jewish residents of Belarus saw in abandoned Jewish property a means to improve their economic situation. In the difficult housing situation in Belarus, which was further aggravated by the war, the houses and apartments of Jews who either had fled into the Soviet interior or were forced into ghettos and/or murdered, became an especially coveted commodity. People who lost their homes during the fighting or simply wished to improve their housing conditions could apply to the housing departments of local auxiliary administrations to request living quarters that had been vacated by Jews.[40] For the local municipal administrations, the sales of Jewish houses and apartments became quite a profitable business, an important resource for filling their treasuries. For example, according to the reports of the financial department of the Mogilev city administration for May and June 1942, income from the sales of Jewish houses constituted between 51 and 65 per cent of the administration's budget.[41]

Regarding the handling of Jewish movable property there were directives of the German occupation authorities and there were real conditions. Officially, money and valuables that were confiscated from Soviet Jews were supposed to be delivered to the Reich's Main Treasury of the Reich Bank, where a body known as the War Booty Office (*Beutestelle*) was established specifically for this purpose. The rest of the property was supposed to be sold and the income from the sales to be placed in the special account of the trusteeship department of German administrative institutions.[42] In reality, however, most Jewish belongings were appropriated by local non-Jewish residents before, during or immediately after murder operations. In this way, the process did not necessarily take the form of robbery. In many cases, prior to their resettlement in ghettos, Jews sold their property or transferred it to their non-Jewish neighbours for safekeeping. Thus, in the city of Borisov and in the Borisov District, Jews sold or transferred to their neighbours domestic animals and home appliances in August 1941 before being transferred to the ghetto.[43] At the same time, in various places, on the eve of the murder operations in the ghettos local non-Jewish residents assembled with wheelbarrows on the streets leading to the ghettos – in anticipation of the moment when the massacres would be over, and it would be possible to enter the emptied ghettos and to start a wild orgy of pillaging. The houses of victims were not only often stripped of their contents, but doors and window frames were taken away as well to serve as fuel.[44] In other cases, after the murder operations residents from localities surrounding the sites of murder assembled at these sites to search through the clothes and other belongings Jews left prior to being murdered. For example, Mikhail Taits, a Jewish boy who survived the massacre of the Minsk Jews in the Minsk suburb of Tuchinka, described how the residents of the villages in the vicinity of the murder site were so preoccupied with searching through the belongings left by the victims of the massacre that they paid no attention to him crawling out of the mass grave covered in blood.[45]

Property left after the murder of the Jews was usually brought to special warehouses, where it was sorted, cleaned and disinfected before it was sold to the local population. These warehouses were often unguarded and open to all. In Bobruisk in late November 1941 the mayor, Stanislav Stankevich, complained to the local commandant about German soldiers and local residents entering the warehouse where the property brought from the ghetto was stored and helping themselves freely to various items.[46] During the occupation of Belarus, when money had lost its value and barter flourished, property that had belonged to murdered Jews often served as a kind of currency. Thus, one woman from Minsk exchanged eggs and poultry she bought at the market for clothes of murdered Jews that were stored in one of the city warehouses, and then she travelled to the western part of the country to exchange these clothes for foodstuffs.[47]

Conclusion: Compromised identities?

It must be admitted that studying the Eastern European Holocaust perpetrators generally and Belarusian perpetrators specifically is quite a daunting task. It provides an enormous challenge for historians dealing with this topic. In a country such as Belarus where the Holocaust occurred in the most personal way and practically before everybody's eyes, the very definition of perpetration and complicity widens almost into the indefinite. It assumed so many forms that it is nigh impossible to trace all of them. Also, the range of the motives for getting involved directly or indirectly in the persecution and annihilation of the Jews is very broad. These motives were defined not only by the conditions created by the German occupation but also by what preceded it, often not by years but by centuries of Jewish–non-Jewish coexistence.

The main obstacle for the historian studying local Holocaust perpetrators in Belarus is the dearth of available primary sources. In the situation in which Belarusian archives, above all the archives of the KGB, are closed hermetically for foreign researchers, it is difficult to draw any firm conclusions about the character of the handling of Belarusian perpetrators of the Holocaust. The unavailability of archival sources coupled with the current political situation in Belarus makes the task of objective study of the involvement in the Holocaust of sections of the Belarusian population all the more difficult, though not impossible. On the basis of the sources that are available for researchers, we can say that perpetration and complicity in the Holocaust in Nazi-occupied Belarus went beyond the bodies that are usually associated with the execution of the 'Final Solution of the Jewish Question'. Broad sections of the Belarusian population were involved in one way or another in the persecution and annihilation of the Jews, whether by denouncing them to the occupation authorities or by taking possession of Jewish property. It is impossible to say with certainty whether all or some of these people felt themselves compromised, but the general context in which the Holocaust in Belarus took place and the history of inter-ethnic relations here allow us to assume that that was very rarely the case.

Notes

1 'The Materials of the Interrogation of David Egof by the KGB', *Yad Vashem Archives* (YVA), M.41/119.
2 The story based on the unpublished memoirs of Dr Ehernfried Schütte is quoted by Bernhard Chiari in *Alltag hinter der Front: Besatzung, Kollaboration und Widerstand in Weißrussland, 1941–1944* (Düsseldorf: Droste Verlag, 1998), 2.
3 Patrick Desbois, *The Holocaust by Bullets: A Priest's Journey to Uncover the Truth behind the Murder of 1.5 Million Jews* (Basingstoke: Palgrave Macmillan, 2008).
4 On the discussion on the problem of categorization, see for example, recently: Mary Fulbrook, *Bystanders to Nazi Violence: The Transformation of German Society in the 1930s* (Jerusalem: Yad Vashem, 2018).
5 See especially Vasilii Romanovskii, *Saudzelniki ŭ Zlachynstvakh* (Minsk: Belarus, 1964).
6 One example is the collection of the documents pertaining to German atrocities in occupied Belarus, including documents referring explicitly to the Holocaust: Zakhar Beluga (ed.), *Prestupleniia Nemetsko-Fashistskikh Okkupantov v Belorussii, 1941–1944* (Minsk: Academy of Sciences, 1965).
7 It is difficult to precisely establish the human losses in Belarus during the period of Nazi occupation. During the Soviet period, it was maintained that 2,200,000 people were killed in Belarus, which constituted one-fourth of the Belarusian population. See for example, Ivan Kravchenko, 'Nemetsko-Fashistskii okkupatsionnyi rezhim v Belorussii', in *Nemetsko-Fashistskii Okkupatsionnyi Rezhim (1941–1944)*, ed. Yevgeni Boltin et al. (Moscow: Politizdat, 1965), 63. This number included 1,409,225 'peaceful inhabitants' and 810,091 Soviet prisoners of war, not all of whom lived in Belarus before the war. These numbers, which originally appeared in the 1944 report of the 'Extraordinary Commission for the Investigation of the Crimes of German-Fascist occupiers' were only revised in the last decades by both Belarussian and foreign historians. In the collection *Narysy history Belarusi* that appeared in Minsk in 1995, the Belarusian historian Alexei Litvin assumed the number of the losses among Belarusian population to be between 1.95 and 2 million people. According to Litvin, this number includes Belarusians who perished on Belarusian territory as well as at the front and as forced labourers in Germany. See: Alexei Litvin, 'K Voprosu o Kolichestve liudskikh Poter Belarusi v Gody Velikoi Otechestvennoi Voiny (1941-1945 gg.)', in *Belarus v XX Veke,* ed. Yakov Basin (Minsk: Vodoley, 2002), 136–37. In the 2002 edition of the study *Zhertvy Dvukh Diktatur* dealing with the tragic fate of Soviet forced labourers in the Third Reich, the Russian historian Pavel Polian quoted the summary report of the Extraordinary Commission of 1 March 1946. The report detailed the losses in Belarus for each of the twelve regions (*oblasts*) that existed at the time (after the war, the Soviet Union transferred a large part of pre-war Bialystok region as well as three districts of the Brest region to Poland. The remnants of the Bialystok region were renamed Grodno region). In this report 1,360,034 people were listed under the rubric 'killed, tormented peaceful citizens'. This number accounted for 22.4 per cent of the total Belarusian population. Pavel Polian, *Zhertvy Dvukh Diktatur* (Moscow: ROSSPEN, 2002), 11.
8 Leonid Rein, *The Kings and the Pawns. Collaboration in Byelorussia during World War II* (New York: Berghahn, 2011), 365f.
9 See for example: 'Appeal of 112th Partisan Detachment to Lithuanian soldiers and to Collective Farmers, Workers and Officials, undated', *Bundesarchiv Berlin* (BAB), R.90/Schr.; 'Appeal of the Lyakhva Clandestine District Committee of the Belarusian

Communist Party to Policemen and Officials of German Institutions', *BAB*, R.90/158.
10. The copies of the files of judicial investigations against Ukrainian collaborators from the Ukrainian Security Service (former KGB) Archives are now also available in the Yad Vashem Archives under the TR.18 signature.
11. Leonid Rein, 'The Belarusian Auxiliary Police', in *The Waffen-SS: A European History*, ed. Jochen Böhler and Robert Gerwarth (Oxford: Oxford University Press, 2017), 183; Martin Dean, *Collaboration in the Holocaust: Crimes of local Police in Belorussia and Ukraine, 1941–1944* (New York: St. Martin's Press, 2000), 75.
12. See for example Franz Kushal, *Sproby Stvarenn'ia Belaruskaga Voyska* (Belaruski Histarychny Agliad: Bialystok, 1999), Dzmitry Kasmovich, *Za Volnuyu i suverennuiu Belarus* (Vilnius: Gudas, 2006).
13. To discredit national Belarusian symbols used by anti-Lukashenko protesters, pro-government media such as the newspaper *Sovetskaia Belarus* claim that these symbols were used during the Second World War by Nazi collaborators and Holocaust perpetrators. Especially active in propagating this idea is the head of the Belarusian Chamber of Representatives for education, culture and science, historian Igor Marzaliuk. See for example his article 'Stiagi propitannye krov'u' (Banners soaked in blood) in *Sovetskaia Belarus* from 10 December 2020: http://sb.by/articles/styagi-propitannye-krovyu.html (Accessed 30 November 2021). Also Lukashenko's opponents use Holocaust imagery and analogies with the Nazi occupation. See inter alia: *2020 Annual Report on Antisemitism of Israeli Ministry for Diaspora Affairs*. https://www.gov.il/BlobFolder/generalpage/report_anti240121/en/anti-semitism_2020%20YEARLY%20REPORT%20-%20FINAL%20(EN)_v7.pdf (Accessed 30 November 2021).
14. Between the ninth century AD and late eighteenth century the territory of present-day Belarus was consecutively part of Kievan Rus, of the Great Duchy of Lithuania and of the Polish-Lithuanian Commonwealth. Hence the history of Belarusian Jews and the relations with their neighbours is as much a history of Russian, Polish and Lithuanian Jewry and of interethnic relations in Russia, Poland and Lithuania. See Antony Polonsky, *The Jews in Poland and Russia* (Oxford: Littman Library of Jewish Civilization, 2010), vol. 1.
15. Documents relating to the short-lived Belarusian National Republic were published in two volumes by a Belarusian émigré organization in Lithuania: Siarhej Šupa (ed.), *Arkhivy Belaruskai Narodnai Respubliki* (Vilnius: Belarusian Institute for Arts and Sciences, 1998–2020), 2 vols.
16. Arkadi Zeltser, 'Inter-war Ethnic Relations and Soviet Policy: The Case of Eastern Belorussia', *Yad Vashem Studies* 34 (2006): 87–124.
17. Mordechai Altshuler, *Soviet Jewry on the Eve of the Holocaust: A Social and Demographic Profile* (Jerusalem: The Center of Research of East European Jewry, 1998).
18. Daniel Romanovsky, 'Soviet Jews under Nazi Occupation in Northeastern Belarus and Western Russia', in *Bitter Legacy: Confronting the Holocaust in the USSR*, ed. Zvi Gitelman (Bloomington: Indiana University Press, 1997), 239.
19. Ben-Cion Pinhcuk, *Shtetl Jews under Soviet Rule: Eastern Poland on the Eve of the Holocaust* (Oxford: Blackwell, 1990), Evgeny Rozenblat, 'Sovetizatsiia i antisemitizm v zapadnobelorusskikh zemliakh, 1939–1941', in *Sowietyzacja i rusyfikacja polnocno-wschodnich ziem II Rzeczypospolitej: Studia i Materialy*, ed. Michal Gnatowski and Daniel Bockowski (Bialystok: Wydawnictwo Uniwersytetu w Bialymstoku, 2003).

20 See Jan Tomasz Gross, *Neighbors. The Destruction of Jewish Community in Jedwabne, Poland* (Princeton: Princeton University Press, 2001).
21 Andrzej Zbikowski, 'Local Anti-Jewish Pogroms in the Occupied Territories of Eastern Poland, June-July 1941', in *The Holocaust in the Soviet Union. Studies and Sources on the Destruction of the Jews in the Nazi-occupied Territories of the USSR*, ed. Lucjan Dobroszycki and Jeffrey S. Gurok (Armonk: M.E. Sharp, 1993), 173–9.
22 Raul Hilberg, *The Destruction of European Jews* (Chicago: Quadrangle Books, 1961).
23 There is limited data available on the size of the local auxiliary administration of occupied Belarus. We know, for example, that in the area of Economic Inspection Center (*Wirtschaftsinspektion Mitte*), the body entrusted to economically exploit the eastern Belarus and western Russia, some 60,000 people served with a local auxiliary administration in mid-1943. See Christian Gerlach, *Kalkulierte Morde: Die deutsche Wirtschafts- und Vernichtungspolitik in Weißrußland 1941–1944* (Hamburg: Hamburger Edition, 1999), 199. We also know that in total some 50,000 people served with the local auxiliary police in the territories under German civilian and military administrations in 1942–1943: 'Report of the Commander of Order Police in White Ruthenia Oberst [Colonel] Klepsch at the Conference of High Functionaries of the General Commissariat for White Ruthenia, 8–10 April 1943', *BAB*, R.93/20; 'Report of the Liaison Officer of the Reich's Ministry for Occupied Eastern Areas at the HQ of Commander of the Rear Area of Army Group Center, Major Müller, 8 October 1942', *BAB*, R.6/76; Gerlach, *Kalkulierte Morde*, 204.
24 Rein, *The Kings and the Pawns*, 131.
25 Leonid Rein, 'Local Collaboration in the Execution of the "Final Solution" in Nazi-occupied Belorussia', *Holocaust and Genocide Studies* 20, no. 3 (2006): 391f.
26 'Activity and Situation Report No. 4 of the Einsatzgruppen of Security Police and SD for the period 1–15 September 1941', in *Die Einsatzgruppen in der besetzten Sowjetunion 1941/42. Die Tätigkeits- und Lageberichte des Chefs der Sicherheitspolizei und des SD*, ed. Peter Klein (Berlin: Hentrich Edition, 1997), 183.
27 Rein, 'The Belarusian Auxiliary Police', 187f.
28 Ibid., 188.
29 'Testimony of Lev Lanskiy, former Inmate of Maly Trostenets Concentration Camp, undated', *YVA*, M.41/100.
30 Rein, 'The Belarusian Auxiliary Police', 188.
31 Rein, 'Local Collaboration in the Execution of the "Final Solution" in Nazi-occupied Belorussia', 394.
32 'Interrogation Protocol of Konstantin Mozolevskiy, 12–13 January 1946', YVA M.41/2838.
33 'Copy of the memorandum of Municipal Inspector Loebel and Reich's Official Plenske Regarding Jewish Property in Minsk, November 16, 1942', *YVA*, M.41/291.
34 Leonid Rein, '"Every Jew Deserves the Gallows": Antisemitism on the Pages of *Belaruskaia hazeta*', in *Distrust, Animosity and Solidarity. Jews and non-Jews during the Holocaust in the USSR*, ed. Christoph Dieckmann and Arkadi Zeltser (Jerusalem: Yad Vashem, 2021), 213–42.
35 'Activity and Situation Report No. 1 of the Einsatzgruppen of Security Police and SD, July 31, 1941', in Klein, *Die Einsatzgruppen in der besetzten Sowjetunion*, 116.
36 Rein, *The Kings and the Pawns*, 264.
37 Albert Lapidus, 'Nas mako ostalos, nam mnogo dostalos', *Vestnik Online* 2, no. 313 (22 January 2003). http://www.vestnik.com/issues/2003/0122/koi/lapidus.htm (Accessed 15 December 2021).

38 'Memorandum of Loebel and Plenske', *YVA*, M.41/291.
39 'Activity and Situation Report No. 11 of the Einsatzgruppen of Security Police and SD for the period 1–31 March 1942', in Klein, *Die Einsatzgruppen in der besetzten Sowjetunion*, 308f.
40 See for example the records of the housing department of Mogilev city administration for the second half of 1941, *YVA* M.41/2820.
41 'Report of the Municipal Financial Department of Mogilev for May 1942'; 'Report of the Municipal Financial Department of Mogilev for June 1942', both *YVA*, M.41/242.
42 See 'Guidelines Regarding Registration, Administration and Utilization of the Movable Jewish Property in the Area of Reich's Commissariat for Ostland, May 19, 1942', *YVA*, M.41/2231.
43 'Report of the Commander of Novo-Borisov Auxiliary Police Bakhanovich to the Borisov District Chief Stankevich, August, 28, 1941', *YVA*, M.41/2396.
44 Leonid Smilovitsky, *Katastrofa Evreev v Belorussii, 1941–1944* (Tel Aviv: Matvey Chorny Library, 2000), 97f.
45 Video Testimony of Milhail Taits, *YVA*, O.93/28947.
46 'Letter of the Mayor of Bobruisk, Stankevich, to the German Military Commandant of Bobruisk, 29 November 1941', *YVA* M.41/2798.
47 'The testimony of Vladimir Kozachyonok, 26 February 1944', *YVA* M.41/2836.

7

Compromising roles

German actresses in German-occupied Minsk[1]

Anne-Lise Bobeldijk

On Friday, 22 January 1943, a young actress from Hamburg arrived in Minsk, where she and her *Kraft durch Freude* (KdF, Strength through Joy) group were housed in the KdF building on the outskirts of the city. Two days earlier she had written to her mother about her journey to the eastern front, where they would perform for the troops. She wrote:

> Dear *Mutti*, everything is as crazy as you would imagine during a tour. We have been on the train continuously since Monday 7am, everywhere we have 6 to 10 hour delays, and at the moment we are sitting in a Red Cross wooden barrack and have not been able to wash ourselves for days. We received rations after Warsaw and have to wait until this afternoon (now 6 o'clock in the morning, about minus 15 degrees) for the connecting train to Minsk, which we were not allowed to board this evening due to danger.[2]

Brigitte was not the only German from Hamburg who was in Minsk during its occupation by the Germans. In November 1941, two trains arrived in Minsk with deported Jews from Hamburg, who were interned in the Minsk ghetto. Of these 2,010 deportees, 15 people survived both their internment in Minsk and the Holocaust. Unlike the German Jews who constantly had to fear for their lives, Brigitte, as a German civilian, was in a completely different and rather privileged position. Although she seemed rather overwhelmed at her arrival in Minsk, due to recent attacks by partisans on the city, Brigitte also seemed to have been excited, writing to her mother that she was facing this new world 'with her eyes wide open'.[3] Women like Brigitte were an important part of the Nazi vision for 'the East'. Early scholarly research into the role of women during the Third Reich established that many of them were active members of the Nazi community, both in the private and the public sphere. This dovetailed with later studies on the ideological commitment of many women, which was consistently found to match that of Nazi male counterparts.[4] Such approaches unleashed considerable controversy, and stimulated further avenues of inquiry in the fields of both gender and the roles of women in the Third Reich.[5] In turn, more recent research has firmly placed women also in the Nazi killing fields and highlighted their functions there.[6] 'When women are there, it becomes a social movement. It's not just men in militia garb', historian Wendy Lower summarized. 'It's society making a claim. Women normalize this behaviour. They provide a certain legitimacy'.[7]

In Minsk, victims and perpetrators from the same cities met far away from their hometowns. Viennese policemen were involved in the murder of Austrian Jews in Minsk and the men of the infamous Police Battalion 101 from Hamburg deported Jews from their home city to Minsk. It is often overlooked that Germans, who were not part of the SS, the police force or the military, were also present in this environment. These civilians had quite an ambiguous position or a compromising role. German actresses, who like Brigitte were employed by the Nazi organization *Kraft durch Freude*, belonged to this group. The position of KdF within the Nazi structure and its role in the Second World War and the Holocaust has been the subject of much analysis in the last twenty years.[8] However, in the literature on KdF, the Holocaust is understood only as the murder of Jews in camps; scholarship has neglected the fact that in Minsk the Holocaust took place through what is called the 'Holocaust by bullets'.[9] The role of KdF in Minsk is therefore more closely connected to the Holocaust than initially appears.

This chapter analyses the roles of civilian German women, mostly actresses, in Nazi-occupied Minsk. By analysing the interconnectedness of the Holocaust in Minsk with the daily life of its inhabitants, including also KdF artists, the paper considers the artists' responsibility and how societal norms of race, class and gender influenced their perception of what took place in Minsk.

Kraft durch Freude and the *Truppenbetreuung*

Although KdF is more commonly associated with state-organized mass tourism in the Third Reich, an important subdivision of the organization was hired by the Wehrmacht and the Ministry of Propaganda for the *Truppenbetreuung*, 'caring for the troops'. This was the task given to the group of German actresses in Minsk. The artists within KdF remained civilian artists, but because of the position of KdF within the Nazi apparatus, their roles became compromised.

KdF was established in November 1933, shortly after the Nazi takeover ten months earlier. The founding of the organization was inspired by the Italian Fascist leisure organization 'After Work' (*Dopolavoro*) and, like its Italian counterpart, KdF organized after-work activities, ranging from holidays and sports to theatre visits.[10] Yet, in the view of KdF leisure was never without a purpose. Its goal was to create a utopian racial community (*Volksgemeinschaft*), and it is this ideological aspect that made KdF key in reinforcing the racial ideology of the Nazis.[11] In his study on how community building within the national socialist system made it possible to commit genocide, Thomas Kühne mentions the role of KdF in creating this *Volksgemeinschaft*: 'Whether applying for a marriage loan from the state or for a vacation trip with Strength Through Joy, virtually every activity was meant to reveal, and make one think about, one's racial origins'.[12] In addition to propagating and cultivating the importance of the *Volksgemeinschaft* through leisure and mass tourism, from 1939 KdF became involved in active propaganda for the Wehrmacht. Following agreement between the Wehrmacht, KdF and the Ministry of Propaganda, KdF was deployed to organize entertainment for the troops. The ministry had an ultimate say in the cultural activities, while the Wehrmacht provided food, housing, transport and other practical matters.[13] Through 'caring for the troops', the programs of KdF were also intended to cultivate cultural superiority over the occupied countries.[14]

Although most of the plays chosen for KdF to perform were not directly written as propaganda, the content of the plays officially had to conform to National Socialist standards and messages.[15] However, historian Julia Timpe shows that in reality many of the performances were mostly light entertainment and did not always concern ideological warfare.[16] Yet, it seems that the larger productions were more propagandistic in nature. The Nazis appropriated different works of Shakespeare, but The *Merchant of Venice* seems to have been the most popular and was recommended for use in both literary classes and lessons on racial science.[17] Actress Inge Stolten appeared in the production of William Shakespeare's *The Merchant of Venice* in Minsk in September 1943. The performance was specifically framed as a way of underlining the racial ideology of the Nazis. The program of the play describes the two of the main Jewish characters in the play, Shylock and his friend Tubal, just as 'Jews', and the footnote to the programme reads: 'The Jews in America and England have pushed for all performances of *The Merchant of Venice* to be banned in England and America!'[18] According to Inge Stolten, the programme also enlightened the reader that the play was performed 'because here in the East we experience the Jewish-Aryan problem even more directly than in the Reich'.[19]

In addition to this clear propagandistic aspect of KdF, 'caring for the troops' also entailed actual caring. According to Alexander Hirt, who compared the role of 'caring for the troops' in both Britain and Nazi Germany during the Second World War, after the invasion of the Soviet Union the task of providing distraction and emotional compensation to the troops became important for their belligerence.[20] Inge writes in her memoirs about a '"cosy get-together" with well-behaved SS-officers', where female SS personnel were also present.[21] Brigitte seems to have been personally more involved in her role of providing emotional support. In one of her letters, she described how two young soldiers came to her room and that of two female colleagues. The men needed both distraction from their life fighting partisan units around Minsk as well as solace from what they encountered, what they had done or what they had seen. Because the men were active in what the Nazis euphemistically called 'fighting bandits' (*Bandenbekämpfung*) in Belarus, it is highly likely that they were actively involved in the brutal treatment of the local population and also in the murder of Jews, which was often carried out under this description. Whether Brigitte knew this or not, she simply took care of them. She elaborated in her letter: 'Hatred burned in their eyes, the hatred of a deadly wounded animal or an abused child. [. . .] He [one of the young men] snuggled up to me and put his head on my shoulder like a big silent child'.[22]

Even though the presence of KdF was clearly valued at the front, its role was not uncontentious. The men who worked in KdF were exempted from military duty and the woman did not have to contribute to the war industry. In some cases, this meant that they were seen as 'shirkers'.²³ In addition, the KdF artists were royally paid for their deployment to the front lines, sometimes up to 100 RM per day. Because the quality of the performances and the artists was not always good, many considered this a problem.²⁴ It even elicited criticism from Goebbels, who was annoyed by the fact that artists could be paid more than those who were active in combat.²⁵ Besides the generous salary, additional privileges came with the job. For example, there was the opportunity to mingle with social groups that were inaccessible for others. Inge Stolten described how she and her companions were invited to a *soirée* at the house of Generalkommissar Wilhelm Kube, and also mentions other get-togethers which before the war had not been accessible for women like her or Brigitte Erdmann.²⁶ Another example is the housing situation, which in the East was often better for KdF artists than for the low-ranking soldiers stationed there.²⁷ Brigitte even mentions that she was able to use the swimming pool in Minsk, which only higher officers were allowed to use.²⁸

Finally, one criticism of KdF related to the women in the East, and more specifically to their behaviour. Some objected that the women of KdF were too loose, dressed too provocatively and that the shows they performed contained too much exposed flesh.²⁹ Sexual relationships between the women and officers in particular were also disapproved of, although KdF did not actively prevent them. Brigitte also reflects on this in her letters to her mother. The letter shows clearly what the deployment to the East meant for a woman's position:

> Although there is only one man for me at the moment, I like to talk, laugh, flirt with all the nice guys and feel my power as a woman, and the knowledge that you can get any man you like is a great confidence booster. Although there's no art in conquering all men (really all of them) here, it's still fun. Just as we women at home long for the men who are not there, the men do the same for us here.³⁰

Women in the East

Brigitte was only one of the many women of German origin who went to the 'East'. Women in a wide variety of jobs were active in Nazi-occupied Eastern Europe. Some women went with their husbands, although this was only a very small number. Many women were part of a group supporting the police, Wehrmacht and local governance in positions as operator or typist, or were involved in social jobs such as teachers, nurses or other jobs that enabled society – a German society – to function.³¹ In other words, they supported the German presence in Eastern Europe and were actively involved in colonizing and Germanizing the occupied territories.

Particularly in Belarus, this colonization was seen as one of the main goals of the civil administration, which was under the command of Generalkommissar Wilhelm Kube. Kube was one of the highly revered 'Old Party Fighters', an honorary title bestowed to long-standing members of the NSDAP (a so-called Alter Kämpfer) with strong national socialist convictions. He had previously been regional leader (Gauleiter) of the Ostmark and Kurmark. He saw it as his personal duty to 'civilize' the Belarusian population. A summary of Kube's speech to a delegation of the Dutch East Company

(NOC), a Dutch national socialist organization that sent Dutch citizens as colonizers to occupied Eastern Europe, shows his commitment. According to the published travel report of an officer of the company, Kube 'underlined the unique civilizing task in the East for the European peoples'.[32] Here the 'European people' included the Dutch. The author of the report explained: 'The leading men of Germanic blood will have to be careful not to mix with the population; in all cities separate urban areas are being set up for the Germanic people from the West, as a result of which cultural centres will be able to grow'.[33] KdF was one of the organizations that had to establish these cultural centres. Bodo Lafferenz, one of the directors of a subdivision of KdF, asserted that the organization had to 'create a "stable order" by restoring German culture', which was originally brought to the region in the Middle Ages by German immigrants but had been undermined by the Slavs for centuries.[34] Kube had similar convictions and even instigated archaeological excavations at his personal estate in Priluki to prove the Germanic roots of the region.

This colonial gaze on Nazi-occupied Belarus and its inhabitants was also present in the views of the women in the 'East'. Anita Kube, Wilhelm Kube's wife, seems to have shared her husband's views on both the racial ideology of the Nazis as well as the country of Belarus. Prior to the war, Kube had met her husband while playing the lead in the play that he had written. Wilhelm Kube's interest in the Germanic roots of the region around Minsk was also on display in this play, titled 'Totila, king of the Goths', about an Ostrogoth king in the sixth century.[35] In their house in Minsk, the Kubes hosted cultural evenings, at which also Belarusian singers took part. In an interview from 1993, in which Kube looked back on her life in Minsk quite positively, she recalled their 'little singer', an opera singer from Minsk, and how the so-called 'Hausjuden' ('domestic Jews') who worked on her husband's estate in Priluki, had, according to her, called her husband their 'protector'.[36] Such attitudes to Belarusians in Minsk were not limited to higher levels of society. The young actress Brigitte also seems to have adapted to the hierarchy within her new environment, one that she, coming from a working-class family, had never experienced before. In one of her letters to her mother she writes: 'A young dental student my age is my special girl. She has to serve only me'.[37]

The motives of the women who went to the East were manifold and are clearly connected to the possibility of social mobility in this new environment. Some believed in the cause of 'Germanization'; some did not really want to go, but felt compelled or felt a sense of duty and went anyway.[38] For others, more opportunistic reasons caused them to enlist for service in the East. After all, the reality of the war caused gender relations to alter and provided women with opportunities that had not been realistic earlier.[39] Particularly in response to Nazi ideology, in which a woman's role was constrained to the small circle of the family and the household, the chance to move outside this restricted realm was tempting for many women. In her article on the motives of Dutch Red Cross nurses who served at the eastern front, Sietske van der Veen argues that many did so from a feeling of duty. However, for some nurses it was a desire for romance and adventure that made them enrol.[40] Similarly, Franka Maubach's study of German women who were enlisted in the Wehrmacht also shows that many of these female auxiliary fighters looked back on this period as the most wonderful time of their lives.[41]

For the women who arrived in Minsk as actresses, similar motives of adventure and a sense of freedom seem to have been pivotal to their recruitment. Inge Stolten, for example, wrote in her biography that one of the reasons to become an actress was that they could wear nice outfits and make up. They, just like the prostitutes in her hometown Hamburg, had more possibilities than other women at the time. She writes about them:

> The independent ones [prostitutes] impressed me, those who did not have a steady boyfriend, who drove them and possibly also beat them up. I wanted to be like them and not like my mother, who worked for the people in the villas to clean and cleaned offices early in the morning to make a living for her paralysed husband and two children. She worked like a slave and despite this we often did not have enough, and had to count every penny. Whores on the other hand had it significantly better. [. . .] Back then I wanted to be a whore or maybe an actress.[42]

The motive of another Hamburg actress was similar. As mentioned earlier, Brigitte enjoyed her power as a woman to seduce any man. In letters to her mother about her 'life of eroticism, love and sensations', she writes elaborately about her feelings for and adventures with the various men she encountered during her tour of the eastern front.[43] In Brigitte's case, the work as an actress involved more than escaping gender norms, and included the desire for social mobility and the wish to outgrow a particular class. In one letter, she discloses how she longed for the opportunity to live a life full of adventure, and gives a glimpse of her social status at the home front: 'If I'm not really reinstated [at the front] then I cannot do anything. There is hardly any market for my art, and then life just starts again in an ammunition factory. Just wait and see'.[44] For her, being sent to the eastern front also meant being able to escape her own environment.

The 'Holocaust by bullets' in Minsk

The women in KdF undoubtedly held a privileged position. However, there is a difference between somehow benefitting from the war and carrying responsibility for the crimes committed by the National Socialist regime the KdF was working for. So how should the role of the KdF actresses in Minsk be interpreted specifically in relation to the Holocaust? In her study of the KdF, Timpe describes how KdF artists performed not only for the Wehrmacht but that there were also KdF events in camps such as Auschwitz, Stutthof and Majdanek, during which the artists performed for SS personnel. By visiting these camps, the artists were able to witness the prisoners, the conditions in the camp and the last stage of the genocide of the Jews.[45] Although these camps were indeed sites where the Holocaust took place, it should not be forgotten that in cities such as Minsk or Riga, in contrast to Western European cities, the Holocaust took place out in the open. The KdF artists were able to witness the destruction of European Jewry taking place here as well.

During the Nazi occupation of Minsk, between late June 1941 and early July 1944, the Nazis imposed a violent and brutal regime on the entire society in Belarus. The estimations are that in total between one and two million people were murdered or otherwise died prematurely in Belarus, and approximately three million people became homeless.[46] However, Jews were primarily targeted: already between August and October 1941, 5,000–6,000 Jews were murdered in Minsk.[47] The Jews in Belarus were most often killed in 'the Holocaust by bullets'. Contrary to the Jews from Western Europe, who were generally sent to camps to be murdered, which is now often symbolized by the image of Auschwitz, Jews in Eastern Europe were shot close to their homes in forests, dunes or gardens.

Minsk, like other cities such as Riga, has a rather peculiar position within the history of the Holocaust. It is a place where the history of the 'Holocaust by bullets' and what in Western Europe is symbolized by 'Auschwitz', interconnects, because in Minsk, Western and Central European Jews were also killed in the 'Holocaust by bullets'. In November 1941, seven trains arrived with over 7,000 Jews who were taken to the Minsk ghetto and imprisoned there. In order to 'make room' for the Western European Jews, in early November 13,000 Soviet Jews from the Minsk ghetto were murdered in the nearby village of Tuchinka. Some weeks later, in late November, another 7,000 local Jews were murdered. Western European Jews from the Minsk ghetto were specifically targeted during massacres from July 1942. In addition to the German Jews already at the Minsk ghetto, in 1942 sixteen trains with Jewish deportees from German cities, as well as Vienna and the ghetto Theresienstadt arrived in Minsk. Almost all of the approximately 15,500 Jews were taken to Blagovshchina forest, on the outskirts of Minsk, where they were either shot or gassed in gas vans on their day of arrival. Only a small group of deported Jews were taken to the camp Maly Trostenets, a forced labour camp located on a former kolkhoz in the village of the same name.[48] Approximately thirty of them managed to escape the camp and survived, as did some local prisoners. The Minsk ghetto was destroyed in October 1943.

The Holocaust in Minsk, both against German as well as against Soviet Jews, was openly visible for many people. Close encounters with victims made it even less of a secret. For example, in November 1941, an Austrian Wehrmacht soldier arrived in Minsk where he and three other soldiers were housed for two weeks by an ethnic German family. In his memoirs, the soldier recalls his time in Minsk:

> There was a lot of laughter and we really had a fun time. We even went to the cinema. In view of the brutal war experiences of the last few weeks, this lightheartedness did us good. On one of these evenings Frau Gareis also told us about a Jewish ghetto that was only a few hundred meters away from us. There was a lot of useful stuff lying around in this camp, she told us, and asked if we couldn't get her some bedsteads from there. Like us, they slept on the cold floor. We promised we'd take a look around.[49]

The memoir goes on to describe how the group of men entered the ghetto, where the lieutenant ran into an old acquaintance from Berlin, his local butcher, whom he had known since childhood. The man asked him what was in store for him, but the lieutenant 'had not had the heart to tell the man the truth'.[50] Although the situation visibly moved the lieutenant, the men went on to find three beds in the ghetto for their landlady, which made her very happy. Meanwhile an SS convoy was already waiting outside the building to take a group of Jewish prisoners away.[51]

This account makes evident how visible the Holocaust was in Minsk: civilians lived only a few hundred metres away from the ghetto, and some of them did not feel restricted by the fact that the possessions they looted were from people who were about to be murdered. The actresses also must have known about the ghetto; an officer of Organization Todt (Nazi civil and military engineering organization infamous for exploitation of forced and slave labour) even asked Brigitte on a date to the ghetto.[52] However gruesome this must seem, such sight-seeing visits by German civilians were common in Eastern European cities.[53] The murder of Jews itself was equally open. Although some larger massacres took place outside the city, killings also took place within it. For example, the Jewish cemetery was used regularly by the SS to murder Jews from the ghetto. After the war a Belarusian woman from Minsk reported that she had been able to witness significant variations between the different massacres that took place in Minsk.[54] Jewish forced labourers too were openly working all over the city. Their work ranged from hard labour at the railway tracks or factories in Minsk, to less physical work in the German hospital and even the theatre. It would therefore have been nearly impossible not to witness the presence and maltreatment of Jews. Encounters between actresses and Jews, who often even came from their hometowns, show that for the KdF artists this was also the case.

The KdF and the Holocaust in German-occupied Minsk

Although it is not clear how many actors and actresses were in Minsk as part of the KdF tours, there seems to have been a stream of visiting groups. There were fewer KdF visits to the eastern front in the year following the invasion of the Soviet Union, and so the KdF attempted to visit the front more often in 1942 and 1943.[55] The visits to Minsk started in the autumn of 1942 and continued until at least the autumn of 1943. It is likely that performances in Minsk continued beyond this point and possibly until the end of the occupation in July 1944, because it was only in September 1944 that Goebbels restricted the activities of KdF, resulting in the closure of all theatres.[56] The KdF artists in Minsk were housed near to, or inside, a *Soldatenheim* (soldiers' recreation centre) in Minsk. Heinz Rosenberg, one of the few Western European survivors of the Minsk ghetto, recalled in his memoirs that German actresses were housed at the *Soldatenheim* in Minsk where he was forced to work. It is possible that the *KdF-Heim* that Brigitte spoke about in her letter was the same *Soldatenheim* where Rosenberg worked. It was here that the artists could have encountered Jews within their own privileged bubble.

Rosenberg recounted how he and other Jews from the Minsk ghetto were told by his superior that they had to assist arriving artists, possibly from KdF. Rosenberg wrote: 'The next day at noon, senior SS and Army officers came to see the arrival of the German artists. Our group consisted of Russian and German Jews. Our clothes were marked with a J and our house number. There were a lot of young ladies among the actors'.⁵⁷ For Rosenberg, this situation radically brought together the gruesome context of the Minsk ghetto with his former life in Germany. From 1934, KdF was active throughout Germany and later in Austria and other annexed territories as well. The *Reichstheaterzug* (Reich Theatre Train) visited places throughout the entire German *Reich* in order to bring theatre and other cultural forms to the masses, even in less accessible places.⁵⁸ Although this was only for 'Aryans', KdF was a visible part of life prior to the war and also visible for people such as Heinz Rosenberg.

In Rosenberg's case, his former life came even closer than mere glimpses of a German society from which he was now brutally excluded. Among the artists that arrived in September 1942 was someone from his former life in Hamburg: a certain Lilli Füchsel. She worked as an actress in Minsk and was an acquaintance, for their sisters had attended the same class in school. Thanks to Füchsel, Rosenberg was able to communicate with his family in Hamburg. Unlike the imprisoned Jews in the Minsk ghetto, she could send letters and packages to the home front. During her four weeks' stay in Minsk, Rosenberg also received a package from Hamburg owing to her privileges. Although the packages did not necessarily save him or his family, Rosenberg conveyed in his memoirs that what she had done meant a lot to him. He also wrote about the theatre group's departure from Minsk: 'When the touring car was packed again with artists and their luggage, I couldn't say a thing anymore. I stood there quietly near the heating room and thought about what a brave human being I had met'.⁵⁹ Although Rosenberg valued the opportunities that Füchsel provided him and possibly also appreciated the normal human interaction they had in his horrific environment, it is impossible to reconstruct what Füchsel thought of their encounter.

We know how other actresses responded to encountering Jews in Minsk. Perhaps more important to them, they were not just Jews in the ghetto but Jews from their own hometown. Brigitte wrote to her mother about her encounter with a Jewish man from Hamburg:

> There's also a Jew from Hamburg working here in the house, who is an artist and who works as a carpenter. Of course, we are forced to discuss some essential things with him (to fix our suitcase and stuff like that), and once that funny man said (I think the only Jew I've interacted with in my life), that he only had one wish: just to be in a hotel once again, to walk into a breakfast room, or to sit in the dining car and stare out of the window. We found him incredibly funny. He also made many pictures that hang here, as he is quite gifted, even though he is a Jew. Don't be angry or afraid, mother. I cannot help it, that I have to speak to Jews here. The staff in the kitchen and many of the maids are Jewish. Thank God we don't have them anymore in the Reich.⁶⁰

Brigitte's letter is disturbing. Not only did she look down on the man, simply for the fact that he was Jewish, but she also could not comprehend that the man was in such a desperate position that his only wish was to have some peace. Brigitte's letter includes language that casts a light on how the process of genocide takes place. According to Gregory Stanton, this process starts with classifying people in terms of 'us' and 'them', and culminates in extermination and eventually denial of a genocide. By presenting herself and her colleagues as 'we' and the man from Hamburg and other Jews in the kitchen as 'them', Brigitte seems really to believe that she is different from the man from her hometown. In her last sentence, 'Thank God, we don't have them anymore in the Reich', she actually agrees with the expulsion and deportation of Jews from Germany. Although her letters reveal a rather naïve young woman, they make evident that she believed in the propaganda that KdF itself circulated, in which an 'Aryan utopian society' was envisaged.

It is more difficult to interpret Inge Stolten's position. She too had an encounter with a Jewish man from Hamburg:

> The young man in civilian clothing, who fixed the lamp in my make-up table and spoke to me, had to know Hamburg well. And he was definitely German, he spoke without any accent. Why wasn't he a soldier, I thought, and asked him whether he was wounded or deployed to the theatre. He did not answer, only shrugged his shoulders. I stood there somewhat helplessly, while he packed his tools. Almost through the door, he turned around and quietly said: 'We are not even good enough to function as cannon fodder.' He was Jewish. There was not a moment of doubt, no one could have understood this sentence any different. Jews were with us in the theatre. That explained all the odd things, it explained what no one said, but everyone knew: deported Jews from Hamburg stood next to us backstage, worked in our workshops and for the administration in the 'House of the Red Army'.[61]

Unlike Brigitte's letter, Stolten clearly reflected on the encounter with the Jewish man from her hometown. Although based on her memoirs Stolten seemed strongly against the Nazi regime, the question can be asked whether in hindsight she might have adapted her role into something more acceptable. She wrote: 'Today I often believe that I also had become accustomed to the fate of the Jews. How did I manage to play this spoiled, cheerful girl Till? And to be Nerissa in "The merchant of Venice", while the Jews had to listen?'[62] Although this reflection seems sincere, Stolten implies in her memoir that she only knew very shortly before the actual performance of *The Merchant of Venice* that she had to take part in it.[63] However, the performance programme shows Stolten as having the part of Nerissa.[64] Also, Stolten does not mention that during the performances of *The Merchant of Venice*, 'real costumes' were used from the depot in Minsk Opera where the possessions of deported Jews were stored and that during one of the performances the Minsk ghetto was being 'liquidated'.[65]

Conclusion

The discussion shows that it is difficult, and possibly unnecessary, to place the individual actresses on the spectrum of perpetration and complicity. But where do we position women who were acting on the eastern front as a group? Criminologist and criminal law scholar, Alette Smeulers, has distinguished several types of female perpetration, ranging from providing moral support to actively taking part in violence or murder. She points out that the largest group of women involved in mass violence are those who are involved as administrative or supporting personnel.[66] Being part of the Wehrmacht apparatus and cheering on the troops would place them in this category. Elizabeth Harvey similarly points out that the German women who were helping 'Germanize' the 'East' 'were deployed to serve a regime of untrammelled force and brutality. [. . .] Whatever the acts of particular individuals or groups, the women [. . .] can be regarded as bearing a share of responsibility for helping maintain a system based on injustice'.[67] This can also be said about the women who were performing in Minsk or on the eastern front as part of KdF.

Although the women might have attempted – and possibly also succeeded in – escaping their own restricted lives by joining the KdF and performing for the troops, they became more implicated in the Nazi system than they might have envisioned: their roles were compromised. The example of the artists in Minsk shows that not just the Wehrmacht, but also the SS was interested in the actors and actresses. Besides this, due to the openness of the Holocaust in Minsk, it was practically impossible not to witness anything. Whether it was by offering emotional comfort to Wehrmacht officers and SS men, seeing the evidence of violence in the city or through encounters with Jews who had to undertake forced labour, there were simply too many channels through which the visiting actresses knew about the reality in Minsk for them to deny awareness of the Holocaust. Timpe writes of KdF performances in concentration camps: 'It could be argued that these camp performances (and their performers) directly supported the crimes of the Holocaust, given that they were intended to entertain and uplift camp personnel. Put briefly, in the camps, the "Strength" created "through Joy" was exercised to help commit the murder of millions in an effective manner'.[68] Although not everyone in Minsk was directly involved in the Holocaust or the active murder of Jews, here too by performing for the troops *and* the SS, by benefitting from the opportunities and by supporting those who were in charge of the crimes committed in Minsk, the artists of KdF as a group had a responsibility for at least sustaining a genocidal system in Minsk.

Notes

1 This chapter is based on a blog written for the Compromised Identities Blog and on a paper presented at the conference, *Compromised Identities? Perpetration and Complicity, Past and Present* in May 2021. I would like to thank Dr Eveline Buchheim (NIOD Institute for War, Holocaust and Genocide Studies) for her feedback on earlier versions of this chapter.
2 Walter Kempowski, 'Letter Brigitte Erdmann, 20 January 1943', in *Das Echelot II, 18.1.-31.1.1943* (Munich: Albrecht Knaus Verlag, 1993), 123.
3 Ibid., 339.
4 Jill Stephenson, *Woman in Nazi Germany* (London: Routledge, 2001); Claudia Koonz, *The Nazi Conscience* (Cambridge, MA: Harvard University Press, 2003).
5 See for example: G. Bock, 'Die Frauen und der Nationalsozialismus, Bemerkungen zu einem Buch von Claudia Koonz', *Geschichte und Gesellschaft* 15 (1989): 563–79; A. Grossmann, 'Feminist Debates about Women and National Socialism', *Gender and History* 3 (1991): 350–8; J. Gehmacher, 'Kein Historikerstreit. . . . Fragen einer

frauen- und geschlechtsgeschichtlichen Erforschung des Nationalsozialismus in Österreich', *Zeitgeschichte* 22 (1995): 109–23.
6 Wendy Lower, *Hitler's Furies: German Women in the Nazi Killing Fields* (Boston: Mariner Books, 2013).
7 Cited in: Marisa Fox, 'Women have Broken Through the Glass of Violent Radicalism', *The Daily Beast*, 28 February 2021. https://www.thedailybeast.com/women-have-broken-the-glass-ceiling-of-violent-radicalism (Accessed 9 August 2022).
8 For example, Alexander Hirt, 'Die deutsche Truppenbetreuung im Zweiten Weltkrieg: Konzeption, Organisation und Wirkung', *Militärgeschichtliche Zeitschrift* 59, no. 2 (2000): 407–34; Shelley Baranowski, *Strength through Joy; Consumerism and Mass Tourism in the Third Reich* (Cambridge: Cambridge University Press, 2004); Frank Vossler, *Propaganda in die eigene Truppe; Die Truppenbetreuung in der Wehrmacht 1939–1945* (Paderborn: Ferdinand Schöningh, 2005); Alexander Hirt, *'Die Heimat reicht der Front die Hand' Kulturelle Truppenbetreuung im Zweiten Weltkrieg 1939–1945. Ein deutsch-englischer Vergleich* (Georg-August-Universität Göttingen, unpublished PhD dissertation, 2009); Julia Timpe, *Nazi-Organized Recreation and Entertainment in the Third Reich* (London: Palgrave Macmillan, 2017).
9 The term was coined by Father Patrick Desbois to refer to the murder of Jews in Eastern Europe nearby their homes. Unlike what is commonly associated with the Holocaust, symbolized by 'Auschwitz' – the industrialized murder of Jews in camp and gas chambers – these Jews were often shot to death. Patrick Desbois, *The Holocaust by Bullets: A Priest's Journey to Uncover the Truth behind the Murder of 1.5 million Jews* (New York: Palgrave Macmillan, 2008).
10 Baranowski, *Strength through Joy*, 42.
11 Ibid., 162.
12 Thomas Kühne, *Belonging and Genocide: Hitler's Community, 1918–1945* (New Haven: Yale University Press, 2010), 36.
13 Timpe, *Nazi-Organized Recreation and Entertainment in the Third Reich*, 120–1.
14 Baranowski, *Strength through Joy*, 204.
15 Vossler, *Propaganda in die eigene Truppe*, 318.
16 Timpe, *Nazi-Organized Recreation and Entertainment in the Third Reich*, 141.
17 Andrew G. Bonnell, *Shylock in Germany; Antisemitism and the German Theatre from The Enlightenment to the Nazis* (London: Tauris Academic Studies, 2008), 141.
18 Programmblatt der Aufführung, 'Der Kaufmann von Venedig', 1943. Staats- und Universitätsbibliothek Hamburg, in: Linde Apel, *In den Tod geschickt. Die Deportationen von Juden, Roma und Sinti aus Hamburg 1940 bis 1945* (Berlin: Metropol-Verlag, 2009), 129.
19 Inge Stolten, *Das alltägliche Exil; Leben zwischen Hakenkreuz und Währungsreform* (Berlin: Verlag J.H.W. Dietz Nachf., 1982), 85–6.
20 Hirt, 'Die deutsche Truppenbetreuung im Zweiten Weltkrieg', 413.
21 Stolten, *Das alltägliche Exil*, 86.
22 Kempowski, 'Letter Brigitte Erdmann, 15 February 1943', 780.
23 Timpe, *Nazi-Organized Recreation and Entertainment in the Third Reich*, 135.
24 Baranowski, *Strength through Joy*, 208–9.
25 Timpe, *Nazi-Organized Recreation and Entertainment in the Third Reich*, 135.
26 Stolten, *Das alltägliche Exil*, 90–1.
27 Vossler, *Propaganda in die eigene Truppe*, 301.
28 Kempowski, 'Letter Brigitte Erdmann, 23 February 1943', 381.
29 Timpe, *Nazi-Organized Recreation and Entertainment in the Third Reich*, 139.

30   Kempowski, 'Letter Brigitte Erdmann, 22 February 1943', 330.
31   Stephan Lehnstaedt, *Okkupation im Osten: Besatzeralltag in Warschau und Minsk 1939–1944* (Munich: Oldenbourg Wissenschaftsverlag, 2010), 65.
32   Hentri Catharinus van Maasdijk, *Nederlandse Mogelijkheden in Het Oosten; Een Reisverhaal van H. C. van Maasdijk* (Den Haag: Nederlandsch Oost Instituut, 1942), 26.
33   Ibid., 25.
34   Baranowski, *Strength through Joy*, 212.
35   The play, officially called 'Totila der Gotenköning', was once performed in Minsk as well, but was not well-received as the Minsker Zeitung wrote that it was the 'work of politicians and propagandists'. Minsker Zeitung Nr. 107, 18 August 1942, as quoted in: Lehnstaedt, *Okkupation im Osten*, 133.
36   Interview with Anita Kube by Paul Kohl, May 1993, private interview collection Paul Kohl, accessed August 2019. The presence of these so-called 'Hausjuden' in the Kube household is also confirmed by Christian Gerlach in *Kalkulierte Morde; Die Deutsche Wirtschafts - Und Vernichtungspolitik in Weißrußland, 1941 Bis 1945* (Hamburg: Hamburger Edition, 1999), 689–90.
37   Kempowski, 'Letter Brigitte Erdmann, 24 January 1943', 340.
38   Elizabeth Harvey, *Women and the Nazi East; Agents and Witnesses of Germanization* (New Haven: Yale University Press, 2003), 13–15.
39   Dagmar Herzog, 'Introduction: War and Sexuality in Europe's Twentieth Century', in *Brutality and Desire: War and Sexuality in Europe's Twentieth Century*, ed. Dagmar Herzog (London: Palgrave Macmillan, 2009), 2.
40   Sietske van der Veen, '"Our Work Was in the Service of the Suffering of Mankind": A Case Study of the Motives of the Easternfront Ambulance Nurses, 1941–1944', *Medicine, Conflict and Survival* 35, no. 2 (2019): 181–82.
41   Franka Maubach, *Die Stellung halten: Kriegserfahrungen und Lebensgeschichten von Wehrmachthelferinnen* (Göttingen: Vandenhoek & Ruprecht, 2009), 73.
42   Stolten, *Das alltägliche Exil*, 8.
43   Kempowski, 'Letter Brigitte Erdmann, 30 January 1943', 331.
44   Ibid., 333.
45   Timpe, *Nazi-Organized Recreation and Entertainment in the Third Reich*, 144.
46   Leonid Rein, 'Local Collaboration in the Execution of the "Final Solution" in Nazi-Occupied Belorussia', *Holocaust and Genocide Studies* 20, no. 3 (2006): 382.
47   Yitzhak Arad, *The Holocaust in the Soviet Union* (Lincoln: Nebraska University Press, 2009), 153.
48   Maly Trostenets is often mentioned as the place of death of the deported Jews from Germany, Vienna and the ghetto Theresienstadt, because it is referred to as an 'extermination camp' or 'death camp'. However, Maly Trostenets was a forced labour camp under the command of the local SS. Only few of the deported Jews were imprisoned here. The large majority of the deportees were murdered in Blagovshchina forest, located three kilometres away from the camp.
49   Luis Raffeiner, *Wir waren keine Menschen mehr; Erinnerungen eines Wehrmachtsoldaten an die Ostfront* (Bozen: Edition Raeta, 2011), 91.
50   Ibid., 92.
51   Ibid., 93–4.
52   Kempowski, 'Letter Brigitte Erdmann, 30 January 1943, Minsk', 613–14.
53   Harvey, *Women and the Nazi East*, 131.
54   'Transcript I. V. Pylilo, Kommissiia po sostavleniiu xroniki Velikoi Otechestvennoi Voiny' (Minsk, 14 August 1944), 116b, NARB, fond 750p, opis 1, delo 118, l. 115–20.

55 Hirt, 'Die deutsche Truppenbetreuung im Zweiten Weltkrieg', 427.
56 Timpe, *Nazi-Organized Recreation and Entertainment in the Third Reich*, 94.
57 Heinz Rosenberg, *Jahre Des Schreckens . . . Und Ich Blieb Übrig, Dass Ich Dir's Ansage* (Göttingen: Steidl, 1993), 55.
58 Timpe, *Nazi-Organized Recreation and Entertainment in the Third Reich*, 90.
59 Rosenberg, *Jahre Des Schreckens*, 58.
60 Kempowski, 'Letter Brigitte Erdmann, 24 January 1943', 339–40.
61 Stolten, *Das alltägliche Exil*, 79.
62 Ibid., 93.
63 Ibid., 85.
64 Programmblatt der Aufführung, 'Der Kaufmann von Venedig', 1943. Staats- und Universitätsbibliothek Hamburg, in: Apel, *Die deportationen von Juden, Roma und Sinti aus Hamburg 1940 bis 1945*, 129.
65 Gerlach, *Kalkulierte Morde*, 738.
66 Alette Smeulers, 'Female Perpetrators - Ordinary and Extra-Ordinary Women', *International Criminal Law Review* 15, no. 2 (2015): 3.
67 Harvey, *Women and the Nazi East*, 16.
68 Timpe, *Nazi-Organized Recreation and Entertainment in the Third Reich*, 147.

8

Gender and transgressive violence in post-war accounts

Stefanie Rauch

'I fired, with a certain gratification, the fifty rounds in the drum through her body. Her belly was gone, but she was instantly dead of course. But that was war.'. This is how, in 2004, a former Wehrmacht soldier from Austria describes his close range killing of a female partisan, who attacked him with a knife after he had initially spared her life. Even though army directives legitimized the killing of female partisans or women aiding 'bandits',[1] the killing of fighting women still required special justification. It threw the role of men as protectors and notions of women as weak, innocent and vulnerable into question. Members of the armed forces considered the killing of men of fighting age permissible, even desirable. The killing of innocent women, children and elderly people was seen as perhaps reprehensible, but as frequently necessary in the context of anti-partisan warfare and genocidal violence. Fighting women constituted a challenge to this order. Felix Römer notes that the troops were particularly incensed and felt threatened by the presence of female fighters. Female Red Army soldiers, denigrated as 'Flintenweiber' ('rifle wenches') were thus often executed immediately upon their capture.[2] During the Second World War, close to one million women served with the Soviet armed forces, including partisans, around half of them at the front, and all were trained to use weapons.[3] Even though most were assigned to positions that were considered non-combatant, losses among women in the Red Army in front-line roles were disproportionally higher than among men.[4] As 'women in battle were not part of German soldiers' frame of reference', they were 'denied the status of true combatants and thus regarded as on the same level as partisans. For that reason, they were more likely than male members of the Red Army to become the victims of excessive brutality.'[5] While the number of women serving in the Soviet armed forces was significant, the threat they posed was also symbolic: female fighters represented 'a perceived perversion of gender norms' and fed 'a traditional German army paranoia with respect to unconventional warfare'.[6] In combination, both factors led to extreme violence, including sexualized violence, against female soldiers and partisans.[7]

After the war, many veterans of Wehrmacht, Waffen-SS and SS maintained that they, personally, never killed anyone never shot anyone or saw little action.[8] Post-war accounts that openly speak of direct perpetration of violence, such as the excerpt cited above, are extremely rare and therefore of particular interest. Why, how and in what context would a former member of the Wehrmacht admit to such extreme, excessive violence against a woman? How would he negotiate actions that would seem to compromise him in the present? In this chapter, I examine the ways in which extreme violence against women, often taboo in the context of public and personal discourse (bar particular male encounters), feature in post-war narratives, to what end and to what extent they can help explain instances of excessive violence directed against female fighters. I focus on two post-war accounts by Austrian Wehrmacht veterans in which they tell of their involvement in transgressive violence during the Second World War, specifically violence against female fighters (either partisans or Red Army soldiers): one is the recording of a talk delivered to a group of students as part of a seminar, the other a narrative oral history interview. I discuss the ways and conditions in which these men recount, frame, (re)negotiate and reflect on their violence in their interactions with others, especially younger generations, in a changed moral landscape after 1945. Oscillating between gendering and un-gendering violence, and between protective and violent aspects of masculinity, their accounts provide insights into how notions of chivalry and camaraderie readily serve as precursor, motivation and justification for the killing of women. These two accounts, both accessed at the Österreichische Mediathek in Vienna, constitute the frankest discussion of direct, and close range, violence against suspected or actual partisans and female fighters that I have come across in the hundreds of oral histories that I examined in different archives. Despite their exceptional status, I use these accounts to raise a set of wider issues, both about the killing of female fighters and how such violence is narrated.

The relative candour with which the two men discussed here speak about their violent wartime conduct must not detract from the possibility (and indeed likelihood) that, as oral history sources co-produced in a particular setting and interaction six decades after the war, the actual events may have unfolded rather differently. They may not even have occurred at all. The interview situation itself presents an opportunity to construct stories about the self that constitute intact, moral identities.[9] From her interviews with violent offenders in the United States, Lois Presser concludes that 'the interview was an event in these men's lives, insofar as it was a setting for construction and reconstruction of the self'.[10] The men whose accounts I am discussing were never charged with a crime, and the violence they perpetrated took place within the context of war. But there is at least one shared feature: the men 'used the interviews' in order 'to construct themselves as morally decent persons'.[11] Here, they do so not *despite* but *through* their stories about excessive violence against female fighters. The construction of moral selves is complicated and at times unsettled by the interaction with the men's audience, who are just as much a part of the 'event' as the veterans themselves. Different contexts of speaking, whether in conversation with fellow soldiers in allied captivity, bugged and secretly recorded, in veterans' gatherings, in court or in conversations with family members or even outsiders, generate different narratives and narrative strategies.

During the war, the killing of partisans was not a taboo subject in wartime soldiers' accounts, such as letters from the front or in the secretly recorded conversations among German and Austrian POWs in British and American captivity. Few however explicitly spoke or wrote about *themselves* personally pulling the trigger. Westphalian Helmut Nick, for instance, wrote to his wife in November 1941:

> The fighting methods of the Russian are different to that of the Frenchman. It is indeed the case that the Russian does not care about death, he is stubborn. Today we again did away with 20 of the partisans, not one of them buckled beforehand. This type of death is as natural to them as any other.[12]

The killing of female partisans features in letters by Berliner Hans Stock, who first saw combat in August 1943 and deserted in February 1945 into American captivity. Aloof from Nazi ideology, Stock felt deeply uneasy about the actions of the troops, especially in Slovenia and Croatia, where they hunted partisans. One of many letters he sent to his family, dated 4 November 1943 in Croatia, describes how the troops requisitioned the homes of civilians, taking their livestock and other foodstuffs without regard for the civilians' ability to feed themselves and their children in the winter. He also details the capture and killing of a group of partisans led by a young female student, further hinting that the latter was assaulted after she was killed:

> They were dragged to the locality where they were 'done away with'. First it was the turn of the girl, a so-called 'partisan wench'. The next day she lay there, slightly exposed, which at least still speaks to our noble mindset, because one wonders that they didn't take the corpse to their beds to work off their lechery. Of course, who did it can't be determined.[13]

In Allied captivity, in secretly bugged cells, some POWs spoke candidly, sometimes boastfully, among themselves about violent incidents, including sexualized and other violence against women, they had witnessed, perpetrated or heard about. Sönke Neitzel and Harald Welzer cite a conversation between two POWs, in which one of them casually mentions raping female forced labourers, in order to illustrate 'the parameters of what can be said and what is expected', that is, the shared but 'historically, culturally, and situatively specific frameworks of reference' among soldiers.[14] These frameworks of reference changed after 1945, certainly in the public sphere; we can only imagine the conversations that took place in the gatherings and reunions of veterans and their associations. Upon their return to civilian life after the war, men integrated wartime transgressions into their post-war narratives in different ways, often responding to pressures from family members, public debates or legal challenge. But few German and Austrian veterans publicly discussed their own participation in the rape or killing (or indeed both) of women during the Second World War. In the following discussion, I examine the context, conventions and discontents of veterans' semi-public narratives about killing women.

The first of the veterans, whom I cited above, is Dr B. Speaking in 2004 to a group of Austrian university students in a seminar organized by his former lecturer, historian Gerhard Botz, Dr B. is frank about several instances of extreme violence.[15] Born in 1927, Dr B. grew up in a nationalist family. His father and uncle joined the NSDAP in 1925 and both rose through the ranks. In 1935 the family moved from Austria to

Berlin, where Dr B. soon happily joined the Hitler Youth. Aged seventeen, he was drafted into the Wehrmacht in 1944 and sent to Yugoslavia, where he volunteered to fight partisans because it promised to be both more exciting and a faster route to promotion. They did not take prisoners, but he insists that they never shot partisans after capture. In special training sessions they learned to stab someone to death, slit throats, use piano wire to cut throats and use any type of weapon. When they raided partisan camps, it was 'kurz und brutal' ('swift and brutal'), and eventually they became numb to their actions. Dr B. believes age was a crucial factor: 'they' relied on young soldiers to carry out these deeds, whereas the older ones, bar those who had previously served in 'special units', simply could not bring themselves to sneak up on someone, put a noose over their head, tighten and twist it until it cut their neck. He and his comrades were no longer fazed by the blood of their victims that would run across their hands, as they were so 'incredibly brutalized' as to be effectively 'dehumanized'. They behaved in this way until the war ended. Amid seemingly indistinguishably brutal anti-partisan campaigns he evokes what he considers his worst experience. Partisans attacked a transport of wounded soldiers and mutilated two female nurses. In response, he and his comrades searched three villages without finding the attackers, but he claims that shots were then fired at them from the first village they had searched. They returned fire and set buildings alight. He used his machine gun:

> You can imagine the resulting bursts of fire [orig.: 'Feuerzauber'[16]]. It was one of the few occasions on which I really shot with fervour and conviction. I held at it until there was no longer any movement. Old people, women, children, partisans, all of it. They no longer moved. All of them, really all of them were killed. Then we pulled out. But we were so exhausted that we could barely walk, and when we returned to camp, we simply lay down, without cleaning the weapons, we didn't clean ourselves, we didn't want to eat, we were done in, all we wanted to do was sleep. Yes, that was partisan warfare, we went through that.

He does not specify why this was the 'worst' of his experiences, whether it was the sight of the nurses and the outrage at an attack on a hospital transport, or indeed his indiscriminate killing of the inhabitants of a village, of men, women and children, both old and young, and the conviction with which he participated in the shooting. The physical exertion and sense of intoxication is also of note: machine-gun use and the killing of all these people took such a physical toll that the soldiers immediately slept after their return to their quarters, as the adrenalin wore off.[17] There is a change in registers too, from the individual 'I' to the passive ('all of them were killed') through to the communal 'we'. While Dr B. narrates this story from his own perspective and personal conduct, he also integrates it into the wider unit as acting and reacting in unison. Thomas Kühne argues in this respect that 'Moral transgression forged bonds', by 'violating civilian, humanitarian norms',[18] while Edward Westermann observes that 'group solidarity and acts of communal performative masculinity' bind perpetrators together.[19] If the experience of 'togetherness'[20] was crucial for participating in violence at the time, the changed moral and normative landscape of the post-war world often required constructing and performing difference, distance and distinction, and indeed reaffirmation of the once disavowed or transgressed bourgeois norms.

After the war, Dr B. was not organized in any veterans' organizations and describes himself as a 'lone wolf'. His father refused to confront the consequences of his own 'fanaticism' and to hear about his son's actions. Dr B. did not speak about his wartime conduct until 1997 when he visited the Wehrmacht exhibition.[21] He began giving public talks, including in schools. The seminar talk was going to be his last. Dr B. criticizes veterans who deny they ever killed anyone. But he insists that, sometimes, they spared the enemy's life, for example, if they were running away. This leads him to the incident in which he killed a woman at close range. He encountered the woman, lying on the ground, one breast exposed, soaked in blood. He decided against shooting her, but she jumped to her feet and stabbed him with a knife:

> And of course I didn't let her live. No one can ask that of me. I fired, with a certain gratification, the fifty rounds in the drum through her body. Her belly was gone, but she was instantly dead of course. But that was war. That was war.

There is much to unpack here. He gallantly let the woman live but instead of showing gratitude, she attacks him. He does not simply defend himself but empties what is left in the drum of his machine gun into the woman's abdomen, and he does so with satisfaction. He closes the story by citing the conditions of war. There are notions of chivalry and humanity: he finds a woman partially exposed and already injured, seemingly helpless and no threat, so he spares her life. But when she attacks him, he strikes her with excessive force, obliterating her abdomen and perhaps pelvis, in what may be seen as a particularly gendered targeting of body parts associated with sexuality and reproduction. But he concludes the narrative by un gendering the violence, bringing it back into the general context of war, and its dehumanizing impact. Later, he returns to the subject by claiming that female partisans were particularly brutal, like the wounded woman who was so 'fanatic' as to attack him. The notion of the fanaticism and brutality of female fighters is also a recurring trope in other post-war accounts.

Dr B. further hints at the under-researched topic of the impact of wartime transgression and brutalization on the post-war period when many veterans struggled with the return to civilian life.[22] Dr B. compensated for the emasculation of defeat, occupation and demilitarization by acting out gendered violence: they beat up an American GI who insulted them and humiliated him by putting his head into a bin, thus reaffirming their dominance and masculinity. When a woman who was friendly with the Americans insulted them, they tracked her down, cut off her hair and beat her, but 'only her buttocks', it was 'not life-threatening'. Another young woman was grabbed by her throat and shoved underneath a train carriage by Dr B. when she called him a Nazi. Eventually, he stopped being violent when he joined the civil service, delivering the post, so not to risk his job if he was caught. Asked by a student whether he has benefitted from his experiences, such as by developing increased self-awareness, Dr B. instead states that he learned 'absolute toughness and endurance' ('absolute Härte und Ausdauer'), both physically and mentally, which helped him in his education and career. Within the postal service, he was known as someone who was able to get jobs done. He was tough towards others and himself. This was also the reason why he began to speak about his experiences and actions in what he considers a 'brutally' honest way, without trying to make excuses. He reflects on feeling unsure as to how much Nazism is still in him, noting his suspicion about his sense of duty, the fact that he would not want to work with disabled people, and that he keeps his distance from a severely disabled nephew. Today he is ashamed that he went to war for Hitler, having truly believed in him. While he may be right in recognizing notions of 'inner hardness' and toughness as key components of celebrated masculinity under Nazism, including among the regular troops, this was certainly not only the case in Nazi Germany.[23]

After nineteen of such talks, Dr B. has become an experienced narrator (who has likely read a significant amount of scholarly literature on the subject), presenting himself as an expert on the period, and a product of the zeitgeist of the times. But there are tensions in the seminar when a female student challenges Dr B. about his wartime conduct towards women, such as when he talked about trading essential goods for sexual services. Conflict also arises over Dr B.'s statement that he was lucky not to have been assigned to shooting Jews. He contrasts his behaviour in the anti-partisan warfare, which he characterizes as 'combat', with the shooting of helpless people. A student now interjects that Dr B. too killed the elderly, women and children in the incident in the village; another student reminds him that he talked 'with glee' about firing fifty rounds into a woman's belly, and that it was not just the partisans who killed and mutilated their enemies. Defensively, Dr B. tells the students that they were not there and thus could not understand. Botz comes to his aid: he acknowledges the students' questions but he emphasizes that it was important to understand the dynamics that bring about such actions, and to respect Dr B.'s willingness to talk about it 'authentically'. Of note is Dr B.'s refusal (or inability) to accommodate his audience: Dr B. does not look for penance, but for recognition. To him, his story is one of war as dehumanizing and brutalizing, a war in which he was also a victim. He seeks to set himself apart from other veterans, who lack his 'courage' to speak out about the violence they enacted. His protest to the students that they were not there is significant as it indicates the inherent disconnect in this inter-generational encounter.

The second source is an oral history interview conducted under the umbrella of the life histories project *Projekt MenschenLeben* at the Österreichische Mediathek, initiated in 2009. Herr W., born in 1917 in Lower Austria, is in the presence of his daughter when he is interviewed in 2011 by an experienced interviewer, who is accompanied by a local history researcher ('Heimatforscher').[24] His daughter seemingly knows most of his war stories, provides cues and laughs with her father about set pieces, such as when SS men had to be rescued by regular troops. Herr W. was drafted in December 1938, served throughout the war, including in Czechoslovakia, Poland, France, Russia and Yugoslavia, was wounded four times and received nine or ten commendations. The daughter raises the subject of the partisan warfare as having been 'the worst'. Herr W. confirms it was indeed the worst, later citing a case of partisans gouging out the eyes of a local SS man. They could hear him scream but were unable to help him. Partisan warfare was 'gruesome', and he still harbours feelings of hatred and revenge against all of 'Yugoslavia'.

As the interview progresses, he volunteers stories that are unknown to his daughter, such as an incident in a small farming village near Vinkovci where they strung up several partisans. The daughter corrects Herr W., insisting he surely must mean that the partisans hung German soldiers, but he clarifies that it was indeed them who strung up the partisans. The daughter repeats this new information without further comment. She is somewhat assured moments later when Herr W. notes that it was the SS who carried out the hangings. When Herr W. critically reflects on using machine guns, which enable killing hundreds of people at a time, as being inherently unfair, the daughter deflects; she seems unwilling to contemplate her father's role in killing people, much preferring the funny or daring stories she is familiar with. She remains silent when he talks about what he knew of the persecution and murder of Jews. Most disturbing for the daughter is Herr W.'s account of killing women in the context of anti-partisan warfare. They were attacked by partisans and began searching a village. In one of the buildings, they encountered a woman who was seemingly ill, and bed bound. Presuming she was harmless, they turned their backs, but she started shooting at them and hit one of their sergeants. In response they blew up the house, 'and the wench ("Weiberleut") too. What a scourge ("Mistvieh")'. As in the case of Dr B., Herr W. too must justify the violence against the woman, which again is excessive: Dr B. empties his drum of fifty rounds into an already injured woman; Herr W. and his comrades use what must have been a substantial amount of ammunition to blow up an entire house to kill one woman. Like Dr B., Herr W. emphasizes their decency and chivalry, how they let go of the woman when they saw she was ill. As in Dr B.'s story, the woman in Herr W.'s account does not show gratitude but attacks them from behind.

The trope of leniency, decency and perhaps weakness, being met with insidiousness and leading to excessive violence is not solely linked to encounters with hostile women. Hans-Georg Borck, born in 1921, joined an armoured division and quickly rose through the ranks, leading a group of 1,000 men by the end of 1943. He claims that they treated the civilian populations well but concedes that things could turn ugly very quickly if they met resistance:

> HGB: [...] the civilian population was taboo for us in every respect. But we could of course be very nasty when civilians resisted us.
> I: Did that happen?
> HGB: As I said before, I experienced that only once and I told you about it already. That was when Lieutenant Stefan died. [...] It broke-. We had behaved in such a fair and clean manner. And then someone [shot him] from a skylight [...]. That caused a lot of bad blood. It certainly caused feelings of revenge in some.
> I: And then some men from your unit...
> HGB: Not from my unit, it wasn't my company, but I witnessed it.[25]

In this incident, the killing of the German lieutenant was met with killing everyone in the building from which shots were fired. It should be stressed here that German soldiers certainly did not need provocation to enact extreme violence on local populations, and that later claims of having been under attack often served as a justification strategy.

Indeed, the 'work of subjugating the eastern territories encompassed the enslavement of local populations, widespread acts of physical abuse, and the routine conduct of mass killing essentially created a colonial mentality among the perpetrators in which new, expanded norms of behavior reigned supreme'.[26] The 'war of annihilation' was embedded in the imperial conquest of supposedly racially inferior populations and of colonizing future 'living space'. This is important for understanding encounters with local populations. As colonial encounters, they were built on a patriarchal and hierarchical relationship. At best, it was paternalistic, but only where local populations recognized the German troops' superiority and hegemony. Where these were put in question, the violence wrought on individuals, families and indeed whole communities could be extreme and disproportionate so troops could reassert their power. Offended and slighted by not being acknowledged as superior, relationships could quickly turn sour, and the conquerors used extreme force: 'What offended them most was the behavior of occupied local populaces. The soldiers thought it was essential to take action against any and every form of noncooperation'.[27] An attack by female fighters would have been considered a particularly grave transgression and offence. In the examples of Borck, Herr W. and Dr B., we also see an expectation to be recognized not only as conquerors, but as chivalrous, humane and as individuals among the wider troops.[28]

Many decades after the war, the men still sought recognition for the latter qualities. But as Dr B. learned in his post-war encounter with the seminar group of young students, veterans' wartime conduct does not easily find sympathetic ears. Such generational conflict can be particularly difficult within families. Herr W.'s daughter came uncomfortably close to discovering a previously hidden, and frightening, side to her father, even more so as he doubles down on the story about blowing up the woman in the house, noting that there were many of such 'wenches' and that he, too, killed one of them:

L.W.: I too had to shoot one of them dead once.
Daughter: Dad!
L.W.: What's the matter?
Daughter: But why?

The daughter is taken aback, her voice sounds distant; her father has not told her this story before, and she clearly struggles with his description of violence against women. It does not fit into her notion of warfare as wrought by men against men, nor her idealized image of her father. Herr W. is surprised by his daughter's reaction and responds: 'Because she was fighting. [. . .] It was war'. Like Dr B., Herr W. cites the conditions of war. Herr W. adds that he would rather kill than be killed: 'That's how it was. In some respects, I wasn't one of the good guys. I admit that'. This statement, however, helps the daughter to bring the story back into line with her image of her father, redirecting his words from a reflection on his conduct and character into a more agreeable notion of soldierly behaviour:

Daughter: You were quite an aggressive soldier.
L.W.: I openly admit to that.

The interview dynamics are interesting in both cases. Herr W. is interviewed by two men, who are local, and they appear to know each other. The interaction with two men situates Herr W. in a familiar frame of reference. This setting, in combination with some perhaps unexpected questions, give rise to his telling of stories that he had not told his daughter. The framework of the partisan warfare is sufficient for Herr W. to fend off notions of untoward behaviour. The daughter complicates the interview dynamics and her presence is both revealing and obstructive. Her reaction not only surprises Herr W., he also appears ready to reflect critically on his own conduct when he is confronted with his daughter's shocked response. He concedes that he was not one of 'the good guys', indicating awareness that, at least by today's standards, he may have pushed the boundaries of acceptable behaviour. It is the daughter who shuts him down and prevents any further revelations when she returns his behaviour to the spectrum of masculine, soldierly conduct. No further questions are asked about his actions, or the context in which he shot a female fighter. While some veterans may not have wanted to talk about the war, in many cases it may have been their children who did not want to hear anything that would challenge their image of their fathers as good people. Unlike Dr B., Herr W. met with his former comrades throughout the post-war period. After the war Herr W. worked for the postal service and was an active Social Democrat in local politics. Herr W. does not feel compromised himself, nor does he think the war affected him that much; trained from a young age, war became a normal, everyday experience. It is his daughter who suddenly needs to grapple with a father whose past, and by extension not only her image of her father but their relationship, may have been compromised. The seminar students interacting with Dr B. have no such personal relationship with him and are thus less reluctant to confront him with his past and the ways in which he represents it in the present, highlighting contradictions in his narrative. Dr B.'s sense of compromise is palpable, but he seeks recognition and rehabilitation for his 'brutally honest' way of confronting his actions, ostensibly not through the lens of the present, but by trying to recount his experiences as he lived through them. The students' reactions challenge his self-representation: unlike Botz, they do not appreciate his 'honesty' and 'authenticity' but instead confront him with their moral judgement of him. Whereas Herr W. had decades building and cementing a usable past through family conversations and veterans' gatherings, Dr B. works through the past in his public talks, yielding mixed, unexpected and, at times, uncomfortable results.

Even Dr B.'s candour had limits, however. A shared feature of post-war accounts about reprisals is that they remain vague as to their exact location. As soldiers moved around, the towns and villages may well have seemed somewhat indistinguishable, their names difficult to pronounce and remember. They also held little regard for the supposedly racially inferior people inhabiting them. But many veterans later consciously withheld detailed geographical information. Dr B. is open about this fact. He explains that he will name neither the locality of the village they wiped out nor his unit, for his 'own protection'. This is not due to concerns over legal repercussions but fear of revenge. He elaborates that after the war he once encountered three men who were from the localities where Dr B. and his comrades had been 'active'; one of them lost his parents in one of their operations and another used to be a member of a partisan unit. While they 'got on well', he stresses that it could have potentially ended badly: 'You know how radical and fanatical they are', how 'impulsive' the people were 'there', that is, in the Balkans, he says without empathy or recognition of his continuation of racialized notions of people in the Balkans (likely reinvigorated during the Balkan wars of the 1990s). This indicates the stability of wartime ideological frameworks over time, as also seen in Herr W.'s continued hatred for the former Yugoslavia.

Dr B. and Herr W.'s stories about killing female fighters add to our understanding of the genesis and aftermath of a type of violence that stands out even in the context of the brutal anti-partisan warfare. Neitzel and Welzer note '"Taking care" of partisans was rationalized with the idea that they ambushed German soldiers. Revenge was a powerful motivator and functioned regardless of individual soldiers' political attitudes'.[29] The stress on insidious behaviour is key as dog whistle for 'feminine crime' and serves to underline the necessity of extreme violence against partisans of both genders, with partisans feminized as 'insidious' ('heimtückisch') and having to be dealt with accordingly. When slighted and humiliated by women, the soldiers retaliated with seemingly disproportionate, excessive violence. Whereas in West German post-war trials especially 'excess perpetrators' were prosecuted and tried, here the excess serves as defence: the behaviour of the women warranted no other response. The excessive force against the women encountered by Dr B. and Herr W. was a response to the humiliation, even emasculation, that the women's attack on them or their comrades represented. In 1942, Lieutenant Peter Geissler, who fought in Yugoslavia, wrote letters home about his disgust and the sense of humiliation at the sight of 'uniformed women': 'Yesterday we had our second black day, we had to leave many dead and badly wounded on a bridge. And when you consider that we suffered these losses at the hands of a *female* Partisan company, it really makes you want to throw up'.[30] Such attacks undermined their authority, power and military honour. In the case of Dr B. and Herr W., it was also an attack on their identity as comrades, as they had been weak when letting the women live, a remnant of bourgeois values. Perhaps the men, at least briefly, recognized the humanity of the women, which renders the latter also 'potentially dangerous and threatening',[31] thus easily giving way to violence where this recognition endangered the troops or soldiers' standing among their comrades. The excessive, transgressive violence – destroying,[32] rather than protecting women (Dr B. destroys the abdomen of the woman, Herr W. and his comrades destroy the woman's house and body[33]) – can be read as 'performative masculinity',[34] demonstrating toughness, comradeship and, not least, their manliness and superiority over supposedly racially inferior, subaltern Eastern women.

To develop these ideas further, drawing on more recent work on masculinities proves insightful. Edward W. Morris and Kathleen Ratajczak consider specific 'manhood acts' through which men assert control over men and women and 'establish masculine credibility', especially when there is an audience.[35] This, in combination with the notion of chivalry – which positions women either as 'damsels in distress' or (possessed by) 'demons' – can account for much of the excessive violence in Dr B. and Herr W.'s narratives, and indeed in other recorded instances. Chivalry called for 'restraint' towards supposedly 'inferiors', who in return 'must keep their place and not offend' the superior soldier.[36] So rather than recognizing the female fighters' humanity, the soldiers saw them through a gendered lens as seemingly helpless women, inferior by both sex and race, and to whom good conduct (restraint) was granted, but only on condition of the women's submission. Analyses of war as a type of 'play' stress the importance of 'a set of rules' and 'the capacity to form communities', both resting 'on the condition that adversaries regard each other as equal, i.e., belonging to some sort of community'.[37] Whereas German troops did not consider Slavic men a part of their community from the outset, female fighters were, however briefly, seen as women to whom restraint might be afforded and thus as part of some type of community and set of rules of play, but the women's 'rule-breaking' violently expelled them from the community, followed by brutal revenge. Upon being attacked by the women, men themselves became feminized victims of violence by 'inappropriately masculine'[38] women, who were seen as an aberration. Moreover, with comradeship 'coded feminine',[39] the men's chivalrous protection of their comrades was also at stake. In response, the soldiers did not merely disable or kill the female fighters but obliterated them as their very presence was threatening: in destroying (parts of) their bodies they also destroyed traces of their sex. This 'compensatory manhood act'[40] was constructive as it reconstituted the soldiers' masculinity and place within the social group. The excessive force used against female fighters may further express heightened anger and aggression at the fact that the men 'had' to kill them 'against' their own values and norms, that the women effectively 'forced' them into this situation.[41] Significantly, the men construct moral selves not despite but through narratives about transgressive violence by *displacing* transgression onto the female fighters, who are perceived to have perverted norms of 'natural' gender relations and chivalrous warfare; the men reset the natural order. Through this mechanism, excessive violence does not constitute criminal or morally compromising behaviour, nor 'moral injury',[42] even six decades later.

Extreme wartime brutality and transgressive violence, against soldiers and civilians, are neither the sole preserve of Wehrmacht, Waffen-SS or SS, nor confined to the Second World War.[43] But the openness with which these two Austrian veterans, who otherwise have little in common, talk about and defend violence against women in a radically different cultural climate is certainly of note. Ben Shepherd highlights that Austrian troops were just as averse to irregular warfare as their German counterparts and prepared to 'employ ferocious brutality when they encountered it'; indeed, some Austrian troops already encountered female fighters during the invasion of Serbia in 1941, where troops enacted severe reprisals against the civilian population.[44] From a judicial point of view there was little they had to worry about after 1945. In Austria, the early post-war People's Courts were concerned with 'domestic political issues', and after 1955 few attempts were made to prosecute more serious crimes; the legal prosecution of Nazi crimes effectively ceased in 1975.[45] Outside the courts, publicly funded veterans' associations actively constructed a positive image of the Wehrmacht and its Austrian troops. Whatever ordinary soldiers may have been involved in, after the war a carefully constructed image of a clean Wehrmacht prevailed.[46] The immediate impact of the Wehrmacht Exhibition cannot be overstated. Widely reported on and discussed, the exhibition was visited by 900,000 people in 33 German and Austrian cities.[47] Hannes Heer argues that the exhibition's explicit association of the war in the East with genocidal and other extreme violence effectively eroded lifelong lies of the war generation and, by extension, their children and grandchildren.[48] Based on his analysis of a series of interviews conducted in Vienna in the mid-1990s, Heer distinguishes between three cohorts of Austrian veterans: Landser (1915–24), recruits and young soldiers (1925–9) and war children (1930–35). Among the Landser cohort – that is, the cohort Herr W. belongs to, – the partisan warfare loomed large, but the majority spoke of it only in vague, general terms, and denied their own involvement in criminal acts.[49] In Dr B.'s cohort of recruits and young soldiers, Heer identified a stronger sense of guilt and condemnation of war, but few reported having personally witnessed violence against Jews, for example.[50] Herr W. and Dr B. both fit and defy Heer's categorization: the partisan warfare is key in both their accounts and they openly talk about themselves as killers, but neither regards their actions as criminal. I suggest that we ought to rethink the longer-term impact that the Wehrmacht exhibition has had on narratives about extreme violence against alleged and actual partisans, male or female, among veterans and indeed wider society. The original Wehrmacht exhibition was met with fierce resistance in certain circles and a campaign to discredit it entirely on account of several wrongly attributed photographs. The backlash led to the closing down and revision of the exhibition, with the second version far less controversial and challenging to the image of the Wehrmacht. Accounts such as those by Dr B. and Herr W. indicate that the exhibition may have done little to disrupt and may have instead reinforced a popular image of the extremely brutal partisan and anti-partisan warfare as regrettable but inevitable facets of the Second World War, and as divorced from the 'war of annihilation' and genocidal violence. While the exhibition was met with denial from many veterans, in the case of Dr B. it helped him verbalize for the first time what he had personally experienced. The Wehrmacht exhibition created conditions in which some veterans can speak about violence, including transgressive behaviour on the eastern front and in anti-partisan campaigns, more openly, effectively stimulating stories about anti-partisan warfare and leading to normalization as backlash to condemnation. It cemented certain stories and brought them into the public sphere, where they could now be told, rather than being unsettled.

Within this wider context, rather than constitute a taboo per se, then, violence against women is constructed and perceived as permissible and indeed necessary if certain criteria of a chivalrous discourse are met: the women were (alleged to be) soldiers, partisans or their helpers; the men spared them, but the women *insidiously* attacked them, thus justifying the use of extreme violence – pointing to wider reaching implications for the involvement of soldiers in direct and indirect killing and living with these actions after the war. The transgressive dimension of the violence was likely less of a consideration at the time, when excessive violence was justified with military necessity and when the transgression was seen in the women's behaviour. Transgression is a particular concern in and of the present, a moral evaluation based on current norms and sensibilities. That extends to the way in which stories about violence are told and whether narrative strategies adhere to cultural scripts and genre conventions that are either acceptable to present audiences or judged as transgressive.

Notes

1. See Ben Shepherd, *War in the Wild East: The German Army and Soviet Partisans* (Cambridge, MA, and London: Harvard University Press, 2004), 125–6, 184–5; Ben Shepherd, *Terror in the Balkans: German Armies and Partisan Warfare* (Cambridge, MA: Harvard University Press, 2012), 121, 143, 220–1.
2. Felix Römer, *Kameraden: Die Wehrmacht von innen* (Munich and Zürich: Piper Verlag, 2012), 331.
3. Reina Pennington, 'Offensive Women: Women in Combat in the Red Army', in *Time to Kill: The Soldier's Experience of War in the West, 1939-1945*, ed. Paul Addison and Angus Calder (London: Pimlico, 1997), 249–52.
4. Ibid., 260.
5. Sönke Neitzel and Harald Welzer, *Soldaten: On Fighting, Killing and Dying. The Secret World War II Transcripts of German POWs* (New York: Alfred A. Knopf, 2012), 317. See for example Pennington, citing a Red Army veteran's report about a nurse taken prisoner by the Germans: 'her eyes had been put out, her breasts lopped off. She had been impaled. It was frosty and she was all very white, her hair completely grey. She was a young girl of nineteen'. Pennington, 'Offensive Women', 260. Hans Prudhoff writes in Russian captivity about Russian medical orderlies lying by the wayside, breasts exposed, clothing ripped from their bodies and shot by the German troops. In: Hannes Heer, *Stets zu erschießen sind Frauen, die in der Roten Armee dienen: Geständnisse deutscher Kriegsgefangener über ihren Einsatz an der Ostfront* (Hamburg: Hamburger Edition, 1995), 80–1.
6. Edward B. Westermann, *Drunk on Genocide: Alcohol and Mass Murder in Nazi Germany* (Ithaca and London: Cornell University Press, 2021), 193.
7. For research on violence against women during the Second World War, see for example Felix Römer, 'Gewaltsame Geschlechterordnung: Wehrmacht und "Flintenweiber" an der Ostfront 1941/42', in *Soldatinnen: Gewalt und Geschlecht vom Mittelalter bis heute*, ed. Klaus Latzel, Franka Maubach and Silke Satjukow (Paderborn: Ferdinand Schoeningh, 2011), 331–51; Regina Mühlhäuser, 'The Historicity of Denial: Sexual Violence against Jewish Women during the War of Annihilation, 1941–1945', in *Gendered Wars, Gendered Memories: Feminist Conversations on War, Genocide and Political Violence*, ed. Ayşe Gül Altınay and Andrea Pető (Abingdon: Routledge, 2016), 29–54; Jeffrey Burds, 'Sexual Violence in Europe in World War II, 1939–1945', *Politics & Society* 37, no. 1 (2009): 35–74.
8. While many men indeed did not see any action, particularly front action, post-war accounts point to patterns of denial among a wide range of soldiers. When talking about violent incidents, they usually distance themselves from any role in the process, instead blaming other units, SS or auxiliaries.
9. For literature on phantasy, and psychoanalytical and psychosocial perspectives on narrative construction, see for example Molly Andrews, *Narrative Imagination and Everyday Life* (Oxford: Oxford University Press, 2014); Karl Figlio, 'Oral History and the Unconscious', *History Workshop* 26 (1988): 120–32; Michael Roper, 'Analysing the Analysed: Transference and Counter-Transference in the Oral History Encounter', *Oral History* 31, no. 2 (2003): 20–32. On oral history and ego-documents, see for example Lutz Niethammer, *'Die Jahre weiss man nicht, wo man die heute hinsetzen soll'. Faschismus-Erfahrungen im Ruhrgebiet. Lebensgeschichte und Sozialkultur im Ruhrgebiet*, Vol. I. (Berlin-Bonn: Dietz, 1983); Gabriele Rosenthal, 'Reconstruction of

Life Stories: Principles of Selection in Generating Stories for Narrative Biographical Interviews', *The Narrative Study of Lives* 1, no. 1 (1993): 59–91; Stefanie Rauch, 'Reconsidering Post-war Narratives of Involvement in Nazi Violence', *Holocaust Studies: A Journal of Culture and History* 28, no. 1 (2022): 67–94; Mary Fulbrook and Ulinka Rublack, 'In Relation: The "Social Self" and Ego-Documents', *German History* 28, no. 3 (2010): 263–72. See also Florian Zabransky's lucid analysis of gender and interview dynamics in an oral history interview with a Jewish survivor who joined the partisans and later the Red Army, and who talks about sexual violence perpetrated by a partisan group against a female farmer: Florian Zabransky, 'Talking about Sexualised Violence: The Presentation of Rape and Male Power in an Oral-History Interview', *EHRI*, If This Is A Woman – EHRI Document Blog Series on Gender Studies and Holocaust History. https://blog.ehri-project.eu/2021/04/26/sexualised-violence-interview/#en-4812-4 (Accessed 18 February 2022).
10 Lois Presser, 'Violent Offenders, Moral Selves: Constructing Identities and Accounts in the Research Interview', *Social Problems* 51, no. 1 (2004): 83.
11 Ibid., 97–8.
12 Museumsstiftung Post und Kommunikation, Feldpost 1939–1945, 'Helmut Nick am 6.11.1941' (3.2002.0274). My translation.
13 Museumsstiftung Post und Kommunikation, Feldpost 1939–1945, 'Hans Stock an seinen Vater am 4.11.1943' (3.2002.1217). My translation.
14 Neitzel and Welzer, *Soldaten*, 3.
15 Österreichische Mediathek, Sammlung Botz Sommer 2019, 255: Interviewee Dr F. B. [c.2004]. All quotations are my translation. See related publication Sandra Paweronschitz, '"Damit der Krieg ein anderes Gesicht kriegt . . ." Herr F. *1927 Westösterreich, 44/45 Partisaneneinsatz mit der Wehrmacht. Öffentlicher Dienst nach 1945', in *Schweigen und Reden einer Generation: Erinnerungsgespräche mit Opfern, Tätern und Mitläufern des Nationalsozialismus*, ed. Gerhard Botz (Vienna: Mandelbaum-Verlag, 2007), 39–46.
16 Term used by soldiers denoting heavy drum fire. See also 'Feuerzauber' in Richard Wagner's 'Die Walküre'.
17 On intoxication, both metaphorical and literal, see Westermann, *Drunk on Genocide*.
18 Thomas Kühne, *Belonging and Genocide: Hitler's Community, 1918–1945* (New Haven: Yale University Press, 2010), 65–6.
19 Westermann, *Drunk on Genocide*, 190.
20 Kühne, *Belonging and Genocide*, 59.
21 1995–1999: War of Annihilation: Crimes of the Wehrmacht 1941–4. Revised version 2001–4: Crimes of the German Wehrmacht: Dimensions of a War of Annihilation 1941–4.
22 For research on soldiers' return to civilian life in more recent contexts, see for example Sarah Bulmer and Maya Eichler, 'Unmaking Militarized Masculinity: Veterans and the Project Of Military-to-Civilian Transition', *Critical Military Studies* 3, no. 2 (2017): 161–81.
23 See for example Westermann, *Drunk on Genocide*, 44; Detlev Peukert, *Inside Nazi Germany: Conformity, Opposition, and Racism in Everyday Life*, trans. Richard Deveson (New Haven, CT: Yale University Press, 1987), 205. On militarized masculinities more generally, see for example Robert A. Nye, 'Western Masculinities in War and Peace', *The American Historical* Review 112, no. 2 (2007): 417–38; Björn Krondorfer and Edward B. Westermann, 'Soldiering Men', in *Gender: War*, ed. Andrea Pető (Farmington Hills: Macmillan Reference USA, 2017), 19–35.

24 Österreichische Mediathek, Sammlung MenschenLeben, 'Oral History Interview mit Herr W.', 10 August 2011/01 September 2011. All quotations are my translation.
25 USHMM, Germany Documentation Project, RG-50.486.0030.02.02, 'Interview with Hans-Georg Borck', 2 July 2007. Transcript (my translation). https://collections.ushmm.org/search/catalog/irn516582 (Accessed 18 February 2022).
26 Westermann, *Drunk on Genocide*, 7.
27 Neitzel and Welzer, *Soldaten*, 274.
28 On the tension between individual identity and modern mass warfare, see Omer Bartov, 'Man and the Mass: Reality and the Heroic Image in War', *History and Memory* 1, no. 2 (1989): 99–122.
29 Neitzel and Welzer, *Soldaten*, 264.
30 Cited in Shepherd, *Terror in the Balkans*, 209. Emphasis in original.
31 Kate Manne, 'Humanism: A Critique', *Social Theory and Practice* 43, no. 2 (2016): 400. More broadly, on misogyny, see Kate Manne, *Down Girl: The Logic of Misogyny* (Oxford: Oxford University Press, 2017).
32 Klaus Theweleit, in his work on the Freikorps, characterizes such destruction as 'the pleasurable perception of women in the condition of "bloody masses"'. Klaus Theweleit, *Male Fantasies. volume 1: Women Floods Bodies History* (Minneapolis: University of Minnesota, 1987), 195. For more recent psychoanalytic approaches to masculinity, see for example Christina Wieland, *The Fascist State of Mind and the Manufacturing of Masculinity: A Psychoanalytic Approach* (London: Routledge, 2015).
33 See also Pennington who discusses the fate of a captured female sniper, whom the Germans 'executed with an anti-tank rifle'. Pennington, 'Offensive Women', 254.
34 See Westermann, *Drunk on Genocide*, 26.
35 Edward W. Morris and Kathleen Ratajczak, 'Critical Masculinity Studies and Research on Violence Against Women: An Assessment of Past Scholarship and Future Directions', *Violence Against Women* 25, no. 16 (2019): 1992.
36 Aldo Scaglione, *Knights at Court: Courtliness, Chivalry, and Courtesy from Ottonian Germany to the Italian Renaissance* (Berkeley: University of California Press, 1991), 287–8, quoted in: René Moelker and Gerhard Kümmel, 'Chivalry and Codes of Conduct: Can the Virtue of Chivalry Epitomize Guidelines for Interpersonal Conduct?', *Journal of Military Ethics* 6, no. 4 (2007): 297.
37 Moelker and Kümmel, 'Chivalry and Codes of Conduct', 294.
38 Morris and Ratajczak, 'Critical Masculinity Studies and Research on Violence Against Women', 1986.
39 Thomas Kühne, 'Comradeship: Gender Confusion and Gender Order in the German Military, 1918–1945', in *Home/Front: The Military, War and Gender in Twentieth-Century Germany*, ed. Karen Hagemann and Stefanie Schüler-Springorum (London and New York: Berg, 2002), 236.
40 Morris and Ratajczak, 'Critical Masculinity Studies and Research on Violence Against Women', 1992. See also Theweleit on 'corrective measures' in Theweleit, *Male Fantasies*, 196.
41 Harald Welzer, *Täter: Wie aus ganz normalen Menschen Massenmörder werden* (Frankfurt am Main: S. Fischer, 2005), 211.
42 On the notion of 'moral injury' among veterans, see for example Philip F. Napoli, Thomas Brinson, Neil Kenny, and Joan Furey, 'Oral History, Moral Injury, and Vietnam Veterans', *The Oral History Review* 46, no. 1 (2019): 71–103.
43 Welzer, *Täter*; Joanna Bourke, *An Intimate History of Killing: Face-to-Face Killing in 20th-Century Warfare* (London and New York: Granta Press, 1999).

44 Shepherd, *Terror in the Balkans*, 30.
45 Mary Fulbrook, 'Reframing the Past: Justice, Guilt, and Consolidation in East and West Germany after Nazism', *Central European History* 53, no. 2 (2020): 302.
46 Hannes Heer, *Vom Verschwinden der Täter: Der Vernichtungskrieg fand statt, aber keiner war dabei* (Berlin: Aufbau-Verlag, 2004), 200.
47 Ibid., 17. See also a documentary about reactions to the exhibition in Austria: *Jenseits des Krieges* (dir. Ruth Beckermann, Austria, 1996).
48 Heer, *Vom Verschwinden der Täter*, 201.
49 Ibid., 204.
50 Ibid., 226–30.

9

Israeli national narratives, complicity and activism

Noam Chayut's *The Girl Who Stole My Holocaust* and Breaking the Silence

Nina Fischer

Breaking the silence's memory activism against the occupation

In her 2017 book *Memory Activism: Remembering for the Future in Israel/Palestine*, Yifat Gutman introduces the term 'memory activism', which she defines as 'the strategic commemoration of a contested past outside of state channels to influence public debate and policy'.[1] Gutman is referring to the remembrance of the *Nakba* [arab. Catastrophe], the 1947–9 period and the end of historical Palestine, the death of 12–15,000 Palestinians[2] and the exile of over 700,000, that is, 80 per cent of Arab inhabitants of the area that became Israel. The interpretation of this time around the founding of the state in 1948, which the Zionist narrative heralds as the nation's virgin birth out of the ovens of Auschwitz, is among the most contested in Israeli society. The social consensus revolves around the notion of self-defence and the local Arabs voluntarily leaving after their leadership had incited to violence against the future Israelis. With the rise of Israel's revisionist New Historians in the 1980s, this narrative was challenged and a more nuanced historiography showed Israel's part in the Palestinian refugee problem. Nevertheless, mainstream Israeli thinking refutes responsibility and silences critical interpretations of history.[3] Other central narratives, for instance, the interpretation of and positioning towards Israel's occupation of Palestinian Territories, also continue to provoke heated debates and activism on both sides of the political divide.

While Gutman focusses on Nakba-related left-wing memory activism, I want to extend the idea of 'memory activism' to Israeli activists who want to influence public debate against the occupation. Primarily, members of Breaking the Silence (BtS), a controversial NGO of Israeli Defense Force (IDF) veterans, record and disseminate testimonies about soldiers' service in the Occupied Palestinian Territories (OPT).[4] BtS's mission is to:

expose the public to the daily reality of the occupation and Israeli military rule over the Palestinian civilian population in the territories, a reality we witnessed firsthand during our military service. By publishing soldiers' testimonies on their service in the occupied territories, we aim to generate opposition to the occupation through meaningful public debate on the significant moral price paid by Israeli society for entrenching the ongoing regime of occupation.[5]

Founded in 2004, BtS attempts to renegotiate the institutionally controlled public debate about Israel's acts and policies in the OPT, the collective and individual complicity of Israelis in the occupation, and the sacrosanct position of the IDF within Israeli society by way of the personal memories of soldiers. These memories of pervasive misconduct put in doubt the national narrative that the IDF solely engages in self-defence. Collections of testimonies have been turned into books that draw a harsh picture of the occupation and aim to sensitize readers to its corrosive effects, on the soldiers tasked with upholding it.[6] In recent years, the concept of moral injury has been applied to Israeli veterans.[7] Moral injury describes the lesser-known psychological effects of battle and its violations of soldiers' sense of justice and core beliefs, including in the good of their own and their nation's acts. Such violations, while causing feelings of remorse, shame, guilt, anger and even suicidal ideation, might also trigger activism, as can be deduced from the testimonies that soldiers shared with BtS.[8] Of course, the format of giving an, in most cases, anonymous witness account is low key compared to other forms of protest. And yet, given that Israel has no plans to end the occupation, any form of speaking out against the realities of being part of an occupying army is at least controversial, if not outright a form of activism.

In addition to collecting testimonies, BtS organizes exhibitions of amateur photographs alongside soldiers' videotaped testimonies, runs tours of Hebron – a flashpoint of the conflict – to demonstrate the actions required to maintain the occupation of an entire population by military force and brings their testimony to anyone willing to listen. The organization is neither anti-Zionist nor committed to Palestinian solidarity work, and yet since its inception it has received hostile responses from many corners of Israeli society, including politicians like Tzipi Hotovely, who called the whistleblowers 'traitors and liars'.[9] In 2018, the Knesset approved a law that prevents members of BtS speaking in Israeli schools and aims to silence any narrative opposing the mainstream. Members of the organization also present verbal and visual testimony around the world to challenge the official Israeli narrative of self-defence against terrorism globally. The goal is to increase international pressure against the occupation, an activity that has escalated official activities against the organization and its supporters, even those abroad.[10]

Veterans' memory activism extended: Noam Chayut's *The Girl Who Stole My Holocaust*

In *The Girl Who Stole My Holocaust*, Noam Chayut, a co-founder of BtS, moves the organization's memory activism into the literary sphere, perhaps echoing George

Orwell's impetus for writing as a 'desire to push the world in a certain direction, to alter other people's idea of the kind of society they should strive after'.[11] Structurally, Chayut extends BtS's testimonial format into a life-writing text that goes beyond portraying his military service and includes a thorough reckoning with his country. He chronicles a complicated process of self-discovery about his own and his nation's complicity in what he came to see as 'crimes in the Occupied Territories'.[12] In this chapter, I argue that Chayut's facing up to complicity and culpability necessitated a re-evaluation of national identity and a rejection of the collective narratives associated with it.

Born in a *moshav*, a cooperative agricultural village, in the Jezreel Valley, and into the heart of Zionist thinking, young Chayut's identity and sense of self were fully aligned with official Israeli narratives. However, when serving as a combat soldier in the West Bank during the Second Intifada, the Palestinian uprising of 2000–05, he experienced situations and behaved in ways that contradicted everything he had been taught about Israel and Israeliness, an upending of deep beliefs that indicates moral injury. This cognitive dissonance triggered the gradual loss of his 'uncompromised identity'[13] which had allowed him to feel 'moral, righteous even. A part of the "Enlightened Occupation"' (127), and which had kept him from seeing his nation's and his own acts as mistreatment of Palestinians.[14] More than that, moral injury and shifting beliefs have him angrily accusing his society of intentionally compromising young Israelis' identities and conceptions of good and bad for the sake of politics. Only such thinking had allowed him to act as commander of Israel's largest checkpoint separating Jerusalem and the West Bank. He:

> believed that all humans were equal, that everyone had the right to live in dignity and freedom. I believed that this situation was temporary and imposed upon us in order to cope with terrorism. Now, as my memory – film-like – replays the events that transpired when I was in charge of Qalandiya Checkpoint, I know this was all a lie, a denial mechanism and distortion of reality, a mechanism and a distortion of reality, a mechanism that enabled me to function without contradicting my own set of values, which in turn were being warped. (232)

As the acerbic title of his memoir indicates, Chayut's reckoning with himself as well as his socialization, the national ethos and the military structures, is harsh. The thesis underlying *The Girl Who Stole My Holocaust* is that Israel's primary reason for rejecting culpability, past or present, is that collective victimhood features centrally in the country's national identity construction. The long history of antisemitism and the Holocaust especially function as evidence that Israel is and will be always in danger, meaning that any act is justified. Alongside the nationalized form of Holocaust memory and the way he sees it as being used for upholding the occupation and giving the army absolute and unquestioned power over Israeli and Palestinian lives, Chayut challenges what he considers a national myth of the IDF as a 'moral army' in which most Jewish Israelis are involved as conscripted soldiers. Finally, he pinpoints mainstream Israel's denial of culpability in the *Nakba* as serving the continuation and increasing normalization of the occupation. All these charges against Israel and how these national narratives function are not Chayut's alone but have long been taken up by critical scholars, public intellectuals and individual Israelis, especially those in activist circles.

The re-evaluation of nation and self is neither a simple nor a linear process for Chayut and is mirrored in the structure of the memoir itself, as if aiming to let the reader experience the author's own path. His introduction describes how, after being injured and forced to stay in one place while on a trip to India, he suddenly felt the need to write his story. Right at the beginning of the text, he pinpoints the moment his sense of self shifted: an encounter with a terrified Palestinian child. Then follow three main sections. The first depicts Chayut's education into mainstream Zionist-Israeli thinking. This section, which could be titled 'The Making of an Israeli', is interspersed with angry commentary against the system he eagerly followed all through his childhood, youth and life as a soldier. The next section is dedicated to a post-army trip hiking the Israel National Trail, a 'purification journey' (111) which offered his first human-to-human encounters with Palestinians rather than occupier-to-occupied. The last section is comprised of Chayut's own soldier's testimony and is intertwined with other BtS testimonies, explicitly raising questions concerning complicity, both collective and individual. Listening to other veterans helped him unpack his own experiences, primarily those that can be read through a moral injury lens. The inclusion of soldiers' testimonies creates a response to the first section, not least in the mode of representation. After all, we encounter much Holocaust memory in testimonial form; so using testimony in a critique of nationalized Holocaust memory strikes a chord. Giving testimony about acts Israelis committed against Palestinians in a form of memory activism creates a new, and challenging, angle to the testimonial genre, the recognizability of which plays into the anti-occupation engagement of *The Girl Who Stole My Holocaust* and of BtS.

The Girl Who Stole My Holocaust is a text with clear political intent. Driven by remorse and anger, the text forcefully aims 'to destroy, to edify [and] to demonstrate' the reality Chayut wants to change.[15] Following Satre's argument that, as a means of communicating, every text functions as an appeal, Chayut's text can be understood as an appeal to activism. Like placards and speeches at a protest, *The Girl Who Stole My Holocaust* shows little interest in complexities, and is driven by absolute convictions and moral clarity. Its publication – much like BtS's dissemination of veterans' testimonies – demonstrates hope that sharing a personal experience can influence readers' hearts and minds. In its original Hebrew, *The Girl Who Stole My Holocaust* became part of internal Israeli conversations. With its translation into English, it aims to influence an international conversation, thus mirroring the political intentions of members of BtS or other Israeli activist organizations going on international speaking tours. Like other memory activists, Chayut believes that challenging the silence around the treatment of Palestinians – past and present – while challenging the sacrosanct position of the IDF and, in his case particularly, exposing the political exploitation of Holocaust memory will benefit, not damage Israel.

Challenging the system through telling a personal story

Chayut mounts a challenge against the entire Zionist belief system, which he subsumes under the term 'my Holocaust'. His main reckoning, however, is with Israeli Holocaust memory, which he depicts as the soil on which his socialization grew. Much research has been done on the role of the Holocaust in Israeli memory and political culture, pointing to the centrality of the genocide to Israeli national identity.[16] Holocaust memory shapes Israeli lives from early on, and is a topic in all levels of Israeli education.[17] In a 2016 Pew Research Center study on the state of Israeli Jewry, 65 per cent of the respondents saw 'remembering the Holocaust' as essential to Jewish identity and more important than any of the other proffered options.[18]

When it comes to political aspects of Israeli Holocaust memory, a particularistic Zionist ethos is often positioned against a universalistic one, a consideration helpful to understand Chayut's case. Uri Ram, for instance, argues that Israel has nationalized Holocaust memory for political purposes, while universal lessons have been ignored.[19] Yaacov Yadgar further differentiates between a universalistic 'peace narrative' and a particularistic 'Jewish narrative', which essentially tells 'a story of Jewish isolation in a hostile world'.[20] This 'us–them' structure culminated in the Holocaust and '[t]herefore, "we" should accept this harsh reality as fact, unite, gain internal strength, and be ready to protect our nation's well-being. As Jews, the narrative tells us, we are eternally bound to fight for our very existence'.[21] Similarly, Esther Benbassa shows how suffering has long functioned as the basis of Jewish identity, crystallized in a 'lachrymose' conception of history from the nineteenth century onwards. She argues that Jewish victimhood as the basis for identity claims today goes hand in hand with the 'direct link forged between the state of Israel and the genocide on both the moral and the political level'.[22] Indeed, 'the obligation to remember was conflated with the defence of Israel at whatever price and in any and all circumstances'.[23] Crucially, the criticism of nationalized Holocaust memory does not disregard the fact that individual Israelis and Israel as a nation suffer from the traumatic past. In the collective case, the Holocaust constitutes a cultural trauma, which influences the community's view of present conflicts and dangers.[24] Raya Morag has coined the useful term of the 'persecuted perpetrator' to depict the complexity of the national identity shaping processes between a security narrative, cultural trauma and a history of persecution interpreted as part of the contemporary political situation of being an occupying power.[25]

Chayut, however, does not engage with such complexities. For him, nationalized Holocaust memory was all-encompassing and the descriptions of being educated into it are lengthy and often emotional, drawing the reader into the experience of emotional immersiveness. Particularly *Yom Hashoah*, Holocaust Memorial Day, and its commemorative rituals, shaped Chayut into the Israeli he was to become. Holocaust memory is all affect for the child; the central emotion is a sense of pride: 'I cried with pride, as I did at all the Holocaust memorials of my childhood [. . .]. That's Holocaust Memorial Day: everyone gets serious, wears a deep and concentrated look and cries together, mourning the "splendor of youth and glory of courage. Do not forget, do not forgive"' (13). Already at this point, Chayut introduces the issue of heroism and with it, an overlap between Holocaust memory, narratives surrounding early statehood and a history of warfare in Israel, culminating in the implicitly taught need for fighting all present and future dangers.

Chayut's description of *Yom Hashoah* indicates another element of nationalized Holocaust memory: historical facts are not the focus. Cultural memory is shaped to serve the nation's Zionist narrative. Young Noam does not really understand what had happened in Europe but learns from 'parents and other authority figures: that the perpetrators were Nazis, were *absolute evil,* and such evil did not *make sense* the way normal people's actions did – and if there was no sense, naturally everything was possible' (18). Thus, the Holocaust stays in the realm of the inconceivable and yet it is a continuation of a longer history of Jews being '[a] nation killed and slaughtered and raped as "the whole world kept silent"' (19). In Chayut's reading, the narrative of Jewish victimhood provides what Jim Wertsch calls a 'mnemonic template', a generalized and schematic narrative element that 'can be used to generate narratives that contain concrete settings, actors, and events'.[26] The template of victimhood continues in Israel, with Chayut taught that 'everything was possible' when faced with 'absolute evil' – now in the guise of Arabs rather than Nazis.

The victimhood logic was further imparted six days after *Yom Hashoah*, on *Yom Hazikaron*, Memorial Day, the commemoration of Israel's fallen soldiers and victims of terror attacks. The two remembrance days are not only linked within the cycle of holidays that structures Israeli lives, by creating a unique and standardized collective memory incorporated into an ideological prism of a Zionist historical narrative, they also have similar rituals and atmosphere. Given their proximity, the youngster's understanding of history and national identity is shaped by the message of both: 'I wondered why I couldn't be born to another people, I imagined a perfectly normal place – just like my village, only its inhabitants were not hated or persecuted or killed or incinerated, as in films shown on Holocaust Memorial Day, or killed in Arab villages on a convoy to Gush Etzyon, lost and helpless' (19). Here, Chayut takes us to the 1947–9 period, the Civil War and then the Arab-Israeli War, the other significant element of Israeli collective memory. For him, the period was filtered through the lens of 'Convoy of 35', a group of *Haganah*[27] fighters who in January 1948 attempted to break the Arab militias' Jerusalem siege to resupply the *kibbutzim*[28] in Gush Etzyon, a group of Jewish settlements south of the city. None of them survived the battle against Arab fighters after their approach was discovered. For Chayut, the two memorial days were hard to disentangle because of their affective power: 'the tale of the Gush Etzyon convoy belongs to that other Memorial Day, naturally, not the Holocaust one. But for me, they both possess one sense-memory' (19). The difference, however, is that while those commemorated on Holocaust Memorial Day are diffuse and impersonal (Chayut only realizes the extent of his family's losses on a high-school trip to Poland), the memory of the fallen fighters is personified in one of the men of Convoy 35, Tuvya Kushnir, who was from Chayut's *moshav*. In the local memories of 1948, Kushnir was a significant figure as someone who lost his life in battle and Noam aspired to be just like this 'loyal son to my people, country, homeland and village' (21).

Possibly the most important and certainly most emotion-driven element of the 'national grooming' (41) of Jewish Israelis is the high-school trip to the former concentration camps, which Chayut takes on too. Jackie Feldman maintains that unlike regular study trips, they function as 'a civil religion pilgrimage. The main aim of this pilgrimage is to establish the foundation or roots of the state of Israel in the Shoah'.[29] The camp visit and return home are a re-enactment of the survivors' journey: survival and *aliyah*, immigration to Mandatory Palestine/Israel. Feldman shows how in this narrative 'Israel serves as an answer, an antithesis' to Jewish victimization and provides a teleological historical narrative for the students about to enter their military service.³⁰

For Chayut, the narratives worked particularly well in the European setting, as he 'began to sense belonging, self-love, power and pride, and the desire to contribute, to live and be strong, so strong that no one would ever try to hurt me' (44). Here, as throughout his upbringing, particularistic messages of victimhood are translated into Zionist themes of security and self-defence, but now the personal joins collective experience. During a remembrance ceremony, Chayut reads out a long list of family members who perished and for the first time in his life balancing diffuse collective memory with historical knowledge about victims he is related to, he is overcome by emotion. His sadness, however, is quickly transformed back into the known space of the collective, where he holds on to national pride as well as 'sweet revenge. I drew power from my Holocaust and this power pushed me on, to want to enlist and serve in a select recon unit' (46), making the Poland trip fuel for his belief in Israel's military strength and the IDF.

At this prominent point in Chayut's life story, where he moves from being moulded by an all-encompassing narrative to seemingly choosing his path of serving his country as a combat soldier, he describes his brain as 'washed with a single dogmatic truth' (50) concerning the necessity and righteousness of the army. Unsurprisingly, BtS, the organization challenging such thinking is first mentioned in this context. Also unsurprisingly, the cathartic moment that ultimately leads to his break with ideology and collective memory culture, is soon revealed; the following chapter portrays the encounter with the titular 'Holocaust Thief'. To set the scene, Chayut describes his initial period of serving in the West Bank, when the reality he encountered still fused with taught narratives. Since these are built on particularistic Holocaust memory, the frame of interpretation is one in which any Israeli choice, including the occupation, is honourable and driven by security concerns. The Palestinians, by contrast, are perpetrators – or at least potential perpetrators. Even in relation to questionable acts, such as ignoring Palestinians' land deeds when their land is taken over for military use or future settlements, he quelled his doubts with his long-taught beliefs about who is right and who is wrong: 'After all, we are no Arabs' (54). Here, Chayut points once again to the power of national narratives and how these function within a group's self-understanding. Dan Bar-Tal and Eran Halperin speak of a 'socio-psychological infrastructure' of cognitive-structural, motivational and emotional factors that 'contribute to the rigid structure of the societal beliefs of the ethos of conflict and collective memory'.³¹ Such a socio-psychological infrastructure ensured that Chayut and his fellow soldiers believed themselves in the right.

But socio-psychological infrastructures can be challenged as the research on moral injury also indicates, and Chayut pinpoints when this happened for him. It is a moment of recognition, when the soldier in full combat gear, machine gun under his arm, steps out of an army vehicle and sees a terrified child stare at him and run off:

> I don't know the name of the thief, but her image is deeply etched in my memory. [...] Her height is that of a ten-year-old and she is thin, very thin. Her shoulder blades protrude. [...] Seeing her run was a familiar sight and seemed

almost natural, so I realized very late that this child had run off with the most precious and emotional possession I had inherited from my forefathers – my Holocaust. (51)

This moment triggers Chayut's slow conversion away from particularistic Holocaust memory which had formerly allowed him to interpret the world according to an engrained mnemonic template. The national narrative is ruptured by the fear in the child's eyes:

> She took from me the belief that I was avenging my people's destruction by absolute evil, that I was fighting absolute evil. For that girl, I embodied absolute evil. Even if I was not as cruel as the absolute – Nazi – evil in the shadow of which I had grown up, I didn't have to achieve its perfection and force in order to fulfil my role in her life. No. I was merely who I was, playing the role of absolute evil in the play of her life. As soon as I realized the fact that in her eyes I myself was absolute evil, the absolute evil that had governed me until then began to disintegrate.[32]

Having grown up with only diffuse historical knowledge about the events of the Holocaust, 'absolute evil' (18) was the basis for all messages that fuelled Chayut's beliefs, including military service as an act of defence against a future Holocaust of Israeli Jews at the hands of Palestinians. But this moment recalls Levinas's insistence on the ethical importance of the face-to-face encounter for recognizing the humanity of the Other and assuming responsibility for them.[33] In such an encounter, everything begins to unravel for Chayut. In the girl's expression, he recognizes that as a soldier of an occupying army, he is not on the side of the victims and those who defend themselves: he is a perpetrator. While clarifying that this realization is no attempt to compare the Holocaust and the Occupation, Chayut draws a universal lesson from Holocaust memory: evil is situational and in this specific situation, he is the one to personify absolute evil in the life of the terrified child.

The scene undoubtedly has problematic aspects. Shira Stav shows that the girl's depiction draws on the intertext of the Jewish child with raised arms in the Warsaw ghetto, thus highlighting the 'problematic limitation of treating the Palestinian story through the prism of "our" Holocaust, as if the Palestinian catastrophe can only be understood when appropriated by the national system of images'.[34] Moreover, the gendered dynamics of this scene are troubling: images of Palestinian resistance normally depict boys and teenagers throwing stones and clashing with Israeli soldiers, as well as suicide bomber videos and their deadly aftermath. Such images of violence are prominent in Israeli and global media representations of Palestinians, curtailing an empathic opening towards them. A little girl, projecting innocence, however, can more easily feature as a victim rather than (potential) perpetrator for Chayut (and his readers).

Nevertheless, it is at this point that Chayut starts reckoning with the IDF and what James Eastwood, in his study of ethics in Israeli militarism, calls the 'moral army mythology'.[35] For Eastwood, the encounter with the Palestinian girl 'marks the moment at which Noam traverses the fundamental fantasy of militarism. The moral justification for his military participation begins to evaporate and the symbolic order of Israeli militarism loses its apparent consistency'.[36] The moment of recognition, and the sense of moral injury, interrupts the memoir, mirroring how it interrupted Chayut's army service and life, even if the effect was slow. Increasingly more uncertainty permeates his thinking as references to his changing perceptions of the situation increase in the text. It is a process that means slipping into uncertainty, and ultimately a complete shift in his sense of self: 'I lost more and more components of my previous identity, mostly based on what I no longer believed in' (163).

Before he finally turns to the work of BtS and his own and other veterans' testimonies, Chayut describes how he started to acknowledge the Palestinians' situation – both today's and the unresolved events of 1948 – as his sense of inherited victimhood recedes and sense of complicity increases. During his hike along the Israel National Trail, he meets a rough, drug-smuggling group of Bedouins who live in the 'unrecognized villages' (183) in Israel's South, and for the first time contemplates Israel's responsibility for their situation. A second encounter, with a man who lived through 1948, takes place in Gush Etzion and links up with his childhood hero, Tuvia Kushnir. From his new perspective, he can now think of Kushnir's death as *'grant[ing] nineteen more years of relative freedom to those unhappy villages'* (141, original italics).

Chayut's growing doubts extend to the events of 1947–49. He is angered by the commemorative plaques dedicated to the Zionist forces that breached the siege of Jerusalem, which he claims 'made me go to the army and commit crimes in the Occupied Territories' (115). His outburst surprises Chayut, for he still thought of Israel as 'enlightened occupiers' and of the occupation as 'moral', and had 'not yet begun to think of my actions in the military as "crimes"' (115).

Chayut begins to question his understanding of the establishment of the state and its implications for Palestinians. Stav's criticism that Chayut's representation of the Nakba in terms of the Holocaust minimizes the Palestinian tragedy by turning it into 'an internal event of Jewish history' is valid.[37] Yet *The Girl Who Stole My Holocaust* nevertheless counters the more common trend of silencing the Nakba, or at least Israeli culpability in it, through 'reflexive denials' in Israeli discourses.[38] Chayut attempts to unpack what had happened in the landscape of his childhood where national narratives that shaped him are linked to the land itself. Beyond Zionist memories of place, he had learned biblical, some Crusader and Ottoman history about the *moshav's* surroundings, but nothing about the centuries of Arab inhabitation. He starts paying attention to

> innocent explanatory texts or signposts directing one's thinking towards the one and only truth. I began rereading them, and the girl who stole my Holocaust forced me to fill in the images with new faces, truths and facts. (150)

In this refashioning of historical narratives, Chayut realizes that the nationalist history he was taught is selective and politically instrumentalized. He starts contemplating the fate of Zar'in, the razed Arab village close to his family home, about which he only knew from heroic tales told during Remembrance Day ceremonies. He wonders what happened in Zar'in when Golani Infantry Battalion 13 entered the village and cleansed its houses of their inhabitants '"because they put up heavy resistance", as the ceremony text put it' (156). He counters the versions he has read about, in which 'the *Palmah* commandoes carried out their secret missions while carefully avoiding unnecessary harm to civilians' with new reflections about the human fates behind the ruins: 'where did that village disappear to? Where did all the people and animals go?' (154) Bringing the Nakba together with his IDF-service, he recognizes that the refugee problem and the occupation are linked: 'I met their children and grandchildren face-to-face in the refugee camps' (158).

The inner workings of the IDF are increasingly thematized, intensifying Chayut's personal struggle. Initially he discusses the 'mistakes' soldiers make, such as when Chayut's unit crushed a pristine old-timer VW beetle with their tank because stone-throwing distracted the driver. They are not reprimanded for the destruction of Palestinian property, and instead the commander jokes that they 'did a nice job on some collectors' item' and that 'Accidents happen' (88). At first, such incidents left Chayut uncomfortable but only when left 'without my feeling of absolute righteousness' (88) did he understand his complicity in what he describes as a pervasive system of impunity. Chayut pinpoints the use of language as an important factor in this system, and gives the example of a commander referring to Arab villagers as a 'malignant cancer', allowing the soldiers to conclude that 'they should be treated like cancer' (141). On the one hand, this sort of implicit order meant that 'no one would back us up when it became known that we had humiliated or harassed them, for that was not what we had been ordered to do – saying "we just said cancer"' (141). On the other hand, Chayut maintains that upholding a military occupation of a civil population is impossible without going beyond the explicit orders he was given. Such acts, however, remain unspoken within the IDF, from small misdeeds all the way to killings, as Chayut later finds out when collecting testimonies for BtS (223). He identifies an unspoken agreement of keeping silent, since 'whoever talks might possibly incriminate himself, and even if not, he might be held accountable for lethal, unbearable complicity' (183). Extending the situation of systematic silencing, Chayut was asked to lie on behalf of the army after he stopped serving (226). Throughout his process of change, he recognized the widespread complicity, but he did nothing about it nor did he betray this system until joining BtS.

Finally, during a three-week stint in Hebron, the cognitive dissonance between reality and taught reality overwhelmed Chayut, who then felt the need to 'tell the nation what was happening [. . .]. I had no doubt that if sane people in this country only knew what went on in Hebron, public opinion would not allow it to continue' (169). BtS is primarily invested in Hebron, and what he felt in that city brought Chayut together with the memory activists about to found the organization. In BtS, once Chayut became active in collecting testimonies of fellow veterans, he comprehended the inevitable complicity of soldiers within a larger, unquestioned structure upheld by the national narratives, and the emotional consequences of this complicity. To his surprise and admiration, some testimonies differed from the majority of veterans who tended to blame others, mostly settlers, for their own acts – as Chayut himself had done. Those accounts were 'deeper, not merely dry descriptions of unpleasant sights, but stories dealing with feelings and emotions, admitting personal responsibility, engaging in self-reflection' (173). He also found that people engaged in anti-occupation activism tended to 'accompany their testimony – bitterly or ironically delivered – with explicit feelings of repentance and shame' (181). This recognition reinforces the argument that moral injury and political activism are or can be linked. Hearing so much, especially from people discussing their complicity and guilt, made Chayut's identity shift unstoppable: 'My own process of shedding my previous self was now leaping from one testimony to the next' (192).

Chayut's memoir, documenting his loss of a particularistic Holocaust memory as well as his belief in a moral IDF, offers insight into how breaking out of an ideological corset and speaking out is necessarily linked to a change in (national) identity: 'I was among the brainwashed who committed crimes in the Occupied Territories, and the quiet struggle over public opinion that BtS is conducting is also a kind of penance for me' (210). Eastwood unpacks Chayut's tendency towards self-punishment and highlights that the original Hebrew for 'penance' is '*kaparot avanot*... atoning for his sins', a direct reference to Yom Kippur, the day of atonement.[39] When asked to elaborate on his use of '*kaparot avanot*', Chayut responded:

> In a different political situation it would mean jail for years. For the violence that I carried out, for the crimes that we carried out. Now, like British soldiers nowadays, like American soldiers nowadays, like strong societies, we don't pay for our violence [...] I do feel that the only way I can try to pay for what we did, for what I did [...] is by letting people know what we did, which are crimes, and I really believe people should pay for them and be responsible for them.[40]

Coda

In late 2021, BtS and its memory activism reached a much wider audience by way of the international award-winning documentary *Mission: Hebron* by director Rona Segal, a filmmaker who used the filmmaking skills taught in the army to create this haunting film. Segal skilfully combined veterans' testimonies and filmed snippets of soldier–settler–Palestinian interactions in Hebron to illustrate the topics they talk about. The documentary is currently streamed by the *New York Times*, exemplifying that discussions around the IDF's role in the OPT, the question of some veterans' guilt and sense of complicity and their need to campaign against the occupation have moved into the global sphere. The international perception of Israel/Palestine, also defined by contested narratives, biases and political position taking, highlights an important aspect in the discussion of compromised identities and complicity: the question is whether the situation causing them is in the past or still ongoing. The fact that the military occupation of Palestinian Territories is unresolved, and its interpretation hotly debated, turns Chayut's memoir and the work of other Israeli memory activists into a political act, challenging historiographies that have decided who the perpetrator and victim are.

The occupation will continue to cause moral injury to soldiers, not least because conflicts necessarily involve narratives meant to boost morale and convince soldiers that they are doing the right thing. However, if a soldier decides to speak about his service in a way that opposes the narrative, doing so becomes an act of activism. BtS has made this their mission and Chayut gives the internal struggle an activist literary form. The extent to which he describes his own struggle, sense of guilt and betrayal allows readers to follow and potentially identify with his thoughts and emotions, bringing an important dimension to memory activism.

Notes

1. Yifat Gutman, *Memory Activism: Reimagining the Past for the Future of Israel-Palestine* (Nashville: Vanderbilt University Press, 2017), 1–2.
2. Like other statistics concerning the Nakba, also the numbers of deaths are contested. The wide range accommodates such historical debates. See Motti Golani and Adel Manna, *Two Sides of the Coin: Independence and Nakba 1948 – Two Narratives of the 1948 War and its Outcome* (Dordrecht: Institute for Historical Justice and Reconciliation, 2011), 138.
3. See: Efraim Karsh, *Palestine Betrayed* (New Haven: Yale University Press, 2010); Nur Masalha, *Expulsion of the Palestinians: The Concept of 'Transfer' in Zionist Political Thought, 1882–1948* (Washington: Institute for Palestine Studies, 1992); Benny Morris, *The Birth of the Palestinian Refugee Problem, 1947–1949* (Cambridge: Cambridge University Press, 1988); Anita Shapira, *Land and Power: The Zionist Resort to Force, 1881–1948*, trans. W. Templer (Oxford: Oxford University Press, 1992); Avi Shlaim, *The Iron Wall: Israel and the Arab World* (New York: W.W. Norton 2000).
4. Cf. Erella Grassiani, 'The Phenomenon of *Breaking the Silence* in Israel: "Witnessing" as Consciousness Raising Strategy of Israeli Ex-combatants', in *The Moral Dimension of Asymmetrical Warfare: Counter-Terrorism, Democratic Values and Military Ethics*, ed. Ted van Baarda and Désirée Verweij (Leiden: Koninklijke Brill, 2009), 247–59; Tamar Katriel and Nimrod Shavit, 'Between Moral Activism and Archival Memory: The Testimonial Project of "Breaking the Silence"', in *On Media Memory: Collective Memory in the New Media Age*, ed. Motti Neiger, Oren Meyers and Eyal Zandberg (Houndsmills: Palgrave, 2011), 77–86; Ruthie Pliskin et al., 'Speaking Out and Breaking the Silence', in *Self-censorship in Contexts of Conflict: Theory and Research*, ed. Daniel Bar-Tal, Rafi Nets-Zehngut, Keren Sharvit (Cham: Springer, 2017), 243–68.
5. Breaking the Silence, 'Who we are and What we Envision', https://www.breakingthesilence.org.il/about/qa (Accessed 1 May 2022).
6. The publications cover the 2009 and 2014 Gaza operations; one contains testimonies of female soldiers and the 2011 booklet details memories of service in the West Bank between 2000 and 2010. Originally in Hebrew, translations were also published in the U.S. and Germany in 2012.
7. Cf. Aviya Ashwal-Malka et al., 'Moral Injury and Cannabis Use Disorder among Israeli Combat Veterans: The Role of Depression and Perceived Social Support', *Addictive Behaviours* 124, no. 1–2 (2022): 107–14; Uri Hertz et al., 'To Shoot or Not to Shoot: Experiments on Moral Injury in the Context of West Bank Checkpoints and Covid-19 Restrictions Enforcement', *European Journal of Psychotraumatology* 13, no.1 (2022). doi:10.1080/20008198.2021.2013651; Yossi Levi-Belz et al., 'Moral Injury and Suicide Ideation among Combat Veterans: The Moderating Role of Self-Disclosure', *Crisis: The Journal of Crisis Intervention and Suicide Prevention*, February 2022. doi:

10.1027/0227-5919/a000849; Gal Schwartz et al., 'Moral Injury and Suicide Ideation Among Combat Veterans: The Role of Trauma-Related Shame and Collective Hatred', *Journal of Interpersonal Violence*, April 2021. doi:10.1177/08862605211007932.
8. Lynd and Lynd count BtS among those Israelis where they see moral injury leading to nonviolent resistance. See Alice and Staughton Lynd, *Moral Injury and Nonviolent Resistance: Breaking the Cycle of Violence in the Military and Behind Bars* (Oakland: PM Press, 2017), 100–1.
9. Joshua Leifer, 'You are All Traitors'. https://www.972mag.com/you-are-all-traitors-the-political-persecution-of-breaking-the-silence/ (Accessed 1 May 2022); Raphael Ahren and Jacob Magid, *Stop "inciting" against Soldiers, Breaking the Silence Spokesman's Mother Urges*. https://www.timesofisrael.com/stop-inciting-mom-of-breaking-the-silence-spokesman-urges/ (Accessed 1 May 2022).
10. Cf. Nitzan Perelman, 'The Development of the Israeli Discourse on Breaking the Silence: When the Sons of the People Become the Enemy of the People', *Confluences Mediterranee* 118, no. 3 (2021): 149–64. Internationally, probably the most problematic diplomatic issue was that in 2017, then Israeli PM Benjamin Netanyahu cancelled a meeting with then German FM Sigmar Gabriel because he had met with members of BtS.
11. George Orwell, 'Why I Write', *Gangrel*, no. 4 (1946). Reprinted in *The Complete Works of George Orwell, Volume 18: Smothered Under Journalism 1946* (London: Secker and Warburg, 2001), 318.
12. Noam Chayut, *The Girl Who Stole My Holocaust*, trans. T. Haran (New York: Verso, 2013), 210. Originally published in Hebrew: *Ganevet ha-shoah sheli* (Tel Aviv: Am Oved, 2010). Page numbers when given in parentheses in the main text are to this book.
13. See the Introduction to this volume, 4.
14. The term 'enlightened occupation' came into use soon after the 1967 War. See Aharon Bregman, *Cursed Victory: A History of Israel and the Occupied Territories* (London: Penguin, 2014), ccvi. Its use is common and often ridiculed by the left.
15. Jean Paul Sartre, *What Is Literature?* (London: Methuen & Co. Ltd, 1950), 13.
16. Cf. Ian Lustick, 'The Holocaust in Israeli Political Culture: Four Constructions and Their Consequences', *Contemporary Jewry* 37, no. 1 (2017): 125–70; Tom Segev, *The Seventh Million: The Israelis and the Holocaust* (New York: Owl Books, 2000); Hanna Yablonka, *Survivors of the Holocaust: Israel after the War* (New York: New York University Press, 1999); Idit Zertal, *Israel's Holocaust and the Politics of Nationhood* (Cambridge: Cambridge University Press, 2005).
17. Since 2014, the national curriculum already covers the genocide in kindergarten.
18. Pew Research Center, Most Israeli Jews say remembering the Holocaust is essential to being Jewish, www.pewforum.org/2016/03/08/identity/pf_2016-03-08_israel-04-10/ (Accessed 1 May 2022).
19. Uri Ram, 'The Future of the Past in Israel: A Sociology of Knowledge Approach', in *Making Israel*, ed. Benny Morris (Ann Arbor: University of Michigan Press, 2007), 211.
20. Yaacov Yadgar, 'From Particularistic to the Universalistic: National Narratives in Israel's Mainstream Press, 1967–1997', *Nations and Nationalism* 8, no.1 (2002): 62.
21. Ibid.
22. Esther Benbassa, *Suffering as Identity: The Jewish Paradigm*, trans. G. M. Goshgorian (London: Verso, 2010), 127.
23. Ibid.

24 Ron Eyerman, *Cultural Trauma and the Formation of African American Identity* (Cambridge: Cambridge University Press, 2004), 2.
25 Raya Morag, *Waltzing with Bashir: Perpetrator Trauma and Cinema* (London: I.B. Tauris), 27–32.
26 James Wertsch, 'A Clash of Deep Memories', *Profession* 8, no.1 (2008): 49.
27 The underground army of the *Yishuv* (the pre-state Jewish community in Mandatory Palestine).
28 Plural of *kibbutz*, the collective Israeli communities, traditionally based on agricultural work.
29 Jackie Feldman, 'In the Footsteps of the Israeli Holocaust Survivor: Israeli Youth Pilgrimage to Poland, Shoah Memory, and National Identity', in *Building History: The Shoah in Art, Memory, and Myth*, ed. Peter M. Daly et al. (New York: Peter Lang, 2001), 53.
30 Ibid.
31 Daniel Bar-Tal and Eran Halperin, 'The Nature of Socio-Psychological Barriers to Peaceful Conflict Resolution and Ways to Overcome Them', *Conflict and Communication online* 12, no. 2 (2013): 5.
32 Chayut, *The Girl Who Stole My Holocaust*, 63. This and similar sections have been read as an 'Israelis are Nazis' simile (cf. Liat Steir-Livny, 'From Victims to Perpetrators: Cultural Representations of the Link between the Holocaust and the Israeli-Palestinian Conflict', *Interactions: Studies in Communication & Culture* 7, no. 2 (2016): 133) and while this problematic comparison might influence Chayut's discussion, it is not central to his interpretation of nationalized Holocaust in creating an 'uncompromised' Israeliness.
33 Emmanuel Levinas, *Ethics and Infinity: Conversations with Philippe Nemo*, trans. R. A. Cohen (Pittsburgh: Duquesne University Press, 1985).
34 Shira Stav, 'Nakba and Holocaust: Mechanisms of Comparison and Denial in the Israeli Literary Imagination', *Jewish Social Studies: History, Culture, Society* 18, no. 3 (2004): 94.
35 James Eastwood, *Ethics as a Weapon of War: Militarism and Morality in Israel* (Cambridge: Cambridge University Press, 2018), 4ff.
36 Ibid., 182.
37 Stav, 'Nakba and Holocaust', 89.
38 Alon Confino, 'Miracles and Snow in Palestine and Israel: Tantura, a History of 1948', *Israel Studies* 17, no. 2 (2012): 39.
39 Eastwood, *Ethics as a Weapon of War*, 183.
40 Ibid.

Part III

Law, complicity and perpetration

10

The constitutive role of Nazi law

Constructing complicity in the Third Reich

Simon Lavis

Adolf Hitler was contemptuous of liberal legality and disdainful of lawyers.[1] Yet he famously resolved to obtain power by (largely) constitutional means[2] and sought to use the form of law to implement Nazi policies when in power.[3] Unsurprisingly, perhaps, given this approach to law, the prevalent Anglo-American academic interpretation of Nazi law has been to view it as the cynical manipulation of the residue of the legal form for instrumental ends; to use the legitimacy of the *Rechtsstaat* to reinforce support and assuage the concerns of sections of the elites and public on the road to power; and to consolidate power and implement policies through using the force of law to repress opposition.[4] Notwithstanding their prolific use of law, this interpretation is associated with the claim that Nazi 'law' was not actually law, that 'Nazis did not write and enforce laws. Nazis plotted and committed crimes'.[5] What the Nazis called law was a system of unlawfulness, barbarity: a state of non-law. While this interpretation has now been challenged on a number of fronts, a strong current of this paradigm endures, particularly when it comes to explaining the role of law in the Holocaust.

In addition to this, the focus of academic attention has generally been on persecutory criminal laws – initially against Jews but also social outsiders, 'gypsies', homosexuals and other groups. This is apparent from the fact that a large proportion of book publications representing the recent increase in interest in the legal history of the Third Reich have been principally in this area.[6] Less attention has been paid to the role of other areas, beyond the founding laws of the regime (the Reichstag Fire Decree, Enabling Act, etc.) and persecutory criminal laws, even though, as Michael Stolleis has claimed, 'Neither the frequently cited land register law, nor the social security or tax laws, nor the law concerning debts, property, family, and inheritance was in any way immune'.[7] Therefore, while the use of individual laws prior to the Holocaust to persecute those considered undesirable by the Nazi leadership has been examined, the concomitant use of law, legality and legal institutions to contribute to fostering a National Socialist identity and implicate German society in Nazi violence is less studied, notwithstanding the growth of a considerable body of 'consent' literature in Nazi historiography.[8]

Finally, there has been a separation, and often opposition, between law and violence in writing about Nazi Germany. While both the ostensibly legal and extra-legal elements of Nazi rule, and the contribution of both of these to the regime, have been studied, these, and the institutions related to them, have generally been regarded as separate and the use of law and violence as two unrelated things. This has started to be challenged in some aspects of Nazi historiography in recent years, with greater understanding and analysis of the complex interrelationships between, for example, the SS (extra-legal) and 'ordinary' judicial system (legal).[9] The opposition of law and violence, if not the complete separation of institutions of state, remains. Extra-legal violence is seen as degrading and destroying the law, and the extreme violence of the Holocaust in particular as happening entirely outside of the law. This relationship, however, can be viewed as mutually supportive; two sides of the same coin of Nazi rule, supporting and reinforcing one another, including in relation to the perpetration of the Holocaust.

These three long-term tendencies in the academic literature – the treatment of Nazi law as both instrumental and non-law, the relative lack of focus on broader aspects of the legal system and the opposition and separation of the legal and extra-legal – leave little room for examination and understanding of the compromised identities that were inevitably at play in those involved in different ways in the implementation of Nazi genocidal policies, specifically in respect of the role of law. There is a persuasive view in the Nazi perpetrator literature that those at the extreme ends of perpetration actively evaded killing or refused to kill and that eager killers were in the minority, even among those tasked with the actual killing.[10] This leaves a large number of primary perpetrators who played a direct role in genocide despite not being 'eager killers', and secondary perpetrators who were otherwise complicit in the Holocaust in a range of ways, but indirectly. This chapter argues that law has a part to play in understanding the normative atmosphere within which mass persecution and extermination was tolerated and carried out by many who would otherwise be reluctant to do so.

Ideology is an important part of this. Among the 'significant minority' that Christopher Browning describes as 'eager killers', it is notable that 'some were transformed by the situation in which they found themselves. But many were ideologically motivated men ready to kill Jews and other so-called enemies of the Reich from the start'.[11] The treatment of Nazi law as non-law or, at best, the instrumentalization of the legal form, neglects the important influence of Nazi ideology on and in the law, which again, it is argued, helped to create societal norms according to which significant numbers of people, albeit a minority, became 'eager killers'. More pertinently to the issue of compromised identities, this influence contributed to the normative atmosphere that enabled very large numbers of people to contribute directly and indirectly to the Holocaust while not compromising their identities completely.

There is now a much greater appreciation of the degree of knowledge and involvement of many elements of Nazi society in the actions of the Nazi state, as bystanders and indirect perpetrators as well as direct perpetrators. As Mary Fulbrook states:

Whatever terms we adopt to describe people's behaviour at the time or later, some things are quite clear. Few who lived through this period could avoid being involved, at some point, on one side or another—sometimes also crossing sides, in complex, ambivalent, and distressing ways, moving from being a committed Nazi to a member of a resistance group, from a victim to a collaborator, from a doubter to a murderer, and from an upright citizen to a shriveled outcast.[12]

This paints a complex and nuanced picture of complicity, both in terms of the extent of those involved and the fluid categories to which they can be assigned. In this context, it is very difficult to understand how the Holocaust could come about without tackling the facets of Nazi society that contributed to such widespread and ambivalent participation by otherwise 'ordinary' Germans. The legal system, this chapter claims, is one of those facets.

This chapter explores how Nazi law and legal institutions helped to construct the atmosphere of ideological consensus within which individually abhorrent and otherwise inexplicable decisions were taken. In addressing the constitutive aspect of the Nazi legal system, this chapter aims to bring the insights of the 'voluntarist turn'[13] in Nazi historiography together with a theoretical understanding of Nazi law that goes beyond its interpretation as 'legal terror' and a concern with whether or not it ought to be considered as valid law. To develop its argument it will make a number of related points: (i) that the dominant academic understanding of the Nazi legal system guards against its ideological role being fully explored, and therefore its influence on normative decision-making by perpetrators; (ii) that part of acknowledging law's own historical complicity with the Nazi project involves accepting its constitutive role in the Holocaust; and (iii) that legal norms did operate to help construct the normative environment within which people acted in the Third Reich. This is in line with Louis Althusser's general claim that law belongs to both what he terms the ideological state apparatus (ISA) and the repressive state apparatus (RSA),[14] and so has a dual repressive and educative function within society. Consequently, it is argued that law inevitably had a substantial role in constructing complicity in the Holocaust and that it is important as researchers to uncover this role in order to understand the relationship between law and violence, past and present.

To advance these claims the next section of this chapter will consider the status and development of academic legal and historical writing about Nazi law to further elucidate the gap in this area in the current literature and the importance of addressing it. The subsequent section will then explore how Nazi laws could be capable of guiding the conduct of those subject to it and, with reference to some related philosophical research,[15] begin to elaborate the extent to which Nazi legal norms did contribute to the complicit conduct of those in the Third Reich.

Law and/in the Third Reich

Until recent years, the Nazi legal system received little dedicated attention from legal and historical scholars of the Third Reich, particularly in the English-speaking world.

While some legal theorists, notably Frederick DeCoste and David Fraser,[16] have been instrumental in highlighting this neglect and addressing the role and nature of Nazi law, mainstream academic discourse about law in relation to the Holocaust predominantly focused on its use in post-war Nazi war crimes trials, and the contribution of the passage of specific laws to the development of the Nazi state and its discriminatory policies (e.g., the role of the Reichstag Fire Decree and the Enabling Act in the consolidation of Nazi power, or of the Nuremberg Laws in the development of anti-Jewish measures). Writing about legal officials in Nazi Germany, as with other types of Nazi officials, tended to focus on the extent to which they attempted to justify their involvement in the Third Rich and were often permitted to reintegrate into post-war German society. In particular, while much was written about law's response to the Holocaust, particularly the Nuremberg International Military Tribunal, little was written about law's direct contribution to the Holocaust, not least because the perpetration of the Holocaust has often been considered to have fundamentally taken place outside of the 'ordinary' legal system, in the extra-legal sphere.

In the first decade of the twenty-first century, scholarly outputs about law in Nazi war crimes trials grew substantially.[17] While many of these, particularly historical accounts, were valuable in focusing on previously under-examined trials or aspects of trials, others sought to cement the status of the Nuremberg IMT as the foundation stone of modern international criminal law, and collectively they reinforced the concentration of academic research on law's response to the Holocaust, rather than law's contribution to it. The last decade, however, has seen a marked increase in volumes either initially published in English or translated into English, dedicated to Nazi law itself, in different ways and across different sub-fields of legal theory and legal history, and including some taking comparative or longer views on the subject.[18] Some of these works have recognized the dominant discursive construction of Nazi law to this point. For example, Thomas Vormbaum has identified that '[t]he agreed-on version in general historiography seems to be: the twelve years of National Socialist rule are twelve dark years that represent a rupture in German history',[19] while Alan Steinweis and Robert Rachlin commented that some readers might 'understand the Nazi regime as a tyranny, characterized by arbitrary rule, enforced through intimidation and terror. The hallmark of Nazi society, as they understand it, was not law, but lawlessness'.[20]

This material also highlights the ongoing reliance in the historical literature on Ernst Fraenkel's dual-state analysis of the Third Reich and its legal system,[21] which continues to be very influential, both for better and worse. While, as Jens Meierhenrich has recently shown,[22] a nuanced examination and application of Fraenkel's model can be fruitful for the understanding of Nazi law and beyond, some uses of the dual-state model are not unproblematic, particularly when an artificial separation between the normative and prerogative states comprising Fraenkel's two systems within the model is constructed. Nikolaus Wachsmann, for example, has identified concerns with the way the dual state has been used to explain the Nazi legal system, arguing that a 'problem with this interpretation of the Dual State is the portrayal of the legal system and the police as two entirely separate entities with opposing agendas, engaged in permanent battle. [. . .] Ultimately they pursued one and the same goal: the fight against "community aliens" in the Third Reich'.[23] This emphasizes the degree to which the historical evidence from the prison system suggests we should not treat the two spheres as distinct and conflictual.

Michael Stolleis makes a related claim about Nazi law with reference to the impact on the residual normative state of the racialized prerogative state, that 'it is a myth that some areas remained entirely untouched by the political claims of the system'.[24] In the first quotation, Wachsmann is concerned about whether the normative state can really be considered normative, in the sense of a continuation of the pre-existing *Rechtsstaat* based on legal norms. As much of a question, however, is how much the prerogative state can actually be considered as extra-legal. This prevalent interpretation of Nazi law can be traced back to Franz Neumann's claim about the unlawfulness of the Nazi legal system,[25] as well as the construction of Nazi law at the Nuremberg trials (itself influenced by Neumann's work),[26] particularly the IMT *Justice case* and, for Anglo-American legal theory, the 1958 Hart-Fuller debate.[27] Unlike Neumann's 'Behemoth' state, Fraenkel's dual state sited both the normative and prerogative states within the broader Nazi legal system, entailing that they both constitute 'law' in some form. This raises the possibility of using it as a framework for discussion of the normative role of law in the decision-making of complicit subjects during the Holocaust, the key elements of which are typically considered to come within the prerogative state.

The issue of whether the prerogative state, or indeed the system as a whole in Nazi Germany, can be considered valid as law has remained the central preoccupation of Anglo-American jurisprudential discussion of the Third Reich, in debates increasingly abstracted from the history under discussion. As Fraser notes, 'much jurisprudential energy has been, and continues to be, wasted by invoking the "what is law?" question'.[28] He goes on to say, '[t]hese debates proliferate, but their utility for historical inquiry and understanding is problematic'.[29] In light of this, one final aspect of the academic discourse around Nazi law to call attention to is the post-war shift away from legal positivism in some areas initiated by Gustav Radbruch's thesis on statutory injustice.[30] This was taken to claim that in extreme cases of injustice the positive law could be invalidated in order to protect justice – the so-called 'Radbruch formula'[31] – because, it was felt, the stringent loyalty to positivism and formalism in the German legal profession was to blame for legal officials blindly following Nazi laws, despite their obvious immorality. The idea of positivism being responsible for legal officials following Nazi laws has since been strongly challenged,[32] and the open-textured and anti-positivistic nature of Nazi law and legal ideology is apparent. Nevertheless, the idea endured as a paradigm of Nazi law and further fuelled academic debates about whether and how Nazi law can be considered law.

The direction and development of academic writing about Nazi law among historians and lawyers has, it can be seen, steered away from a systemic discussion about its constitutive role in the advancement of Nazi ideology and policies and towards its treatment as a repressive instrument of terror because it has been shaped by certain events (primarily the Nuremberg Trials) and debates (primarily around the validity question). The treatment of Nazi law as 'non-law' on a systemic level guarded against the emergence of an English-language legal history of the Third Reich. It largely excluded attempts to explain Nazi law through an ideological lens – because it was precisely irrational Nazi ideology that invalidated its legality – and means there are very few attempts to examine the history of the Holocaust specifically from a legal perspective.[33] This chapter seeks to move beyond a univocal view of Nazi 'law' as a repressive instrument of terror and overcome the temptation to become embroiled in the 'validity question' while addressing the nature of the Nazi legal system as a whole: first by accepting generally that it is 'law' and specifically that the decrees, rules, norms, orders and directives of the Holocaust can also be treated as law in a broad sense; and second by grounding the discussion in the history of the Third Reich.

Law, ideology and complicity in the Nazi state

Referring to the voluntarist turn in Nazi historiography, Dan Stone asserts:

> what recent scholarship has shown is, first, that the institutions that were 'murderous' were more numerous than historians have long thought, and second, that even if not outright conspiracy theorists, most Germans during the Hitler years subscribed more or less willingly to the dictates of the regime, that is, allowed themselves to be *gleichgeschaltet* ('co-ordinated').[34]

In applying the voluntarist turn to Nazi law, it is the role of law in the decision-making of those complicit in (and coordinated by) the Nazi state who were not 'outright conspiracy theorists' that is the concern here. Stone elsewhere states that '[t]he "return of ideology" to the historiography of the Third Reich and the Holocaust is most visible in the sphere of Nazi racism and the way in which Nazism sought to racialize the everyday lives of the Germans, both those who were part of the *Volksgemeinschaft* and those who were excluded from it'.[35] Similarly, while it has long been the perception that Nazi racialization of life, particularly in relation to the Holocaust, was done in such a way as to take it outside of the legal realm, it is this very racialization of Germans who were part of the national community through the law that is of interest and has great explanatory power in terms of understanding the compromised identities of direct perpetrators and others indirectly complicit in the Holocaust.

The question of whether Nazi laws helped to guide the actions of those complicit in Nazi racial policies and programmes needs to be approached from (at least) two points of entry. First, whether the laws passed by the Nazi regime were capable of contributing to the racialization of the everyday lives and decisions of the population, beyond creating obligations, the compliance with which was secured by force; and second, whether and how laws acted on the minds of those subjected to the laws. On the first point, there have been some recent examples of research that recognizes the ideological content of Nazi law, its consistency at least in terms of alignment with broader Nazi ideological aims and its potential for constituting what could be seen by some people as a system of 'good' (or at least legitimate) law, which is instructive in terms of applying the voluntarist turn in this area.

Harry Reicher, for example, has made the claim that 'the extent to which there was actually an internal logic to the legal system implemented by the Nazi regime is striking. There was an underlying ideology at the heart, driving the regime'.[36] The infusion of Nazi law with the moral standards of the regime is supported by Herlinde Pauer-Studer's research, which refers to the Nazi ideal that 'ethical principles should be embedded in law'.[37] Carolyn Benson and Julian Fink have gone further to summarize the ideological aim of Nazi law: 'the primary Nazi standard of "good law" was taken to be the advancement, purification and collective properties thought to be essential to the flourishing of the German "Blood-community" (*Blutsgemeinschaft*)'.[38] The regime was engaged in 'reversing liberal principles',[39] and Benson and Fink have also identified four legal developments that they consider encapsulate the departure of Nazi law from the rule of law:

(i) the establishment under Nazi rule of a new *ultimate justificatory standard of* 'good' law;
(ii) the validation of distinctively *political* and *non-formal sources of law* (Rechtsquellen);
(iii) the degradation of the written law in favour of vague ideological standards; and
(iv) the denial of the *separation* between law and Nazi 'morality'.[40]

The recognition of these points as intrinsic to the Nazi legal system is essential to both challenging the previously dominant representation of Nazi law and understanding its role in the Holocaust. This is because a combination of these same factors may be cited as the reason that Nazi law should not be considered valid law. The rejection of the rule of law in favour of an alternative standard of good law has been a problem for natural lawyers, who have also, along with positivists, often overlooked the challenge presented by the fact that the Nazis denied law was separate from morality, rather than merely manipulating law cynically as an instrument of power.[41] Points (ii) and (iii) pose a problem for the regularity and formality of law because the commonplace use of a range of legal forms and sources, including oral decrees, and the reliance of law on often ambiguous and amorphous ideological principles were features of much of the system, and particularly the implementation of the Holocaust, which have been used to call into question its status as law.

The particularities and perversities of Nazi law and its underpinning ideology became part of a legal system accepted as legitimate, and so highlighting its failure to meet a series of formal and/or moral criteria associated with certain types of law alone fails to address the underlying issue of how law contributed to the element of consensus now undeniable in the execution of the Nazi project. As Pauer-Studer claims, the '"ethical recognition" of the Führer's orders by officials and judges was [. . .] crucial for the inner stability of the Nazi state in the pre-war years'.[42] It is vital, therefore, for understanding how law became part of the Nazi armoury – as opposed to the armour against Nazism – to examine the nature and operation of Nazi law as law, as well as to comprehend how law can and might be used in a similar way in the future.

The racial, ideological content of many laws passed under the Nazi regime is often very clear to see in the legal texts themselves, as may be illustrated with reference to a small number of examples. This intention is evident as early as 1920, in point 19 of the NSDAP 25-point Party Programme, which demanded that Roman law 'be replaced by a German common law'. Actual, post-1933 Nazi laws incorporated ideology both in terms of creating specific legal rules to ensure ideological imperatives were realized and setting laws within the context of the newly dominant moral universe of the state, and sometimes these two aspects overlapped. Examples of the former include the compulsory retiring of civil servants of 'non-aryan descent', restricting citizenship to those of 'German or kindred blood', legislating against the breaking up of hereditary farms and making the study of National Socialism part of the requirement for qualifying for public offices.[43] Examples of the latter approach may include references to the NSDAP as 'the bearer of the concept of the German state', the idea that 'the German people have attained an indestructible internal unity superior to all internal subdivisions and conflicts of a political character', being '[m]oved by the understanding that purity of German blood is the essential condition for the continued existence of the German people', justifying a law 'as a defensive measure against communist acts of violence endangering the state', and a desire to 'preserve the peasantry through the ancient German method of inheritance as the blood source of the German people' or to 'create a true national and productive community of all Germans'.[44] Examples of laws conflating the two approaches – specific rules to enforce ideological goals located within the framework of Nazi ideology – might include the dismissal of civil servants unable to 'act in the interest of the national state at all times and without reservation', or making being 'willing and able to faithfully serve the German people and Reich' a condition of citizenship.[45]

We can see from these examples that Nazi laws were not only, from the start of the takeover of power, suffused with ideological tenets and references, but also that they appear to be intended to act as a guide to behaviour for those viewed to be part of the *Volksgemeinschaft*, which goes beyond mere rule-following. For example, a criminal law prohibiting certain, specific conduct on pain of imprisonment (or worse) may just be followed because: (i) it is passed and supported by the coercive power of the state; and (ii) it contains a strong deterrent in the form of a sanction. But how should a subject of the law view the preamble to such a law, which declares the moral purpose of that law in National Socialist terms, or the content of a non-criminal law that attaches conditions around acting a certain way or studying the (nazified) history of the German nation to certain ends? Even if at first a law is accepted notwithstanding its stated, underlying purpose, or behaviour is modified instrumentally simply to adhere to a stated stipulation, it is possible for that purpose to become normative and that behaviour to become socialized, over time. It appears that Nazi laws could be capable of acting normatively on people's decision-making. The next question is to what extent they actually did.

Pauer-Studer argues that 'under conditions like the Third Reich morality becomes contested ground since moral ideas and principles are deeply involved in ideological moralising'.[46] In their 2011 article 'Distortions of Normativity',[47] Pauer-Studer and Velleman sought to analyse 'the thoroughness with which the Nazi regime transformed the conventional moral order, causing its citizens to lose their moral bearings'.[48] They argued that '[i]n order to understand the perverse application of moral standards under the Nazis, we must understand how people perceived their circumstances and how they interpreted abstract moral concepts',[49] because abstract moral principles alone are not sufficient to safeguard against corrupted morality. Rather, they 'must be given a socially relevant interpretation, and they must then be applied by agents with socially inculcated habits of moral perception'.[50] Moral standards, they claim, 'though present within every agent, cannot be applied without moral knowledge that is socially constructed and conveyed'.[51] The Nazi perpetrators they examine, however, 'mischaracterized their situations and consequently misinterpreted and misapplied the guidelines of their conventional morality'.[52] Their conclusion was consequently that 'morality became distorted in the Third Reich at the level of its social articulation'.[53]

> What concerns us is not so much the behaviour of the perpetrators at the top of the Nazi hierarchy as that of the ordinary people who were directly involved in the shooting and gassing. The reason why the latter perpetrators were not deterred by morality, in our view, is that moral principles were filtered through socially conditioned interpretations and perceptions that gave events a distorted normative significance.[54]

Three Nazi perpetrators are discussed in the article: Johann Paul Kremer, who served at Auschwitz for a period; Felix Landau, who was a member of the SS; and Karl Kretschmer, who served in a *Sonderkommando* on the eastern front.[55] Pauer-Studer and Velleman are concerned here with the inversion of moral principles in the conduct of perpetrators in the Third Reich, but already from their study, some interesting insights about the role of law in distorting normativity can be gleaned. For example, the authors make the following comment in relation to Kremer:

> Kremer's failure to comment on the criminality of the gassings cannot be attributed to fear of criticizing the regime in his diary, since he was shortly to write a polemic against the notion that there is such a thing as 'Jewish science'. He was not young and inexperienced, nor incapable of defining ideals in opposition to those around him. Finally, he never expressed any hatred or contempt toward the victims.[56]

The explanation given for this is that his professional self-understanding as a physician in a particular workplace situation overrode moral considerations. It is interesting, however, that the gassings in Auschwitz are referred to as criminal whereas they would not have been considered as such in the environment in which Kremer was operating. This explanation, convincing though it is in part, elides the possibility that the normative legal environment contributed to distorted decision-making on an individual level, even if Kremer apparently did not assimilate Nazi ideology in full.

The comment made by Pauer-Studer and Velleman about Landau is also instructive: 'Landau did not dehumanize Jews, nor does he seem to have hated them. His attitude towards Jews was simply the one that was mandated by the National Socialist state'. They quote Landau reacting to anger at his dismissal of a Jewish worker: '[t]he gentleman forgets that we have introduced the race law into the National Socialist state'.[57] Landau is also quoted as writing in his diary: 'Fine, so I'll just play executioner and then gravedigger, why not? Isn't it strange, you love battle and then have to shoot defenceless people. Twenty-three had to be shot'.[58] Ultimately, Landau's conduct is largely explained by pride in 'doing a good day's work'.⁵⁹ Landau specifically makes reference to a legal provision in these extracts and his response to it is instructive. The use of the language of obligation in the other quotation ('*have to* shoot defenceless people') is mirrored by the authors' explanation of Landau's attitude being simply 'mandated' by the state. And it might be argued that his decision to dismiss the worker is purely because that was what the law required. Yet there is a lot of possible ground between hating Jews wholeheartedly and only acting in a certain way because one is forced to. There is no sense here that Landau is fearful of the consequences of not following the law and, elsewhere, he is quoted as referring to a Wehrmacht Major as being 'the worst kind of state enemy' and being 'put into preventative detention immediately' for remarking that 'the Jews fall under the protection of the German Wehrmacht'; 'That's no National Socialist'.⁶⁰ This seems to go far beyond simply following orders in terms of compliance with the Nazi state, and the relationship between legal rules and ideological imperatives in the subject's own mind is worthy of further examination.

Finally, in fighting on the Eastern Front, Kretschmer appeared to accept 'the ideological characterization of the operation as one of racial self-defense',⁶¹ which Pauer-Studer and Velleman relate back to Nazi propaganda he would have heard. We have already seen how ideological justifications such as self-defence made their way into legal instruments and so it is not out of the question to hypothesize that socially articulated legal norms, or even ideologically infused legal orders, contributed to Kretschmer's own thinking. The authors also comment that in Kretschmer's case:

> The resulting moral inversion was not at the level of fundamental moral principles; it was brought about by an ideological re-interpretation of moral concepts such as equality, respect, and even the Aristotelian mean. These re-interpretations left Kretschmer with a normative framework that was utterly consistent, so that he could continue to view himself as a principled moral agent.⁶²

This analysis has interesting parallels to the Nazi legal system, in part because a concept such as 'equality' is both a moral and a legal one, and partly because Nazi law also co-opted and re-purposed pre-existing legal concepts and principles, re-interpreting them for Nazi means. Again here, the potential for law to contribute to a justificatory normative framework should be taken seriously as a possible contributory explanation for the conduct of perpetrators.

Conclusions

More research needs to be done in the area of the individual and social interpretation and application of Nazi legal norms, especially related to Nazi racial policy and the Holocaust, to fully explicate and understand the impact the law had on the normative decision-making of those ordinary Germans that became complicit in the Nazi project. Pauer-Studer and Velleman argue: 'Living in a normative system like the Third Reich, perverted as it was, offered individuals the resources to see themselves as principled'.⁶³ That is, such a system offered people the means to ignore the fact that their identities as good people had the potential to be compromised by the acts they were carrying out and their consequences. The thesis this chapter has sought to begin to develop is that law was one of those resources. It has also aimed to set out why the constitutive role of law in Nazism is an important issue to explore for both legal and historical academics alike, with reference to the dominant narratives and pre-existing literature that has tended to eschew such questions. In a moment when Anglo-American academic interest in Nazi law has increased markedly and the voluntarist turn in Nazi historiography has not yet passed, the time is ripe for these issues to be tackled. Two decades ago Dan Stone wrote 'in order to think through Nazism, we must recognize an inevitable complicity with it',[64] something that much of the legal academy continues to shy away from. The remaining aspect of complicity that can be illuminated by further research into the constitutive role of law in the Third Reich is that of the concept of law itself with the Holocaust.

Notes

1 Robert D. Rachlin, 'Roland Freisler and the Volksgerichtshof: The Court as an Instrument of Terror', in *The Law in Nazi Germany: Ideology, Opportunism, and the Perversion of Justice,* ed. Alan Steinweis and Robert D. Rachlin (New York: Berghahn, 2013), 67–8.
2 Jeremy Noakes and Geoffrey Pridham (eds), *Nazism 1919–1945 Volume 1: The Rise to Power 1919–1934* (Exeter: University of Exeter Press, 1998), 36–7.
3 Richard Lawrence Miller, *Nazi Justiz: Law of the Holocaust* (Westport CT: Praeger, 1995), 1.
4 See for example Miller, *Nazi Justiz* 2; cf. Simon Lavis, 'Nazi Law as Pure Instrument: Natural Law, (Extra-)Legal Terror, and the Neglect of Ideology', in *Modernisation, National Identity, and Legal Instrumentalism: Studies in Comparative Legal History (Vol. II: Public Law)*, ed. Anna Klimaszewska and Michał Gałędek (Leiden: Brill, 2020): 192.
5 Miller, *Nazi Justiz,* 2. On the predominant treatment of Nazi law as non-law, see: David Fraser, *Law After Auschwitz: Towards a Jurisprudence of the Holocaust* (Durham: Carolina Academic Press, 2005); David Fraser, 'Evil Law, Evil Lawyers? From the Justice Case to the Torture Memos', *Jurisprudence* 3, no. 2 (2012): 391; Simon Lavis, 'The Distorted Jurisprudential Discourse of Nazi Law: Uncovering the "Rupture Thesis" in the Anglo-American Legal Academy', *International Journal for the Semiotics of Law* 31 (2018): 745.
6 For example, John J. Michalczyk (ed.), *Nazi Law: From Nuremberg to Nuremberg* (London: Bloomsbury, 2018); Thomas Vormbaum, *A Modern History of German Criminal Law* (Berlin: Springer-Verlag, 2014); Kai Ambos, *National Socialist Criminal Law: Continuity and Radicalization* (Baden-Baden: Hart Publishing, 2019); Stephen Skinner (ed.), *Ideology and Criminal Law: Fascist, National Socialist and Authoritarian Regimes* (Oxford: Hart Publishing, 2019).
7 Michael Stolleis, 'Law and Lawyers Preparing the Holocaust', *Annual Review of Law and Social Science* 3 (2007): 213, 216.
8 For example, Nathan Stoltzfus, *Hitler's Compromises Coercion and Consensus in Nazi Germany* (New Haven: Yale University Press, 2016); Lisa Pine, *Hitler's 'National*

Community': Society and Culture in Nazi Germany (London: Bloomsbury Academic, 2017); Michael Wildt, *Hitler's Volksgemeinschaft and the Dynamics of Racial Exclusion: Violence Against Jews in Provincial Germany, 1919–1939* (New York: Berghahn, 2014); Martina Steber and Bernhard Gotto, *Visions of Community in Nazi Germany: Social Engineering and Private Lives* (Oxford: Oxford University Press, 2014).

9   For example, on research around the development and nature of the concentration camps, see Jane Caplan and Nikolaus Wachsmann (eds), *Concentration Camps in Nazi Germany: The New Histories* (London: Routledge, 2010).
10 Christopher R. Browning, *Nazi Policy, Jewish Workers, German Killers* (Cambridge: Cambridge University Press, 2000).
11 Ibid., 175.
12 Mary Fulbrook, *Reckonings: Legacies of Nazi Persecution and the Quest for Justice* (Oxford: Oxford University Press, 2018), 9–10.
13 Identified by Dan Stone in Dan Stone (ed.), *The Holocaust and Historical Methodology* (Oxford: Berghahn, 2012), 44–60, and Dan Stone, *Histories of the Holocaust* (Oxford: Oxford University Press, 2010).
14 Louis Althusser, 'Ideology and Ideological State Apparatuses (Notes Towards an Investigation)', in *Lenin and Philosophy and Other Essays*, ed. Louise Althusser (London: Monthly Review Press, 1971).
15 Particularly a related philosophical endeavour in Herlinde Pauer-Studer and J. David Velleman, 'Distortions of Normativity', *Ethical Theory Moral Practice* 14 (2011): 329.
16 See for example Frederick DeCoste, 'Law/Holocaust/Academy', *Modern Law Review* 62 (1999): 792; Fraser, *Law After Auschwitz*. Michael Stolleis, in particular, had already been writing about this area in German; see for example Michael Stolleis, *The Law Under the Swastika: Studies on Legal History in Nazi Germany* (London: University of Chicago Press, 1998).
17 See, as just a few examples: Kevin Jon Heller, *The Nuremberg Military Tribunals and the Origins of International Criminal Law* (Oxford: Oxford University Press, 2011); David A. Blumenthal and Timothy L. H. McCormack, *The Legacy of Nuremberg: Civilising Influence or Institutionalised Vengeance* (Leiden: Martinus Nijhoff, 2008); Rebecca Wittmann, *Beyond Justice: The Auschwitz Trial* (Cambridge, MA: Harvard University Press, 2005); Hilary Earl, *The Nuremberg SS-Einsatzgruppen Trial, 1945–1958: Atrocity, Law, and History* (Cambridge: Cambridge University Press, 2009).
18 See Michalczyk, *Nazi Law*; Jens Meierhenrich, *The Remnants of the Rechtsstaat: An Ethnography of Nazi Law* (Oxford: Oxford University Press, 2018); Steinweis and Rachlin, *The Law in Nazi Germany*; Michael Stolleis, *History of Social Law in Germany*, trans. Thomas Dunlap (Berlin: Springer-Verlag, 2014); Vormbaum, *A Modern History*; Ambos, *National Socialist Criminal Law*.
19 Vormbaum, *A Modern History*, 172.
20 Steinweis and Rachlin, *The Law in Nazi Germany*, 1–2.
21 Ernst Fraenkel, *The Dual State: A Contribution to the Theory of Dictatorship* (New York: Octagon Books, 1969 [1942]).
22 Meierhenrich, *The Remnants of the Rechtsstaat*.
23 Nikolaus Wachsmann, *Hitler's Prisons: Legal Terror in Nazi Germany* (London: Yale University Press, 2004), 380.
24 Michael Stolleis, 'Law and Lawyers Preparing the Holocaust', *Annual Review of Law and Social Science* 3 (2007): 213, 216.
25 Franz Neumann, *Behemoth: The Structure and Practice of National Socialism 1933–1944*, 2nd ed. (London: Frank Cass & Co, 1967).

26 See: Kim C. Priemel and Alexa Stiller (eds), *Reassessing the Nuremberg Military Tribunals: Transitional Justice, Trial Narratives, and Historiography* (New York: Berghahn, 2012); Christiane Wilke, 'Reconsecrating the Temple of Justice: Invocations of Civilization and Humanity in the Nuremberg Justice Case', *Canadian Journal of Law and Society* 24, no. 2 (2009): 181; and Fraser, 'Evil Law, Evil Lawyers'.
27 Primarily comprising H. L. A. Hart, 'Positivism and the Separation of Law and Morals', *Harvard Law Review* 71, no. 4 (1958): 593; and Lon Fuller, 'Positivism and Fidelity to Law — A Reply to Professor Hart', *Harvard Law Review* 71, no. 4 (1958): 630.
28 David Fraser, 'Review of Maksymilian Del Mar and Michael Lobban (eds), *Law in Theory and History: New Essays on a Neglected Dialogue*', *Modern Law Review* 81, no. 6 (2018): 1096, 1099.
29 Ibid.
30 Gustav Radbruch, 'Statutory Lawlessness and Suprastatutory Law (1946)', *Oxford Journal of Legal Studies* 26, no. 1 (2006): 1.
31 Cf. Thomas Mertens, 'Nazism, Legal Positivism and Radbruch's Thesis on Statutory Injustice', *Law and Critique* 14 (2003): 277.
32 Not least in Vivian Grosswald Curran, 'Fear of Formalism: Indications from the Fascist Period in France and Germany of Judicial Methodology's Impact on Substantive Law', *Cornell International Law Journal* 35, (2001/2002): 101.
33 For the beginnings of one such attempt, see David Fraser, 'Criminal Law in Auschwitz: Positivism, Natural Law and the Career of SS Lawyer Konrad Morgen', in *Ideology and Criminal Law: Fascist, National Socialist and Authoritarian Regimes*, ed. Stephen Skinner (Oxford: Hart Publishing, 2019).
34 Dan Stone, 'Holocaust Historiography and Cultural History', in *The Holocaust and Historical Methodology*, ed. Dan Stone (Oxford: Berghahn, 2012), 51.
35 Stone, *Histories of the Holocaust*, 162.
36 Harry Reicher, 'Evading Responsibility for Crimes Against Humanity: Murderous Lawyers at Nuremberg', in *The Law in Nazi Germany*, ed. Steinweis and Rachlin, *The Law in Nazi Germany*, 143.
37 Herlinde Pauer-Studer, 'Law and Morality under Evil Conditions: The SS Judge Konrad Morgen', *Jurisprudence* 3, no. 2 (2012): 367, 371.
38 Carolyn Benson and Julian Fink, 'Introduction: New Perspectives on Nazi Law', *Jurisprudence* 3, no. 2 (2012): 341, 342.
39 Douglas G. Morris, 'Discrimination, Degradation, Defiance: Jewish Lawyers under Nazism', in *The Law in Nazi Germany*, ed. Steinweis and Rachlin, *The Law in Nazi Germany*, 107.
40 Benson and Fink, 'Introduction', 342.
41 Lavis, 'Nazi Law as Pure Instrument'.
42 Pauer-Studer, 'Law and Morality under Evil Conditions', 373.
43 Respectively, the Law for the Restoration of the Professional Civil Service, 7 April 1933; the Reich Citizenship Law, 15 September 1933; the Hereditary Farm Law, 29 September 1933; and the Decree on the Qualifications for the Offices of Judge, Public Prosecutor, Notary Public, and Lawyer, 4 January 1939. All translations of the laws are from the German Historical Institute, Washington, DC; United States Holocaust Memorial Museum; or Jeremy Noakes and Geoffrey Pridham (eds), *Nazism 1919 - 1945 A Documentary Reader* (Exeter: Exeter University Press).
44 Respectively, the Law to ensure the Unity of Party and State, 1 December 1933; the Law for the Reconstruction of the Reich, 30 January 1934; the Law for the protection of German Blood and German Honour, 15 September 1935; the Decree of the Reich

President for the Protection of the People and the State (Reichstag Fire Decree), February 28, 1933; the Hereditary Farm Law, 29 September 1933; and the Decree on the Nature and Goals of the Labour Front, 24 October 1934.
45 Respectively, the Law for the Restoration of the Professional Civil Service, 7 April 1933 and the Reich Citizenship Law, 15 September 1935.
46 Pauer-Studer, 'Law and Morality under Evil Conditions', 370.
47 Pauer-Studer and Velleman, 'Distortions of Normativity'.
48 Ibid., 333.
49 Ibid., 336.
50 Ibid., 334.
51 Ibid., 335.
52 Ibid., 334.
53 Ibid., 329.
54 Ibid., 340.
55 Ibid., 340–50.
56 Ibid., 344.
57 Ibid., 346.
58 Ibid., 347.
59 Ibid., 348.
60 Ibid., 346–7.
61 Ibid., 349.
62 Ibid., 351.
63 Ibid., 350.
64 Dan Stone, *Constructing the Holocaust: A Study in Historiography* (London: Vallentine Mitchell, 2001), 241.

11

Public execution in your community

The summary courts of 1945 Germany

Bastiaan Willems

For the majority of the German population, the year 1945 was the most traumatic year of the entire war. Not only were they under attack from the entire might of both the eastern and western allies, but this also proved to be the year in which the regime publicly turned on its own citizens. The clearest manifestation of this was the introduction of legislation establishing summary courts. Initially these courts were military affairs,[1] but their scope was steadily expanded so that by February 1945 different summary courts, which were to operate 'in areas that were immediately threatened by the Allied advance', had jurisdiction over 'all criminal acts that threaten the German fighting strength and determination to fight'.[2] This type of summary court knew only two judgments: acquittal or a death sentence. Their widespread implementation is commonly seen as proof that 'the terroristic repression of the Nazi regime functioned to the last',[3] and, in sharp contrast to other Nazi crimes, little effort has been put into retracing the motivations of those involved.

Many of the men who in 1945 were part of these summary courts were brought to trial in the immediate post-war years. As with other Nazi crimes the prosecution tended to go after 'small fry',[4] but contrary to large-scale genocidal crimes, which tended to require many 'moving parts' and therefore involved a larger number of people, the public executions were often cases of direct violence. Defendants could not as easily hide behind the bulk-standard excuses of 'orders are orders', or the fear that disobeying a command would imperil themselves. Personal agency was of decisive importance in these summary executions. During the post-war trials defendants often readily admitted that they had taken part in the killing of the person or persons of which they stood accused, but (unsurprisingly) seldom framed their behaviour as rooted in radicalized National Socialism. The first goal of this chapter is therefore to reconstruct the setting in which the summary executions took place, and address how in the post-war years the different protagonists explained their behaviour in the light of the events of 1945. Which moralities and motivations did these men hope that the courts would infer from their testimonies? Few of these men acted on their own, as most of them were part of larger groups, and therefore this chapter's second goal is to show how in post-war court proceedings the members of these groups managed to recast their roles by styling themselves as 'witnesses'. These men, who had often passively or actively contributed to the summary executions, were now 'helping the prosecution', in the process shaping the myth of Germans as victims of National Socialism.

If we want to gauge to what extent the exclusionary practices that defined the Nazi regime can be detached from their racist motivations, the summary executions of 1945 offer a window to look 'beyond the racial state' which has so far not been acknowledged. The summary courts neither merely targeted social outsiders, nor did the regime have much opportunity to directly enforce summary justice or demand ruthlessness of the members of summary courts. As such, these executions could offer a comparison with other acts of exclusion from communities, and reconstruct how different mindsets of societal conformity developed once the regime was no longer able to enforce the legislation underpinning its ideologies. Another major advantage compared to other Nazi crimes is that it is comparatively easy to create a comprehensive social profile of those involved in these executions. For crimes committed abroad, notably in Poland and the Soviet Union, it has proven hard to find witnesses for the prosecution: German bystanders and perpetrators closed ranks, leading to what Hannes Heer has called, 'crimes without perpetrators'.[5] This de-personification of crimes did not happen to the same extent when it concerned public killings in Germany: many of those involved could be tied to them and were subsequently made to justify their actions in court.

As part of the prosecution of Germans charged with Nazi crimes against social outsiders or foreigners, witness testimony initially only played a subordinate role, while those witnesses who were eventually called up sometimes had to endure bullying or were openly harassed by defence lawyers during trials.[6] In stark contrast, the credibility of witnesses to late-war German-versus-German violence was seldom called into question. In the manslaughter case against a former *Feldwebel* (sergeant) accused of killing an officer near the town of Neubukow in Pomerania in late April 1945, the judge stressed that the 'clear statement by witness K. must be given full credit', even though she 'could no longer say with certainty at the main hearing whether the defendant facing her is the same person'. The witness identified the defendant by his southern German dialect, and the court stressed that 'it is easy to understand that she can no longer clearly picture [him], since the accused, according to his own admission, did not have a beard during the war – in contrast to today – and because people in uniform are known to have a different appearance than in civilian clothes'.[7] Put differently, much less of the court's time needed to be spent establishing whether or not the defendant had participated in the crime of which he stood accused, forcing the defence to address the motivations behind his actions and relate them as favourably as possible.

The final stage of the war and the mindsets underpinning intra-ethnic violence

There are few individuals or groups whose motivations to carry out killings in the name of the Nazi regime have been as poorly understood as those Germans who took part in the public executions of their compatriots in the final stage of the war. In the post-war years, the emphasis on the criminality of the 1945 summary court proceedings helped shape, to some extent, a 'comforting' public discourse of a Nazi regime that had not only victimized Jews, Roma, gays and innumerable other social and racial outsiders, but that ultimately also brutally targeted ordinary Germans. Imagery of arbitrary summary justice is part of the German memory culture of 1945,[8] but portraying those involved merely as 'settling old scores', and as having had a 'private lust for power [and] pathological bloodthirst'[9] ignores most of the much more widely held beliefs and motivations that underpinned these executions. The extreme violence of these summary courts was not merely a knee-jerk reaction to the events of 1945; the readiness of the different perpetrators to consider corporal punishment appropriate for an increasing number of crimes had come about gradually. There was – and still is – little doubt that for a law to be obeyed there needs to be social consensus and support.[10] That by the final stage of the war there was widespread preparedness to pass death sentences on 'Aryan' compatriots is best illustrated by the practice of military courts, which by late 1944 had sentenced to death close to 20,000 German soldiers.[11] In the decades prior, the application of the death penalty had been subject to constant change and reinterpretation by subsequent systems of government, and since the German unification of 1871 debates had gone in both directions. During the Third Reich corporal punishment was considered warranted, with Nazi officials solidifying its use during the peace years, and significantly expanding it during the war.[12] 'Killing as punishment' was an integral part of the vocabulary of many of the eventual perpetrators, and although their regurgitation of the regime's murderous objectives should not necessarily be conflated with an actual propensity to kill, among the people around them were some who realized that this could translate into actual deadly behaviour. A clear example is that of Theobald Droll, who as part of the staff of the local *Kreisleiter* oversaw the establishment of the *Volkssturm* militia and the construction of defences in Coesfeld in Westphalia in March 1945. The opening page of the brief of his 1947 trial features the statement that 'among the *Volkssturm* men there was a strong animosity against him, because he often used the word *Umlegen* ("bump off"), and they concluded that he would be quick to resort to shooting'.[13] A similar sentiment was expressed by one of the witnesses to a summary execution in Stollberg in late April 1945, who remarked that 'by this time *Erschiessen* ("shoot them") had become a common idiom of *Oberleutnant* Schwalbe', which was not meant to be acted on literally, but rather understood as a warning.[14]

Although in the post-war trials numerous witnesses for the defence claimed to have been opposed to such language, it was never challenged in 1945 and was part of common parlance. The boasts and subsequent actions of these men reveal a clear presence of what is known as 'availability bias': the incessant Nazi propaganda time and again broadcast examples of a threatened German people, which was coupled with an emphasis on the use of lethal force as a viable means to deal with threats.[15] In the midst of a chaotic and unfamiliar situation, large sections of the population had little opportunity to critically judge the information that reached them, making them susceptible to these kinds of narratives which inflated the risks of a collapsing German society. Crucially, lauded examples of 'resolute action' were readily available to German audiences, ensuring that some came to view these as 'representative' and accepted behaviour in times of danger. Having to make a judgement in times of extreme uncertainty, Germans could very well believe the rumours and reports ubiquitous at the time that such violent behaviour had in fact become the norm elsewhere, and was representative of the situation in Germany as a whole.[16]

These trends in reaction and behaviour went in both directions. Many communities in 1945 were cut off from the rest of their country; whether physically (as a result of the Allied advance, bombing of transport systems or disruption of communication lines) or mentally, Germany experienced an 'islandization' of society,[17] which meant that there were vast local differences. For every group of actors caught in the grip of an existential scare, another was informed by 'positive' information – such as an uneventful change of power after the arrival of Allied troops in a neighbouring town – which greatly diminished the chance of an escalation of violence. Indeed in the establishment of the different summary courts we see an implicit acknowledgement of a development that had plagued the Third Reich from 1943 onwards: the regime's incapability to provide centralized rule.[18] Different centrifugal developments in the latter half of the war brought more power into the hands of provincial leaders (*Gauleiter*), who in turn delegated many important aspects of the war effort to their subordinates.[19] Eventually even the responsibility for executions was pushed down the Nazi Party hierarchy. The small number of people needed to carry out a summary execution, juxtaposed to the high number of summary executions carried out, against the backdrop of crumbling Nazi rule, lends itself particularly well to Christian Gerlach's examination of 'extremely violent societies'. Gerlach argues that violence, even in a totalitarian state such as Nazi Germany, was not perpetrated based on centralized and homogenous ideas. It was rather 'coalitions of violence', consisting of 'fairly unstable alliances between social groups with overall diverging political goals', that determined the situation on the ground.[20] These no longer needed to judge supposed crimes solely along Nazi principles; increasingly there was room for community-specific considerations to be inserted into the summary court proceedings.

The profile of those who served as judges and executioners in the 1945 summary courts reflects this decentralizing tendency. Whereas the selection process for the role of state executioner was closely guarded by Nazi officials – with the last applicant for the function turned down in 1945[21] – those overseeing and carrying out the public summary executions came from different backgrounds and strata of the local community. Even though the legislation underpinning the establishment of summary courts indicated that the different functions in these courts could only be taken up by party and military officials,[22] civilians played an active role in the way summary executions played out. Thus even the little that had remained of due process was effectively discarded. Many Nazi officials served on these summary courts, but even though the 'radicalized Party official' is often the one-dimensional lynchpin of 1945, few defendants identified their Party function as their main occupation.[23] Many of these men, although certainly not all, were party members, but tying a propensity to execute fellow countrymen to party affiliation creates a false equivalence. Perpetrators came from all walks of life, and among their numbers we find teachers,[24] artists,[25] members of the local *Mittelstand*[26] ('shopkeepers and the independent artisans of the "old" middle class'[27]), blue-collar workers[28] and many other ordinary Germans.

Further complicating the top–down 'Party-versus-civilian' dichotomy was that holding a high party position did in itself not make one impervious to suspicion. In the last week of the war, on 3 May 1945, three men of the *Volkssturm* (Nazi Germany's last-ditch militia) shot the local *Ortsgruppenleiter* after he had felt it in his right to open an anti-tank barrier.[29] In Riddagshausen, a village near Braunschweig, *Landrat* Dr Bergmann, the local *Kreisleiter*, was shot shortly before the arrival of American troops because his failed suicide attempt was judged to be a sign of defeatism.[30] During the final storming of the East Prussian capital Königsberg in early April 1945, two party officials were publicly shot after they were caught trying to evade the fighting in the city – only one day after they themselves had condemned to death two deserters for the very same 'crime'.[31] That party officials are well represented among these cases is not surprising: they helped determine whether or not a town would surrender, and those party officials articulating the wish to spare their community risked being labelled defeatists. In turn, the men in their immediate circle were more likely to be familiar with the relevant legislation that called for their execution. The 'wavering' attitudes of these officials fed into the fears of their peers, since it had long been 'established' that even among party members there was generally little willingness to shoulder the burdens of war.[32]

The age profile of the perpetrators further calls into question the correlation between exposure to National Socialist teachings and the preparedness to kill in 1945. Neither the age bracket 1900–09, which included the members of the 'uncompromising generation', nor the age bracket 1910–19, which came of age during the Nazi regime – and obviously not the even younger age groups – provided the largest number of men involved in these executions. Instead, it is the age bracket 1890–99, that is, those whose moralities and identities had been formed well before the coming of the Third Reich, who were most commonly tried for their part in the execution of their *Volksgenossen*.[33] In a number of cases, the maturity of the perpetrators is specifically alluded to. In the 1947 trial against three men of the Sontheim *Volkssturm*, the presiding judge stressed that 'the defendants are men with life-experience'.[34] 'Life experience' would be flagged up by the prosecution as a way to show that the defendant knew the difference between right or wrong, albeit not as part of a legal argument but rather as a rhetorical device to imply that by 1945 the defendant could have known better.[35]

These are clear indicators of the persistence of long-established community structures which the Nazi regime had still not broken, nor had necessarily intended to break.[36] Especially in smaller towns and villages social control still played an important role as a determining factor for behavioural patterns. The idea that the members of these communities had a 'joint responsibility' was still strong.[37] The Nazi regime fairly successfully instrumentalized these popular sentiments and managed to encourage its citizens to police conformity (markedly in cases of denunciation) until the final stages of its rule.[38] The repeated emphasis on the idea that in defeat every German was 'in the same boat' further strengthened this sense of community.[39] At the same time, the changing tide of the war led many to abandon the idea that 'community' referred to the

German people as a whole, and instead chose to interpret it in a much narrower sense, such as the members of their own *Heimat*.[40] Beyond the debates of the function and value of this community lie the different interpersonal connections of its members, and on occasion we find instances where perpetrators had to weigh their role in the Nazi community (manifested in a preparedness to pass summary judgement) against long-standing personal relationships. In Munich, the committed National Socialist Alfred Salisco offered an old acquaintance, Major Günther Caracciola-Delbrück, an opportunity to escape, which the latter declined with the words 'comrade, you are the father of two children yourself, I won't flee'. Later that day Salisco would oversee the major's execution and would give him the *coup de grace*.[41] The head of a summary court in Weidenau was heard saying: 'I brought the execution squad with me right away. One is already hanging in Klafeld. I have another eleven men on my list, among them my friend Becker'.[42] In Königsberg, the chief editor of the local newspaper asked one of the men involved in the executions about his motivations:

> The drumhead courts that were deployed for these culprits only knew one punishment, even for small thefts: death through hanging. One of the assessors, an *Ortsgruppenleiter* of the Nazi Party who normally oversaw the administration of a large hospital, otherwise known as an unusually good-natured man, in answer to the question of whether he could justify such judgements for his conscience, said: 'It's what's best for them and us, and that is what determined my decision'.[43]

As defeat started to loom, the purpose of this *Volksgemeinschaft* was no longer to merely contribute to a Nazi vision; rather it was used as an 'emergency organization' whose validity lay only in its members surviving the war.[44] Safeguarding this local community was often presented as a main reason for perpetrators to order a summary execution, and little evidence suggests that the perpetrators saw their behaviour as paradoxical or contradictory. Nazi principles were not necessary to motivate this kind of intra-ethnic violence: to many of the men who carried out summary executions the killing of an individual who, due to his unpredictable behaviour and lack of understanding of his community, threatened the community as a whole, was considered to be the only sensible thing to do. Unwittingly echoing Goethe's 1793 dictum 'Better to commit an injustice than to countenance disorder', they claimed that in their preparedness to doggedly defend the values of their communities, sometimes regardless of their personal convictions, they had been led astray by National Socialism.

Whether or not different communities agreed with the summary justice, or whether its members merely fell in line because they felt terrorized, is hard to gauge. Whereas Ian Kershaw maintains that the public nature of these summary executions suggests that there was widespread complicity until the very end, Edgar Wolfrum indicates that summary courts often operated against the will of bystanders, most of whom had, by 1945, turned their backs on the Nazi regime.[45] Little outrage in the face of these summary executions was reported at the time,[46] but case briefs in the *Justiz und NS-Verbrechen* sometimes note a 'hostile mood' towards summary justice, and occasions on which crowds even had to be dispersed at gunpoint.[47] Conversely, it is relatively easy to find voices from workers, party officials and soldiers alike agreeing with the executions.[48] On trial for his role in a summary execution in Klafeld in April 1945, Friedrich Jäger attested that as his men attached a rope to an oak tree 'spectators (*Zuschauer*) from the local population encouraged the execution by shouting "hang him"', and possibly even helped provide a table or chair as a platform for the execution.[49]

Finally, the most obvious marker of National Socialist exclusionary practises – discrimination along the lines of 'Jewishness' – played only a limited role in these executions. Whereas Nazi authorities used the chaos of 1945 to clear their camps and prisons of their enemies,[50] in the public sphere minority groups were not being singled out with the same rigour (of course, by 1945 most Jews had disappeared 'East', while those still alive realized that their best chance to outlive the regime was to keep a low profile). The suspicion and paranoia towards Jews that had been cultivated during the Nazi regime nevertheless continued to play a role, such as in the case of a Gelsenkirchen man who was killed shortly after he had attested that 'his wife is Jewish and is in a concentration camp',[51] or that of a boy accused of theft who, according to his killer, 'had a Jewish appearance and was therefore not able to live' (*nicht lebensfähig gewesen*)[52] – but these are exceptions.

The perpetrators' lack of attention to Jews (and other social outsiders) should not be interpreted as a move away from the core tenets of the community that the regime had sought to create – although some of them undoubtedly felt it did. The summary executions were physical manifestations of the deep-felt fear which informed many of Nazi Germany's wartime decisions: a collapse of the home-front, as had happened in 1918. Yet, whereas the collapse of the home front in 1918 could be pinned on Jews and leftists, this was no longer the case in 1945.[53] Since the regime was adamant that the different racial and social minority groups had been ruthlessly expelled from the German community and been denied their agency, the Nazi home front could by its very nature only be shaped by the behaviour of fellow compatriots, who were therefore looked upon with increasing distrust. To alleviate the tensions on the home front, the regime occasionally managed to 'introduce' new enemies: it quickly learned that many Germans could easily be swayed to heap their anger upon an 'invisible enemy made visible', such as downed allied airmen or the 'clique' of 'criminally stupid officers' of 20 July.[54] These manifestations of public outcry, which were presented as spontaneous and which often took place in the public sphere, bolstered a sense of community and temporarily shifted the blame away from the regime and the German High Command. It discouraged potential perpetrators to critically question Germany's chances to win the war, and instead allowed them to retreat into perverted notions of 'guardianship' and 'doing one's duty'.[55] The perpetrators themselves seldom denied having taken part in the summary executions (in contrast to perpetrators of genocidal crimes in death-camps or on the eastern front), but would stress that their brutality should be framed as 'tough love' – as inflicting pain in the present so to save their community from a much greater pain in the future. These sentiments were well understood during the war and were not widely opposed at the time, but fell into disfavour as soon as Nazi Germany had been defeated.

From 'accomplice' to 'witness' in the post-war world

Is it possible for a member of the German *Volk* to be a mere witness to violence during the Nazi era? Not only is it important to establish to what extent Nazi ideology informed exclusionary (and even brutal) bystander behaviour; it is equally necessary to establish how much agency individuals living in a dictatorship had. Ascribing their unwillingness and inability to interfere to what social psychologists consider 'the very natural human tendency to stay silent in the face of bad behaviour'[56] does not in itself answer the question of why throughout the Third Reich the public space could be used for crimes with such impunity. The large grey zone that existed for 'bystanders' during the Third Reich was actively used in later years, such as in the 1948 trial against three Mannheim police men who on 28 March 1945 had been involved in the summary execution of three civilians found hiding in a house that flew a white flag. Earlier that day the local police commander, *Polizeipräsident* Habenicht, had passed on Himmler's infamous 'flag order', emphatically stressing that all men above the age of fourteen found in a house flying a white flag had to be shot 'on the spot'. Habenicht was not prosecuted as he had not been present during the summary execution itself, but the court nevertheless considered it necessary to highlight that 'Habenicht is not a witness (*Zeuge*), but one of the main culprits'.[57] Many of the men involved in summary executions managed to distance themselves from them, and this section will probe the defensive strategies they used.

In contrast to the Nuremberg trials, during which different Nazi figureheads were charged with newly defined categories of crimes ('crimes against humanity', 'crimes against peace' and 'war crimes'), the West German judges who oversaw cases against defendants involved in the 1945 summary executions adhered to the principle of *nulla poena sine lege* ('no punishment without a law'). This meant that the court adhered to a pre-existing legal definition of 'murderer', namely the one established in 1941 as 'someone who out of lust for murder, to satisfy the sexual instinct, out of greed, or for other base motives; in an malicious or cruel manner [. . .] kills a person'.[58] The decision to prosecute defendants under the 1941 criminal code meant that for a case to go to trial, public prosecutors had to establish the personal guilt of a suspect beyond a reasonable doubt and build their case proving defendants' 'base motives'. 'Doing justice' to the victims of summary courts meant ensuring a guilty-verdict and putting 'the perpetrator' behind bars for this crime; it did not mean reconstructing a broad historical picture. Events that did not directly have an impact on a case fell outside the remit of the prosecutors. Critically, prosecutors depended on the testimonies of members of the very communities they investigated, even though many community members were themselves often deeply implicated. The inherent friction between establishing the 'historical truth' and 'building a case' lies, as Michael Wildt succinctly puts it, in the fact that 'whereas historians normally talk *about* protagonists, prosecutors talk *with* them'.[59] Eager to put some distance between themselves and the criminality of National Socialism, many 'bystanders' became 'willing witnesses', safe in the knowledge that as long as they portrayed themselves only as indirectly involved they would have little to fear by way of future prosecution.

Some men claimed to have taken part in summary killings because they were ordered to, although once on trial – in contrast to the prosecution of other Nazi crimes – few of them maintained that they were 'simply following orders'. Rather, they stressed that they did not know that they had played a role in an illegal process that would eventually lead to an execution. The seventeen-year old Hitler-Youth boy H. joined a '*Werwolf*' Nazi partisan chapter operating out of Wilhelmshaven, where on 2 May 1945 he was part of a group that carried out a summary killing. The group had, since November 1944, operated on the general principle 'that people who in the face of the enemy commit treason or intend to do so are to be eliminated (*beseitigt*) by *Werwolf*. During the car ride to the eventual killing H.'s superior asked him 'whether he's even seen a person die'. Yet despite these facts, H. claimed ignorance of his superior's intentions and was acquitted.[60]

> As always, he followed Lotto's instructions and followed him to [the victim's] hotel. Here he witnessed an act which he did not suspect and which he did not demonstrably approve of. He became a reluctant spectator (*Zuschauer*). He should be believed when he states that witnessing such an act at such a young age caused him to be in a state of mind that later caused him to cry in a car, and that all other memories [of that day] remain shrouded in darkness.

In another example, the witness testimony of the police man H. played a critical role in the prosecution of the former military commander of the village of Hechtsheim. H. stated that he had been dispatched, together with another police man, to take down a white flag that had appeared over a school. Upon arrival they encountered two locals who had hoisted the flag, and told them that what they did was forbidden and, given the situation, a very dangerous thing to do. Their names were noted, but they were not arrested. Only later that day did the incident gain traction, when the village's military commander and its local police commander were informed about the incident. Since the two police men could identify the culprits they were ordered to arrest them with the help of a third police man. Upon their arrest the two flag raisers indicated that they had been instructed to do so by a certain Adam Schuch, who, since he had served with one of the police men, was told to make himself scarce. Schuch was nevertheless arrested shortly thereafter, and the three men were charged with defeatism and shot that same day.[61] It remains unclear why H. and his colleague did not warn the three men to 'get lost', even though they knew that their inaction could lead to the death of multiple people. By offering himself up as a witness against the Hechtsheim battle commander, H. could evade questions regarding his motivations during that day.

Another large group of 'witnesses' consisted of people who voiced protest against the killings and expressed disagreement, but nevertheless had no real intention of interfering. Some of them went along and became accessories to murder, while others were 'clever' enough to distance themselves from the act. The summary execution of hairdresser Hermann Masalsky in Lüdenscheid on 13 April 1945 shows the unwillingness of bystanders with agency to interfere in the process. During lunch on the day prior to the American arrival in the city (which was expected to fall without a fight) the officer Karl Wilhelm Wülfing drew attention to Masalsky's repeated defeatist remarks and told his comrades that he wanted to report him. When they realized he was serious, they 'urged him to quit such nonsense', brushing it off by telling him that he was agitated because he had been drinking. Wülfing persisted and enquired with other officers. The first officer he met dodged the issue by stating, it was 'none of my business', another told him, 'kiss my ass', while a third let him know, 'if he were a man he'd go to the front'. When he finally found a willing officer senior enough to order a subordinate to assist in the execution, Wülfing went out to find Masalsky and immediately ordered his execution. During Wülfing's 1947 trial his comrades' negligent ambivalence came to light, prompting the court to conclude that 'although they knew what was going on, none of them did anything'.[62]

That some of the witnesses nevertheless felt compromised is illustrated by the post-war behaviour of the defendant K., who was charged with 'accessory to manslaughter' for his role in a summary execution in Ingelheim in March 1945. Initially, in a June 1946 letter to the public prosecutor, he stated that he thought that he had been part of a 'legally sound special court', but K. changed his defensive strategy once on trial in 1953. There he testified that 'he stayed at a noticeable distance and watched the scene from the outside staircase of the school next to the police station', and that he 'only acted as a spectator (*Zuschauer*) during the execution'. The court accepted his account of the events, although it noted that since K. 'had already become aware of the illegality of the so-called conviction that preceded this execution, he was fully aware of the illegality of this execution'.[63]

Conclusion

In the form of hundreds of summary courts, a wave of intra-ethnic violence swept over Germany in 1945, the likes of which the country had not experienced since the Thirty Years' War. The Nazi regime advocated the use of the death penalty, and increasingly passed death sentences for minor offenses. At the same time, it celebrated brutal resoluteness, which it expected from its soldiers and officials alike. Certainly not every German bought into these narratives, but there were large segments of the population that did. Among them were many men who in 1945 were given the task of defending their communities, and their brutalizing attitudes lay at the foundation of different 'coalitions of violence' that emerged throughout the country. To these men, summary execution was available as one of the tools that could help shape the fate of the communities they defended. The threat of summary execution was meant to stamp out defeatism, although among the different coalitions there still existed varying attitudes towards executions, as some of their members doubted the proportionality, and not all were willing to personally see them through. Once the decision was made to execute someone, few were willing to challenge it, as doing so meant risking being branded a defeatist yourself. Those pushing to set up summary courts, moreover, seemingly had the law on their side.

After the war, knowing that the prosecution had to prove 'base motives', many of those involved in the executions styled themselves as mere 'witnesses'. In practice this meant that they would not deny their involvement, but rather stress that they were unaware of the criminality of the act, or had been mentally opposed to it, as such underlining that their motives had not been 'malicious or cruel'. This left only a small number of supposed 'real' perpetrators, whose motivations – by the very nature of the charges levelled against them – were detached from the historical context in which their crimes took place. These men could therefore readily be presented as criminal individuals whose actions did not represent their community's values. This meant, moreover, that the wider question of the complicity in the communities where these summary executions had been carried out was considered to be sufficiently dealt with after the trials had come to a close. The number of people compromised by their actions in the final stage of the war extended far beyond the narrow definitions set out after 1945. Wider local and societal motives that underpinned the 1945 summary executions were left out of the post-war courtrooms, allowing former bystanders, prosecutors and judges alike to skirt around painful questions regarding wartime conformity and complicity.

Notes

1 Peter Lutz Kalmbach, 'Fliegende Standgerichte. Entstehung und Wirkung eines Instruments der nationalsozialistischen Militärjustiz', *VfZ* 69, no.2 (2021): 211–39.
2 The 'Decree on the Establishment of Summary Courts' of 15 February 1945 counted a mere 250 words and was read out in its entirety over the radio. See Reichsgesetzblatt Teil I, Nr. 6: 20 February 1945. 'Verordnung über die Errichtung von Standgerichten', 30.
3 Ian Kershaw, *The End: Germany 1944–45* (London: Allen Lane, 2011), 3–5.
4 Mary Fulbrook, *Reckonings. Legacies of Nazi Persecution and the Quest for Justice* (Oxford: Oxford University Press, 2018), 266.
5 Hannes Heer, *Vom Verschwinden der Täter: Der Vernichtungskrieg fand statt, aber keiner war dabei* (Berlin: Aufbau-Verlag 2004), Ch. 2; Dirk Rupnow, *Aporien des Gedenkens. Reflexionen über Holocaust und Erinnerung* (Berlin: Rombach Verlag, 2006), 80.
6 Julia Wagner, 'The Truth about Auschwitz: Prosecuting Auschwitz Crimes with the Help of Survivor Testimony', *German History* 28, no.3 (2010): 348–54.
7 Band II, Lfd. Nr. 052, 412–13.
8 For example in movies such as *Der Untergang* (2004) and *Der Hauptmann* (2017), which both reached international audiences, as well as in the acclaimed ZDF TV-series *Tannbach* (2015).
9 Klaus-Dietmar Henke, *Die amerikanische Besetzung Deutschlands* (Munich: R. Oldenbourg Verlag, 1996), 847.
10 Max A. Shepard, 'Law and Obedience', *The American Political Science Review* 33, no.5 (1939): 783–810, 785: 'Any rule, to be law, must be generally obeyed, or otherwise it is mere counsel'.
11 Manfred Messerschmidt and Fritz Wüllner, *Die Wehrmachtjustiz im Dienste des Nationalsozialismus. Zerstörung einer Legende* (Baden-Baden: Nomos Verlagsgesellschaft, 1987), 78–9.
12 Richard Evans, *Rituals of Retribution. Capital Punishment in Germany, 1600–1987* (Oxford: Oxford University Press, 1996), Chs. 8–16.
13 Band I, Lfd. Nr. 024, 533.

14 Band XII, Lfd.Nr. 408, 699.
15 On the normalization of death during the Third Reich, see Jay Baird, *To die for Germany: Heroes in the Nazi Pantheon* (Bloomington: Indiana University Press, 1990), Ch. IX.
16 Daniel Kahneman, *Thinking, Fast and Slow* (London: Penguin Books, 2011), Chs. 12,13, Appendix A.
17 Wolfgang Franz Werner, *'Bleib übrig!': Deutsche Arbeiter in der nationalsozialistischen Kriegswirtschaft* (Düsseldorf: Schwann, 1983), 329.
18 Hans Mommsen, 'The Dissolution of the Third Reich: Crisis Management and Collapse, 1943–1945', *Bulletin of the German Historical Institute* 27 (2000): 9–23.
19 Eleanor Hancock, *The National Socialist Leadership and Total War, 1941–45* (New York: St Martin's Press, 1991), 156–7, 163.
20 Christian Gerlach, 'Extremely Violent Societies: An Alternative to the Concept of Genocide', *Journal of Genocide Research* 8, no.4 (2006): 455–71.
21 Klaus Hillenbrand, *Berufswunsch Henker. Warum Männer im Nationalsozialismus Scharfrichter werden wollten* (Frankfurt a.M.: Campus Verlag, 2013), 18; Evans, *Rituals of Retribution*, 665–7.
22 The 'Decree on the Establishment of Summary Courts' called for a presiding criminal judge, as well as a higher NSDAP official or functionary, and an officer of the Wehrmacht, Waffen-SS, or police as assessors.
23 We should keep in mind that at least for some of them, the efforts to distance themselves from their party duties was part of their defence strategy. (Band II, Lfd.Nr. 072, 769. The defendant Hans Hoffmann is referred to as 'saddle maker and former *Kreisamtsleiter der NSV*', but had been the NSDAP mayor of Forchheim since 1933). Moreover, not all party positions were full time.
24 For example, Band I, Lfd.Nr.020, 411: Before joining the army in 1935, Major a.D. K (b. 1896) had been a high-school teacher. Band II, Lfd.Nr.037, 49: Alfred Salisco (b.1894) had been a high-school teacher until 1943, when he became the *Rektor* of the *Schule am Hart* in Munich. Band II, Lfd.Nr.059, 521: The defendant S. was a head teacher (b. 1901) and was acquitted; Bd.III, Lfd.Nr.098, 419: The defendant A. was a high-school teacher (b. 1985) and was acquitted.
25 Band II, Lfd.Nr. 65, 669: Dr F., Painter and former Gau Department Head; Band II, Lfd. Nr. 070, 745: Painter A.; Band V, Lfd.Nr.163, 193, 195: Painter H. became a state prosecutor in 1939 and returned to art after the war. Band III, Lfd.Nr.078, 67: Widowed author.
26 Among the defendants we find: Lfd. Nr. 001: Farmer; Lfd. Nr. 002: Commercial assistant; Lfd. Nr. 019: Gardener; Lfd. Nr. 033: Innkeeper and vintner; Lfd. Nr. 034: Merchant, Lfd. Nr. 035: Apothecary; Lfd. Nr. 039: Grocer; Lfd. Nr. 062: Commercial clerk; Lfd. Nr. 071: Master tailor.
27 Mary Fulbrook, *A History of Germany 1918–2014. The Divided Nation*, 4th ed. (Chichester: Wiley Blackwell, 2015), 53.
28 Among the defendants we find: Lfd. Nr. 016: Miner; Lfd. Nr. 019: Mechanic; Lfd. Nr. 023: Carpenter, Lathe operator; Lfd. Nr. 027: Electrician; Lfd. Nr. 036: Construction worker; Lfd. Nr. 038: Carpenter; Lfd. Nr. 039: Mechanic, crane operator, specialist worker; Lfd. Nr. 048: Worker; Lfd. Nr. 061: Electrician.
29 Band I, Lfd. Nr. 019, 401.
30 Band I, Lfd. Nr. 021, 438.
31 Armin Fuhrer and Heinz Schön, *Erich Koch, Hitlers brauner Zar: Gauleiter von Ostpreussen und Reichskommissar der Ukraine* (Munich: Olzog, 2010), 179.

32 Hancock, *The National Socialist Leadership and Total War*, 142.
33 These men were part of the so-called 'front generation' that experienced the Great War, emerging from it with a heightened sense of guardianship. See Mary Fulbrook, *Dissonant Lives: Generations and Violence through the German Dictatorships* (Oxford: Oxford University Press, 2011), 12, 40–5.
34 Band I, Lfd. Nr. 019, 404.
35 *Lebenserfahrung* features in: Band II, Lfd. Nr.038, 100; Band V, Lfd. Nr. 173, 444.
36 Jill Stephenson, 'The Volksgemeinschaft and the Problems of Permeability: The Persistence of Traditional Attitudes in Württemberg Villages', *German History* 34, no. 1 (2016): 49–69.
37 Geoffrey Hosking, 'Trust and Distrust: A Suitable Theme for Historians?', *Transactions of the Royal Historical Society* 16 (2006): 98.
38 Robert Gellately, *Backing Hitler* (Oxford: Oxford University Press, 2001), Ch. 10.
39 Peter Fritzsche, *Life and Death in the Third Reich* (Cambridge, MA: Belknap Press of Harvard University Press, 2008), 284–6.
40 Celia Applegate, *A Nation of Provincials: The German Idea of Heimat* (Berkeley: University of California Press, 1990), 225–7.
41 Band II, Lfd.Nr. 037, 51-3. See also: Volker Ullrich, *Eight Days in May: How Germany's War Ended* (London: Penguin, 2021), 11.
42 Band X, Lfd. Nr. 335, 257.
43 Bastiaan Willems, *Violence in Defeat: The Wehrmacht on German Soil, 1944–1945* (Cambridge: Cambridge University Press, 2021), 254.
44 Clemens Vollnhals, 'Disillusionment, Pragmatism, Indifference, German Society After the "Catastrophe"', in *The Legacies of Two World Wars: European Societies in the Twentieth Century*, ed. Lothar Kettenacker and Torsten Riotte (New York and Oxford: Berghahn, 2011), 186.
45 Kershaw, *The End*, 3–5; Edgar Wolfrum, 'Verbrechen am Ende des Zweiten Weltkriegs', in *Terror nach Innen: Verbrechen am Ende des Zweiten Weltkrieges*, ed. Cord Arendes, Edgard Wolfrum and Jörg Zedler (Göttingen: Wallstein, 2006), 7–14.
46 Earlier in the war, the public outcry against the euthanasia program had prompted Nazi officials to temporarily halt it and continue it clandestinely. See Nathan Stoltzfus, *Hitler's Compromises: Coercion and Consensus in Nazi Germany* (New Haven: Yale University Press, 2016), Ch. VI.
47 Band I, Lfd. Nr. 027, 609; Band V, Lfd. Nr. 180, 580.
48 Nicholas Stargardt, *The German War. A Nation under Arms, 1939-45* (London: The Bodley Head, 2015), 523–4; Willems, *Violence in Defeat*, 249–58.
49 Band VIII, Lfd. Nr. 279, 422.
50 Nikolaus Wachsmann, *Hitler's Prisons, Legal Terror in Nazi Germany* (New Haven: Yale University Press, 2004), 319–38; Gerhard Paul, '"Diese Erschießungen haben mich innerlich gar nicht mehr berührt": Die Kriegsendphasenverbrechen der Gestapo 1944/45', in *Die Gestapo im Zweiten Weltkrieg: 'Heimatfront' und besetztes Europa*, ed. Gerhard Paul and Klaus-Michael Mallmann (Darmstadt: Primus, 2000), 543–68.
51 Bd.I, Lfd. Nr.016, 298.
52 Band I, Lfd. Nr. 002, 15–16.
53 Michael Geyer, 'Endkampf 1918 and 1945: German Nationalism, Annihilation, and Self-Destruction', in *No Man's Land of Violence: Extreme Wars in the Twentieth Century*, ed. Alf Lüdtke and Bernd Weisbrod) Göttingen: Wallstein, 2006), 35–68.
54 Georg Hoffmann, *Fliegerlynchjustiz: Gewalt gegen abgeschossene alliierte Flugzeugbesatzungen 1943–1945* (Paderborn: Ferdinand Schoeningh, 2015), Ch. 3;

Karl Heinrich Peter (ed.), *Spiegelbild einer Verschwörung: Die Kaltenbrunner-Berichte an Bormann und Hitler über das Attentat vom 20. Juli 1944* (Stuttgart: Seewald Verlag, 1961), 1–11.

55 On the Nazi appropriation of the Kantian sense of duty, presented as a German virtue, see Wolfgang Bialas, *Moralische Ordnungen des Nationalsozialismus* (Göttingen: Vandenhoeck & Ruprecht, 2014), 47–53.
56 Catherine A. Sanderson, *The Bystander Effect: The Psychology of Courage and Inaction* (London: William Collins, 2020), xi.
57 Band II, Lfd. Nr. 063, 627.
58 Reichsgesetzblatt, Teil I, Nr. 101, 8 September 1941. 'Gesetz zur Änderung der Reichsstrafgesetzbuchs', 549.
59 Michael Wildt, *Die Ambivalenz des Volkes: Der Nationalsozialismus als Gesellschaftsgeschichte* (Berlin: Suhrkamp, 2019), 351–8.
60 Band III, Lfd. Nr. 091, 311.
61 Band II, Lfd. Nr. 070, 745–7.
62 Band I, Lfd. Nr. 027, 606–8.
63 Band X, Lfd. Nr. 344, 436–7.

12

Excess and normality

West German and Austrian media and Nazi crimes trials from the 1950s to the 1980s

Christoph Thonfeld

'There, but for the grace of God, goes John Bradford', is a phrase attributed to the sixteenth-century religious reformer of the same name, advocating trust in God rather than human judgement to see justice done. It was also meant as a humble recognition of human beings' moral fallibility. Interestingly, the phrase appeared twice in German weekly *Die ZEIT*'s coverage of Nazi crimes trials. In 1957, it was used as a form of protest against the few remaining outcomes of alleged Allied 'victors' justice'.[1] Then, in 1982, it was employed by a different but equally high-profile editor to point out how easily any German or Austrian adult could have become involved in crimes during the Nazi era.[2] He advocated against claiming any moral high ground with the benefit of hindsight or handing out overly harsh judicial verdicts against perpetrators almost forty years later. While in 1957 Nazi perpetrators were referred to as 'war convicts', as had become customary in the 1950s, in 1982 they were openly addressed as 'murderers'. However, in the 1950s the guiding principle for the assessment seemed to have been that they had atoned enough while in the 1980s it rather seemed questionable whether they had been culpable in the first place. Both texts frame the time span under investigation in this chapter and give us an idea of the trajectory of media coverage of Nazi crimes trials.

For the first two and a half decades after the Second World War, radio and newspapers were still the leading media until television firmly took over that position around 1970. This also holds true in general for coverage of Nazi crimes trials despite singular peaks like the Eichmann and Auschwitz trials in the 1960s, which turned into early huge television events. However, when it came to opinion leadership in the public sphere, audiovisual media were already in the process of taking it over around the mid-1960s.[3] During the Nazi era, radio had taken up the role of leading media, which became even more pronounced immediately after the war[4] when most newspapers were either shut down or had run out of paper. Throughout the 1950s, the relation between radio and newspapers tilted more towards the papers while television became the newcomer in the German and Austrian mediascapes around 1960. Over time, newspapers, radio and later television all played their role in shaping public opinion on Nazi crimes trials and, in turn, were the sites where changes in public opinion were most prominently reflected. They were also contested opinion-forming sites during that era where relevant actors or observers of the trials would make their voices heard. Media were not simply mirroring the events they were covering but rather presented their own view of things, influenced by a variety of interests and agendas.

When the big Operation Reinhardt camps trials and euthanasia murder trials began in West Germany in the 1960s, there was much less coverage in Austria. Austria also developed a pluralistic mediascape, albeit one that seemed to have been more rigidly politically compartmentalized than the one in West Germany. However, due to the pervasive conviction – only seriously challenged since the mid-1980s – that Austria was the first victim rather than part of the Nazi perpetrator state and society, printed media as well as broadcasters seemed to pay much less attention to Nazi crimes trials at home and abroad.[5] As of the late 1940s, corresponding coverage in East Germany was firmly in the grip of the Socialist Unity Party. Therefore, East Germany does not lend itself for a straightforward comparison. There, media reports became mainly a tool to fuel competition between the East and West German political systems, which had been in full swing since the late 1950s.[6] Using coverage of the aforementioned trials as point of departure, this article shows how perceptions and representations of Nazi perpetrators were negotiated within post-war media and society.

From the late 1950s to the late 1960s

In 1957, liberal weekly *Die ZEIT* questioned Allied verdicts in Nazi crimes trials mainly in two respects: allegedly, they had been too harsh and the defendants had been chosen rather arbitrarily. What these offenders had done many others had done as well and, therefore, prosecution of the few created injustice in the face of many others who were left untried. However, editor Rudolf Walther Leonhardt's choice of case examples was not particularly well informed as there was pertinent evidence at hand against both, the former Organisation Todt doctor Erika Flocken and the former Goslar NSDAP Gauleiter Wilhelm Pfeiffer.[7] Leonhardt's contribution shows how *Die ZEIT* still had a distinctly national liberal outlook which was only to change in the 1960s. Indeed, Leonhardt himself has been credited for being a driving force in this change. In the late 1950s, though, public criticism of a number of lenient verdicts in contemporary Nazi crime trials and first signs of generational change in the media also triggered a shift in newspaper coverage. Television too showed early signs of promoting a public confrontation with Nazi crimes through critical documentaries.[8] However, especially in 1950s and 1960s West Germany and Austria many Nazi perpetrators still held similar positions or represented similar institutions as they had before 1945, so the need to negotiate the justifications and explanations for their involvement in Nazi crimes became more acute. Media played an active role in this negotiation process and made it digestible for mainstream society. A more critical note started to appear in the early 1960s when the lenient sentences for Nazi-era perpetrators seemed to expose systematic flaws in court procedures: 'Thus, the Council of the Evangelical Church of

Germany discovered "a disproportion between some judgements on crimes from the Nazi era and judgements on crimes from our days".⁹ Coverage of courtroom events and historical background, which from then on was often based on moral indignation about the period of silence and impunity for perpetrators during the 1950s, soon became mingled with a voyeuristic view of crimes, for example: 'The murder factories were adorned with geraniums'.¹⁰

In the 1960s, coverage of Nazi crimes trials had to compete for scarce public attention. One problem was that the trials were not made for providing entertainment. A lack of suspense had already been criticized by reporters at the International Military Tribunal (IMT) in Nuremberg in 1945/46. Since then, the mediascape had grown enormously in size and variety. In light of this development, West German magazine *Der SPIEGEL* summed up proceedings of those trials as a 'monotony of horror',¹¹ which indicated how quickly the public curiosity for shocking details of the past could be overfed. Therefore, even at the height of public interest in the trials in the late 1940s and the mid-1960s, a few major trials overshadowed all the others: 'The Frankfurt trial stole the limelight from the Düsseldorf trial, Auschwitz prevailed over Treblinka'.¹² Apart from market pressures, coverage of Nazi crime trials often had to deal with a not overly welcoming societal atmosphere. Newspapers and magazines also felt the increasing competition presented by the advance of television during the 1960s. Due to its television presence, the first Frankfurt Auschwitz trial had a unique status among all German and Austrian Nazi crimes trials after the IMT.¹³ That trial in a number of ways became the benchmark for what was to follow not only in West German courtrooms, but also in terms of media coverage and the crimes that had to be reported: 'The [. . .] indictment shows that no less gruesome details will be brought up in this Düsseldorf [Treblinka] trial than in the Frankfurt Auschwitz trial', *Frankfurter Allgemeine Zeitung* (*FAZ*) wrote in its 1964 pre-trial coverage.¹⁴ The mere reference to 'Auschwitz' by now seemed sufficient to invoke corresponding images of Nazi atrocities. The trials came to stand for the former camps and, thus, for the crimes that had been committed there and their corresponding status in public consciousness.

Coverage of Operation Reinhardt crimes trials

Although crimes had undeniably been committed, those who were involved, as well as the wider society around them, attempted to distance the majority of offenders from their deeds, with the courts sentencing only a small minority. Media played an important role in the process of determining the lines between those who were guilty and not guilty, and in considering if and how crimes should be faced publicly. One way to avoid a head-on confrontation with crimes in extermination camps was to localize them in a space beyond this earth or beyond human imagination: 'Report from the hell of the extermination camp'¹⁵ was one version of that trope. On the other hand, following the courts' focus on cruel and excessive perpetration,¹⁶ newspapers concentrated on such outrageous atrocities while the 'orderly' daily mass murder was more often than not allowed to fly under the radar of news coverage. Furthermore, the widespread institutional and organizational support that had been required to commit crimes largely stayed out of the media limelight.[17] One strategy to emphasize the idea of individual abnormal perpetration was to portray particularly gruesome details of actions the defendants were accused of, for example: 'Baby hurled against a post'.[18] Additionally, especially the more colourful magazines showed a strange penchant for pairing horrible news stories with obviously innocent advertisements like: 'Be considerate in traffic'.[19] Without overstating the connection between text and advertisements, it can nevertheless be seen as one of the patterns of normalization that helped to integrate coverage of Nazi crime trials into the daily life of post-war West German society.[20] Advertisements aside, illustrated magazines established themselves as platforms for serious debates in the mid-1960s,[21] thereby not only diversifying the mediascape but also strengthening the position of printed media as opinion leaders at a time when the competition with television was increasingly gaining traction. Another strategy of normalization was to highlight the successful reintegration of defendants into post-war society. This also served to rationalize the awkward question of why it had taken (and was taking) so long to bring those accused of the horrific crimes to trial: 'All the accused, who had returned to Germany in civilian clothes, unrecognized and unhindered immediately after the end of the war, and who until a few years ago had returned to their former professions as respected citizens, could only be located in recent years'.[22]

Newspapers' close scrutiny of how participants comported themselves in courts included meticulous observation of signs of emotional involvement. In relation to defendants, there was particular interest in whether their display of emotion might constitute contempt of court, while, the behaviour of judges and prosecutors was examined for signs of potential bias for or against the parties involved. With the victim–witnesses, emotional involvement was linked to the reliability of their evidence, The *Rheinische Post* wrote of a prosecution witness that his outburst 'prevents his swearing in because, as the defence puts it, he "made his feeling known and is not willing or able to distinguish objectively"'.[23] The tension and mistrust prevailing in the relationship between journalists and witnesses for the prosecution seem to have been mutual as not every testifying survivor was comfortable with press inquiries and even challenged the journalists at times.[24]

Since the days of Allied military tribunals immediately after the war, the German public had been concerned about what and how witnesses would testify against German defendants in courtrooms. One especially strong worry was whether witness statements were 'directed'.[25] Such suspicions came up several times during the Treblinka main trial. None of them were ever substantiated. However, it shows how widespread the suspicion was that witnesses were colluding against the German defendants who were, therefore, sometimes seen as victims of so-called Jewish revenge. This trope had already gained popular traction immediately after the war and remained part of an exculpatory discourse by defendants in Nazi crimes trials well into the 1960s. And by spreading news about the court cases, papers and radio stations created a further dimension to this line of defence. Some survivors of Operation Reinhardt camps who later appeared as witnesses were alleged to have heard about the judicial proceedings only through news coverage; only there had they picked up names and events. This supposedly had an effect on their memories of the camps.[26] As far as defence lawyers were concerned, mistrust went even further than that. Some of them alleged that witnesses only reproduced knowledge gained from reading newspapers, which by divulging content relevant to the historical events, provided incriminating evidence against the defendants. An *FAZ* report on the trial of Kurt Franz, the main defendant at the first Düsseldorf Treblinka trial, claimed that many witnesses 'described everything they had read about Franz in an Israeli newspaper article long before the interrogation'.[27]

The fragility of the relationship between courts and the public is discernible in how the courts easily felt pressured or feared undue meddling in their affairs if they had immediate contact to the outside world. Photographs in court were only allowed before the start of proceedings, while audio recordings were rare. There are only two major examples of extant audio documents of Nazi crimes trials. One is the announcement of the verdict in the 1958 Ulm Einsatzgruppen trial. This recording was apparently the result of a compromise to avoid a more wide-ranging call for documentation, since the court emphatically rejected radio and television broadcasting: 'The courtroom is not a show stage'.[28] The other originated from the first Frankfurt Auschwitz trial. It was explicitly requested by the judges and authorized by the Federal Supreme Court. This recording was meant as a memory aid for the court and was intended to be destroyed afterwards, which – in contrast to the Düsseldorf Treblinka trial where recordings were actually destroyed – was later prevented through intervention of Auschwitz survivors and their organizations.[29]

In the 1970s

In the 1970s, publicized views of the Nazi past were no longer considered mainly a matter of journalists and historians in courtrooms, but more broadly (again) also of psychologists, writers and theologians outside of them. Taking special interest in perpetrators' alleged paths of trial and tribulation leading to their crimes, they were looking for universal lessons that could be drawn from the past or for insights about human nature more generally. Radio chimed in with this trend in a roundtable talk about the former Treblinka commandant Franz Stangl,[30] based on Hungarian journalist Gitta Sereny's study about her interviews with him in Düsseldorf prison in Spring 1971. She described her views of Stangl as a person and the structure of his character in the light of his childhood and youth in Austria. The other members of the podium then analysed what they saw as the deeper reasons and motivations behind his career as a manager of mass murder between Spring 1942 and Summer 1943, drawing on psychological and sociological insights. Writer Paul Schallück, who enjoyed a successful career in media in the 1960s,[31] voiced concern about a potential sociopolitical legacy of the Nazi era: 'Does the structure that produced Stangl still extend into our present? What else can it still make possible?' Swiss theologian Franz Boeckle argued that society as a whole also needed to acknowledge the suffering of the individual person that allegedly preceded their acts of perpetration: 'A society that is aware of its structures must also see perpetrators as victims'. Sereny went even further in her plea to let society benefit collectively from former perpetrators instead of punishing them individually, arguing that 'society must use the perpetrators to learn'. And she admitted of Stangl that 'I don't know if I could still find him guilty in a criminal sense'.

Beginning in the late 1960s, the debate about reform of the West German criminal code started to play into the hands of imprisoned Nazi perpetrators. There was general agreement at least in parts of society and the judiciary that most no longer posed any risk and that they had stayed away from crimes for more than twenty years. Thus, both the need for atonement and prevention no longer seemed relevant in their cases. Indeed, social–liberal reform policies intended to enable early releases for prisoners with a 'favourable prognosis'[32] were explicitly aimed at convicted Nazi criminals. Defence counsels in their pleadings as well as convicts themselves in their petitions made ample use of the new ideas. The former head of the Gestapo in Minsk, Georg Heuser, who applied for early release in 1969, cited the prevailing 'talk about reform and rehabilitation' and claimed the 'interest of re-integration into society' as a priority.[33] The West German and Austrian societies were eager to open a new chapter, turning from the long shadow of the wartime past to a brighter future of continuous democratic reform and development. They no longer saw old Nazis as a security threat but as members of society who deserved a second chance. The security threat in West Germany was by now firmly located on the political left where radical discourse and action seemed to endanger the social democratic reform agenda.[34] This shift in attention also influenced coverage of Nazi crimes trials. Problematic issues raised by the trials, such as the unimaginability of hundreds of thousands of victims murdered in extermination camps were now contrasted with more current court matters. Coverage thereby even implicitly exculpated German mainstream society from the charge of lacking empathy with Nazi victims: 'On the same day that Franz Stangl heard his verdict, the chief detective Karl-Heinz Kurras was acquitted in Berlin of the charge of negligently killing the student Benno Ohnesorg. This one death stirred the emotions. It was imaginable. [] But 580,000 or 500,000 or 400,000 dead Jews remain a number, nothing else'.[35]

One consequence of this changed outlook on Nazi perpetrators was that the idea of culpability was also fundamentally shifted. The focus should no longer be on individuals committing crimes but on a society which enabled such crimes. The individual had to be seen as the victim of social and political circumstances and of the burdens of upbringing and socialization. This went together with psychology and sociology becoming new leading sciences and psychiatric expertise was soon in high demand in courtrooms. This shift in emphasis worked in support of perpetrators like former Sobibor SS-Corporal Hubert Gomerski in his re-trial after twenty-seven years. *Die ZEIT* reported the Frankfurt neurologist and psychiatrist, Dr Schumacher's warning against 'privatising genocide and persecution as the actions of individual perpetrators'. Not only could the criminalization of the individual have the effect of decriminalizing the wider society, but punishing individuals could 'unconsciously serve to provide a convenient alibi' for the many who had supported National Socialism.[36]

Also in the 1970s, the ageing process of defendants and witnesses became a major issue. The press frequently mentioned the problem of fading memories roughly thirty years after the events. That argument had first been brought up in connection with Nazi crime trials around 1948 to question whether memories could be accurate some three years after the crimes had been committed. Now that ten times this period had elapsed, the notable gap seemed insurmountable: 'Further difficulties arose from the fact that the action had taken place some 30 years ago, so that even witnesses who themselves had nothing to hide had to take into account memory weaknesses after such a long period of time'.[37] Altogether, media showed increasing scepticism about whether justice could be achieved with ever more costly and time-consuming trials against Nazi perpetrators. Additionally, it became increasingly difficult – given the limitations and interim changes of the German criminal code – to arrive at convincing guilty verdicts that would last beyond the appeal proceedings in front of the Federal Supreme Court. Even moderate left-wing newspaper *Frankfurter Rundschau*, which was generally considered very supportive of judicial attempts to hold perpetrators responsible for Nazi crimes,[38] admitted: 'The proof of guilt becomes less comprehensive and more fragile, indeed, sometimes it is no longer possible at all, as in the case of the former SS-Corporal Alois Frey, who had to be acquitted in the Auschwitz Trial No. 5, not least because the main incriminating witness had died during the trial'.[39] This reflected the eroding legitimacy that a continuation of Nazi crimes trials was met with from the mid-1970s. Apart from mounting costs and less convincing results, it was also their increasing length which reduced public acceptance of those trials. This applied especially to re-trials that became necessary due to some procedural flaws in previous proceedings. As a Frankfurt public prosecutor commented on the case of Hubert Gomerski, 'retrials are seen by the public as a sign of failed justice'.[40]

It was only after the main Auschwitz and Operation Reinhardt camp trials that recognition and even appreciation of the pivotal contribution of victim-witnesses through their evidence in court became more acknowledged in printed media. The *FAZ* recognized that investigations into Sobibor and Treblinka had for years 'been based on the few dozen prisoners who managed to escape during the uprisings'.[41] However, the outright appraisal was probably a point only made in a few quality papers. And it was around 1970, too, that doubts about collusion among witnesses for the defence started to be voiced more openly. Hitherto, such collusion had barely caught media attention or was even tacitly taken for granted. The *FAZ*, for example, reported how the former SS accountant and Treblinka staff member Willy Häusler 'read newspapers in these four weeks since the beginning of the trial, reports that have described the image of the brutal Christian Wirth and the gentle innocent Franz Stangl'.[42] This change indicated an overall more balanced perception of the various groups of actors in Nazi crimes trials. Nevertheless, courts also had to deal with the problem that witnesses from mainstream society were even less willing to cooperate than before. This was a major problem for cases where there were hardly any people who were not personally either massively affected or heavily compromised by past events and/or had a vital interest in obfuscating evidence in order not to incriminate themselves. This was certainly an issue in West Germany but even more problematic when it came to Austrians: 'Many witnesses no longer want to have anything to do with this past and the Austrians who are to be heard cannot be forced to make themselves available to courts in the Federal Republic [West Germany]'.[43]

Apart from a lack of cooperation between witnesses and courts, the immediate participation of the public as audience in courtrooms in the 1970s showed a serious decline compared to the big trials of the 1960s, reverting closer to the situation of the 1950s. And there were other notable changes to courtroom attendance during the 1970s, too. First, school classes were becoming the main audience, and concentration camp survivors still showed up regularly but only in small numbers. Journalist Lothar Bewerunge had embarked on a career as a political correspondent for *FAZ*. Based in Düsseldorf, he was *FAZ*'s special reporter at the trial against the second Treblinka commandant Franz Stangl, where he observed: 'The trial days, twice a week, with practically no audience unless school classes appear, give the impression of treading water'.[44] Although more sympathetic towards the political establishment than many of his peers at major papers,[45] he kept Nazi crimes trials firmly on the news agenda for a number of years and contributed to more self-reflexive forms of accounting for the past in the West German public sphere. Secondly, for the trial against Stangl, at least, there was still sustained media presence and coverage, also in Austria, even while the public no longer showed much active interest: 'After about fifty journalists followed the opening phase of the trial, the spectator benches remained sparsely occupied'.[46] At a time when television claimed the position as leading media, radio programme-makers re-developed a targeted interest in Nazi crimes trial coverage.[47] This, in turn, alerted more newspapers to send special reporters again, at least for the bigger trials, and to re-create international attention for them. Thirdly, foreign media interest in trials concerning crimes committed during German occupation could also spur German papers into more active coverage. Finally, the Majdanek trial, which lasted from 1975 until 1981, saw continuously flagging newspaper coverage while right-wing extremists started to become more visible in the audience.[48] However, another change of generation led to renewed interest in bringing specific Nazi crimes to trial around 1980 in the context of growing societal attention for so-called forgotten victims. As the number of reports about Nazi crime trials in dailies went down in general, pertinent coverage in quality magazines and weeklies with mass distribution, which targeted a more elite readership, started to add pressure on law enforcement agencies to look into euthanasia crimes in particular: 'From the end of the 1970s, the reporting on the Nazi doctors in *Der SPIEGEL* and *Die ZEIT* showed direct media effects: Courts started investigations, doctors were removed from their posts'.[49]

In the 1980s

When *Die ZEIT* turned to Reformation-era martyr John Bradford for inspiration yet again in 1982, it was once more in order to question a judicial verdict in a Nazi crimes trial: this time the 1971 judgement against the by-now-deceased former Treblinka commandant Franz Stangl. However, now the emphasis lay on the question of individual guilt, which allegedly could not be ascribed to Stangl due to his traumatic childhood experiences and adverse political circumstances in his adult life. Thus, the legitimacy of bringing Nazi perpetrators to justice was finally undermined. The reasoning went that Western governments and the pope could have intervened against the mass murder of the Jews of Europe and did not, but Franz Stangl could not.[50] The argument was underscored by the alleged total powerlessness of the individual in a dictatorship. This was paired with the purportedly ill-fated process of individuals unwittingly making initial decisions which eventually put them on an irreversible trajectory: 'Without already knowing it, Stangl chose crime. His chance lay in the first resistance. There lies also – if we ever find ourselves in the same situation – our chance, the chance of those who must not believe to have been created so much better than Stangl'. Gerd Bucerius, author of this article, was a co-founder of *Die ZEIT* and one of its most influential long-term editors. He – like Leonhardt – personified the weekly's turn towards a more liberal outlook as he had left the centre-right CDU in 1962 over the party's repeated attempts to pressure him into using his influence on *Die ZEIT* and other papers and magazines under his editorship to its advantage.[51] Due to the iconic status as a paradigmatic Nazi perpetrator that Franz Stangl seemed to have achieved posthumously in the 1970s, he still occupied journalists' imagination well into the 1980s when he became the object of a radio play. The title of the documentary play, Commandant in Treblinka – The obedient life of Franz Stangl, 'hints at what in the conversation with Stangl proved to be exemplary for the behaviour and thinking of many people in a system of injustice: The concentration camp commander [. . .] was, according to his own statements, an apolitical, fearful, law-abiding and order-loving person'.[52] Similarly generalizing and normalizing assessments of Stangl could be read in Austria, but they attracted less attention: 'Stangl as an individual case, a "special monster"? Hardly'.[53]

This kind of generalizing assessment of individual and collective behaviours of Germans and Austrians during the Nazi era still dominated public opinion in the early 1980s. However, growing attempts of the fledgling 'Dig where you stand' movement in West Germany started to challenge such apologetic blanket assumptions about individual scopes of action and responsibility in the Nazi era by looking into concrete cases in their local environment. In the 1980s, societal and media approaches towards the Nazi past in West Germany changed insofar as most of those, who had been involved in Nazi crimes and later took over senior positions within functional elites, had retired. As a result, more open views of their roles during the Nazi era could be voiced without fear of offending senior staff in the police, judiciary, universities and other relevant public institutions and private companies. At the same time, evaluations of the Nazi past became newly understood as the analysis of yet another part of the longer trajectory of German history, a process of historicization which created further distance to concrete events. This perspective was epitomized by retrospectives framed by the fifty-year-remembrance cycle of the Nazi regime, starting in 1983. In 1986, a radio feature observed the 40th anniversary of the International Military Tribunal at Nuremberg. In it, former Düsseldorf public prosecutor Alfred Spieß pointed to the newly predominant function of trials to collect historical evidence and to enable further research into Nazi crimes instead of mainly bringing perpetrators to justice.[54]

Additionally, a more critical attitude developed in the press towards the assessments of defendants' fitness to stand trial. During the 1960s, defendants' state of health was not yet considered a contentious issue. The Düsseldorf court at the beginning of the 1964/65 Treblinka trial considered installing an Eichmann-style glass cabin built for the trial of Willi Grossmann, who had been sick with tuberculosis. The court decided against the idea and instead quashed his indictment without triggering any notable public reaction. In the 1970s, health had become a vital argument to declare defendants unfit to stand trial and at the same time victims' and witnesses' health was also declining. Printed media were still more dutifully reporting what they considered facts rather than questioning this as a defence strategy to delay procedures or even prevent their conclusion, thus averting a final sentence. When procedures against euthanasia doctor Georg Renno were suspended in March 1970, the *Frankfurter Neue Presse* was sympathetic. Now that Renno's 'general clinical condition has [. . .] been aggravated by an acute kidney inflammation, it is obvious that neither a continuation nor an imminent restart of his proceedings can be expected, which will thus remain interrupted for an indefinite period of time'.[55] But by the mid-1980s, the tide was decidedly turning when previous practices of assessing defendants' health status were now considered to have unduly favoured them. Although trial coverage would not necessarily take sides in those conflicts, newspaper headlines still included those like, 'Court aids mass murderer'[56] when proceedings were suspended because of the defendant's apparent mental distress.

Conclusion

Particularly within printed media, representations of perpetrators changed from the 1950s to the 1980s. With renewed public interest in Nazi crimes trials in the 1960s, specifically West German papers contributed to sensationalizing representations of the few indicted perpetrators while normalizing the many who were not brought to trial. In the 1970s, societal attitudes towards the Nazi past fundamentally changed. The focus was transferred from defiant social solidarity with the majority of perpetrators[57] towards abstract empathy with their alleged psychological and social predicaments past and present as well as political concern for their reintegration. However, the image of a minority of allegedly demonized perpetrators still functioned as a tool to mark the 'true culprits'. The discourse with which to communicate abominable crimes to mass audiences had to be reinvented by the media, which navigated between the struggle for attention, the need for credible distancing from criminals and the drawing of acceptable moral borders. Thus, the ongoing normalization of the vast majority of Nazi perpetrators remained an integral part of otherwise shifting representations. The constitutive elements of this representational shift were fourfold. First, critical attention for courtroom actors was more evenly distributed. An attitude of othering the victim-witnesses or even us-versus-them reflexes in mainstream society gave way to more balanced views at press level. Second, all three successor societies of the Nazi regime turned over a new leaf in their political history in the early 1970s. Especially in West Germany, Nazism was no longer seen as an imminent threat but rather a distant legacy to be dealt with in innovative ways. The media reacted by turning actual perpetrators into objects of in-depth analysis instead of seeing them mainly as defendants in courtrooms. Third, this caused a shift in ideas of culpability. In the 1960s public discourse on Nazi crimes had been dominated by the opposition between perpetration as acting upon orders versus voluntary individual excess perpetration. In the 1970s, this became overlaid by the opposition between seeing perpetration as a product of an individual disposition or as an outcome of the impact of the dictatorial superstructure. Fourth, in the 1970s, courtroom audiences were dominated by school classes and press people. Dealing with the Nazi past became mainly an educational issue, or one providing merely pieces of news; it was no longer the urgent issue of mainstream society as in the 1960s.

There are a couple of oppositions within the mediascapes under consideration. There is a gap between national papers or magazines and regional or local papers both in terms of focus and density of coverage and in terms of depth and quality of their coverage of Nazi crimes trials. These oppositions happened synchronically but also have a diachronic dimension. For example, while national papers in the mid-1960s already adopted a more open-minded and critical approach to defendants' defence strategies, local papers still tended to describe things from a more traditionally nationalistic point of view.[58] Also the stance of individual papers and magazines changed over time, especially when *Die ZEIT* – corresponding to its own trajectory – turned into a kind of seismograph for changes in societal attitudes and views. *Der SPIEGEL* underwent an even broader shift, from being instrumentalized by former Nazi functionaries in the early 1950s[59] to being at the centre of the single-most-influential confrontation between state and press in West Germany in the 1962 'SPIEGEL affair', and to becoming an outspoken centre–left adversary of a succession of governments from then on. In Austria, media discourses and reflections on Nazi crimes trials happened altogether on a smaller scale. The few trials in Austria were either apologetically minimalized or ruthlessly scandalized. The 1970s saw an almost complete lack of legal action against former Nazis and a corresponding lack of coverage, apart from a few peak events like the West German trial against the Austrian Franz Stangl. This included odd references to Nazi crimes, for example: 'Franz Stangl was [. . .] commander of the Treblinka extermination camp in its golden age from August 1942 to August 1943'.[60] An openly critical attitude towards average Nazi perpetrators in Austrian mainstream papers took even longer to develop. Only the controversial public debate about the Nazi past of presidential candidate Kurt Waldheim in 1986 put into question previous media practices of regarding formerly influential Nazis as mere contemporary witnesses or even victims.[61]

Especially in the 1970s, social and political developments in West Germany and Austria suggested an emerging new era, which emphasized future opportunities over continued efforts at dealing with the past. The historicizing effects of this re-orientation led to waning interest in bringing former Nazis to justice. This was complemented by shifting assessments of the defendants' health status. Hardly an issue in the 1960s, stronger interest in medical examinations of perpetrators accompanied the psychological and sociological investigations of the 1970s before turning firmly into a point of accusation against them in the following decade. In the 1980s, the renewed activities to highlight acts of perpetration within their local environment put individual perpetrators back into the limelight, unsettling a prevailing trend towards generalizing and exculpating assessments of Nazi crimes as impersonal manifestations of 'evil'. At the same time, attempts at putting the Nazi past into the longer perspective of respective (West) German and Austrian national histories gained momentum, while commemoration and remembrance attained new prominence in social and political debates. Thus, the broader public focus moved towards accounts of the Nazi past as experience and emotionalized memory. At societal level, this also opened up new discursive space for coming to terms with Nazi crimes in the public sphere.

Notes

1 Cf. Rudolf Walther Leonhardt, 'Wir leben – sie büßen . . . Neunzig "Kriegsverurteilte" werden noch von den Alliierten zurückgehalten', *Die ZEIT*, 28 March 1957.
2 Cf. Gerd Bucerius, 'Wem steht das letzte Urteil zu? Gedanken nach der Lektüre eines Buches über den Lagerchef von Treblinka', *Die ZEIT*, 5 February 1982.
3 Cf. Christina von Hodenberg, *Konsens und Krise: Eine Geschichte der westdeutschen Medienöffentlichkeit 1945–1973* (Göttingen: Wallstein Verlag, 2006), 289.
4 Cf. Inge Marszolek, '"[. . .] täglich zu Dir kommt das Radio" – Zur Repräsentation der NS-Vergangenheit in Sendungen von Radio Bremen 1946–1952', *Tel Aviver Jahrbuch für deutsche Geschichte* 31 (2003): 163f.
5 Cf. Renée Winter, *Geschichtspolitiken und Fernsehen. Repräsentationen des Nationalsozialismus im frühen österreichischen TV (1955–1970)* (Bielefeld: transcript Verlag, 2014), 198ff. and 221.
6 Cf. Cord Arendes, *Zwischen Justiz und Tagespresse. 'Durchschnittstäter' in regionalen NS-Verfahren* (Paderborn/München: Ferdinand Schöningh, 2012), 135.
7 On crimes of Dr Erika Flocken, see National Archives Microfilm Publications Pamphlet Describing M 1093, United States Army Investigation and Trial Records of War Criminals, *United States of America v. Franz Auer et al.*, National Archives and Records Administration, Washington DC On those of Gauleiter Wilhelm Pfeiffer in Vienenburg, see Kevin T. Hall, *Terror Flyers: The Lynching of American Airmen in Nazi Germany* (Bloomington: Indiana University Press, 2021), 167ff.
8 Cf. Frank Bösch, 'Der Nationalsozialismus im Fernsehen: Geschichtsschreibung im Fernsehen, 1950–1990', in *Public History. Öffentliche Darstellungen des Nationalsozialismus jenseits der Geschichtswissenschaft*, ed. Frank Bösch and Constantin Goschler (Frankfurt aM: Campus Verlag, 2009), 75.
9 'Diese Bestien', *Der SPIEGEL*, 24 July 1963, 26.
10 Heinz Höhne, 'Der Orden unter dem Totenkopf. Die Geschichte der SS (12th sequel, caption)', *Der SPIEGEL*, 2 January 1967, 52.
11 Cf. Arendes, *Zwischen Justiz und Tagespresse*, 164. See also the assessment of the Düsseldorf Treblinka trial as 'a long and tedious procedure with few highlights', Heinz Schweden, 'Alle beschuldigen Franz', *Rheinische Post*, Düsseldorf, 14 October 1964.
12 Cf., also on the following, 'Fagott geblasen', *Der SPIEGEL*, 8 September 1965, 61.
13 Cf. Arendes, *Zwischen Justiz und Tagespresse*, 166f.
14 Lothar Bewerunge, 'Lupinen über dem Vernichtungslager', *Frankfurter Allgemeine Zeitung [FAZ]*, 18 September 1964.
15 'Augenzeuge unzähliger grausamer Verbrechen', *General-Anzeiger Bonn*, 10 September 1964.
16 Cf. Sara Berger, *Experten der Vernichtung. Das T4-Reinhardt-Netzwerk in den Lagern Belzec, Sobibor und Treblinka* (Hamburg: Hamburger Edition, 2013), 377.
17 Cf. Rebecca Wittmann, 'Tainted Law. The West German Judiciary and the Prosecution of Nazi War Criminals', in *Atrocities on Trial. Historical Perspectives on the Politics*

of Prosecuting War Crimes, ed. Patricia Heberer and Jürgen Matthäus (Lincoln: University of Nebraska Press, 2008), 219f.
18 'Baby gegen Pfosten geschleudert', *Rheinische Post*, Rheinhausen (special report), 12 November 1964.
19 'Treblinka-Prozeß: Elf Angeklagte', *Mettmanner Zeitung*, 31 August 1964.
20 Cf. Jan Erik Schulte, '"Namen sind Nachrichten": Journalismus und NS-Täterforschung in der frühen Bundesrepublik Deutschland', in *Public History. Öffentliche Darstellungen des Nationalsozialismus jenseits der Geschichtswissenschaft*, ed. Frank Bösch and Constantin Goschler (Frankfurt aM: Campus Verlag, 2009), 36.
21 Cf. Hodenberg, *Konsens und Krise*, 340 and 360.
22 Hasso Ziegler, 'Mord an 700.000 Menschen ruft nach Sühne', *Neue Ruhr-Zeitung*, Essen, 10 September 1964.
23 Eduard Neumaier, 'Tote in drei Schichten', *Rheinische Post*, Krefeld, 26 March 1965.
24 Lothar Bewerunge, 'Aus der Gaskammer zurückgekrochen', *FAZ*, 4 June 1965.
25 Cf. 'Wurden Aussagen gelenkt?', *Neuß-Grevenbroicher Zeitung*, 20 August 1965.
26 Lothar Bewerunge, 'Wer bei der Auspeitschung schrie, wurde erschossen', *FAZ*, 12 Februar 1964.
27 Lothar Bewerunge, '"Treblinka hat 1933 angefangen"', *FAZ*, 8 October 1965.
28 Cf. Baden-Württemberg State Archives, Ludwigsburg State Archive, Fond: Staatsanwaltschaft beim Landgericht Ulm: NS-Verfahren, EL 322 II DO 1, *Tonbandaufzeichnungen des Urteils im Prozess gegen ein NS-Einsatzkommando vor dem Schwurgericht Ulm I*, tape 2, at 10:30 min.
29 Cf. Werner Renz, 'Anmerkungen zum Tonbandmitschnitt im 1. Frankfurter Auschwitz-Prozess', in *Tonbandmitschnitte des Auschwitz-Prozesses (1963–1965)* (September 2013). https://www.auschwitz-prozess.de/materialien/T_03_Der _Tonbandmitschnitt_des_Auschwitz-Prozesses/ (Accessed 11 December 2021).
30 Cf. Westdeutscher Rundfunk [West German Broadcasting Corporation, WDR] Corporate Archive, 6075093101.1.01, '*Er wurde Kommandant in Treblinka. Diskussion über den KZ-Kommandanten Franz Stangl*', 21 November 1971.
31 Cf. Hodenberg, *Konsens und Krise*, 286.
32 Cf. BT 5. WP DS [West German Federal Parliament, 5th Legislative Period, Printed Matter] V-4094, Report of the Special Committee on Reform of the Criminal Code (Modification of § 26 StGB – Early Release), May 1969, 13.
33 Cf. Jürgen Matthäus, '"No Ordinary Criminal": Georg Heuser, Other Mass Murderers and West German Justice', in *Atrocities on Trial. Historical Perspectives on the Politics of Prosecuting War Crimes*, ed. Patricia Heberer and idem (Lincoln: University of Nebraska Press, 2008), 201f.
34 Cf. Wittmann, 'Tainted Law', 223. On the following, see ibid., 211.
35 Dietrich Strothmann, 'Tragödie von Treblinka. Der banale Böse: Stangl', *Die ZEIT*, 1 January 1971.
36 'Persönliche Schuld an Völkermord und Verfolgung?', *FAZ* (dpa), 27 April 1977.
37 'Euthanasie-Urteile gefällt', *Frankfurter Rundschau* [*FR*] (bi), 28 May 1970.
38 'Sobibor-Urteil rechtswidrig', *Deutsche National-Zeitung*, München, 11 April 1980.
39 Norbert Leppert, 'Richter müssen gegen Krankheiten ankämpfen', *FR*, 4 March 1976.
40 'Herr über Leben und Tod der Juden', *Frankfurter Neue Presse* (tn), 11 May 1977.
41 Lothar Bewerunge, 'Franz Stangl bald vor Gericht', *FAZ*, 12 March 1970.
42 Lothar Bewerunge, 'Der Burgherr von Treblinka', *FAZ*, 15 June 1970.
43 Heinrich Schott, 'Tausende von Vergasten klagen an', *Garmisch-Partenkirchner Tagblatt*, 21 January 1970.

44　Lothar Bewerunge, 'Die Zeugen unter Eideszwang nach 28 Jahren', *FAZ*, 21 September 1970.
45　Cf. his obituary in Landtag intern, *State Parliament of North Rhine-Westphalia* [Online], 7 September 1989, 19, https://www.landtag.nrw.de/portal/WWW/dokumentenarchiv/Dokument?Id=ZLANIN8914%7C19%7C19 (Accessed 27 November 2021).
46　'Stangl: Nur die Pflicht erfüllt', *Die Presse*, 14 May 1970.
47　Cf., also on the following, Heiner Lichtenstein, 'NS-Prozesse und Öffentlichkeit', in *Vereint vergessen? Justiz- und NS-Verbrechen in Deutschland*, ed. Landeszentrale für politische Bildung Nordrhein-Westfalen (Düsseldorf: Self-Publishing, 1993), 71ff.
48　Cf. Wittmann, 'Tainted Law', 224.
49　Arnd Schweitzer, 'Sadistische Einzeltäter oder Kollektivschuld eines ganzen Standes? 50 Jahre Berichterstattung über NS-Verbrechen von Ärzten in SPIEGEL und ZEIT' (Diploma Thesis, Hochschule für Musik, Theater und Medien, Hanover, 1997), 60. This reference is relevant also for the discussion that follows.
50　The article was actually a review of Sereny's book on Franz Stangl, Gitta Sereny, *Into that Darkness. From Mercy Killing to Mass Murder* (New York: Mc Graw Hill, 1974). Cf. Bucerius, 'Wem steht das letzte Urteil zu'. This reference is relevant also for the discussion that follows.
51　Cf. Hodenberg, *Konsens und Krise*, 326.
52　Wilfried Mommert, 'Blick in den Abgrund', *Frankenpost*, 29 March 1984.
53　'Es war eigentlich wirklich schön. Das gehorsame Leben des KZ-Kommandanten als Hörspiel', *Ausweg*, September 1984, 13.
54　Cf. WDR Corporate Archive, 6108358201.1.01, 'Forum West. Vierzig Jahre danach - Eine Bilanz der NS-Prozesse. Alfred Spieß im Gespräch mit Heiner Lichtenstein', 4 October 1986.
55　'Verhandlung ohne Renno', *Frankfurter Neue Presse* (mm), 26 March 1970.
56　'Gericht hilft Massenmörder', *Rhein-Zeitung*, Koblenz, 29 June 1984.
57　Cf. Berger, *Experten der Vernichtung*, 379.
58　Cf. 'Heute: Prozeß wegen Beihilfe zum Mord von 360.000 Juden', *Solinger Tageblatt* (AP), 18 January 1965.
59　Cf. Schulte, 'Namen sind Nachrichten', 30.
60　'KZ-Kommandant Stangl verhaftet', *Wiener Zeitung*, 3 March 1967.
61　Cf. Heinz P. Wassermann, *'Zuviel Vergangenheit tut nicht gut'. Nationalsozialismus im Spiegel der Tagespresse der Zweiten Republik* (Innsbruck/Vienna/Munich: Studien Verlag, 2000), 436f.

13

Pinochet's accomplices

Perpetration, civilian complicity and individual versus institutional culpability in domestic atrocity crime accountability

Francisco Bustos, Cath Collins and Francisco Ugás

Introduction

This chapter discusses the potential of domestic courts to comprehensively address the responsibility of direct and indirect perpetrators of grave and systematic human rights violations perpetrated by past authoritarian military regimes. It does so through a participant observation-informed[1] case study of legal pathways employed in Chile to address atrocity crime accountability in domestic courts. Breakthroughs in the country's formal justice sphere since 1998 have seen prosecutions, civil claims and other judicially arbitrated actions over killings, disappearances and other repressive crimes committed by the 1973–90 military dictatorship.[2] These breakthroughs have generated a considerable criminal and civil caseload.[3] They have also seen the courts increasingly resorted to in efforts to address collusion, shape the symbolic landscape, deepen acknowledgement and change the present-day discourse of institutional actors including the armed forces. While this expanded legal repertoire has had uneven and sometimes contradictory outcomes, its very existence speaks to the relative richness of the domestic legal arena as a venue for addressing past atrocity crimes.

Two themes emerge with particular force: individual versus collective agency in the attribution of responsibility, and consistency of state acknowledgment across institutions and over time. Each has evident broader comparative and theoretical importance. These themes are explored via four lines of enquiry. Lines one and two explore how Chile's courts have understood perpetration, with particular reference to treatment of civilian perpetrators. Taken together, these two lines demonstrate tension between the intrinsically diffuse, systemic nature of mass violations and traditional criminal liability approaches focused on tangible individual acts. Next, lines three and four consider legal responses beyond criminal law: civil claims, increasingly resorted to by survivors, and novel types of legal action that aim to address the ongoing duty and responsibility of collective entities, including commercial concerns and state institutions. This chapter argues that beyond their contingent outcomes these novel recourses, unique to the domestic legal sphere, offer particular potential synergy with the truth-telling, reparation and reform dimensions of transitional justice. The conclusions return to the question of what is or can be distinctive about domestic legal venues as a site of post-atrocity accountability.

How Chilean courts construe perpetration

Osiel observes that '[m]ass atrocity could not occur without the organized cooperation of [...] both soldiers [...] and sympathetic civilians', adding that 'a satisfactory method for ascribing particular harms to specific defendants is not always readily at hand'.[4] To date, a conservative approach to criminal liability for past mass violations has seen Chilean higher courts preferring to prosecute action rather than omission, moreover emphasizing direct physical participation by named individuals in visible harms to bodily integrity. This narrow focus emerged early in the post-1998 accountability revival, when the Supreme Court tried to restrict new investigations to cases involving deaths or disappearances. All other grave violations were to be treated as still subject to amnesty and/or statutes of limitation.[5] The new investigations did not, however, exclusively target low-level foot soldiers; there was some readiness to convict based on membership of collectivities, at least as regards semi-secret, specially created repressive apparatuses. Nonetheless, the Chilean courts have proved generally averse to the novel joint criminal enterprise theories espoused by international criminal tribunals. Instead, a preference for chains of events linking individual perpetrators in time and place to specific victims has often facilitated absolutions where circumstances strongly suggest shared criminality but do not clearly delineate the exact contribution of each suspect.[6] Overall, this approach favours atomistic, individualized approaches to guilt, blame and punishment.[7]

Many of these features are rooted in a rigid understanding of the principle of legality, one which betrays, as Torelly notes, a generally beneficent view of even authoritarian-era legality as wholly legitimate, or at least, not to be lightly set aside.[8] However, the principle of legality poses difficulties for post-hoc atrocity accountability anywhere and everywhere, since it entails the prohibition on retroactive application of changes in law often referred to as *lex praevia*. In Chile, *lex praevia* has been read as requiring any allegedly criminal act to be tried under existing criminal law at the time of the offence. When this preference is combined with a marked disinclination to directly apply international law,[9] the criminal law in question becomes that of the domestic dispensation of the day. International norms are invoked, but only to consider whether the threshold for an internationally defined crime against humanity has been met.[10] We are left with a version of the 'Nazi legality' dilemma that so vexed the architects of Nuremberg: how to 'translate' modern conceptions of atrocity crime into the entirely extemporaneous language and codifications of authoritarian-era criminal law. For

Chile, a civil law tradition country, this has moreover meant relying on the letter of a Criminal Code dating back to 1874.

Despite subsequent updating, this Code retains notably anachronistic features. Rooted in a world long predating the post-1945 'atrocity paradigm',[11] it offers few tools adequate for grappling with state-instituted mass atrocity. The development of such tools for Chile lay far into the future.[12] The old code does, of course, offer a range of norms that have been pressed into service to judicialize some approximation of the crimes at the heart of dictatorship-era repression: kidnap (*secuestro*) for enforced disappearances; and homicide (*homicidio*) or – in its aggravated version – *asesinato*, for extrajudicial executions.[13] The question of torture, inflicted not only on absent victims but also at least 40,000 acknowledged survivors, is more complex. Available charges are woefully inadequate even in name: 'torments' (*aplicación de tormentos*) or 'illegitimate pressure' (*apremios ilegítimos*). Hence many survivors' preference for civil claims.[14]

Articles 14–17 of the Code delineate subtypes of possible criminal participation, with Articles 15, 16 and 17 dealing with authors (*autores*), accomplices (*cómplices*) and accessories after the fact (*encubridores*). Article 14 presents three hypotheses of authorship: *autor ejecutor*, *autor mediato* and *coautor*, roughly equivalent to perpetration, perpetration-by-means and co-perpetration. Authorship is quite broadly drawn, comprising those who seek to prevent the avoidance of a crime, directly force or induce another to commit it, knowingly and intentionally provide the means or are present at its commission, with knowledge and intent, even if they do not take 'immediate' part. Despite their habitual literal-mindedness, Chilean higher courts have moreover also been known to admit a version of perpetration-by-means through control of an organized power apparatus, following Claus Roxin.[15] This has mainly been deployed against high-ranking members of the Direccion de Inteligencia Nacional, DINA, a powerful secret police set up at Pinochet's direct behest in the early 1970s. The result has been repeated conviction of the DINA's most notorious figures, many now serving decades of accumulated prison sentences. Nonetheless, other doctrines considered progressive in international criminal justice circles have not been taken up by Chilean domestic courts, despite case litigants' best efforts. These include the joint criminal enterprise (JCE) thesis first made explicit by the International Criminal Tribunal for the former Yugoslavia, ICTY.[16]

This judicial resistance to doctrines that promise to expand modes of liability cannot be attributed solely to an at least respectably rigorous adherence to *lex scripta*. This is because in issues favourable to the defendant the courts have shown themselves much readier to apply requirements not strictly speaking demanded by the old Criminal Code. Thus for example, the Santiago Court of Appeal generally leans towards the physical presence requirements discussed above, despite the relative breadth of scope of Article 15 regarding authorship. Here, the same legality principle elsewhere adduced to declare international law precepts inapplicable is watered down. Convictions have consequently been overturned even when all valid *de iure* elements of the crime are indisputably present.[17] Courts have also vacillated as to whether civilians – that is, private individuals who were neither members of the Armed Forces nor civilian agents formally recruited into security service apparatuses – are imputable as full perpetrators (see below).

As we have seen, these rather retrograde examples of Appeals Court logic do not stand up to doctrinal scrutiny even from the limited perspective of now-superseded domestic law at the time of the offence, suggesting that legality and positivism are not the only drivers. This pattern presents a greater problem for legal pluralists sympathetic to a municipal 'margin of appreciation' than that presented, per se, by the reliance on an outdated domestic criminal code. Yang, for example, rightly observes that 'international labels' (e.g. 'enforced disappearance') need not be present for domestic atrocity crime prosecution to be considered satisfactory.[18] However, he also wants domestic outcomes to be positively valued as 'permissible pluralism', even if they are so far at odds with international venues' prevailing interpretations as to appear 'unreasonably lenient'.[19] Osiel offers a similar defence of the virtues of 'untrammelled discretion'[20] in choosing among alternative methods and sites of atrocity crime response, albeit presuming each to demonstrate a certain 'internal coherence and rule-boundedness' that is not really visible in the erratic and legally opaque outcomes discussed above. The question of whether and how domestic judicial practice can be shaped into a more coherent and rule-bounded form from within then becomes particularly pressing. The recent Chilean experiences analysed here suggest this is possible, but not guaranteed.

Civilians as perpetrators

We have already seen, above, how an early judicial filter attempted to limit the operational definition of human rights violations to killings and disappearances only. The extreme selectivity that this entails should not be laid entirely at the door of Chile's justice system; it faithfully maps explicit or implicit victim hierarchies prevalent throughout Latin America and beyond. During the dictatorship, Chile's incipient domestic human rights movement echoed this emphasis on individual right-to-life violations.[21] One corollary has been a focus on ex-uniformed personnel as perpetrators, as killing and disappearance was overwhelmingly the preserve of agents from the armed forces and police, grouped into 'intelligence' organizations of dubious legality.[22] Some civilians were recruited by these organizations as informants, support staff or agents. These individuals have in the recent period run greater risk than formerly of conviction alongside their uniformed counterparts.[23] The possible criminal liabilities of other classes of civilians have however been addressed in quite a limited manner, if at all.[24]

The only civilians not attached to security agencies who seem to run any real risk of prosecution are those physically present when killings or disappearances took place. Even here, complicity figures are preferred, with some courts asserting that civilians ipso facto cannot exercise direct or functional control over human rights violations.[25] One departure from this logic, and the first ever confirmed conviction of a non-security-service-agent civilian, came in 2017, when the Supreme Court ratified a 20-year sentence against landowner Juan Luzoro for direct perpetration (*autoría*) of multiple aggravated homicides.[26] This departure, like the relatively substantial sentence, is susceptible to various particularist explanations including the undoubted diligence of the investigative magistrate and the fact that Luzoro, who had repeatedly boasted of having personally shot some victims, was the only perpetrator still alive to be sentenced by the time the case concluded. A second civilian currently convicted (at Appeals Court level) in a related case was however also sentenced for *autoría* despite the fact that numerous former Army officers were available to shoulder the lion's share of the blame, had the Court seen fit.[27]

A small cluster of criminal cases has emerged in recent years addressing willing facilitation, a class of collaboration in which pro-coup businesses lent practical and logistical support, including singling out union-linked employees for torture or elimination.[28] To date, however, investigations have pursued former directors or managers – rather than addressing collective or corporate decision-making – and continue to emphasize direct physical connection to chains of events leading to deaths or disappearances. One such iconic case, over the 1973 massacre of nineteen workers from the CMPC paper company, did initially see three former company executives and a driver charged alongside former police officers. The January 2020 verdict (currently under appeal) however absolved all four civilians of accomplice charges, despite finding that they had plied the police officers with alcohol, lent them a vehicle, identified employees to be taken away and provided quicklime later used to destroy human remains. Individual civilians, then, are rarely being charged, and even more rarely being convicted, even where the facts and available domestic law clearly permit it.

Across our first and second categories of example, then – criminal sanction and treatment of civilian versus uniformed perpetrators – the capacity of inherently unwieldy legal figures and categories to deliver consistent, proportionate sanction has been further vitiated by interpretive conservatism plus occasional pro-defendant judicial activism. This uneven state of affairs is perhaps encouraged by the absence of binding legal precedent in the Chilean system, which offers broad scope to judges' personal discretion ('inner conviction') as a legitimate basis for adjudication.[29] There is little sign of sentencing consistent enough to serve any broader social function, whether dissuasive, punitive or communicative in the sense suggested by Antony Duff, that is, rationally signalling collective reproach for harm done to agreed values.[30]

There is also a strongly individualizing dynamic at work in relation to case bringers as well as defendants.[31] Most currently active criminal investigations were set in train not by state prosecutors, but by relatives or survivors submitting a criminal complaint (*querella*) before an investigative magistrate.[32] The closest this dynamic has come to recognizing a collective complainant identity has been in allowing relatives' associations, rather than solely family members, to submit *querellas*, and in allowing survivor cases for torture to be brought by small groups of affected individuals.[33] Here, though, it is not unknown for a group that has acted together throughout a case to be subsequently divided at the verdict stage, with courts deciding that some complainants have a better claim to victim status than others, and/or awarding widely differing amounts of compensation, frequently without explanation.[34] Meanwhile the argument that cases can and should be initiated without the need for activism by or on behalf of any named victim – investigating, for example, the structure of clandestine detention centres, or the command decision to routinely use torture – has simply not prospered.

The next two sections consider how other (i.e. non-criminal) types of legal action have begun to broaden the domestic accountability landscape beyond the frame of criminal law, and potentially also beyond the frame of the individual as sole or principal infractor. While the results, as we will see, are similarly mixed – and indeed at times arguably counterproductive – the very fact that the domestic legal sphere offers these avenues is undoubtedly one of its distinctive features as an accountability venue.

Civil claims: Individuation, collectivization and state attitudes to liability

As Osiel states, where redress for mass atrocity is at issue, '[a] single question is central and distinctive [. . .] whether to regard the dramatis personae – perpetrators, victims, and beneficiaries – chiefly as individual persons or instead as collectivities'.[35] Civil claim-making tends to bring this question into particularly sharp focus, catalysed as it is by victim-driven perceptions of who should be held liable for what. This represents an oft-ignored but substantial potential advantage of domestic justice systems over international venues: while atrocity crime justice in the international space is almost exclusively criminal,[36] domestic justice systems offer a range of possible points of entry. Considering, moreover, the less exacting standard of evidentiary certainty usually applied to civil, as opposed to criminal, proceedings, we see that civil claims can make a potentially unique contribution to the truth-telling and economic reparations dimensions of states' transitional justice obligations. At least as practised in Chile, civil claim-making also introduces a collectivizing dynamic to accountability, since claims almost invariably name state entities, rather than individual perpetrators.

Empirically, in Chile, although criminal cases often entail a damages component, victims can also file standalone civil claims. Most of Chile's growing universe of civil claims are against the state per se, with a smaller proportion naming a specific institution (usually a branch of the Armed Forces).[37] The majority seek reparation of moral harm through monetary indemnization. The Treasury (*Fisco*) appears as respondent. These suits usually deal with violations whose veracity, and state-sponsored nature, the state has already acknowledged.[38] Notwithstanding, the Chilean state invariably vigorously contests liability, adducing arguments both general and case-specific. Initially, the state simply invoked statutes of limitation, which are of shorter duration for civil than for criminal liability. This application of ordinary legal precepts to extraordinary harm was however rejected by the relevant Supreme Court bench, who found domestic statute, the Constitution and international law to render statutes of limitation inapplicable to civil as to criminal remedy for crimes against humanity.[39] Faced with this relatively progressive jurisprudence, the state began to contest the factual basis even of incidents amply documented previously by a truth commission. The outcome is thus paradoxical: while most claims currently find in the claimant's favour, this is despite express opposition from state legal representatives. The transformation of the courts into a route to reparation has therefore entailed one branch of state expanding the scope of remedy, while another reacts defensively by reneging on previous acknowledgement.

A third, currently largely unsuccessful, strand of argument softens this contradiction, and the symbolic violence it inflicts, by adducing '*excepción de pago*': the state contends that reparations schemes introduced after the 1990 transition satisfy its obligations. Here, at least, responsibility for the original violation is not openly denied. One might argue that these civil claims therefore on balance expose the collective nature of regime terror better than their criminal equivalents. Notably, though, it is the present-day state, rather than the actual perpetrating institution, that provides the redress.[40]

Overall, and despite some activation of international legal precepts foregrounding systematicity, Chile's atrocity crimes are still being judicialized in a rather improvised domestic idiom, the organic result of multiple private activisms. State-initiated criminal investigations make up the minority of extant cases for absent victims, do not respond to any cohesive prosecutorial strategy and feature not at all in the caseload for crimes against survivors, meaning Chile's ex officio duties to prosecute atrocity crimes are at best incompletely fulfilled. In civil claims, the state moreover balks at allowing prior acknowledgement to stand as an admission of liability. Despite the incipient collective responsibility implied by findings of liability against the state, the basic 'units' of judicialization – episodes, victims, perpetrators – continue to betray an atomized configuration, delineated by largely incidental temporal or geographical circumstances. Judicial reasoning in verdicts rarely explicitly locates the facts of a case within the overall sweep of state terror, beyond an initial examination of whether they formed part of a systematic and/or widespread attack on the civilian population.[41] The myopia inherent in such an approach is deftly exposed by Osiel, counselling against understanding mass atrocity as 'a series of discrete acts of *mano-a-mano* violence'.[42]

Is the systemic, corporate nature of mass atrocity adequately captured by the matrix of criminal and civil proceedings described above? Is state crime unduly disaggregated, taking on the semblance of a mere accumulation of morally bankrupt personal choices, or does conviction after conviction of former uniformed officers somehow add up to the passing of judgement on their institutions? Is state responsibility underlined by repeated findings of financial liability, or has the state's desire to defend its coffers de-natured this aspect of the present-day accountability caseload? Discussion, below, of more novel types of legal action complements these reflections by allowing us to see how relevant entities and institutions have behaved in the face of real or perceived attribution of collective blame.

Other uses of the courts

More recent privately instigated actions have used the courts to address newer arenas of responsibility, such as inciting, planning and financing the coup, or knowingly publishing regime propaganda and falsehoods.[43] In transitional justice terms it might be argued that these actions constitute a search for symbolic reparation, truth-telling and/or guarantees of non-repetition, since they usually seek changes to the public and institutional landscape rather than criminal or pecuniary remedy. Resort to the courts for such purposes is striking, given their patchy record even in what could properly be considered their core functions (criminal and civil justice). It may, then, say more about the dearth of alternative vehicles for pursuing transitional justice goals. Notwithstanding, these new types of action have obliged the courts to pronounce on issues that undoubtedly matter for national self-understanding, perhaps bearing more symbolic weight even than the now-habitual drip-feed of criminal or civil verdicts.

The principal objects of these alternative legal actions have been civilian instigators of, and cheerleaders for, the dictatorship: private media outlets, spurious dictatorship-era military tribunals and the present-day armed forces.[44] We can trace an increasingly collective character to the object of action, from private media moguls to their companies or conglomerates, and from past agents of now-defunct irregular security agencies towards the current military high command. Targets for these creative departures from the 'who did what to whom' focus of earlier criminal and civil actions have included Agustin Edwards, the now-deceased newspaper magnate behind right-wing broadsheet *El Mercurio*. Relatives' associations denounced him to the National College of Journalists, and to the criminal courts, over his active sabotage of the 1970–73 government and proactive support for the 1973 coup. Although the College of Journalists' ethics tribunal finally agreed to expel Edwards, the legal complaints, initiated in 2012 and 2013, did not prosper. In truth, the legal panorama was never promising, and these attempts can be read as a form of social, political and ethical accounting as much as a genuine effort to achieve sanction through the courts.

The complaints also described how *El Mercurio* and its sister papers had lied about and covered up human rights violations, through selective silence and the printing of regime propaganda known to be false. In 2018, family members of two victims demanded that the *La Tercera* newspaper be ordered to publish a retraction of a dictatorship-era article. Prompted by a 2017 criminal case verdict, the families invoked constitutional and human rights principles to challenge the newspaper's previous characterization of the men as 'extremists', and their murders as lawful. The Supreme Court duly ordered the retraction.[45] A similar recourse was brought in 2019, this time over a notorious 1975 front page headline in the *La Segunda* paper, crowing that fifty-nine left-wing activists had died 'like rats' in supposed internecine confrontations. In fact, they had been forcibly disappeared in an international state terror operation. The sister of one victim took out a writ of protection and in August 2020 the Santiago Appeals Court ordered a full-page retraction, citing explicit Constitutional protection of personal and family honour.[46] Similar cases are in train, and the accountability frame is thereby being expanded to include Constitutional and administrative law alongside criminal or civil codes. Interestingly, also, the 'collectivization' of the object of these actions is accompanied by a time shift towards the present day, since the focus is not (only) on past press misdeeds, but on the ongoing offence entailed by the failure to retract.

This same question of ongoing or inherited responsibility is latent in each of the final clusters of examples considered here. The first speaks to the courts' own undoubted dereliction of duty throughout the dictatorship, since a steady stream of recent legal submissions features survivors looking to overturn spurious convictions imposed by dictatorship-era courts-martial. Requests accelerated after an Inter-American Court of Human Rights (IACtHR) verdict in September 2015 ordered a legal remedy to be provided.⁴⁷ Chile's Supreme Court later decided on a motion for revision (*recurso de revisión*) as the most appropriate remedy, duly granting dozens each year since late 2016.⁴⁸ Resolutions rarely if ever make reference to individual perpetrators, beyond decrying the 'general system of physical and mental degradation, and affronts to dignity' endemic in the military courts of the time.⁴⁹ While there is certainly collective blame apportioned here to military justice and/or the armed forces of the day, we might also interpret this novel line of recourse as a collective historic reproach to the justice system as a whole.⁵⁰ While the Court's reasoning may be robustly collectivizing in this sense, individuation is however still at work inasmuch as each survivor or their family must individually submit a motion. Pressure to have the Court institute a collective solution, dissolving or revising these verdicts wholesale, has not prospered. This habit of individuation remains a marked tendency in Chile's transitional justice practice, reflecting an unfortunate tendency to treat accountability for past atrocity as a private grievance between relatives, survivors and often elderly ex-military perpetrators.⁵¹ This tendency is partly exacerbated by the same relative openness to direct participation in legal actions by victims, survivors or their representatives that has allowed novel legal actions to be generated, again creating an element of paradox in valuing the space different domestic legal systems and traditions afford to privately initiated accountability action.

A final cluster of legal actions challenges highly unrepentant attitudes on the part of the state institution(s) with most direct perpetrating responsibility: Chile's armed forces. Refusing to distance themselves from figures indelibly associated with the worst manifestations of state terror, the services have instead seemed bent on continuing to wrap these figures in an institutional mantle, making a 'rotten apple' defence much harder to sustain. In one instance the institution seemed to prevail, as the Supreme Court refused to challenge the presence of a statue of an ex-member of the dictatorship-era military Junta outside the national Naval Museum.⁵² However, two weeks later, the same court ordered the army to remove artefacts paying homage to deceased former DINA director Manuel Contreras.⁵³ Both resolutions were prompted by legal actions initiated by a former political prisoner. Invoking constitutional and international norms, including explicit references to the right to reparation and guarantees of non-repetition, the plaintiff argued that psychological harm was being caused to him, fellow survivors and society in general, by the continued presence of such elements. In case one, the Navy's arguments for retaining the statue included the contentions that it was not a public monument and its subject 'has never [. . .] been convicted of a crime', rather a low bar.⁵⁴ In case two, the then-Commander in Chief of the army maintained that framed photographs and a plaque did not constitute a homage, and were anyway counterbalanced by unspecified 'contents of a humanitarian nature'.⁵⁵ It further held that, since military installations are not open to the public, the psychological harm alleged by the plaintiff could not exist.⁵⁶ In both, it is notable that a State legal representative appeared before the Court to actively defend the army's and navy's positions. A final pair of examples from this cluster involve the commission of new crimes to obliterate traces of the old. The first was clearly instigated by the institution per se, rather than merely taking place within its confines. In February 2020, three Army officers were charged over the systematic destruction of microfilmed archives from a now-defunct dictatorship-era intelligence service. The incident betrayed a perverse ésprit de corps which does not simply refuse to disown past perpetrators, but orders further lawbreaking to actively protect them. In example two, the army repeatedly refused to reveal the identities of two serving soldiers who vandalized a memorial to victims of disappearance.[57] The arguments presented by the services clearly suggest that we are not in the presence of a chastened, or even minimally self-critical, set of former perpetrating institutions, suggesting that duties of acknowledgement, symbolic reparation and guarantees of non-repetition are at best unevenly recognized or supported across a disaggregated state apparatus.

Conclusions

This chapter has shown how Chile's increasingly varied domestic legal repertoire for addressing past atrocity crime accountability distinguishes it from the necessarily limited ambit of international criminal justice as practised in international venues. Section one, exploring how Chilean courts address criminal responsibility for past atrocity crimes, argued demonstrable tendencies to construe modes of liability even more narrowly than the letter of the law requires. Section two, focused on civilian perpetrators, discerned a preference for apportioning greater blame to uniformed agents. Section three highlighted the twin capacity of civil claim-making to contribute to broadening avenues of accountability, but also to provoke defensive reaction from the state. Section four explored novel recourses which further expand the available legal repertoire. These have seen modest success in achieving retraction by media sources guilty of past collusion, but have exposed apparently defiant, or at least unrepentant, attitudes on the part of perpetrating institutions (the Armed Forces).

Across these four sections, the chapter looked for atomism versus holism in the attribution of criminal and civil responsibility, and the consistency or otherwise of acknowledgement by the present-day state of past crimes and its responsibility for them. Findings revealed a mixed picture, with the courts having proved ready to contradict not only one another but also other branches of state and certain established principles of law; state legal representatives vigorously contesting civil liability but supporting some criminal prosecutions, and all types of legal response and recourse overwhelmingly triggered by private activism rather than proactive state initiative. Overall, a selective borrowing from international law has led to some progress in creating crimes-against-humanity exception to domestic impunity and amnesty, one which allows some space for justice and economic reparation but stops far short of comprehensive state repudiation of, and amends for, past crimes. Mixed signals over civil liability, and defiance from the Armed Forces, limit the 'signalling function' of verdicts and sentences by demonstrating that present-day state espousal of its duties in truth, justice, reparation and guarantees of non-repetition is neither unqualified nor unanimous.

Beyond these specific outcomes, which may prove malleable, the mere existence of this more varied 'accountabilityscape' is nonetheless of interest from a transitional justice perspective. It fleshes out prevailing criminalization-focused understandings of the justice dimension of the transitional justice matrix, offering concrete ways in which the oft-asserted interrelationship between justice, truth-telling, reparations and guarantees of non-repetition could be reflected in domestic court practice as well as in policy or non-governmental circles. We nonetheless observe significant gaps in addressing the role of the private sector, whether in bodily integrity harms or in structural, economic and/or cultural harms. The relative dearth of expansive economic, cultural, political and even moral accounting for the Pinochet period in Chile to date[58] may even have been inadvertently exacerbated precisely by the recent partial success of court-focused activism, reinforcing a tendency for law and the courts to be regarded as not just a proper place, but the only place, for rehearsal of such matters. Recent turns in transitional justice toward a transformative concern with the socio-economic and social justice legacies of mass violence would doubtless find the current courts-based repertoire wanting in this regard, while also posing new questions as to where on the individual–institutional–collectivization axis these other kinds of harms and responsibilities should be conceptualized as occurring.[59]

Further research could usefully explore under what circumstances the distinct types of legal action analysed here may help dismantle enclaves of denialism in post-transitional public life, and/or whether the inherently adversarial nature of such proceedings can instead trigger retrenchment. One might argue that there is considerable scope for domestic jurisdictions to be prompted to develop more inclusive and sophisticated theories of perpetration and liability. This would probably encompass greater readiness to hold civilian collaborators and 'cheerleaders' of grave violations to account in various ways, some of these in and through the courts, challenging and where necessary changing the actions and attitudes of collective and corporate entities as well as individuals. Nonetheless, there are of course limits to the proportion of any such moral, social, political and economic accounting that should or could fall to the courts to resolve. The justice system is not the only, nor necessarily always the best, domestic venue for attending to the present-day reverberations of collectively perpetrated past atrocity.

Notes

1 Two of the chapter's co-authors currently litigate domestic accountability cases. One formerly headed the principal state agency concerned with criminal prosecution and administrative reparations for dictatorship-era violations. All are members of Chile's Transitional Justice Observatory, whose detailed case database, in-house publications and work with key actors provide the empirical grounding of this chapter.

2 The year 1998 became a critical juncture for various reasons, including the UK arrest of former dictator Augusto Pinochet. See: Cath Collins, *Post-Transitional Justice: Human Rights Trials in Chile and El Salvador* (University Park: Penn State University Press, 2010); Cath Collins, 'The Politics of Prosecutions', in *The Politics of Memory in Chile from Pinochet to Bachelet*, ed. Cath Collins, Katherine Hite and Alfredo Joignant (Boulder: Lynne Rienner, 2013), 61–90; Cath Collins, 'Human Rights Policy under the Concertación', in *Democratic Chile: The Politics and Policies of a Historic Coalition*

1990–2010, ed. Kirsten Sehnbruch and Peter M. Siavelis (Boulder: Lynne Rienner, 2014), 143–72.

3   Since 1998, Chile's domestic courts have resolved just over 400 criminal and 75 civil cases. Approximately 1,500 criminal investigations and 100 civil claims were ongoing as of December 2021, with over 1,000 former regime agents convicted and sentenced. Many criminal cases also contain a civil component, but the figures given here represent standalone civil claims. See Observatorio de Justicia Transicional, 'Justicia transicional como justicia constituyente', in *Informe Anual DDHH en Chile 2021* (Santiago: Universidad Diego Portales, 2021), 29–101.

4   Mark Osiel, 'The Banality of Good: Aligning Incentives against Mass Atrocity', *Columbia Law Review* 105, no. 6 (2005): 1752–3.

5   Challenging this sui generis, indeed arbitrary, edict is an ongoing task. Although serious harm to survivors is now generally also construed as a crimes-against-humanity exception to amnesty, the amnesty law itself remains in force. Even cases for extrajudicial killing have at times been abandoned if judges decide they amount to mere 'ordinary' homicide.

6   Examples include two soldiers who admitted shooting at the same victim. As it could not be forensically determined which had fired the fatal shot, both were acquitted. Similarly, higher courts have fully or partially overturned mass convictions by a first instance judge over a long-running operation that killed or disappeared 119 regime opponents. Observatorio Justicia Transicional, 'Negacionismo en la Era de la Pos-Verdad', in *Informe Anual DDHH en Chile 2018* (Santiago: Universidad Diego Portales, 2018), 17–105; and Observatorio Justicia Transicional, 'La Memoria en los Tiempos del Colera', in *Informe Anual DDHH en Chile 2019* (Santiago: Universidad Diego Portales, 2019), 23–132.

7   The exigencies of space make it impossible here to do full justice to more progressive judicial opinion and action, but see Observatorio Justicia Transicional, *Jurisprudential Milestones in Human Rights Cases: Chile 1990–2020* (Santiago: Universidad Diego Portales, 2020). https://derechoshumanos.udp.cl/publicacion/major-jurisprudential-milestones-in-human-rights-cases-chile-1990-2020-2/, and Cath Collins, 'Legitimation Narratives, Resistance, and Legal Cultures in Authoritarian and Post-authoritarian Chile', in *Comparing Transitions to Democracy. Law and Justice in South America and Europe*, ed. C. Paixão and M. Meccarelli (Cham: Springer, 2021), ch. 8.

8   Marcelo Torelly, 'Domestic Rule of Law Gaps and the Uses of International Human Rights Law in Post-Atrocity Prosecutions', *Teoría Política, Nuova Serie, Annali* 7 (2017): 345–61.

9   See Ibid.

10 Where this threshold is met, amnesty and statutes of limitation are set aside.

11 Lawrence Douglas, 'From IMT to NMT: The Emergence of a Jurisprudence of Atrocity', in *Reassessing the Nuremberg Military Tribunals*, ed. Kim Priemel and Alexa Stiller (Oxford: Berghahn, 2012), 281.

12 It was not until 2009, almost two decades after the end of the dictatorship, that Law No. 20.537 fully domestically typified crimes against humanity and war crimes, prompted by Chile's ratification of the Rome statute. Given the strong version of non-retroactivity already described, the 2009 law is however universally regarded in Chile as inapplicable to dictatorship-era crimes.

13 Código Penal (CP) arts. 141 and. 391, respectively.

14 CP Art. 150. Again, replacement was not achieved until long after the dictatorship ended.

15 See discussion in Jain, including cogent critiques by Ambos and by Osiel: Neha Jain, 'The Control Theory of Perpetration in International Criminal Law', *Chicago Journal of International Law* 12, no. 1 (2011): Art. 8.
16 ICTY Appeals Bench, *Tadic*, 15 July 1999.
17 Alternatively, aggravating circumstances are dissolved. Examples include a heavily criticised verdict, delivered in April 2020, aspects of which have been deemed 'fallacious', 'oxymoronic' and 'bordering on [the] perverse' by one prominent Chilean jurist (See: J. P. Mañalich, 'Comentario a la sentencia de la Corte de Apelaciones de Santiago en el caso "Villa Grimaldi"', *Revista de Estudios de la Justicia* 32 (2020): 209–27, our translation). Notwithstanding, a similar argument was adduced by the same Court in a November 2020 case. See Observatorio de Justicia Transicional, 'Justicia transicional como justicia constituyente'.
18 Justin Su-Wan Yang, 'The Evolution of International Criminal Justice – The Incorporation of Domestic Legal Pluralism in the Current Practices of the International Criminal Court', in *The Nuremberg Principles in Non-Western Societies*, ed. Ronald Slye (Nuremberg: The Nuremberg Principles Academy, 2017), 258.
19 Yang, 'The Evolution of International Criminal Justice', and see generally 251ff.
20 Mark Osiel, 'Choosing Among Alternative Responses to Mass Atrocity Between the Individual and the Collectivity', *Ethics & International Affairs* (September, 2015), 1. http://www.ethicsandinternationalaffairs.org/2015/choosingamongalternative-responses-mass-atrocity-individual-collectivity/.
21 Oriana Bernasconi (ed.), *Resistance to Political Violence in Latin America: Documenting Atrocity* (London: Palgrave McMillan, 2019).
22 Pablo Policzer, *The Rise and Fall of Repression in Chile* (Notre Dame: University of Notre Dame Press, 2009).
23 Despite a marked reluctance to imprison female civilian agents: Observatorio Justicia Transicional, *Jurisprudential Milestones in Human Rights Cases*, and interviews for: Cath Collins, 'Transitional Justice from Within: Police, Forensic and Legal Actors Searching for Chile's Disappeared', *Journal of Human Rights Practice* 10, no.1 (2018): 19–39.
24 Particularly in comparison to Argentina, where clergy, judges, businesspeople and journalists have long been actively targeted, and corporate actors are now in prosecutors' sights. See Juan Pablo Bohoslavsky, *¿Usted También Doctor? Complicidad de jueces, fiscales y abogados durante la dictadura* (Buenos Aires: Siglo XXI, 2015).
25 Santa Barbara-Quilaco case, Concepción Appeals Court, 13 June 2019, consideration number 58. The court argued that the civilians involved acted under the army officer present, despite abundant evidence that the group acted in concert. Applicable Chilean criminal law moreover reserves the category of accomplice for much more residual forms of collaboration.
26 Caso Paine, episodio Collipeumo, 16 November 2017. See Jara Bustos and Ugás, 2018.
27 Caso Paine, episodio Principal, San Miguel Appeals Court, 10 November 2020. Luzoro, meanwhile, was subsequently sentenced in another case alongside a former Army officer: the two received roughly equivalent sentences.
28 Examples include the firms Pesquera Arauco, whose refrigerated trucks were used to secretly transport kidnapped prisoners, and paper producer CMPC – see below.
29 Daniela Accatino and Cath Collins, 'Truth, Evidence, Truth: Testimony, Archives and Technical Data in Domestic Human Rights Trials', *Journal of Human Rights Practice* 8, no. 1 (2016): 81–100.

30 On Duff and collectivism, see Daniela Accatino, 'Por qué no a la impunidad? Una mirada desde las teorías comunicativas', *Política Criminal* 14, no. 27 (2019): 47–64.
31 In Chile, criminal responsibility can generally only be attributed to natural persons.
32 Case litigants tended initially (in 1998) to be victims' relatives, represented by pro bono private human rights lawyers. Direct survivor casebringing gathered pace from around 2005. Gradually, a state Human Rights Programme – a transitional justice unit in all but name – also began to adhere to cases and, after 2009, to act directly. However, it can act only over deaths or disappearance. See Cath Collins, 'Human Rights Trials in Chile During and After the "Pinochet Years"', *International Journal of Transitional Justice* 4, no. 1 (2010): 67–86; Collins, 'Transitional Justice from Within'.
33 A practice that began as a self-help measure among survivors wanting to ensure mutual support.
34 Observatorio de Justicia Transicional, 'Justicia transicional como justicia constituyente'.
35 Osiel, 'Choosing Among Alternative Responses to Mass Atrocity Between the Individual and the Collectivity', 1. Lecture 22 June 2015 at SOAS Centre on Conflict, Rights and Justice. MS on file with Cath Collins, quoted with permission, and visible at https://www.soas.ac.uk/ccrj/events/22jun2015-individual-and-collective-in-the-response-to-mass-atrocity.html.
36 With regional human rights courts as the only significant exception.
37 It is also possible to sue an individual perpetrator. Individual perpetrators found liable have rarely paid up, however, and the state is the principal target.
38 In one of Chile's two official Truth Commission reports, and/or in a criminal case verdict.
39 Observatorio Justicia Transicional, 'La Memoria en los Tiempos del Colera'. This position is not, however fully settled: Observatorio Justicia Transicional, *Jurisprudential Milestones in Human Rights Cases*.
40 See Osiel, 'The Banality of Good'. Osiel recommends, in such circumstances, collective economic sanction of the Armed Forces.
41 Used as the threshold test for crimes against humanity, and therefore for exemption from statutes of limitation or amnesty.
42 Mark Osiel, 'Who Are Atrocity's "Real" Perpetrators?', *Ethics & International Affairs* 28, no. 3 (2014): 287.
43 Observatorio Justicia Transicional, 'La Memoria en los Tiempos del Colera'; Observatorio Justicia Transicional, *Jurisprudential Milestones in Human Rights Cases*.
44 Specifically, the latter's predilection for continuing to defend and even celebrate past perpetrators.
45 Case Jorge Oyarzún Escobar and Juan Escobar Camus, Rol. 84.116-2018, 12 April 2019.
46 Santiago Appeals Court, Rol Protección 183.699-2019; ratified on 9 October 2020 in Supreme Court Rol 112/391-2020.
47 IACtHR, *Omar Humberto Maldonado Vargas and others v. Republic of Chile*, 2 September 2015.
48 Observatorio Justicia Transicional, *Jurisprudential Milestones in Human Rights Cases*; Boris Hau, 'Consejos de guerra y justicia transicional', *Anuario de Derechos Humanos* 17, no. 2 (2021): 355–80; Francisco Bustos, 'Los Consejos de Guerra de la Dictadura Militar y su Anulación', in *La Justicia Como Legalidad*, ed. Nicolás Acevedo et al. (Santiago: Universidad de Chile, 2020), 149–75.

49 Representative quote from Supreme Court ruling Rol 29.937-2019, 6 January 2020, our translation.
50 The past sins referred to are also the Supreme Court's own, since it voluntarily renounced, quite early in the dictatorship, its supervisory role over military justice and the latter's blatant illegalities.
51 Collins, 'The Politics of Prosecutions'.
52 Supreme Court Rol 15.310-2020, 19 February 2020.
53 Supreme Court, Rol 14.720-2020, 5 March 2020.
54 Santiago Appeals Court, Rol Protección 79183-2019, 22 January 2020 (Authors' translation).
55 Santiago Appeals Court, Rol 79.631-2019, 26 December 2019.
56 Santiago Appeals Court, Rol 79.631-2019, 26 December 2019.
57 The incident took place while the men were in uniform. The Army defied repeated access-to-information court orders over the subsequent four years ordering them to reveal the men's identities and any disciplinary action taken against them.
58 Pietro Sferrazza and Francisco Bustos, 'Complicidad económica y Derecho chileno', in *Complicidad económica con la dictadura chilena*, ed. Juan Pablo Bohoslavsky, Karinna Fernández and Sebastián Smart (Santiago: LOM, 2019), 437–51.
59 Daniela Accatino argues that Chile's 2021 constitutional 'moment' is a 'transitional justice moment', in which a newly assertive collective political subject seeks to expose and revert some of the more socially pernicious and long-lasting harm caused to the social fabric by the dictatorship's radical neoliberal economic project. See: Daniela Accatino, 'The Chilean Crisis as a Transitional Justice Moment', *Special Issue: 'It Is Not 30 Pesos, It Is 30 Years': Reflections on the Chilean Crisis', Social & Legal Studies* 30, no. 4 (2021): 627–68.

Part IV

Framing the past

14

Perpetrator memory and the fascist exile in Argentina

A case study[1]

Zoltán Kékesi

In 1978, György Oláh, an émigré journalist, received a package from a friend in his home near Córdoba, Argentina. The package contained a 1930 anniversary publication of the newspaper *The Hungarian* (*Magyarság*, 1920–44) where he had started his career more than half a century before. The publication celebrated a decade of counterrevolutionary regime, and concurrently, reflected on the first decade of *The Hungarian* itself, a prestigious organ of the regime's radical, pro-fascist, faction. The old copy represented a precious gift, a true rarity from a remote past and homeland. For its recipient, it had historical and personal significance. Leafing through it, he would find his own portrait as a young man, placed among portraits that showcased a who's who of counterrevolutionary journalism. The gift made him reminisce about his early career and reflect on how the politics of his youth had shaped him—and what it meant for him in exile.[2]

In this chapter, I follow Oláh's career in interwar Hungary and his trajectory as an émigré journalist. As fascist regimes collapsed in Europe, post-war consensus across the Allied-dominated world turned his commitment to the fascist cause into complicity. In exile, Oláh and like-minded intellectuals were challenged to redefine what they represented and reclaim respectability and moral authority. Argentina, in particular, I argue, did not merely provide them with protection and somewhere to settle but a renewed sense of their place in the world. For Oláh and fellow émigrés, a combination of social and ideological factors – including their status as European immigrants, the legacy of colonialism, and Hungarian and Argentinian intellectual traditions of Christian-national ideology – enabled a new self-definition and political vision.

In what follows I argue that Oláh's reminiscences about the past and his political commentary on the present were inseparable. Bridging interwar Europe and Argentina's Dirty War, his long career as a journalist sheds light on entangled histories and unexpected continuities. Furthermore, it allows a multifaceted account of what it meant to confront post-war consensus in exile and beyond the confines of Western societies. Finally, while there is a robust scholarship on especially the German national socialist exile in Argentina,[3] my chapter highlights the pro-fascist exile from outside of the Rome–Berlin Axis. As for Hungarian perpetrators in particular, confronting complicity had to account for anti-Jewish and pro-fascist policies prior to and collaboration during the country's German occupation in 1944. Oláh's case shows how a limited willingness to reckon with the catastrophe opened up ways to reformulate past political commitments in a changed time and space.

Perpetrator memory and pro-fascist journalism

By covering the pre- and post-1945 career of a pro-fascist journalist, this chapter proposes a combination of perpetrator studies and memory studies. Since the 1980s, Holocaust perpetrator studies focused primarily on perpetrator biographies prior to 1945 in order to understand what led ordinary men and women to their crimes. Memory studies, on the other hand, has been preoccupied with conceptualizing the emerging, transnational, memory of the Holocaust and tracing its genealogy in the post-war West. While perpetrator studies largely excluded the dimension of memory, memory studies has been interested in *representations* of perpetrators – less so in perpetrator memory *per se*. Some recent initiatives, however, demonstrate an interest in perpetrator memory, while debates mostly centred on testimonies produced in a legal context and foregrounded the question of whether and how to use them for historical purposes.[4]

In this case study, I look at memory produced outside of the legal context and use it as a lens to understand perpetrator biography and moral-intellectual trajectory. By doing so I am proposing a way to see a more detailed picture of both perpetrator experience and post-war memory. At the same time, considering perpetrator memory may present one way to transcend a separation of pre- and post-1945 histories and to refocus on as yet untraced transformations of biographies and ideologies. This chapter accentuates social and ideological components of past acts and later memories in order to understand notions of moral and political commitment at work when participating in and remembering the fascist project. Furthermore, the chapter draws the attention to a particular group of Holocaust perpetrators, fascist and pro-fascist intellectuals, including journalists, publishers and writers. In discussing Holocaust perpetrators, scholars commonly focus on political leadership, state administration or, in a now decades-long tradition of perpetrator studies, the 'ordinary men' of mass murder. Yet, journalists did the daily work of propagating and *imagining* fascism. They were complicit in some key areas of racist practices in particular, including elaborating and transmitting the language of racism, creating a hostile climate and mobilizing for exclusionary policies.[5] Some of them, like Oláh, were quite popular in their time, and their reports, weekly columns and book publications were widely read. Similar to him, many occupied positions in professional and political organizations, state administration and legislation.

For émigré journalists, the need to reclaim respectability and moral authority after the war did not come merely from the stigma of their names being tied to the collapsed regime. More specifically, it came from the contemporary perception that regarded their role in crimes committed prior to 1945 as instrumental. Post-war judgement confirmed, though negatively, their own self-perception of playing a prominent part in creating what they had called 'racial Hungary'. Indeed, post-war justice saw their responsibility in social and political terms and included war propaganda and racial incitement in its set of legal definitions of what constituted war crimes and crimes against the people, in contemporary parlance. As a result, some of the high-profile cases at the People's Tribunals were high-ranking officials in charge of press and publishing. For example, Mihály Kolosváry-Borcsa (1896–1946), head of the National Press Chamber (1938–44) and government commissioner for press and publishing during the German occupation in 1944 was sentenced to death and executed. Ferenc Fiala (1904–88), head of the Arrow Cross press office spent some ten years in prison before emigrating to West Germany in 1956.

Editors and columnists, too, were seen as prominent enough to be 'wanted men', Oláh included. Similar to him, many had realized the need to flee before the Red Army liberated Budapest. Hiding in and around the refugee camps of post-war Europe, they would soon see their names in the newspapers as reports were coming out on extradition requests and trials *in absentia*. They would see pictures of their colleagues and superiors extradited and tried. The memoir of journalist Lajos Marschalkó (1903–68), *Red Storm*, written in Munich and published in Buenos Aires in 1952, documented their experiences. Looking back at his route through Allied-occupied territories, Oláh, too, remembered his internment as a moment that shattered whatever had tied him to his social status and moral standing.[6] Although the Cold War soon put an end to extraditions and émigrés eventually settled in western Europe, the Americas or Australia, they still had to reframe and explain their past vis-á-vis post-war consensus in the 'free world'.

Oláh, on his part, escaped internment for Italy where, aided by the Catholic Church, he boarded a ship to Argentina in 1946. He resumed journalism around 1949 and published regularly until 1958 and then from around 1971 until 1981, residing in Argentina but publishing across the diaspora press. For this chapter, I surveyed the pieces he sent to the *Hungarian Path* (*Magyarok útja*, 1948–55), a Buenos Aires-based biweekly that printed national-conservatives and pro-fascist radicals,[7] as well as newspapers in the United States, Canada and the United Kingdom, including moderate-conservative periodicals such as Toronto-based *Chronicle* (*Krónika*, 1975–93) and radical outlets such as *Bridgehead* (*Hídfő*, 1948–86), one of the longest standing journals of the Hungarian fascist exile, published in London.

From contempt to prestige: A career in counterrevolutionary journalism

In 1930, the anniversary edition of *The Hungarian* celebrated the first decade of the counterrevolution. By then, a conservative authoritarian regime had been installed in Hungary. The regime emerged from the collapse of the Monarchy and annulled the policies introduced by the revolutions in 1918 and 1919. Under the regency of Miklós Horthy (1920–44), it restored the power of the old political and economic elite and introduced a parliamentary system that secured the hegemony of the ruling conservative circles. Although the regime enabled a multiparty system, it restricted democratic institutions and pre-empted political and social reform. While it despised liberal democracy and had a decidedly authoritarian character, the ruling elite disliked the rising dictatorships in Italy and later in Germany as well. Anxiety of social movements and mass politics – whether in the form of democratic participation or fascist mobilization – shaped their attitudes and the political culture of the regime.[8] The new regime under Horthy regarded itself as 'Christian' and 'national' – a composite that had varying implications, including anti-Jewish connotations that somewhat faded away as an 'era of moderation' set in during the early 1920s.[9]

In 1930, *The Hungarian* commemorated the act that in 1920 had opened the new, counterrevolutionary era: Horthy entering Budapest on a white horse in order to take command of the 'sinful city' where the revolutions had erupted. Yet, the newspaper's anniversary reflections harboured discontent as well. *The Hungarian* came into being in 1920 as an organ of the far right – the 'racial defenders' (*fajvédők*), as they were called, a movement that formed in the midst of White Terror. They propagated radical anti-Jewish policies, social reforms and military-type dictatorship. As a time of moderation set in during the early 1920s, they were either pushed to the margins or had to adopt a more moderate stance. In 1930, *The Hungarian*'s anniversary edition praised Mussolini's 1922 *Marcia su Roma* as 'a most momentous date in European history since the Great War' and effused about fascism's 'eternal charisma'. For them, Horthy's entry to Budapest in 1920 compared to Mussolini's March on Rome as the opening act of an incomplete, even suppressed, revolution. 'Counterrevolution' in their parlance constituted a revolution against the revolution – anti-Communist, 'Christian', 'national' and 'social'.

Like many in the 'racial defense' circles, György Oláh (1902–81) came from the 'traditional', ethnic-Hungarian, *magyar* middle class. He joined a paramilitary organization in 1920 and participated in the counterrevolution. Subsequently, he studied economics in Budapest before joining *The Hungarian* in 1924.[10] With a father in the higher echelon of the judiciary, starting a career in journalism was anything but natural. Leafing through the newspaper's 1930 anniversary publication in 1978, he reminisced about how anxious his parents were about his choice to become a journalist – especially in Budapest. In the eyes of the 'old Christian middle class' journalism ranked as 'one of the most disrespected professions', he remembered. His parents wanted him to enter public office, preferably in one of the Ministries. Since the emergence of the modern tabloid press around 1900, journalism, he recalled, had been a 'breeding ground for shaky, shady, anti-social characters'. Journalism was synonymous with the 'streets of Pest' (the more modern and mondaine half of the capital), moral decline, political unrest and Jewishness. The press was widely seen as responsible for the Leftist revolutions and as a sphere dominated by Jewish professionals and 'Jewish capital'.

What in the eyes of the young Oláh restored the prestige of journalism was the counterrevolution, a founding event of his life story. During his years as a student, he felt entranced by the intellectuals of the far right that had formed in its wake. Especially

István Milotay (1883–1963), chief editor at *The Hungarian*, had a lasting impact on him. Later in the exile, he recalled how Milotay's newspaper became a magnet for him and other 'children of the counter-revolution'. He remembered Milotay as one of their 'prophets' and related how *The Hungarian* attracted a new 'spiritual elite'. Milotay's newspaper instilled into them the belief that it would be *their* mission to help the nation 'revive' from the 'abyss of collapse'.[11]

Looking through the anniversary edition, Oláh compared *The Hungarian* to the tabloids of the 'streets of Pest'. While the tabloids subordinated themselves to capitalist interests, *The Hungarian* had a national mission. Instead of sensationalism, *The Hungarian* exhumed the 'spiritual legacy' of the nation's past. Instead of being a 'business enterprise' of rapacious, 'soulless capitalists', *The Hungarian* represented 'Christian-national regeneration'. Finally, Oláh recalled the roomy office of the chief editor as a 'sanctuary' and a 'focal point of the country's spiritual life'. Being allowed to attend the daily meetings that were being held there was an 'honor for a young journalist'.

Thus, journalists at *The Hungarian* felt respectable *because* of the newspaper's radical program. While it was precisely the latter that turned into a stigma for post-war consensus, it guaranteed social prestige in an era where press professionals, especially inside the Christian middle classes, were often seen as morally and politically suspicious, and ultimately, un-Hungarian. Press legislation in post-revolutionary Hungary reflected such suspicions and introduced stronger state control as press and publishing were made responsible for having incited the revolutions.[12]

Journalists around the radical paper were privileged dissidents of a conservative-authoritarian regime, positioned at the same time inside of and in opposition to it. They took a more radical stance but shared the regime's fundamental principles – anti-Communism, anti-liberalism, ethnic-Christian nationhood and territorial revisionism – and their leaders were well integrated into the political elite and state administration. Their status as inner dissidents made them protected compared to opposition coming from outside the regime. The latter included, from the early 1930s on, national socialist groups as well. Compared to the pro-fascist faction of the regime, these groups – among them, most prominently, the Arrow Cross – had a more plebeian outlook, less respect for the regime and more determination for revolutionary solutions. Thus, a conjunction of class difference and political stance made the regime's radical faction seem more respectable than the plebeian Arrow Cross – or, of course, the stigmatized Left. These differences still mattered decades later – especially in Argentina where many Hungarian immigrants came from state administration and middle- and upper-middle-class strata – and helped some émigrés demarcate themselves from both 'Communists' and 'Nazis'.

Looking back at his early years as a journalist, Oláh emphasized his upbringing in a 'traditional' middle-class home, his career at a respectable, Christian-national newspaper, and, finally, earning a decent income. At thirty years of age, he remembered, his earnings were comparable to his father's benefits after retiring from his position at the *Kúria*, the Supreme Court. At the newspaper they all felt, so he remembered, financially secure, despite the economic crises and the rising unemployment in the educated middle and lower middle classes. As to why they did so, he mentioned the newspaper's 'loyal readership', committed to the cause of 'Christian-national regeneration', and their expectation that 'a new Press Chamber and proper press legislation would secure a decent retirement'. And 'by then, we will have national fame', they speculated.

Indeed, these expectations for expanding market share and protective state intervention were mostly fulfilled by the late 1930s. In 1938 a newly established National Press Chamber created a new regime of privileges in which membership – and thereby the license to pursue journalism – depended on political adherence and 'racial', non-Jewish, belonging. Membership policies adhered to legislation that from 1938 until 1941 gradually restricted Jewish participation in all possible occupational fields, including press and publishing. While the country's territorial losses and economic difficulties had previously created a shrinking market, rising unemployment and sinking wages in journalism, anti-Jewish legislation restructured the profession. In a field where Jewish participation had been significant,[13] the expulsion of Jewish professionals reduced competition and opened up career opportunities. At the same time, new regulations installed pre-publication censorship that further tightened state control and increased the market chances of pro-governmental outlets. This process culminated in 1944, as German occupation introduced total coordination of the press, banning all opposition papers, excluding, interning and deporting Jewish and Leftist professionals. Members of the Press Chamber, on the other hand, became 'witting beneficiaries' and often 'willing facilitators' of a racial regime.[14]

Reading the old copy of *The Hungarian*, Oláh remembered the Chamber fondly, without mentioning its racial and political component explicitly. He did not feel the need to explain, scrutinize or question the ever expanding system of privileges that the Chamber helped create alongside anti-Jewish legislation.

In the late 1930s, Oláh himself became a member of the parliament and supported anti-Jewish laws. At the same time, he opened a new chapter in his career in journalism as chief editor of *We Are Alone* (*Egyedül Vagyunk*, 1938–44), a monthly publication dedicated to 'the revolutionary ideas of fascism and national socialism'.[15] Established in the context of the First anti-Jewish Law, the newspaper cultivated an excessive language that made it into a true medium for radical transgression. In 1939, Oláh received the Order of the German Eagle for promoting national socialism. In 1944, he supported Hungary's German occupation and celebrated the mass deportations of Jewish Hungarians in an elated tone, stating, 'Finally, we can enjoy being among ourselves, without all the foreign scum'.[16]

Vision for a new era: A career in exile journalism

In 1980, Zsuzsánna Haynalné Kesserű (1938–), a niece, journalist, librarian and community organizer visited Oláh in his home near Córdoba. Driving up from Buenos Aires, she recorded an interview for *Chronicle*, a Toronto-based Hungarian monthly. Their conversation took place in 'a living room-cum-study', among 'overcrowded bookshelves, scattered newspapers, piles of uncut books that all show: we are in the home of an active writer with a restless inner life'.[17] Writing from his home, she enthused, Oláh had been sending articles to émigré newspapers 'in all quarters of the globe', his contributions making him a well-known voice throughout the Hungarian diaspora.

Their conversation revolved around the two 'collective catastrophes' that shaped Oláh's career: the period around 1918/1920, including the revolutions and the disintegration of Greater Hungary, and the 'Russian invasion', as they called it, in 1945. Although they certainly conceived both periods as catastrophes of a national scope, they emphatically described the latter as a collective cataclysm of the 'exiled Hungarian Christian middle class' where they hailed from. Remembering the past was thereby framed by a sense of ethnic-Hungarian, Christian belonging, political stance and class consciousness.

The interview contained no reference to anti-Jewish policies, sentiments or, for that matter, Jews. Nonetheless, excessive language lingered in their conversation, as the interviewer mentioned the diaries of Cécile Tormay (1875–1937), a popular author of the counterrevolutionary era. Tormay's potent, passionate language deliberately transgressed earlier norms of Christian middle-class antisemitism, and helped it adopt a more radical tone.[18] Published in 1923 and reprinted multiple times before 1945, her book became a classic of anti-Communist and anti-Jewish literature of interwar Hungary. By calling it 'moving reading', the interviewer reinforced Tormay's authority.

While driving back home to Buenos Aires, the interviewer still reflected on the conclusion of their conversation. In the fifth year of the military dictatorship, her last question invoked the 'ongoing social transformation', perhaps in reference to what the junta called National Reorganization Process, and asked Oláh: 'Do you too believe that our future is here?', to which he responded:

> Yes, I do. It is becoming my belief that once recklessness and Latin bravado end – these signs of immaturity of a young society – it will be here where the white man will find his future refuge from the cataclysms that are threatening the globe.[19]

His response condensed expressions of white supremacy, Euro-centrism, (East-) Central European consciousness *vs* Latin 'mentality' and the prospect of a racial apocalypse. These notions had been elaborated in his writings throughout his exile career and were central to re-formulating notions of the Self as well as interpreting the émigré trajectory from interwar Hungary to post-war exile.

Back in 1951, in a first piece ever published under his byline in exile, Oláh reconsidered the recent war as the outcome of a moral decline of western, European, Christian civilization.[20] Writing for the *Hungarian Path*, he addressed an émigré community in and beyond Buenos Aires and Argentina. His piece reformulated radical conservative and pro-fascist concepts from his youth and read as a program of some sort for a new era. He claimed that the post-Enlightenment age had led to a decline of traditional Christian culture, unchaining the 'barbarian', 'instinctive' or 'animalistic' tendencies in humankind. Certainly, he blamed Marxism and psychoanalysis for releasing these tendencies, but regarded them as symptoms of a wider tendency towards mass society, materialism and technological progress. For Oláh, the unprecedented brutalities of the war testified to the destructive forces that had long compromised

European–Christian civilization. While his diagnosis condemned some of the crimes committed by Nazi Germany, including the concentration camps, it incriminated the entire post-Enlightenment era and eventually restored the claim of the radicals of his youth for an all-encompassing anti-Enlightenment renewal.

His condemnation of the camps did not exclude some sort of moral concern about past deeds. Nonetheless, it came limited to Hitler's last, 'lunatic', period and to an extremely restricted admission of non-German agency: 'There is no shame in admitting that [. . .] we were wrong [. . .] that we were entranced [. . .] and in the agony of war and in the fire and smoke of our burning cities we did not see what the Christian world has to be ashamed of today'.[21] At the same time, he depicted the early post-war period as a time of 'penance' and 'painful reflection' when Christian Hungarians eventually realized the magnitude of the crimes committed by Hitler, a leader they had been so 'entranced' by. In a manner common to post-war apologists, he turned complicity into a sense of being betrayed and unjustly persecuted. Finally, he memorialized the 'martyrs' of the War Tribunals in a pseudo-religious vocabulary. Although he made some concessions and condemned Nazi crimes, he eventually exonerated his readers and offered a perspective that restored their moral standing.

What is more, he maintained that émigré intellectuals should spearhead a post-war renewal of 'Christian civilization'. He claimed that they were predestined to be the heralds of a moral renaissance both in their status as immigrants and intellectuals – being white, educated and European. Coming from the 'most ancient and most cultured continent', Oláh maintained, they were envoys of European–Christian civilization in the most remote corners of the globe. Furthermore, living as outsiders, they were in a position to replace the national lens and see 'the fate of the white man' instead.

It was this new vision of being part of a more encompassing cause – the rescue and renewal of white, European, Christian civilization – that helped him restore a sense of moral superiority and a strong sense of purpose. Throughout his career in the exile, from around 1951 to 1981, he remained consistent in propagating this vision. The legacy of European colonialism, the construction of whiteness and Hungarian and Argentinian versions of Christian-national ideology made his claims seem reasonable for his readership. Their notions of a 'Christian nation' resonated well with traditions of their new home (more so than the views of their German or Italian counterparts).

Although many post-1945 Hungarian immigrants were privileged in being white-European, Christian and anti-Communist,[22] their social status and middle-class standing had been shattered by exile. With that, an important part of what had constituted their sense of respectability had been lost too. Although the 1950s would later be seen as a 'Golden Age' of Hungarian journalism in Argentina,[23] émigré publications and journalists struggled to stay afloat. Respectability had to be reconstituted on moral grounds.

In a lecture given at the recently established Free University of the Hungarian diaspora in Buenos Aires in 1953, Oláh talked about how the modern press had once contributed to the 'collapse of Western civilization'.[24] By becoming a mass product exposed to market mechanisms, he told his audience, the modern press and its sensationalism played a part in moral decline by unleashing inferior instincts in the masses. The heroes of his youth, he reminded them, the journalists around *The*

Hungarian, revolted against the materialism of the press and propagated a 'moral renaissance'. Now, three decades later, he claimed, émigrés were witnessing a second renaissance of journalism. Diaspora newspapers were predestined to resume the work of counterrevolutionary press: talking to small audiences in dedicated émigré communities, they escaped the mechanism of mass media and the materialism of the market. For Oláh, émigré journalists were destined to be the harbingers of a new age in their status as professionals: they were called on to continue what had been cut off by collapse and catastrophe.

From counterrevolution to counterrevolution

Throughout the 1970s, Oláh's writings responded to the profound cultural and political transformations that had unfolded during the previous decade – including decolonization in the Third World, desegregation in the United States and the emergence of the New Left. Locally, the latter presented a challenge to Argentina's conservative culture, racial order and prevailing political traditions of Christian-national ideology. Previously, Peronism had opened up ways for non-white populations to participate in the country's modernization, although it had not questioned the prevailing self-perception of Argentina as a white nation. Despite the racism of the military regime that ousted Peron in 1955, Leftists of the 1960s (among them Left-leaning Peronists) challenged the hegemony of the white middle class and Argentina's self-understanding as a white nation, highlighting social inequality and the misery of non-white multitudes. In the late 1960s and early 1970s, mass protests made these multitudes ever more visible.[25] Oláh's anxieties were further exacerbated by the emergence of Leftist-revolutionary movements elsewhere on the continent. In 1971, discussing the Tupamaros in Uruguay and Allende's presidency in Chile, he pictured Argentina as being 'caught in a red vise'.[26] In the face of these transformations, Oláh's writings cemented notions of white supremacy, colonialism, Christian nationhood and resolute anti-Communism.

Anxieties of a 'reddening' continent were intertwined with white panic and the belief that Leftist revolutions would endanger the racial order on the Southern Cone. Oláh described the region encompassing Chile, Uruguay and Argentina in a colonialist language as the most precious 'for the future of the white man'. Due to 'its moderate climate, extensive, yet unpopulated, fertile zones and a European population less mixed with Indios', he wrote, it is the most suitable 'for European settlement' and for becoming an 'enormous future colony for Western white civilization'.[27] His writing reinforced biological termini that had been progressively discredited since the collapse of the Third Reich, more recent decolonization, and political and social transformations in Argentina itself.

In terms of open and excessive racism, anti-Indigenous and anti-Black racism replaced antisemitism in his post-war writing. While antisemitism lived on in more coded ways (such as references to a Freudian-Marxist conspiracy) his vocabulary grew ever more violent when it came to America's Indigenous population. In relation to the northern part of South America, he wrote about 'underdeveloped, dominantly Indio, dark-skinned caricatures of a republic'.²⁸ In reference to Juan José Torres's socialist presidency in Bolivia (1970–1), he pictured a 'frenzied mob, small, Eskimo-looking Aymaras, and Mongoloid, mongrel Quechuas'.²⁹ He compared indigenous peoples of South America to peoples in the Arctic and used the old term 'Mongoloid' as ways to denigrate them and to suggest racial stereotypes that readers across the diaspora were aware of. Similarly, he despised Bolivian immigrants in Argentina and lamented over the immigrant population of his home province, with Córdoba at its centre – a city which in the previous decade became second only to Buenos Aires in the size of its migrant population.³⁰

For Argentina, Oláh envisioned 'a new, enormous immigration from preferably non-Latin elements of the white race', to counterbalance the all-too 'emotional' and 'passionate' Latin population and remedy the country's 'degenerated biological design' that resulted from European-Indigenous mixing. These categories offered racist explanations for political and social phenomena such as instability, unrest or violence. The country's future, Oláh claimed, was a 'biological' rather than 'merely political' matter.

In an age of decolonization, he reinforced long-standing colonialist visions and its local, Argentinian, expressions that perceived, historically, European immigration as a means of 'whitening' the country and established, since the early twentieth century, the notion of Argentina as a white country.³¹ The so-called 'conquest of the desert' that in the late nineteenth century led to the displacement and murder of Indigenous populations lived on in memory as a national achievement. At the same time, the self-perception that maintained that Argentinians were merely 'Europeans in the Americas' contributed to 'a feeling of superiority over the rest of Latin America'.³² Oláh, on his part, did not see himself as merely a white immigrant in a country that privileged whiteness, he saw himself as superior for coming from Europe and for being therefore more fully white.

In the 1970s, Oláh travelled extensively and reported on the signs of what he regarded as a decline of 'Western civilization'. In 1971, while preparing the anniversary celebrations of the 1956 Hungarian Revolution, he visited bookstores throughout Buenos Aires in search of anti-Communist literature and expressed his frustration vis-à-vis the many titles that he encountered on 'Gandhi, the Black Panthers, the martyr Martin Luther King, the "liberation" of the American Negroes and especially Fidel Castro's partisan-prophets'.³³ In 1973, touring Hungarian communities in Miami, Pittsburgh, Cleveland, Chicago and Toronto, he presented his new book that blamed Communism and 'the destructive dominance of the Negroes' for the end of 'Christian civilization'.³⁴

In 1976, following the coup d'état that established Argentina's last military dictatorship, Oláh celebrated the turn. The country joined 'the circle of anti-Communist regimes', he wrote in reference to the coups that had established the Uruguayan dictatorship and the Pinochet regime in Chile in 1973.³⁵ In 1981, he praised the 'enormous effort' put into fighting 'international red terror organizations' and 'restoring peace, the rule of law, and security' in the country.³⁶ By then, the National Reorganization Process, as the junta called it, had led to the establishment of concentration camps throughout the country and to the detention, torture and 'disappearance' of tens of thousands.

His view that Argentina would become a 'future refuge for the white man from global cataclysms' corresponded to how the junta defined its 'Dirty War' against a 'conspiracy against Civilization'. Drawing on a *nacionalista* tradition of seeing Argentina as 'the scene of a millenarian struggle between communism and Christianity', the junta presented its cause in reference to 'transcendental trans-historical forces'.[37] At the same time, they 'reaffirmed the idea of Argentina as a homogenous society founded on European-ness and whiteness'.[38]

In the context of these social and political conflicts Oláh returned once again to his reminiscences of his youth. In 1981, shortly before his death, he sent an open letter to Ferenc Fiala, former head of the Arrow Cross press office, then an émigré in West Germany and editor of London-based *Bridgehead*. In his letter, published in three instalments, he again looked back at his career, claiming that 'we were among the first in Europe to stand up uncompromisingly and with revolutionary passion against the global destruction that is now threatening the fate of the entire Western Christianity. [. . .] We shall be proud of being the children of the Hungarian counterrevolution and remaining that way until today'.[39] His life story, as he saw it, led him from counterrevolution to counterrevolution.

Conclusion

During Argentina's last military dictatorship, the most inhuman manifestations of antisemitism were clandestine as they were confined to the detention centers where references to Auschwitz were applied as techniques of torture on Jewish detainees. That way the junta produced a historically unique situation where 'perpetrators present[ed] their actions [. . .] as a reenactment of the Holocaust',[40] using the memory of the Holocaust to frame genocidal acts. Although public manifestations were less excessive, they were explicit in presenting Jews as alien 'others' and the nation's enemies. However, public manifestations somewhat softened over time as Argentinian Jewish communities managed to reach out to members of the political leadership. Ironically, in 1981, the regime eventually granted permission to air the 1978 American TV-series *Holocaust*.[41]

Although Oláh rarely mentioned Jews and their persecution explicitly, he did not seem to *deny* the Holocaust, as it had been by then widely named. Reviewing Ferenc Fiala's 1979 memoir, he rather lamented what he regarded as unequal recognition:

> Television, cinema, popular pundits, political memoirs published in hundreds of thousands of copies, the propaganda that permeates the free world today, after thirty-four years – they all rejoice in the victories over the Germans, and it is the same that they ruminate on behind the Iron Curtain as well. Of course, there is plenty of ballyhoo about the Palestinians. The series *Holocaust* is aired everywhere, over and over. In the meantime, one has to remain silent on the martyrdom of thousands of decent, devout, educated patriots; about them, no bestseller can be published.[42]

Here, he juxtaposed unrecognized émigrés – portrayed as decent, cultured and educated – and the non-Christian, non-white subjects of Western and Eastern recognition. It is not that he denied the latter's sufferings altogether but he claimed Christian-white émigrés to be more deserving subjects of recognition. The underlying biases were cultural and racial and transformed pre-1945 perceptions of the Self and its Others in the context of a competition for symbolic recognition.

This chapter argues that studying perpetrator memory may offer a more detailed picture of moral and political commitments at work when pursuing the fascist project. At the same time, it helps us see post-war memory beyond the confines of mainstream, mostly Western, publics and retrace unexpected transformations. To be sure, Oláh, a prominent propagator of fascism, did not recognize his own complicity, except in a very limited way. Nonetheless, I argue that there is more to learn from perpetrator discourse if we refocus from instances of denial or distortion.

For Oláh and like-minded émigrés, their interwar and wartime career did not merely represent a remote past that needed to be remembered and defended or obscured, denied and explained away. Although he certainly remembered his homeland and his pre-exile past nostalgically, he claimed continuity despite collapse and resisted much of the moral and political consequences of 1945. The experience of exile impacted him in profound ways and his new home on the American continent opened up new political dimensions. While he continued to be committed to a national agenda, his exile writings were informed by a wider political imaginary shaped by the global Cold War and its Latin American context, the legacy of colonization and Argentine *nacionalismo*. Remembering his pre-exile past remained eminently political and embedded into the social and ideological conflicts of the present. While he was deeply invested in preserving what he regarded as the national-ethnic heritage of the émigré community, he was just as interested in the political issues of his present time and his memory work evolved in relation to these. By remembering his own past, he reclaimed moral authority in addressing the present. His notions of respectability were tied to (past) status and class, profession, political commitments, white-European, Christian ancestry – as well as to ways of remembering, preserving and reclaiming them in the exile. Though he presented their cause as 'martyrs of communism' as he claimed moral recognition, he did not speak as a mere victim – and he certainly refused to do so as perpetrator. Rather, he spoke as a political–ideological subject that reclaimed his past while pursuing a radical – and disastrous – agenda in the present.

Notes

1 Funding for this research has been generously provided by the Alexander von Humboldt Foundation.
2 György Oláh, 'Szegény, szegény emigráns szerkesztő', *Krónika*, April 1978, 16–18.
3 See especially Holger M. Meding, '*Der Weg*'. *Eine deutsche Emigrantenzeitschrift in Buenos Aires 1947–1957* (Berlin: Wissenschaftlicher Verlag, 1997); Gerald Steinacher, 'Argentinien als NS-Fluchtziel. Die Emigration von Kriegsverbrechern und Nationalsozialisten durch Italien an den Rio de la Plata 1946–1955. Mythos und

Wirklichkeit', in *Argentinien und das Dritte Reich*, ed. Holger M. Meding and Georg Ismar (Berlin: Wissenschaftlicher Verlag, 2008), 231–54.
4   Christopher R. Browning, *Collected Memories. Holocaust History and Post-War Testimony* (Madison: The University of Wisconsin Press, 2003), 3–36; Jonathan Dunnage (ed.), 'Perpetrator Memory and Memories about Perpetrators', *Memory Studies* 2 (2010): 91–4; Sibylle Schmidt, 'Perpetrators' Knowledge: What and How Can We Learn from Perpetrator Testimony?', *Journal of Perpetrator Research* 1, no. 1 (2017): 85–104.
5   For these categories, see the website of the project 'Compromised identities? Reflections on perpetration and complicity under Nazism', https://compromised-identities.org.
6   György Oláh, 'Tíz éve vándorolunk', *Magyarok útja*, 19 July 1954, 3.
7   For the newspaper, see Judit Némethy Kesserű, '*Szabadságom lett a börtönöm'. Az argentínai magyar emigráció története 1948–1968* (Budapest: A Magyar Nyelv és Kultúra Nemzetközi Társasága, 2003), 90–3, 133–5.
8   For the regime, see Levente Püski, *A Horthy-rendszer* (Budapest: Pannonica, 2006).
9   For the notion of the Christian nation, see Paul A. Hanebrink, *In Defense of Christian Hungary: Religion, Nationalism, and Antisemitism 1890–1944* (Ithaca and London: Cornell University Press, 2006).
10 For a brief biography, see Rudolf Paksa, *A magyar szélsőjobboldali elit az 1930-as évek elejétől 1945-ig* (Budapest: ELTE, 2011), 162.
11 György Oláh, 'Reakciósak lettünk!', *Hídfő*, April 1981, 4.
12 See Balázs Sipos, *Sajtó és hatalom a Horthy-korszakban* (Budapest: Argumentum, 2011).
13 See Gábor Gyáni and György Kövér, *Magyarország társadalomtörténete a reformkortól a második világháborúig* (Budapest: Osiris, 2006), 180–1.
14 See Mary Fulbrook in Chapter 3 in this volume.
15 György Oláh, 'Mérleg', *Egyedül Vagyunk,* August 1940, 23–5.
16 György Oláh, 'Történelmi elégtétel', *Egyedül Vagyunk,* June 1944, 1.
17 Zsuzsánna Kesserű Haynalné, 'Beszélgetés Oláh György íróval', *Krónika* July-August (1980): 6–9.
18 See Éva Bánki, 'Lobogó sötétség. Tormay Cécile: Bújdosó könyv', *Múltunk* 2 (2008): 100.
19 Kesserű Haynalné, 'Beszélgetés Oláh György íróval', 9.
20 György Oláh, 'Új enciklopédisták felé', *Magyarok útja*, 1 December 1951, 5–6.
21 Oláh, 'Tíz éve vándorolunk', 3.
22 See Raanan Rein, 'Argentina, World War II, and the Entry of Nazi War Criminals', in *Argentine Jews or Jewish Argentines? Essays on Ethnicity, Identity, and Diaspora* (Leiden: Brill, 2010), 79–80, 86–7.
23 Ádám Anderle, 'Magyarok Latin-Amerikában', *Külügyi Szemle* 3 (2008): 177.
24 György Oláh, 'Az újság-üzem ördögei', *Magyarok útja*, 15 September 1953, 6–7.
25 For the latter, see Eduardo Elena, 'Argentina in Black and White. Race, Peronism, and the Color of Politics, 1940s to the Present', in *Rethinking Race in Modern Argentina*, ed. Paulina Alberto and Eduardo Elena (Cambridge/New York: Cambridge University Press, 2016), 184–209.
26 György Oláh, 'Néhány szó a latinamerikai vitához', *Chicago és környéke,* 11 June 1971, 7.
27 Ibid.
28 Ibid., 7.
29 György Oláh, 'A bolíviai ellenforradalomról', *Chicago és környéke,* 17 September 1971, 7.

30 See Luis Alberto Romero, *A History of Argentina in the Twentieth Century* (University Park: The Pennsylvania State University Press, 2002), 158.
31 Ignacio Aguiló, *The Darkening Nation. Race, Neoliberalism and Crisis in Argentina* (Cardiff: University of Wales Press, 2018), 41–4.
32 See Federico Finchelstein, *The Ideological Origins of the Dirty War. Fascism, Populism, and Dictatorship in Twentieth Century Argentina* (Oxford and New York: Oxford University Press, 2014), 24, 157.
33 György Oláh, '1956 évfordulóján a nagy süllyesztőről', *Chicago és környéke*, 19 November 1971, 7.
34 György Oláh, 'Az antikrisztus itt jár közöttünk', *Magyarság*, 7 September 1973, 5. On his tour, see *Magyarság*, 11 May 1973, 2; 22 June 1973, 2; 29 June 1973, 2; 13 July 1973, 4; 27 July 1973, 5; 10 August 1973, 7; 24 August 1973, 5; 7 September 1973, 5.
35 György Oláh, 'Délamerikai napló', *Chicago és környéke*, 17 July 1976, 9.
36 György Oláh, 'Nobel-díj a gerillának', *Katolikus Magyarok Vasárnapja*, 18 January 1981, 1.
37 Finchelstein, *The Ideological Origins of the Dirty War*, 126, 127, 142.
38 Aguiló, *The Darkening Nation*, 49.
39 Oláh, 'Reakciósak lettünk!', 4.
40 Finchelstein, *The Ideological Origins of the Dirty War*, 143.
41 See Emmanuel Nicolás Kahan, '"Memories that Lie a Little". New Approaches to the Research into the Jewish Experience during the Last Military Dictatorship in Argentina', in *The New Jewish Argentina. Facets of Jewish Experiences in the Southern Cone*, ed. Adriana Brodsky and Raanan Rein (Leiden and Boston: Brill, 2012), 293–313.
42 György Oláh, 'Koronatanú', *Katolikus Magyarok Vasárnapja*, 7 October 1979, 3.

15

Complicity versus cooperation

Zygmunt Bauman's *Modernity and the Holocaust* and Claude Lanzmann's *Shoah* and its outtakes

Sue Vice

In this chapter, I will ask to what extent the sociologist Zygmunt Bauman and the filmmaker Claude Lanzmann share a conception of the Holocaust as the product of modernity's rational tendencies. Such tendencies most strikingly include the elicitation of complicity on the part of the genocide's facilitators and cooperation by its victims, even in situations where this is contrary to the subjects' own ethical beliefs or interests. I compare approaches to the same instances of these kinds of participation as they are addressed in both Bauman's classic study *Modernity and the Holocaust* (1989) and Lanzmann's documentary *Shoah* (1985) and the outtake footage excluded from the film's final version.[1]

In their respective portrayals of complicity, Bauman and Lanzmann enlist the example of Nazi correspondence between an engineer and an SS commander about the gas vans to convey the transformation of everyday work-practices into those of mass murder. The notion of cooperation on the victims' part is typified for Bauman in *Modernity* and Lanzmann in the *Shoah* outtakes by the selectivity of self-rescue among the Jews, within the context of a genocide that targeted everyone. While Lanzmann's outtake archive reveals his extensive engagement with the efforts of the Budapest Rescue and Aid Committee in wartime Hungary, Bauman cites its leader Rezső Kasztner in support of his critique of Jewish Council leadership in the ghettos. There seems to be accord between the two in relation to complicity, while Lanzmann's archive includes interviews which address the very instances of cooperation that preoccupy Bauman. However, the artistic heterogeneity of the outtakes ultimately distinguishes Lanzmann's filmic oeuvre from that of the sociological argument.

Complicity versus cooperation

In *Modernity*, Bauman contrasts the notion of complicity with that of cooperation. His claim that the mass murder of Europe's Jews was not an aberration but a paradigmatic expression of aspects of life within modernity makes these versions of collusion central to the argument that both were 'brought into being by the thoroughly modern art of rational action'.[2] For Bauman, 'the technological tools' and 'scientific management as embodied in bureaucratic organization' (228) were crucial to complicity in murder. The genocide's occurrence equally exposes modernity's central features of the division of labour and dissipation of personal responsibility, which Bauman views as underlying the 'moral indifference' to a mass murder undertaken for the sake of '*an artificial social order*' (65, Bauman's italics). As he summarizes this convergence in genocide of modern means with 'grand' ambition, '*The design gives it the legitimation; state bureaucracy gives it the vehicle; and the paralysis of society gives it the "road clear" sign*' (114).

Throughout his study, Bauman examines the 'social production' (244) of both killers and assenters in a 'vicious' (16) system like that of Nazism. His fullest engagement with the term 'complicity' appears in relation to Stanley Milgram's postwar experiments on obedience to authority and the binding quality of 'sequential' or repeated actions (157–59). In this context, Bauman describes complicity as the effect of an 'ingenious system' where 'the degree to which the actor finds himself bound to perpetuate the action, and opting-out difficult, grows with every stage' (157). Bauman likens complicity, even to an act that the subject 'admit[s] is criminal' (158), to a bog or swamp. Once an individual is within it, every effort at extrication simply results in 'one's sinking deeper into the mire' (157). Thus, 'the subject is trapped by his gradual commitment' to actions even if their continuation causes increasing 'moral torments' (158, quoting Sabini and Silver).

The invocation of a bog implies that falling foul of such a system is an everyday experience readily understood by 'everyone who once inadvertently stepped' (157) into a geological feature of this kind. The downplaying of agency ('inadvertently') and assumption that readers will recognize themselves in this plight contrasts with Bauman's describing as 'cooperation' another kind of gradualism on the part of the system's victims (117–50). Those targeted by the Nazi genocide, in contrast to those who enacted it, were 'solicited' into making 'rational calculations' about survival in actions that both hastened their own destruction and betrayed their 'moral duty' (143).

Although complicity is represented as a machine or natural obstacle that engulfs those in its thrall, Bauman's analysis of cooperation suggests that more resistance is expected of the victims of a system such as Nazism. Their ethical 'dehumanization' (147) in the enactment of the murder directed against them prompts Bauman's greatest censure, not only of the mechanism that was established for that purpose, but of the Jews who were induced to abandon 'solidarity' (133) through choosing whether 'to die or to let others die' (144). Bauman's analysis thus contradicts the celebration of survival as this characterizes Holocaust remembrance and lacks any proposal for alternative action other than assenting to one's death. Yet his considerations are shared by Lanzmann as these emerge in *Shoah* and in the footage excluded in the process of the film's making. While a Baumanian engagement with modernity's complicity-inducing effects is evident in *Shoah*, it is the excluded outtake interviews which address questions of cooperation.

Bauman concludes *Modernity* with acknowledgement to what he calls Lanzmann's 'monumental' (249) documentary. This might seem surprising in relation to the concerns of *Shoah* as it stands, since the film memorializes those who died, as implied by its opening epigraph from Isaiah, 'I will give them an everlasting name'.[3] This is far from conveying the ethical disaster which Bauman claims befell the Jews' efforts to stay alive in the face of Nazi genocide. However, *Shoah*'s centring on what Lanzmann calls the 'machinery of death' means the features that Bauman places at the heart of modernity also appear in the film.[4] Thus, the editing of *Shoah* to emphasize murder's present-day traces entails showing those phenomena that Bauman claims were foundational to the Jews' isolation and murder: 'modern industry, transport, science, bureaucracy, technology' (188).

These categories as listed by Bauman might put us in mind of *Shoah*'s sequences showing Germany's industrial Ruhr valley, the many travelling shots of trains, emphasis on developments in the methods of killing by gas and, in Lanzmann's last release *The Four Sisters* (2017), Ruth Elias's undergoing in Auschwitz the extremity of 'value-free' scientific research (Bauman, 126). Considered from the perspective of Bauman's assertion of the Holocaust's 'normality' (119) within modernity, these features in *Shoah* take on a new significance. The location outtakes of Germany in Lanzmann's archive increase this impression with their focus on locations including the Thyssen factory complex at Duisberg and neon-lit Berlin. Such footage's visual layering of past and present suggests an ominous continuity. This is evident in the distant view of East Berlin's Fernsehturm television tower framed by the arch of Grunewald Station (Figure 15.1), from which German Jews were deported during the war, as if in cinematic corroboration of Bauman's argument that modern working practice still risks '*the denial of the moral significance of non-technical issues*'(160, Bauman's italics).

Indeed, in some cases *Shoah* seems to have inspired the examples on which Bauman's argument rests. It is hard not to recall Raul Hilberg's bringing to light, in Lanzmann's film, the murderous significance of the train timetable 'Fahrplananordnung 587' to Treblinka when reading Bauman's description of the 'detached, abstract awareness' on the part of 'bureaucratic functionaries', the 'final outcomes' of whose work when 'graphically or numerically represented' appear reassuringly 'devoid of substance'.[5]

Figure 15.1 Layers of history in Berlin.

Likewise, Lanzmann's discussing with Hilberg the fact that, although the Jews were made to pay for their journeys east, children under four 'went free' and had, as the director says, 'the privilege to be gassed freely', is echoed by Bauman's observation that 'the leaders of the doomed communities [. . .] mobilized the financial resources needed to pay for the last journey'.[6]

Yet the object of Lanzmann's sardonic remark is the architects of the genocidal infrastructure and the Reichsbahn who profited from it, while Bauman's sarcasm is directed at the Jewish leaders who relieved their captors of tasks which, as he puts it, would otherwise have stretched the Nazis' 'ingenuity or resources' (118). This variation in target points to a larger difference. For Bauman, the elements of modern life which enabled the genocide also shaped the ways in which the victims responded. For Lanzmann, revealing the continuity between the technologies of murder and of contemporary life makes the victims' fate visible in the cinematic present. Rather than expose the 'instrumental rationality' (18) that Bauman claims engulfed the quest for survival on the victims' part in its 'call[ing] for non-resistance to the other's destruction' (203), Lanzmann's film takes for granted their entrapment in a system from which there was no escape.

Bauman and *Shoah*

As Bryan Cheyette recounts, Zygmunt Bauman and his wife Janina first saw *Shoah* in the shortened, three-hour version broadcast on Polish television in the year of its release.[7] Bauman's familiarity with the film in its entirety is evident in his detailed commentary on some of its central eyewitnesses, and *Modernity*'s appearing just four years after *Shoah*'s release entails a reliance on the same sources at a time before the end of the Cold War, the opening of Soviet archives and subsequent developments in historiography.[8] Both *Modernity* and *Shoah* evidence a debt to Hilberg and Hannah Arendt, while the historian Henry Feingold and theologian Richard Rubenstein, both frequently cited by Bauman, also feature in Lanzmann's outtake interviews.

Despite his attentive response to *Shoah*, it is unlikely that Bauman was aware of the extra interviews that Lanzmann recorded during its filming and which were cut out during the editing process. These outtakes amount to over 220 hours of encounters with many eyewitnesses, historians and others who do not appear at all in the finished version. The outtake interviews differ from the final film by engaging so definitively with what Bauman calls the 'unsightly and disturbing' questions about 'solicitation' (9) of the victims' cooperation that this could be considered the most pressing reason for their omission. For both the sociologist and the filmmaker, these include actions by the Judenräte in the ghettos of Łódź, Vilna and Amsterdam, where arguments to 'rescue through work' (129) or 'save what you can' (137) depended on the protection of some lives at the expense of others.

As shown by the examples discussed here, bearing in mind Bauman's arguments while considering episodes from *Shoah* and its outtakes has a variety of implications. It provides a frame within which we can consider such elements as *Shoah*'s emphasis on technology, including the gas vans' significance as a 'crucial' step towards the 'systematic mass murder' in the death-camps which is the final film's concern.[9] This emerges in relation to Lanzmann's citing a letter about 'improving' these vehicles for their new purpose, its impersonal tenor arising from what Bauman, in his analysis of the same document, calls the 'deadly logic of problem-solving' (74). The letter's role in *Shoah* as a document testifying to functional complicity on the perpetrator side is, as I will argue, clarified in relation to similar material that was not used. Lanzmann's outtake interview with the Israeli lawyer Shmuel Tamir poses ethical questions about the victims' response to genocide. The interview addresses the attempted rescue in Hungary by the Budapest Aid and Rescue Committee, headed by the individual to whom Bauman pre-emptively refers as 'the notorious Rezső Kasztner'.[10] While Lanzmann and Bauman seem united in their negative judgement on the selectivity of such initiatives as the Kasztner Train, the very fact of the exclusion from *Shoah* of Tamir's interview and the question of self-rescue reveals that the film's priority lay elsewhere.

The complicity of expertise

In *Shoah*, Lanzmann reads aloud a memorandum sent by the engineer Willy Just to the SS commander Walter Rauff. The letter describes the 'technical changes' required to make the murderous task of those operating the gas vans at Chełmno easier.[11] Extracts from the same letter appear in *Modernity*, Bauman's extract and Lanzmann's both edited to emphasize its impersonal tone by concluding with Just's recommendations about improving the vehicles' drainage. The source Bauman draws on is Christopher Browning's essay on the role of the gas vans.[12] However, it seems possible that Lanzmann's voicing of this haunting text in *Shoah* prompted Bauman's including it in his book.[13] The passage from Just's memorandum chosen for both contexts uses the passive constructions and oblique wording typifying what Bauman calls 'the neutral language of car-production technology' (197). This discourse highlights by its very occlusions the horrifying reality of murder by gas, as the respective versions of the same extract show:

> *Shoah*
>
> For easy cleaning of the vehicle, there must be a sealed drain in the middle of the floor. The drainage hole's cover [. . .] would be equipped with a slanting trap, so that fluid liquids can drain off during the operation. During cleaning, the drain can be used to evacuate large pieces of dirt.[14]
>
> *Modernity*
>
> The floor should be slightly inclined, and the cover equipped with a small sieve. Thus all 'fluids' would flow to the middle, the 'thin fluids' would exit even during operation, while 'thicker fluids' could be hosed out afterwards.[15]

In the passage from *Modernity* above, what Bauman presents as a verbatim citation 'at length' (197) from Just's memo is, rather, Browning's summary of the letter in a free indirect style. Bauman therefore mistakenly views the quotation marks as Browning's intervention in Just's text to highlight the presence of 'metaphors or euphemisms' (197). However, the quotation marks' role is to signal the sole direct citations, showing that Browning agrees with Bauman's conclusion that Just uses 'the straightforward, down-to-earth, language of technology' to eliminate 'moral inhibitions' or humane awareness (196–97). Yet it is only Lanzmann's spoken rendition that makes plain the document's chilling integration of phrasing and meaning. The fact of the director's recitation of Just's words places the whole utterance within notional quotation marks while defying the original's designation of 'Secret Reich Business' through its filmic release.[16]

Bauman argues that, rather than the 'passion' of virulent racism, Just's letter reveals how the atomized work patterns of modernity allow murder to 'masquerade' as a 'routine' function of 'orderly society' (245). In this case, distancing enabled the conduct of mass murder. In addition to the Jews' ejection from social life, Bauman claims that a psychological distance was necessary when 'perpetrators had to meet the victims face-to-face', or could not avoid considering the 'effects of their actions' (196) on them. The tendency of Just's letter supports Bauman's conclusion, 'Such a method is provided by a specifically modern form of authority – expertise', in relation to which 'personal responsibility dissolves in the abstract authority of technical know-how' (196). Lanzmann's choice of extract equally highlights the aspect of the gas van correspondence as elucidated by Bauman's conclusion: 'The fact that the load consisted of people about to be murdered and losing control over their bodies, did not detract from the technical challenge of the problem' (196).

It might therefore seem that Lanzmann's reading out Just's words in *Shoah* has the same purpose as Bauman's citation. It reveals the mindset responsible for the atrocities witnessed from a victim's perspective by the Chełmno survivor Simon Srebrnik, whose testimony is heard immediately beforehand in *Shoah*. But the role of Just's memorandum in Lanzmann's film differs from that in *Modernity* through its use of the material as part of an artwork. The letter's being preceded by Srebrnik's words reveals a logic of ironic juxtaposition reliant on the viewer's intuition, by contrast to Bauman's of cumulative argument. The effect of Just's language as decoded by Bauman is experienced by the viewer at this point in *Shoah* through Lanzmann's voicing its words and its position in relation to the film's other elements. Just's letter concludes *Shoah*'s 'first era', its recitation a transition to the second era's focus on the gas chambers which opens with Franz Suchomel's recall of Treblinka. Suchomel's SS guard perspective is set against that of the Treblinka survivor Abraham Bomba in a montage that is not available in the case of the gas van murders. Despite Lanzmann's efforts to film the former gas van driver Gustav Laabs, the director was unable to interview any eyewitness of Chełmno from the perpetrator side. We could consider his reading of Just's letter to offer, in the unusual form of ventriloquy, this missing perspective.

Shoah's outtakes show that Just's letter, cut down to establish particular emphases, was chosen from among several eyewitness reports on the gas vans which were also recited by Lanzmann.[17] The archive includes several takes of Lanzmann reading the whole of Just's letter to Rauff, these recordings' existence solely in the form of audio tracks suggesting that they would have been matched with separately filmed location footage. Footage of the failed interview with Laabs includes repeated readings by the director of another letter sent to Rauff on 16 August 1942.[18] Lanzmann describes this letter's author, Dr August Becker, as 'the inventor of gas trucks, or more exactly the system that allowed the exhaust gas to kill'.[19] The disavowal of the humanity of the vans' 'cargo' expressed in Just's letter also pervades Becker's, in this case through the mechanism of perpetrator self-pity or what Bauman calls 'strain on the participant'.[20]

In this example of a memo to Rauff, Becker demands more staff because of concern for the gas van operators' well-being. His assertion, 'I ordered that during all actions, our men stand as far as possible from the gas trucks so that their health is not jeopardized by any leaking gas', gives terrible irony to the disregard for the victims. It also bears out Bauman's claim that an 'atmosphere of the office' (195) characterized the responses of functionaries in their genocidal roles. In keeping with Becker's earlier involvement in the T4 programme, his letter is more explicit about the killings. He not only exhibits Just's concern to redress 'faults in [his] product' but asserts the need to make up for poor workplace provision.[21] The role of perpetrator self-pity in moving from hands-on to more 'remote' (193) mass killing, as analysed by Bauman, is revealed through Lanzmann's act of verbatim voicing.

While the 'ethically blind' nature of what Bauman calls 'the bureaucratic pursuit of efficiency' (15) is forcefully conveyed in both examples of wartime correspondence with Rauff about the gas vans, Lanzmann's description of Just's as 'more unbelievable' (*plus incroyable*) than Becker's, through its exclusively functional view of the need for the vans' 'improvement', explains his decision to include it in the finished film.[22] There was a contrasting rationale for Lanzmann to exclude from *Shoah* the footage of himself reading a third, very differently oriented text about the gas vans, the affidavit from February 1945 by a German forester in Poland, Heinrich May.[23] May's record of horror at what he witnessed in his role of providing wood from the Chełmno forest for the burning of corpses on pyres reveals that he did not take refuge from acknowledging atrocity in a specialized activity. Unlike Just, May's fulfilling his 'ordinary duties' (Bauman, 153) accompanied his retaining awareness, as his testimony shows, of the human status of the victims of gassing, and the foundational human potential for an 'ethicality of being' (224) that Bauman invokes. While it might be true of Just, as a mechanic with no previous involvement in mass murder,[24] that modernity's detachment and division enabled engagement in actions that his 'nature would otherwise prevent' (Bauman, 95), May describes those who carried out the killings from the perspective of someone whose 'nature' was indeed affronted.

Yet, despite his 'despair' (232) at the crimes, May falls within Bauman's category of those who '*passively watched*' (205, Bauman's italics). The adherence to 'the rationality of self-preservation' (143) at the expense of all other obligations, as Bauman identifies it in the context of the victims' cooperation, also characterized the responses of those unwilling contributors to the killing-process like May. Although Bauman gives as an example the failure to shelter a Jewish family on these grounds of self-preservation by their non-Jewish Polish neighbours (201–2), this uncomfortable assertion is much more extensively examined in relation to the victims.

Unlike Just's letter, Lanzmann's recitation of May's testimony has a synchronous image-track showing the Chełmno forest. The mise-en-scene of Lanzmann, clad in a green waterproof coat and standing on a muddy path in front of a thicket of trees like

Figure 15.2 Lanzmann reads aloud in the Chełmno forest.

those May was ordered to plant to disguise the mass graves, emphasizes the materiality of this setting about which he reads aloud (Figure 15.2).

The marking up of May's transcript in Lanzmann's archive reveals that the director's plan for the testimony was to focus on the killings' secrecy. However, rather than considering this in relation to the German public, as does May in his conviction that the murders' clandestine nature explained the lack of protest, Lanzmann's concern lies with the deception of the victims and the erasure of crimes committed against them. For Bauman, the anatomy of the victims' 'cooperation in their own destruction' depends on his assumption, as he claims of the Judenräte members, that 'at a relatively early stage ... [they] knew – or at least could know, unless they tried hard not to – what was the true purpose of the "selections" they were commanded to make' (140). For Lanzmann, redressing the wartime concealments is a factor central to his cinematic emphasis on 'the traces of traces' in the present. Yet, as we will see in relation to the case of the Kasztner Train rescue in Hungary, the notion of the manipulation of facts by the Jews among themselves adds to Lanzmann's conviction of aspects of the victims' culpability.

Cooperation in Hungary

For Lanzmann and Bauman alike, crucial questions about the practical and ethical pitfalls of Jewish self-rescue are exemplified by the Kasztner Train rescue in wartime Hungary. This initiative resulted in 1684 passengers leaving Hungary in June 1944 on a train to Switzerland, following negotiations conducted between the Budapest Aid and Rescue Committee and SS officials including Adolf Eichmann. The event raises such questions as how those who journeyed to safety were chosen by the Committee and what its members' attitude was to those who were left behind. While Bauman cites Kasztner to support his broader claim about Jewish leaders' accession to Nazi demands, Lanzmann's interview with Shmuel Tamir contrasts Kasztner's selective rescue efforts with the more eclectic actions of Rabbi Michael Weissmandl in Slovakia to imply that patterns of response were not predetermined.[25]

Lanzmann's focus on the Kasztner Train is one element in his filmic project to reveal the near impossibility of rescue, while for Bauman it exemplifies how the victims were drawn into cooperation with the Nazis' design. The distinction between these emphases is conveyed by the phrasing each uses to sum up the response of the victims. While Bauman sees Kasztner's actions as an instance of the 'rationality' of choice, for Lanzmann, they convey the 'tragedy' of being made to choose in a context of communal doom.[26] Bauman's is the harsher verdict, although his examples of cooperation focus in more detail on the practice of the ghetto Judenräte than this one-off rescue mission. It is Lanzmann who dwells at length on the Kasztner Train, in discrete interviews with the committee member Hansi Brand and rescuee Hanna Marton, and several hours of dialogue in encounters with other testifiers including Rudolf Vrba and Raul Hilberg, none of which appears in *Shoah*. The director chose to interview Tamir on the Kasztner rescue despite the lawyer's perspective being that of an onlooker rather than an eyewitness. In 1954, Tamir had represented the defendant Malchiel Grünwald in a libel suit brought against him by Kasztner, whom Grünwald had accused of 'collaboration' with the Nazis for the sake of a selective rescue which he claimed cost the lives of thousands of others in wartime Hungary. Although the verdict was initially found in Grünwald's favour, it was overturned on appeal – by which time Kasztner had been murdered in Israel by members of a right-wing militia.

In his anatomy of cooperation, Bauman cites Kasztner's *Report* of 1946, an account of wartime events in Hungary.[27] He does so to demonstrate Kasztner's awareness that, as Bauman contends, for the Jews under Nazi rule, 'Once self-preservation had been chosen as the supreme criterion of action, its price could be gradually yet relentlessly increased – until all other considerations have been devalued' (143). Kasztner is thus quoted describing the escalation of Nazi demands, by which, as he phrases it, at first 'relatively unimportant things were asked [of the Jewish Council], replaceable things of material value' such as the Jews' 'personal possessions'. Bauman concludes by quoting Kasztner's observation, 'Later, however, the personal freedom of human beings was demanded. Finally, the Nazis asked for life itself' (143).

Bauman's adding 'of the Jewish Council' in square brackets, to quotations taken not directly from the *Report* but from Isaiah Trunk's 1972 study *Judenrat*, makes Kasztner's utterance fit *Modernity*'s thesis about the success of deportations from the ghettos of Poland and Lithuania 'in instalments' (139). At this stage in the *Report*, Kasztner puts forward the different point that 'ma[king] compliant' the Judenräte did not occur in Hungary, where the speed of events prevented the councils having to take the actions he describes.[28] Kasztner wanted to make clear in his *Report* the hazards facing the rescue committee and ensure that he gained credit for his role in the Train's success.[29] Bauman, however, sees these words in the opposite sense as Kasztner's 'tormented admission' (143) of his role in the oppressors' design.

Lanzmann also quotes from Kasztner's *Report* during his encounter with Tamir. He does so, like Bauman, to demonstrate what he calls Kasztner's 'lucid' comprehension that the rescue committee's having to place their trust in the Germans meant that they began a 'game of roulette with human lives'. Tamir's indignation at Kasztner's invoking 'roulette' leads him to conclude that this notion of gambling with 'the lives of hundreds of thousands' reveals that Kasztner 'simply lost [. . .] the last senses of values'. Here and throughout, Tamir's eloquence confirms his experience as a lawyer and politician, the interview's performative nature acknowledged by the crew's applause heard as the camera stops rolling. The arguments about Kasztner's 'betrayal', and the guilt Tamir takes as given, as if the trial's original judgement had not been overturned, are ones he is clearly accustomed to making. While Bauman sees Kasztner's action as emblematic of cooperation, for Tamir, who refers to it throughout as 'collaboration', his behaviour is untypical, having nothing in common with that of the Judenräte where 'people under agony tried to save lives'. In phrasing that accords with his avowedly psychological approach, Tamir concludes that 'under Nazi pressure', Kasztner 'developed a fanatical egomaniac attitude' and became what he calls 'a dangerous victim'.

Lanzmann's counterargument to Tamir is that, since it was 'impossible to save everybody', Kasztner was 'perfectly right to choose'. Yet neither Tamir nor Lanzmann, who claims to be quoting witnesses for Kasztner's defence, agrees with this argument's seeming cogency. In this respect, the interview's representation of Kasztner's actions corresponds with Bauman's. However, while Tamir uses the analogy of the captain of a sinking ship, claiming that such a leader should not offer selective access to a lifeboat but give the passengers responsibility for their own fate, Bauman does not suggest what course of action should instead have been taken. His accolade for the 'dignified departure' (141) by suicide on the part of the Warsaw Ghetto Judenrat leader Adam Czerniaków, also perhaps inspired by his recalling Lanzmann's *Shoah*, and for the Judenrat members in the Bereza Kartuska ghetto, all of whom killed themselves rather than agree to Nazi deportation demands, suggests that for Bauman the only ethical response to a situation where no good choice was available was permanently to remove oneself from it.

Bauman's using Kasztner's words in relation to selective decisions by such Judenrat leaders as Jacob Gens in Vilna does not acknowledge the different circumstances of attempted rescue in Hungary, since, as Yehuda Bauer emphasizes to Lanzmann in their outtake interview, the Kasztner Train was seen by the Budapest rescue committee as a test case for further such journeys.[30] It is Lanzmann's encounter with Tamir which brings out the extra accusation that, beyond choosing between people, this mission involved the deception of those excluded. Lanzmann claims that concealing the destination of deportations from 'the masses' ensured the peaceful departure of the Kasztner Train to safety for a chosen few. This position accords with Bauman's, since he concludes his argument as exemplified by Kasztner's rescue mission by claiming it shows 'the rationality of self-preservation', once it had been 'chosen as the supreme criterion of action', to be 'the enemy of moral duty' (143). Lanzmann's interview with Tamir elicits negative judgements of just this kind. However, its unedited status gives it a plurality of possible significance beyond such finality.

Despite its extensive engagement with the Kasztner Train rescue, Lanzmann's interview, with this interlocutor whose renown arose from his defence of the accused in the Kasztner libel trial, is not only concerned with events in Hungary. Lanzmann's dialogue with Tamir hints at the possibility of a different response to the threat of genocide, beyond either cooperation or Bauman's invocation of suicide. Indeed, Kasztner's mission is introduced as a foil to the efforts at rescue taken in Slovakia under the leadership of Rabbi Weissmandl, with whose history the encounter opens. The mise-en-scene for Tamir's interview testifies to this priority, since he is shown seated at a table on which is visible, in varying degrees of close-up, a copy of Weissmandl's posthumously published testimony *Min Ha-Meitzar* [From the Straits] of 1957, from which he reads aloud the late rabbi's wartime harangues against the unresponsive 'countries of freedom'. As if the volume personifies its author, Lanzmann can be heard instructing his interviewee to 'look at the book' during his account of meeting Weissmandl, and, looking as if swearing an oath, Tamir rests his hand on it while describing what he calls Kasztner's 'collaboration with the death machine' (Figure 15.3).

For Tamir and Lanzmann, Weissmandl's stance is free from the ethical compromise besetting the Kasztner initiative. Beyond his affirmation of Czerniaków's death by suicide, Bauman does not address the possibility of exceeding the structural grip of modernity's 'adiaphoria' (215), that is, its morally neutral or indifferent practice, in relation to the victims' efforts to stay alive. Yet Weissmandl's rescue campaign ranged across the 'whole spectrum' of activities including negotiations with the Nazis, raising money, helping people hide or flee, advocating information campaigns and demanding the Allies bomb the train tracks and crematoria at Auschwitz, seeming thus to evade the binary of cooperation or suicide.

Figure 15.3 Shmuel Tamir with Rabbi Weissmandl's memoir.

Beyond the variety of his actions, in Weissmandl's case an answer can be given to Bauman's judgement of Jewish leaders, 'Playing God was made easier by self-interest', while, 'It is impossible to say how many of those who chose to "foul their hands" did hope to survive' (144). A very different train journey to that arranged by Kasztner was the setting for Weissmandl's survival, since he escaped from a transport to Auschwitz, where the rest of his family perished, with the avowed intention to continue his rescue mission on behalf of others. Yet Lanzmann's omission from *Shoah* of all these matters, including the attempted rescue of the Hungarian Jews and efforts by Weissmandl, on both of which he had claimed the final film would centre,[31] suggests that comparison between the modes or morality of survival was too tangential to the genocide which his film was committed to representing.

Conclusion

The cases of Willy Just and Rezső Kasztner are used by both Lanzmann and Bauman to exemplify questions of complicity and cooperation in the Holocaust world. However, as we have seen, their practice in relation to eyewitness utterance is symptomatically different. Where Bauman summarizes testimony and quotes it selectively or second-hand to support his thesis, Lanzmann constructs a self-conscious filmic relationship between voice and body. If a witness cannot speak on their own behalf, the enactment of ventriloquism makes that plain. That this formal and generic distinction is also an ethical one is revealed by Lanzmann and Bauman's respective approaches to the Sonderkommando, those 'special squads' of Jewish prisoners kept alive to be 'grotesquely tasked with the running of the crematoria in the extermination camps'.[32] In this case, Bauman's source for his examples is Lanzmann's *Shoah*.

For Lanzmann, the Sonderkommando members were crucial to his cinematic vision for their ability 'to describe in detail how the machinery of death functioned'.[33] Thus, the best-known testifiers in *Shoah*, including Michael Podchlebnik, Filip Müller and, as we shall see, Richard Glazar and Abraham Bomba, were sought out for the sake of their Sonderkommando perspective. Lanzmann's inclusion of Müller's recalling that he was urged to remain alive by those about to be killed to transmit their story shows that there were motivations beyond what Bauman disapprovingly calls an 'irresistible compulsion to live' (147).

For Bauman, the utterance of two of *Shoah*'s Sonderkommando testifiers has a significance quite different to that customarily drawn from Lanzmann's film. Bauman cites, although does not name, Glazar and Bomba, who were enslaved at Treblinka in the tasks, respectively, of processing clothes from those who had been murdered and cutting the hair of those about to be killed. Bauman does so in support of his consistent argument that 'obedience' on the part of Sonderkommando members 'was rational', even at the cost of 'non-resistance to the other's destruction' (202–3). While Glazar is said by Bauman to have relied on the enactment of deportation and murder for his survival, Bomba is described as ensuring that his fellow Jews complied in the process of their own murder. Bauman claims that such cooperation arose from the conviction that 'everything that served self-preservation was right', following the hierarchy of destruction through which some were spared death longer than others.[34] He concludes that the actions of the Sonderkommando, like those of the Judenräte leaders and individuals who strove to survive at the expense of others, disrupted the unambiguous division between 'murderers and the murdered' (122) as that usually characterizes genocide.

In evidence for his thesis, Bauman cites Glazar's description of 'the dead season' (147) in Treblinka when no transports, and therefore no food, arrived in the camp. Glazar's testimony in *Shoah* of his 'helplessness' and 'shame' that life 'depended on [...] the slaughtering process at Treblinka'[35] is invoked but not quoted directly in *Modernity*. Bauman's attention focuses on the Sonderkommando prisoners seeming to gain not just from the arrivals at the camp but from the entire structure of persecution, as he puts it: 'Their prospects of survival brightened when new Jewish populations were rounded up and loaded into trains destined for Treblinka' (201). The use of everyday phrasing – 'prospects brightened' – implies the pettiness of the goal of survival, as well as Bauman's own revulsion that it came at the cost of abandoning, in his words, 'moral scruples' and 'human dignity' (147).

The summary in *Modernity* of Abraham Bomba's testimony also depends on Bauman's idiosyncratic 'way of remembering' this sequence.[36] It takes an unexpected perspective on an interview which is usually valued for eliciting Bomba's 'involuntary memory'[37] of an atrocious past as he recounts cutting women's hair on the gas chamber's threshold. By contrast, Bauman focuses on the barber's 'obedience' to the Nazi design that this action reveals. Bomba's almost 10-minute testimony is condensed by Bauman:

> A former Sonderkommando member, now a Tel-Aviv barber, *reminisces* how, while shaving the hair of the victims for German mattresses, he kept silent about the purpose of the exercise and *prodded* his *clients* towards what they were made to believe was a communal bath. (201, italics mine)

Bauman's phrasing minimizes the painful nature of Bomba's recall ('reminisces') while exaggerating his agency ('prodded') and making his actions sound even more regrettable through bathos ('his clients'). The experience of hearing Bomba's utterance in *Shoah* – which Bauman, in the absence of direct quotation, summarizes as his 'keeping silent' (201) to ensure his own survival – is likely to have a different significance for the viewer. Bomba's words' importance as edited for the finished film lies rather in his proximity to those who cannot testify for themselves, even as he speaks in the third person about himself and his fellow barbers encountering women whom they knew:

> BOMBA: They could not tell them this was the last time they stay alive . . . they tried to do the best for them, with a second longer, a minute longer, just to hug them and kiss them, because they knew they would never see them again.[38]

Bauman's argument here that 'rational defence of one's survival' at the expense of others' lives depends on the claim that *Shoah* reveals 'how few men with guns were needed to murder millions'.[39] What Bryan Cheyette calls this 'reductive' view of Lanzmann's film sums up the difference between Bauman's approach and the director's.[40] Bauman sees *Shoah* as supporting his thesis, but the notion of what he calls the 'terrible, humiliating truth' of rational obedience is offset even in the more cooperation-focused outtakes. Lanzmann's excluded interviews and location footage address the wider context that Bauman's *Modernity* has been accused of omitting.[41] Bauman's focus lies on the abstract workings of modernity as these produced the most intimate dramas of life-and-death located at the far end of a chain of influence and power. By contrast, Lanzmann's outtakes confront inaction on the part of allied and neutral nations and institutions, including the fruitless refugee conferences at Evian and Bermuda, the late establishment of the United States' War Refugee Board and negligence by the Red Cross.[42] Of these factors, only the significance of closed borders is mentioned by Bauman. He fleetingly acknowledges that the genocide might not have occurred if the Nazis had been able to achieve a '*judenfrei* Germany' through enforcing emigration, had 'other countries' been 'hospitable to Jewish refugees' (15).

In both *Modernity* and *Shoah*, the killing is shown to be the outcome of an elaborate 'process' or 'machine'.[43] But Lanzmann has consigned to the repository of his archive those questions about the Jews' conduct in the face of insuperable forces which are central for Bauman. Whatever might have been Lanzmann's plans for the interview with Tamir and its focus on cooperation, viewers are able to envisage for themselves its potential to be 'created anew on the editing table'.[44] This might follow Lanzmann's editing of Hanna Marton's interview in *The Four Sisters*, which enables the answering back by one of the Kastzner Train passengers to the director's leading questions on the selectivity of this rescue. Not only does Marton conclude by observing that she is the only member of her family to have survived, but the very existence of the film and of its protagonist is the outcome of the mission which she is asked to evaluate. The director's own editorial practice reveals this, in giving Marton the last word in *The Four Sisters*: 'what always bothers me is that people forget [. . .] it's the Nazi system that forced people to choose'.[45]

Notes

1 The outtakes were created by Claude Lanzmann during the filming of *Shoah* and are used and cited by permission of the US Holocaust Memorial Museum and Yad Vashem, the Holocaust Martyrs' and Heroes' Remembrance Authority, Jerusalem.
2 Zygmunt Bauman, *Modernity and the Holocaust* (1989; repr. Cambridge: Polity, 2021), 118. Page numbers when given in parentheses in the main text are to this book.
3 Claude Lanzmann, *Shoah: An Oral History of the Holocaust* (New York: Pantheon, 1985), v.
4 Claude Lanzmann, *The Patagonian Hare: A Memoir*, trans. Frank Wynne (2009; repr. London: Atlantic Books, 2012), 422.
5 Lanzmann, *Shoah*, 138; Bauman, *Modernity*, 99.
6 Lanzmann, *Shoah*, 142; Bauman, *Modernity*, 118.
7 Bryan Cheyette, 'Afterword', in *Revisiting Modernity and the Holocaust: Heritage, Dilemmas, Extensions*, ed. Jack Palmer and Dariusz Brzeziński (London: Routledge, 2022), 233.
8 Ibid., 237.

9 Christopher Browning, *Fateful Months: Essays on the Emergence of the Final Solution* (1985; repr. New York: Holmes & Meier, 1991), 57.
10 Bauman, *Modernity*, 143: Bauman misspells Kasztner's first name as 'Resvö'.
11 Lanzmann, *Shoah*, 103.
12 Browning, *Fateful Months*, 64–5.
13 Lanzmann, *Shoah* 103.
14 Lanzmann, *Shoah*, 194.
15 Bauman, *Modernity*, 197, quoting Browning.
16 Lanzmann, *Shoah*, See also Mark Ward, *Deadly Documents: Technical Communication, Organizational Discourse and the Holocaust: Lessons from the Rhetorical Work of Everyday Texts*, Amityville: Baywood 2014, 157–8.
17 Claude Lanzmann, 'Lettre Just', United States Holocaust Memorial Museum. https://collections.ushmm.org/search/catalog/irn1005028 (Accessed 5 April 2022).
18 Claude Lanzmann, 'Chełmno', United States Holocaust Memorial Museum. https://collections.ushmm.org/search/catalog/irn593675 (Accessed 5 April 2022).
19 Lanzmann, 'Lettre Just'.
20 Bauman, *Modernity*, 103, 155, quoting Milgram.
21 Ibid., 195, quoting Browning.
22 Lanzmann, 'Chełmno'.
23 Ibid.
24 See Browning, *Fateful Months*, 66.
25 Claude Lanzmann, 'Shmuel Tamir', US Holocaust Memorial Museum. https://collections.ushmm.org/search/catalog/irn1004453 (Accessed 5 April 2022).
26 Bauman, *Modernity*, x, Lanzmann, 'Shmuel Tamir'.
27 Rezső Kasztner, *The Kasztner Report: The Report of the Budapest Jewish Rescue Committee, 1942–1945*, trans. Ruth Morris and György Novák (1946; repr., Jerusalem: Yad Vashem, 2013).
28 *Kasztner Report*, 170–1.
29 László Karsai and Judit Molnár, introduction to *Kasztner Report*, 37–8.
30 On its status as a 'Muster Zug', or 'demonstration train', see Daniel Brand, *Trapped by Evil and Deceit: The Story of Hansi and Joel Brand* (Boston: Academic Studies Press, 2020), 126–7.
31 See Lanzmann's letter to Roswell McClelland, quoted in Jennifer Cazenave, *An Archive of the Atrocity: The Unused Footage of Claude Lanzmann's 'Shoah'* (Albany: SUNY Press, 2019), 5; and the Weissmandl-related interviews with André Steiner, Herman Landau and Peter Bergson among Lanzmann's outtakes.
32 Anne Karpf, foreword to *Testimonies of Resistance: Representations of the Auschwitz-Birkenau Sonderkommando*, ed. Nicholas Chare and Dominic Williams (Oxford: Berghahn, 2019), ix. See also Williams' discussion in his 'From Understanding Victims to Victims' Understanding: Rationality, Shame and Other Emotions in *Modernity and the Holocaust*', in *Revisiting Modernity*.
33 Lanzmann, *The Patagonian Hare*, 144.
34 Bauman, *Modernity*, 202, 147.
35 Lanzmann, *Shoah*, 148.
36 Williams, 'From Understanding Victims', 59.
37 Philippe Mesnard, 'The Sonderkommando on Screen', in Chare and Williams, *Testimonies*, 337.
38 Lanzmann, *Shoah*, 117.
39 Ibid., 202–3.

40 Cheyette, 'Afterword', 233.
41 Bauman, *Modernity*, 201; see Griselda Pollock's close reading of Bauman's phrasing, 'Reading *Modernity and the Holocaust* with and against *Winter in the Morning*', in *Revisiting Modernity*, 184–6.
42 See Sue Vice and Dominic Williams, 'Memory as Practice: Editing Claude Lanzmann's Location Outtakes', *ViewFinder*, October 2021.
43 Bauman, *Modernity,* 118; Lanzmann, *The Patagonian Hare*, 422.
44 'Ruth Beckermann', in *Ruth Beckermann*, ed. Eszter Kondor and Michael Loebenstein (Vienna: Austrian Film Museum, 2019), 28.
45 Claude Lanzmann, 'Hanna Marton', United States Holocaust Memorial Museum. https://collections.ushmm.org/search/catalog/irn1003917 (Accessed 5 April 2022).

16

Challenging the museum visitor? Complicity and perpetration during and beyond the Second World War in contemporary museum exhibitions

Stephan Jaeger

Introduction and theoretical framework[1]

In permanent and special exhibitions today, how can museums successfully represent complicity and perpetration during the Second World War and the Holocaust? How can they deal with the ethical, legal and aesthetic factors, as well as the risks and repercussions of such representations? Is it possible for museums to allow their visitors to have an experiential understanding of perpetration and complicity, while avoiding simplistic forms of identification and thereby attracting right-wing groups? Are there ways to exhibit the 'banality' of perpetration without reducing visitors' critical capabilities and moral compass? Or can museums only depict perpetration from a historiographical distance that mainly allows visitors to passively read and observe data and information?

Museums generally depict four – often overlapping – historical situations of feeling morally compromised or uncompromised. The first three of these situations typically relate to a historical person, a generic individual or a constructed collective; they also either refer solely to the historical period of complicity and perpetration, or integrate historical stages of remembrance concerning former attitudes and acts of complicity and perpetration. First, museums can depict the self-perception of the historical subject through these situations. Second, historians and curators/researchers can present their analytical conclusions on how a historical person, a generic individual or a constructed collective perceived themselves as (un-)compromised. Third, museums can aim to immerse today's visitors in the past, in order to make them identify with personified feelings of being (un-)compromised. Fourth, museums can let visitors experience historical situations or structures that lead them to feeling (un-)compromised – this often allows visitors to reflect upon the possible personal implications involved in historical decision-making. The first two scenarios here usually encourage distance between the historical subject–matter and the curator–researcher or visitor. In contrast, the final two scenarios lead to an increased proximity between museum visitor and historical subject-matter. This article employs three theoretical concepts in order to analyse how exhibitions use representational strategies to make visitors cognitively, emotionally and ethically understand and relate to complicity and perpetration during the Second World War and the Holocaust: narrative empathy, experientiality and agonistic memory.

The concept of empathy is comprised of feeling, intellect and imagination (Lanzoni 2018: 280). It has a positive learning connotation in numerous disciplines. Lanzoni notes that empathy 'dares us to move beyond the habitual borders of the self to reach toward another human being'.[2] Jason Endacott and Sarah Brooks define historical empathy in pedagogical settings as follows: 'Historical empathy is the process of students' cognitive and affective engagement with historical figures to better understand and contextualize their lived experiences, decisions or actions'.[3] When we look at museums, we need to analyse the aesthetic and narrative techniques that trigger empathetic reactions in museum visitors in order to understand the curatorial possibilities, challenges and limitations of using empathy in historical representations.[4] In doing so, theories of narrative empathy are particularly useful; they highlight the temporality of creating empathy while reading, viewing, hearing or imagining narratives that relate to others' situations and conditions. Here, the imaginative potential of entering story worlds and siding with another is foregrounded. For example, Suzanne Keen discusses empathy in the narrative techniques of literary texts 'such as the use of first-person narration and the interior representation of characters' consciousness and emotional states'.[5] These techniques offer insight into how storytelling, the multi-perspectivity of historical witnesses and experiential settings can work in museums. To understand how narrative empathy can be utilized in exhibitions on complicity and perpetration, Fritz Breithaupt's definition of empathy as 'the coexperience of another's situation' proves particularly valuable.[6] Breithaupt argues that empathy is not simply emotion-sharing, but also the focus on the situation of the other in some or all of its emotional and cognitive aspects. This makes decision-making in multiple possible and imaginary worlds a particular important component of empathy. Consequently, empathy does not simply make human beings morally good, but it 'widens the scope of our experiences [. . .] and enables a rich and complex co-experiencing of our joint world'.[7]

Empathy can help us understand how the decisions of perpetrators and their supporters start to become regarded as legitimate – meaning that perpetrators feel uncompromised – in certain historical situations. Empathy is a paradox that visitors are inside and outside simultaneously; it allows museums to explain a framework of understanding and decision-making to visitors, while enabling them to maintain a moral compass within their own ideological settings. To avoid over-identification and to move beyond simplistic black-and-white thinking, museums could use Breithaupt's focus on complementing multiple perspectives and worlds to create a better understanding of how historical complicity and perpetration emerged and was justified during the Second World War. Narratives can elicit the visitors' empathy so that they 'align in various and often uncomfortable ways with [the perpetrators'] perspective even as we become aware of their violent actions'.[8] This chapter explores current and potential ways of how exhibitions can create experiential structures and perceptions that allow visitors to understand and relate to perpetration and complicity, while maintaining an analytical and ethical distance. To achieve this, museums can trigger visitors' imaginations, which then allows them emotional access to the worlds of collaborators and perpetrators – even if such worlds contradict their own world views and ideologies. Dominick LaCapra has developed the term of empathetic unsettlement 'that creates a certain discomfort in "inhabiting" the experiences of others' during such experiences.[9]

Whereas narrative empathy facilitates the co-experiencing of another's situation and decision-making, the concept of experientiality allows us to analyse historical museum exhibitions as aesthetic responses, which possess various potentialities that exceed the intent of museum curators and architects.[10] Experientiality provides us with a tool to help analyse museums' effects on visitors that supersede a mimetic re-production of possible past experiences (by individuals or collectives). The visitor – entrenched in their own cultural memory and possibly being challenged to reflect on their own implications and biases – becomes a mediating consciousness in the museum space (an anthropomorphic experiencer), activating the different potentialities of artefacts, spaces and constellations. This can include a wide range of cognitive, affective, ethical and aesthetic responses. In particular, regarding the focus of this chapter, experientiality allows us to understand how exhibitions simulate structures of complicity and perpetration, of feeling morally compromised or uncompromised, without relating back to the experiences of a specific individual. Such representations avoid the danger of visitors over-identifying with the value system of a perpetrator, while simultaneously enabling the visitor to understand the potentiality of being complicit in perpetration. Potential visitor interactions with museum exhibits vary on a sliding scale between restricted experientiality, primary experientiality (which is focused on the experiences of actual people or collectives) and secondary/structural experientiality (which only exists within the simulation). In understanding perpetration and complicity, it is particularly important to analyse whether there are master narratives present that restrict experientiality. It is also important to look at whether an exhibition encourages its visitors to understand its networking effects and draw connections between structural constellations and relationships – these allow for multiple viewpoints and critical thinking. Unlike some perpetrator fiction in literature and film, museums shy away from creating immediate empathy with perpetrators. However, exhibitions can simulate experiential structures that depict how the stage was set for the occurrence of wartime atrocities, as well as the Holocaust. It is also crucial to note that structural experientiality integrates forms of distancing, as well as representational meta-reflection. This means that museums can simulate structures of perpetration without running the risk that visitors will identify or empathize with the perpetrators' opinions or perspectives themselves.

The concept of experientiality allows us to understand the degree to which museums enable visitor participation, as well as the ways in which they steer their visitors towards either restricted or dynamic/critical forms of interaction with experiences and structures of complicity and perpetration. The concept of agonistic memory supplements the understanding that narrative empathy and experientiality provide us with. Agonistic memory differs from antagonistic and cosmopolitan memory.¹¹ Antagonistic memory primarily positions adversaries, often nations, in patterns of 'us vs. them' or 'good vs. evil'. Cosmopolitan memory universalizes the story and highlights the perspective of victimhood; in other words, it is prone to excluding any in-depth discussion of complicity or perpetration. In contrast, Anna Cento Bull and Hans Lauge Hansen define agonistic memory through four features: first, it avoids setting good against evil by acknowledging the human capacity for evil within specific historical circumstances; second, it relies on testimonies from a wide array of historical actors, including victims and perpetrators, in order to understand their experiences and motivations; third, it recognizes how important affect and emotions are and advocates for empathy towards victims – in other words, it tries to prevent empathy with perpetrators; finally, it pays attention to the historical contexts, the sociopolitical struggles as well as the individual and collective narratives that led to the perpetration of mass crimes.¹² To avoid misunderstandings in the discussion on the perpetration of mass crimes, many agonistic memory discourses apply a multi-perspectival approach to their narratives: 'This approach allows for the voice of the perpetrators to speak out in their own right, but opposes their self-understanding to that of other agents such as victims, by-standers and/or historical successors. Through this dialogic juxtaposition of different discourse positions, the reader/listener/spectator is enabled to take a qualified stand'.¹³

Complicity and perpetration in current Holocaust exhibitions

Susan Macdonald argues that in museums, it has become considerably easier, more prevalent and internationalized to depict 'difficult heritage in the sense of publicly acknowledging crimes in one's own history'.¹⁴ She also notes that though 'not so often seen as a major disruption of contemporary collective identities [. . .] it is still difficult in the moral and representational challenges that it poses'.¹⁵ When we look at current German and European permanent and special exhibitions, there is no doubt that critical heritage is often acknowledged as part of one's cultural and, usually, national memory. However, a closer analysis also reveals how restricted such representations are. Despite the recent attention towards perpetrator research, a detailed analysis of museum representations of Fascism, the Second World War and the Holocaust reveals that the depiction of perpetration and complicity in most museums worldwide is still relatively subdued.¹⁶ They mostly have an evidentiary function to prove that atrocities, genocide and war crimes truly took place. Major perpetrators are represented from a distance through a biographical narrative of their lives, clearly marked as evil. This (intentionally) makes it hard for visitors to understand the motives that lead people to commit acts of perpetration. Similarly, complicity is most often depicted through the lens of an anonymous collective who are deemed guilty, such as 'the Germans', 'the French' or the 'Catholic Church' – and rarely through individual stories. In countries that were under occupation, exhibitions might mention collaboration, but normally as a mere misguided exception to the true values of the national collective. In other words, morally compromised subjects during the Holocaust are clearly marked as such by the museums' perspectives. Visitors are steered to believe that perpetrators perceive themselves as uncompromised, while being undoubtedly complicit in the eyes of the curators and, by extension, the majority of today's museum visitors. The case studies in this chapter suggest ways that museums can go beyond the ordinary acknowledgement of complicity and perpetration during the Second Word War and the Holocaust. This chapter first analyses the representation of morally uncompromised and compromised identities in museums. It then takes a look at exhibitions' use of empathy and multiperspectivity and, lastly, the creation of experientiality through structures of complicity and perpetration. The conclusion reflects upon agonistic memory and the challenges and visions for representing perpetration and complicity in museums.

Morally uncompromised and compromised identities

The *Verzetsmuseum* (Dutch Resistance Museum) in Amsterdam opened its former permanent exhibition in 1999.[17] It allows visitors to become kind of time travellers through the conditions of the German occupation. The exhibition presents historical topics and decision-making during the time of occupation in mostly chronological order. The question 'Cooperate?' leads most closely to collaboration (though the museum avoids this terminology): according to this section, in order to prevent the Dutch Nazi Party NSB from taking over power, officials remained in their positions 'as long as Dutch interests are being served'. There is no doubt here that 'Dutch interests' are anti-German and refer to one unified group. The exhibition then depicts the foundation and quick growth of the *Nederlandse Unie* (Netherlands Union), which is willing to cooperate with the Germans to prevent the NSB from gaining power; in other words, their collective identity is clearly depicted as uncompromised. The exhibition does not present different choices and conflicts, and is therefore limited to a clear black-and-white pattern. Why would individuals choose to become members of the *Unie*, or even the NSB? The conflict faced by *Unie* members is presented in the form of collective, rational reasoning: what is the better strategy for the Netherlands against the German enemy during the occupation? Visitors do not get the slightest idea why revenge is taken against collaborators after the war. The Dutch Nazi Party is the enemy within the Netherlands, and the typical Dutch perpetrator is mainly described through the ideology and actions of the party's leaders. Consequently, the exhibition remains mostly antagonistic.

The current trend of museums representing a country's crimes against its own population and acknowledging collaboration has been widely heralded as innovative. However, this acknowledgement is most often made without exhibitions seriously engaging with the shades of grey between good and evil, between victimhood, resistance, collaboration and perpetration. The closest museums usually come to depicting complicity is when they target morally questionable or criminal acts by their own populations. This is exemplified in the original version of the *Muzeum II Wojny Światowej* (MIIWŚ, Museum of the Second World War) in Gdańsk, which opened in March 2017.[18] It places the perpetration of the Holocaust and all other atrocities together in a scheme with clear concepts of right and wrong. This mere reflection on Polish perpetration seems, on the surface, to be an advancement in mediating Polish public memory. The limitations of this approach, however, become clearer when we take a closer look at one of the two concrete stories of Polish perpetration featured in the MIIWŚ. The pogrom in the village of Jedwabne on 10 June 1941, during which several hundred Jews were murdered, is situated in the context of other pogroms around Europe. The text reads: 'Poles were persuaded by the Germans, probably following a pre-existing German plan to round up their Jewish neighbours in the market square. They humiliated, beat and killed them there'. This section focuses fully on the victims. No Polish perpetrators are mentioned by name, nor does the overall display mention the deep divide in Polish society or the question of antisemitism in Poland. In the end, the only explanation that remains of why Polish people participated in the pogroms is that the Germans manipulated them to do so – confirming an antagonistic pattern and maintaining a Polish collective identity that is morally uncompromised.

The *Mémorial de Caen* (Memorial Museum Caen) in France, which was founded in 1984 and considerably revised between 2009 and 2010, is a good example for a museum approach depicting (un-)compromised identities for the visitor from a cognitive distance. In its section 'France in the dark years', the exhibition pits the two extremes of resistance and collaboration against each other. Focusing on Vichy France, it defines collaboration and different motivations behind it (self-interest, tactical, strategic, ideological) with the use of long text panels. It does so while explaining how the actions and motives of the Vichy regime's leadership supported collaboration through long quotations and excerpts of speeches. The exhibition's tone remains neutral – although today's observer can clearly recognize that the regime's dreams of working together with the Nazis were bound to fail and take moral sides. This representation creates distance and avoids storytelling; it does not depict the voices of ordinary French citizens; however, it allows for a cognitive understanding of why political leaders chose to collaborate without immediately morally assessing such choices as misguided. We saw a similar approach above in the Resistance Museum in Amsterdam.

The temporary online exhibition *Compromised Identities?*[19] at the UCL Institute of Advanced Studies (2020), part of the same larger research program as this book, provides a more in-depth context of complicity and perpetration under National Socialism and the Second World War. It is particularly rich in material for understanding German and Austrian complicity. It functions like a multi-modal history book and is more educational than experiential. It highlights structures of complicity and perpetration and often illustrates these through case studies. It does so while reflecting upon the characteristics of how individuals perceive their own un-(compromised) identities when remembering and narrating the past. The basic structure of the exhibition is chronological. The visitor scrolls through eight systematic chapters on understanding perpetration and complicity in Nazi Germany from the 1930s up until the latest trials and forms of remembrance today. Online visitors are strategically made to understand the exhibition's historical contents and context, as well as its analysis from a distance. This is most evident in the thirty 3.5–5.5-minute long video segments that form the backbone of the exhibition. They are either interviews interspersed with commentary from the exhibition curators/researchers,[20] or their narrative voice-over[21] – often filmed at historical locations today – about historical case studies, supplemented with historical photo material. Visitors can have affective reactions to the films, especially segments on eyewitness testimonies or story-telling through voice-over narration. However, the UCL exhibition does not provide its visitors with the freedom to understand structures of perpetration for themselves. Mainly, they are presented with a cognitively oriented expert analysis that leads them to understand historical constellations of complicity, as well as the mechanisms of remembrance and storification of complicity. The witnesses' self-perception of their own uncompromised identities becomes evident. Unlike in the previous examples, this representational mode allows for an in-depth understanding of shades of complicity.[22]

For example, four of the curators/researchers discuss the case of a young librarian in Vienna who describes her sadness at telling a Jewish customer wearing the yellow star for the first time that she is not allowed to let him borrow books any longer. She talks about the situation of exclusion and deportations in Austria without reflecting upon her own agency. The researchers discuss this and conclude that she exemplifies somebody feeling honestly sad, not guilty or complicit, since she did not do anything actively wrong – although she indirectly supported the policies of the regime. In another example, a former German Wehrmacht soldier defends his father who, as a railwayman, was instrumental in logistically supporting the deportations to Auschwitz. The discussion between the curators and researchers identifies and explains the numerous contradictions in the man's testimony; it also highlights different layers present in his defence of his and his father's uncompromised identities. The format allows for negotiations on the compromises and complicities of the interviewees, as well as how the patterns of remembering their actions could be generalized.

The curators/researchers attempt to negotiate subjective perceptions of complicity, tensions between the witnesses' performances in official roles and their personal, possibly uncompromised identities as human beings.[23] These negotiations are carried out in a demonstrative-analytical mode that places visitors in a passive observer position. It is from this position that they take in the stories being told and, particularly, the interviews expertly dissected for contradictions and possible meanings. However, this distance also prevents visitors from developing their own experiences – whether in connection with narrative empathy or structural experientiality – within the exhibition space. The online exhibition proves to be a hybrid of critical and analytical top–down history education and offers us the potential to think further. However, its potential for experientiality, agonism and implication is restricted – the exhibitions almost seem to shelter visitors, as observers, from becoming experientially immersed in its structures of complicity and perpetration.

Empathy and multiperspectivity

The examples from Caen and London in particular demonstrate that exhibitions with sufficient emphasis on complicity and perpetration can represent more in-depth case studies on the (un-)compromised identities of individuals and collectives. However, they intentionally restrict their representations to a cognitive understanding of how such identities emerge and are negotiated and remembered. Visitors remain at a cognitive distance from the historical subject-matter, which is mediated by curators and historians. This section probes innovative approaches from museums that try to interweave cognitive and affective understandings of complicity and perpetration, and question the limitations of narrative empathy regarding collaborators and perpetrators.

If we briefly return to the final part of the section on collaboration-resistance in the *Mémorial de Caen*, despite its overload in text, there is also an affective dimension that allows visitors to empathize with the atmosphere of a war-torn France under the conditions of occupation. This section of the exhibition raises doubts around simplistic black-and-white narratives of good and evil by spelling out in white large fluorescent letters above its entrance: '40 Million Collaborators, 40 Million Resisters?' – meaning the entire population of France in 1940 could see themselves either as resisters or collaborators with the Nazis. Visitors then walk through a set of house facades, in which they are simultaneously confronted with announcements about the occupation in France and acts of resistance. For example, visitors see Nazi posters announcing the conviction and execution of a Breton butcher for 'an act of violence against the German army', overlapping with graffiti by resistance fighters calling for the shooting of collaborationist politician Pierre Laval. Consequently, visitors can empathize with the atmosphere in the street and the publicly displayed tensions between supporting and resisting the Germans. However, there is neither major learning for the visitors beyond this experiential display on the atmosphere in France at the time nor empathetic unsettlement and empathizing with the decision-making of collaborators. Visitors either passively perceive the atmosphere or remain morally on the right side, which presumably allows them to empathize with Nazi victims and resisters.

One of the most elaborate displays creating narrative empathy can be found in the Dutch Resistance Museum. Its permanent Junior Exhibition from 2013 is built around the real-life stories of four Dutch children who experienced the Nazi occupation. Eva is Jewish, Jan has parents in the resistance, Henk comes from an everyday family and plays with his war toys to defeat the Nazis and, finally, Nelly is in the Youth Organization of the Dutch Nazi party and her father is the local party leader in her village (Figure 16.1). The characters tell their true stories through original objects, photos and documents in animations, audio clips and interactive games. Young visitors in particular (the recommended minimum age is nine) can empathize with Nelly's perspective: she excels as a Nazi Storm trooper, is shunned by friends and enthusiastically listens to NSB leader Anton Mussert as part of a large crowd. The story is told in the voice and with the vocabulary of a teenage child. At the end of the war, the family flees to Germany. They are arrested and Nelly is briefly interned in Camp Westerbork, one of two transit camps used for the deportation of Jews from the Netherlands. The exhibition tells Nelly's story in an audio–video installation. Her story then is spatially reinforced through a reconstructed living room from Nelly's family home, containing everyday items, particularly NSB propaganda, and short quotations reinforcing Nelly's story (Figure 16.2). A computer station titled 'Nazi propaganda' helps visitors understand propaganda slogans and their impact by allowing them to match the correct propaganda image to different slogans, such as 'Jews are bad', or 'The NSB is for all Dutch people'. This is contrasted to the part of the exhibition where Nelly's father is arrested and she writes him loving letters. These empathetic techniques

Challenging the Museum Visitor? 243

Figure 16.1 Nelly's House, Junior exhibition, Dutch Resistance Museum, Amsterdam; photos by author 2015; courtesy of the Dutch Resistance Museum.

Figure 16.2 Damaged GAMA tank toy and war toy parade, permanent exhibition, Bundeswehr Military History Museum, Dresden; photo by author 2019; courtesy Militärhistorisches Museum der Bundeswehr.

allow the visitor to reflect on how children can be manipulated by propaganda on the one hand, but still operate with the same feelings of love as everybody else on the other.

The exhibition provides further complexity through the temporality of empathy created in its final room. Here, it displays video testimonies by the real people on which the four protagonists are based. The real Nelly remembers her story from the perspective of an 86-year-old woman. She highlights that she does not feel guilty about her choices during the occupation and that she only heard about the 'terrible' fate of the Jews in the Netherlands after the war. Her statement, 'You shouldn't tease others because they are different. I personally experienced what it is like to be different and I would not wish that on anyone else', opens space for debate and the validity of different viewpoints – especially since visitors have also been immersed in the fate of the Jewish girl Eva and the two other children's perspectives. How should we or how can we see Nelly as a victim? Nelly's story offers an immersive inroad into understanding complicity. However, it plays with ideas of immersion and sympathy; due to the fact that Nelly is a child, she does not know any better. This also reveals the limitations of the Dutch Resistance Museum in understanding complicity and collaboration. In the adult world, the perpetrators are all NSB members. The visitor cannot experience the ways in which these perpetrators are complicit in the decisions that, for example, enabled the German occupation and deportations of Jewish people. This means that the exhibition mainly returns to an antagonistic model, in which empathy is impossible.

Experientiality – structures of complicity and perpetration

The limitations that museums have in steering their visitors towards empathy with complicity and perpetration in the Holocaust leads to the theoretical concept of structural experientiality. By employing this concept, we can analyse historical museum exhibitions for various potentialities that exceed mimetic representation of possible past experiences. First, this analysis returns to the Museum of the Second World War in Gdańsk. In its original exhibition – the parts analysed here are still mostly displayed – the complimentary transnational comparative framework allows for a structural understanding of complicity and perpetration. This is due to the fact that its Polish master narrative avoids taking a heroic or emphatic tone, while underscoring universal values such as freedom, dignity and life. The exhibition explicitly features a section on collaboration under German occupation that discusses German occupation policies, as well as the forms and causes of collaboration. Unlike the *Mémorial de Caen*, it creates a tableau of nine countries under occupation from the Channel Islands, to Poland and the Soviet Union. This section of the exhibition does not attempt to understand the ambiguities of any topic in depth – Polish or otherwise – including specific case studies or personal stories. Visitors can identify both universal and nation-specific elements in human behaviour under occupation. Although this section does not challenge the general assumption that there is good victimhood on the one hand, and bad totalitarian regimes on the other, visitors receive a varied picture of the conditions under occupation, as well as distinct National Socialist policies. Because the MIIWŚ foregoes making a moral assessment, visitors are enabled to draw their own conclusions about how specific actions and attitudes during occupation should be assessed. Does it make a difference if an existing police force collaborates with the occupier? How important is it that collaboration is voluntary? Can one demand that everybody supports the resistance? Since visitors first learn about the various occupation policies in different countries, they can judge whether informing on other people is the same in all occupied countries, or whether there are explicit differences on a case-by-case basis. The comparative approach in the MIIWŚ creates structural experientiality by triggering potential structural comparisons on what collaboration, or in other sections, what perpetration means. The exhibition's almost exclusively historical point of view does not allow its visitors to feel immersed or implicated from today's perspective.

Generally, complicity is best depicted by museums when they aim to simulate the perceptions of a specific historical collective that is matched by their main target audience. There is also a tendency for more dynamic and focused approaches to the topics of complicity and perpetration to be found in special exhibitions – with the exception of very few institutions, such as the Topography of Terror in Berlin, which almost exclusively documents such topics.[24] This is, for example, evident in the special exhibition *Americans and the Holocaust* in the United States Holocaust Memorial Museum in Washington, DC, which opened in 2018 (still on display, ongoing). The exhibition examines the motives, pressures and fears that shaped responses from the American people to Nazism, war and the persecution and murder of European Jewry during the 1930s and 1940s. The exhibition employs historical opinion polls to illustrate how the American public answered specific questions regarding fears of a depression, boycotting the 1936 Olympics in Berlin, letting more Jewish refugees into the country, America's entrance to the war, as well as knowledge about the mass killings of Jews in extermination camps. The results of these opinion polls are presented on large vertical displays that the visitor can rotate. On one side, the polling question is asked; on the other side, the responses – yes or no – appear proportional in size to the percentage each choice received. For example, the exhibition presents the results of two public opinion polls taken after the so-called 'Kristallnacht' in November 1938, which show that 94 per cent disapprove of the treatment of Jews in Nazi Germany. Large white letters on a bright blue background emotionally document the strikingly clear answer. However, before and after visitors are presented with other answers: the question 'Should we allow a larger number of Jewish exiles from Germany to come to the United States to live?' is answered 'Yes' by 21 per cent of the poll's participants and 'No' by 71 per cent; in January 1939, a more specific poll gauging acceptance for plans to bring 10,000 refugee children from Germany to the United States was carried out, resulting in 66 per cent of participants choosing the option 'No'.

The opinion boards are further contextualized through photographs and quotations from newspaper editors and letters to the editor. These present a wide range of opinions spanning from whether the American people come first, to whether humanity should prevail. For example, the Yes and No opinion board on the initiative to allow refugee children into America features quotations by Eleanor Roosevelt supporting the bill, and Democratic North Carolina Senator Robert Reynolds rejecting it. The latter reads 'My heart goes out in sympathy to the refugee children, but, I repeat, my heart beats in sympathy first for American sons and daughters'. The strength of the exhibition here is that it avoids taking sides and judging any opinions directly. A variety of contemporary perspectives are shown and historically contextualized. On the one hand, the blatant gap in opinion between the American disapproval at the Nazi treatment of Jews and possible American action allows for criticism of the US immigration policy and the possible latent antisemitism in American society at the time. On the other, it encourages visitors to think about similar immigration policies and helping refugees and targets of genocide today. They do not simply empathize with one specific group, but are experientially confronted with multiple strands of complicity that challenge them cognitively and affectively to reconcile their own positions with the tensions and paradoxes displayed.

Lastly, structural constellations that do not directly simulate a role or perspective from the past can produce experientiality regarding complicity and perpetration. Whereas the permanent exhibition of the *Militärhistorisches Museum der Bundeswehr* (Bundeswehr Military History Museum in Dresden) from 2011[25] seems limited in representing the complicity of ordinary Germans, we see the Wehrmacht's complicity in atrocities and the Holocaust; perpetration and acts of atrocity are present throughout the museum, mostly in abstract structural forms. For example, in the display cabinet 'The Economy of War in World War II' on the German armament industry and the war economy, a variety of objects create a space showcasing the war effort, forced labour, the Holocaust and the German economy. The cabinet does not merely document the links between these elements; instead, it makes them present in a way that leaves the visitor with no doubt about the historical complicity of German society and industry in the Holocaust, or the interwovenness of the war effort and the Holocaust.[26] Another feature in the exhibition targeting perpetration and complicity are short tabular biographies spread throughout the chronological exhibition. These challenge visitors to fill in gaps and explore the shades between good and evil. These biographies link contrasting pairs of people who lived during the same period, but took divergent routes in similar situations. The tensions between the many tabular biographies of leaders, everyday people, victims, bystanders and perpetrators, provide the visitor with room to consider differing life trajectories, as well as what justifies and alters these under certain circumstances.

The museum's combination of anthropological structures of warfare with its chronological exhibition featuring many constellations that visitors can potentially connect, create structural experiential forms of complicity. One striking example of this is the display of a toy tank made by the company GAMA (Figure 16.2).[27] The tank was damaged during the bombing of Dresden on 13 February 1945. The description notes that these tanks, which sent out showers of sparks, were among the most popular toys in the Third Reich. The exhibition also informs visitors that such toy tanks were reproduced in West Germany in the 1950s. Opposite the tank is a parade of toy soldiers and vehicles from the seventeenth century to the present; these span from tin soldiers, to Lego soldiers, to space warriors – all of which seem to be marching together into battle against the burnt-out tank. The fact that the tank is a concrete artefact from firebombed Dresden intensifies its authenticity and gives the impression that it stands metonymically for the real war. Here, visitors are encouraged to enter an experiential state in which they are challenged to connect the past with their present attitudes, or those from their childhood. The tank is ambiguous, oscillating between being a 'victim' of the Allied fire bombings and a 'perpetrator' metonymically pointing to German atrocities; between being a symbol of evil defeated and a symbol of that evil's afterlife in post-war West Germany; as well as between play and reality. Visitors are led not only to question their memory of and attitude towards war toys, but also the complexity of interwoven forms of perpetration and victimhood. In this way, visitors could potentially feel complicit for participating in similar forms of play that support real-life violence in the present.

Conclusion

Clearly, museum exhibitions on the Second World War and the Holocaust could do more to depict perpetration and complicity. Too often, they reflect on the extremes of good and evil, as well as victim, resister and perpetrator. They do so without providing visitors with insights into how complicity and perpetration emerge societally. One of the challenges, the first key feature in agonistic memory, is to actively explore the grey zones of perpetration and complicity. Even well researched and reflected exhibitions such as those in Gdańsk, Caen and the former exhibition in Amsterdam, tend to reaffirm extreme black-and-white/right-or-wrong patterns. Museum representations that are able to penetrate the grey zones in between are either self-reflective, like the one in London, or require an active visitor who can draw different conclusions and is allowed to find different comparative angles in order to understand multiple perspectives, such as those in Dresden and (to an extent) Gdańsk. One of the biggest challenges for museums is finding a balance between cognitive and affective representation. Whereas an almost exclusively cognitive and analytically designed exhibition like *Compromised Identities?* can document grey zones, visitors are allowed to stay passive at a safe distance. As we have seen through the concepts of empathy, experientiality and agonism, an affective component is needed to challenge the visitor's own subject-position. In contrast, exhibitions that are mostly based on affect – like the empathetic Junior exhibition in Amsterdam – run the risk of simplifying the complexities of complicity and perpetration. At the same time, they positively demonstrate that empathy and empathetic unsettlement can be an important pedagogical tool if they simulate decision-making. Concrete stories and artefacts representing multiple viewpoint and story-lines are needed for an emotional connection to the displays. They are also needed as a moral corrective, providing visitors with a wide range of possible decisions and actions. This avoids visitors perceiving complicity as an almost deterministic choice. Consequently, it is particularly important that there is space – beyond historical facts – for visitors to reflect upon and connect perceptions and opinions. How do certain groups or individuals in a society come to follow certain ideologies and beliefs? Agonism only works if exhibitions let visitors experientially understand and challenge how varying antagonistic and cosmopolitan world views become the predominant ideology and value system for a specific group. As we have seen, this works better in the form of structural experientiality, as used in Washington and Dresden, which connects the past and present. Fictitious elements that support historical storytelling, such as ones used in the Junior exhibition in Amsterdam, hold great imaginative possibilities to explore the potentialities of complicity and perpetration. As highlighted in the concept of agonistic memory, it is necessary for exhibitions to maintain a moral compass for inclusion, democracy and justice, as well as an emotional connection and empathy for victims; this is important so that when exhibitions perform structures of complicity and perpetration, this does not lead the visitor towards an unguarded identification with complicit subjects. Critically immersing visitors and having them engage with the complicity of large groups in society, as well as encouraging them to understand how their actions, value systems and forms of remembrance emerge, is highly promising. This requires some courage by museums to experiment and empower their visitors to negotiate their own way through multiple viewpoints, stories and scenarios, as well as empathize with different types of decision-making.

Notes

1 I am grateful to Emma Mikuska-Tinman for proofreading and editing this manuscript.
2 Susan Lanzoni, *Empathy: A History* (New Haven: Yale University Press, 2018), 280.
3 Jason Endacott and Sarah Brooks, 'An Updated Theoretical and Practical Model for Promoting Historical Empathy', *Social Studies Research and Practice* 8 (2013): 41.
4 Cf. also Silke Arnold-de Simine, *Mediating Memory in the Museum: Trauma, Empathy, and Nostalgia* (Basingstoke: Palgrave Macmillan, 2013).
5 Suzanne Keen, 'A Theory of Narrative Empathy', *Narrative* 14, no. 3 (2006): 213.
6 Fritz Breithaupt, *The Dark Sides of Empathy*, trans. A. B. B. Hamilton (Ithaca: Cornell University Press, 2019), 10.
7 Ibid., 227.
8 Erin McGlothlin, 'Empathetic Identification and the Mind of the Holocaust Perpetrator in Fiction: A Proposed Taxonomy of Response', *Narrative* 24, no. 3 (2016): 258.
9 Dominick LaCapra, *History in Transit: Experience, Identity, Critical Theory* (Ithaca: Cornell University Press, 2004), 41.
10 Cf. Stephan Jaeger, *The Second World War in the Twenty-First-Century Museum: From Memory, Narrative, and Experience to Experientiality* (Berlin: De Gruyter, 2020). The original concept of experientiality was developed for fiction and life-writing by narratologist Monika Fludernik as 'the quasi-mimetic evocation of "real-life experience"'. Monika Fludernik, *Towards a 'Natural' Narratology* (London: Routledge, 1996), 12.
11 This is based on Chantal Mouffe's discussion of an 'agonistic approach to the future of Europe', wherein she argues for a 'pluralization of hegemonies'. Chantal Mouffe, 'An Agonistic Approach to the Future of Europe', *New Literary History* 43, no. 4 (2012): 629, 639. Cf. Anna Cento Bull and Hans Lauge Hansen, 'On Agonistic Memory', *Memory Studies* 9, no. 4 (2016): 390–404.
12 Cento Bull and Hansen, 'On Agonistic Memory', 399.
13 Anna Cento Bull, Hans Lauge Hansen, Wulf Kansteiner and Nina Parish, 'War Museums as Agonistic Spaces: Possibilities, Opportunities and Constraints', *International Journal of Heritage Studies* 25, no. 6 (2019): 614.
14 Susan Macdonald, 'Is "Difficult Heritage" Still "Difficult"?', *Museum International* 67, no. 1–4 (2015): 20.
15 Ibid.

16 Cf. Jaeger, *The Second World War in the Twenty-First-Century Museum*, 221–64.
17 The museum re-opened with a completely redesigned exhibition on December 1, 2022.
18 In April 2016, the Polish Ministry of Culture and National Heritage announced a new administrative structure. This was done with the intent of creating a more Polish, heroic, battle-oriented museum and a less civilian-based, transnational museum. Cf. Paweł Machcewicz, *The War That Never Ends: The Museum of the Second World War in Gdańsk* (Berlin: De Gruyter Oldenbourg, 2019).
19 UCL Institute of Advanced Studies, *Exhibition Compromised Identities* (2020). https://compromised-identities.org/ (accessed 16 October 2021). I am grateful to Stefanie Rauch who discussed the framework and production conditions of the exhibition with me in June 2021. The exhibition was conceptualized as a physical travelling exhibition that was redesigned for an online format because of the COVID-19 pandemic.
20 Stephanie Bird, Mary Fulbrook, Stefanie Rauch and Christoph Thonfeld. A varied model of this mode is a roundtable discussion with supplementary footage used to explain theoretical concepts such as 'Perpetration and complicity'.
21 Here Fulbrook and Thonfeld.
22 For example, Thonfeld's 3:45-minute video narrative about Nazi hunter Simon Wiesenthal's story is able to dissect a more complex story of Wiesenthal's insistence despite a lack of interest and support from the American and particularly the Austrian governments. In contrast, the MIIWŚ in Gdańsk briefly documents Wiesenthal's achievements in aiding the capture of Adolf Eichmann and Franz Stangl as a straightforward success story, eliminating any complexities of pitching good against evil.
23 See especially Fulbrook in the roundtable 'Choices, Chance or Circumstance?'
24 Cf. Jaeger, *The Second World War in the Twenty-First-Century Museum*, 160–71.
25 For further context, see ibid., 129–49, 246–7 and 261–2.
26 Stephan Jaeger, 'Temporalizing History Toward the Future: Representing Violence and Human Rights Violations in the Military History Museum in Dresden', in *The Idea of a Human Rights Museum*, ed. Karen Busby, Adam Muller, and Andrew Woolford (Winnipeg: University of Manitoba Press, 2015), 238.
27 Cf. Jaeger, *The Second World War in the Twenty-First-Century Museum*, 3–7.

17

Compromised identities? Reflections on perpetration and complicity under Nazi rule

An exhibition[1]

Stephanie Bird, Mary Fulbrook, Stefanie Rauch and Bastiaan Willems

In Holocaust education, musealization and commemoration, an (understandable) focus on victim voices and the top echelons of power and repression predominates. The broad spectrum of perpetrators, beneficiaries and facilitators of persecution remain underrepresented, as does the wider social context. A 2016 survey by the UCL Centre for Holocaust Education established a serious lack of knowledge and understanding of these issues among a majority of young people in the UK. Although the Holocaust Memorial Day Trust wrote that bystanders 'enabled the Holocaust, Nazi persecution and subsequent genocides', their voices were largely missing from the Trust's 2016 Holocaust Memorial Day's 'Don't Stand By' materials and ceremonies. Moreover, the focus often presupposes a degree of individual choice that was not available to many people at the time. The relative absence of 'perpetrator perspectives' adversely affects teaching and public understanding of the conditions under which genocide was possible and means of addressing its legacies.

We set out to curate a research-based exhibition that would help transform this situation: first, by developing a differentiated, interdisciplinary analytic framework for understanding patterns of involvement in state-sponsored violence, and the interplay between changing contexts and self-representations; and secondly, by opening up perspectives and developing materials for further research and study. The aim was to create an exhibition that would discuss sources and approaches, and facilitate understanding of complicity and perpetration as well as subsequent efforts to engage with a violent past.

Context and conceptual approach

Exhibitions about perpetration and complicity in Nazi crimes have come in a wide variety of shapes, forms and locations. Our aim here is not to provide a comprehensive survey, but rather to contextualize the particular challenges we faced and the choices we made in constructing our own web-based exhibition. While there is no one 'right' way to exhibit both essential facts – key developments, dates, incidents – and experiences and patterns of involvement, there are clear distinctions with regard to intended impact as well as degrees of emphasis, omission or distortion. Many exhibitions about Nazi crimes are based in authentic 'sites of memory', such as former concentration camps, where the site itself is integral to the display and shapes criteria for choice of objects and emphasis. Historical exhibitions in museums are also influenced by their context in other ways, from Yad Vashem which opened in 1953 on Mount Herzl in Jerusalem, through the United States Holocaust Memorial Museum (USHMM) which opened in Washington, DC, in 1993, to the Jewish Museum designed by Daniel Libeskind which opened in Berlin in 2001. Many such museums, including the re-opened Holocaust Gallery at London's Imperial War Museum, or, albeit on a smaller scale, the Holocaust Exhibition and Learning Centre at the University of Huddersfield, are able to devote considerable resources to comprehensive displays drawn from extensive source collections as well as using the latest audiovisual technology and mapping programmes. There is by now a significant interdisciplinary body of literature on sites of memory and museological approaches.[2] There are also lively discussions among professionals and practitioners internationally, with growing cooperation, as evidenced for example in bodies such as the International Holocaust Remembrance alliance (IHRA) and the European Holocaust Research Infrastructure (EHRI), or in the networks and interconnections between individual experts based at institutions in widely differing national contexts.

Everywhere, wider contexts have made a significant difference to the narratives conveyed in exhibitions. Supposed 'lessons for the future' have varied dramatically, with striking differences in both eastern and western Europe during and well beyond the Cold War. Selected heroes and martyrs have been variously highlighted, while other groups were marginalized or excluded. The uses of 'authentic' sites for post-war political and national purposes after the war varied enormously; but it was always easier to focus on victims, martyrs and heroes, and clearly identifiable enemies as the 'other', rather than to problematize local complicity or involvement of wider groups. The pressure from survivors and relatives to ensure places for remembrance was indeed initially how some sites, such as the Chełmno death camp, or more belatedly as in the case of Dachau concentration camp, became significant places to be preserved for remembrance, rather than simply disused buildings to be variously destroyed, repurposed or plundered. Official emphases ranged from explicit celebration of communist heroes in places such as Sachsenhausen and Buchenwald in the GDR, to the conservative nationalists of the 1944 July Plot in West Germany, or resistance heroes in France. Monumental celebrations of 'Soviet patriotism' on sites of former forced labour camps, such as Salaspils near Riga, were combined with the near obscurity of murdered Jews in overgrown mass graves in nearby Rumbula. After the collapse of communism, in Lithuania and Latvia local antisemitic political activists could be reconfigured as nationalist heroes against Soviet oppression.[3]

The representation of perpetration and complicity on such ground remains controversial for other reasons too. Despite massive changes in the twenty-first century, many such sites remain even now a form of 'sacred' ground, where people come not only to learn but also to remember and mourn. Some incorporate a sense of being collective graveyards, where the bones and ashes of innumerable unnamed victims are scattered, as on the paths of Treblinka, or in the lake of ashes at Auschwitz-Birkenau and the nearby Vistula and Soła rivers. Displays at such sites – particularly if they include disturbing graphic images of victims, or powerful representations of former perpetrators – may be subject to pressure for modification out of respect for continuing sensitivities, with commemoration or political priorities displacing or shaping pedagogic considerations. But some sites, such as Buchenwald, Ravensbrück and Neuengamme in Germany, or Mauthausen and selected subcamps in Austria, have nevertheless been developing strategies for incorporating material on perpetration at the sites and on the involvement and knowledge of people in the wider locality. The focus is often on camp personnel, including medics, or adjacent industry, and the involvement or 'knowledge' of local people witnessing arrivals and slave labour. Displays about perpetrators on historically significant sites have tended to concentrate primarily on the specific perpetrators and points of particular relevance to the site, while also organizing special events and temporary exhibitions about selected wider questions. Such sites include, for example, the Topography of Terror, on the site of the former headquarters of the Reich Security Main Office (RSHA) in central Berlin; the Nuremberg Trials Memorial, focusing on the principal defendants at the IMT and successor trials, and their crimes; the 'euthanasia' institutes in six sanatoria in Germany and Austria; the Villa ten Hompel, formerly the regional headquarters of the order police, and in the post-war years used for denazification and compensation; Hitler's 'Eagle's Nest' in the Bavarian Alps above Berchtesgaden; or the villa on the shores of Lake Wannsee where Nazi officials came to deliberate on the coordination of the 'Final Solution of the Jewish Question' in January 1942. There are of course innumerable locations associated with the exercise of Nazi power and violence, and only a tiny minority have been both marked and transformed into memorials with exhibitions; many have simply passed unnoticed into later re-use for quite other purposes, or even been consciously passed over for fear of becoming shrines for right-wing sympathizers with Nazism, as in the case of the ruins of Hitler's former bunker in Berlin. The selection of specific locations for exhibitions therefore already intrinsically embodies a history of recognizing distinctive groups, and the pre-selection of those deemed worthy of attention in a later era. This is highlighted by the example of the Forced Labour Documentation Centre in Schöneweide, Berlin, based in the barracks of a relatively intact former internment camp; most such locations had simply been re-used for other purposes after the war, and indeed even here industrial concerns and a café have taken over six of the thirteen barracks. This exhibition, run by the Topography of Terror, focuses directly on complex interactions between millions of German civilians and foreign forced labourers, whose status as victims worthy of compensation was only officially recognized more than half a century after the end of the war.

Given the ubiquity of quotidian complicity, this is something not so readily 'located' and exhibited in quite the same way as those involved in site-specific or relevant perpetration, quite apart from the potential data protection and legal implications of naming those never publicly brought to account for their actions. For this, a far wider historical compass is necessary. One major example outside of historic sites is the watershed 1995 *Wehrmachtsausstellung*, the touring exhibition about the involvement of regular Wehrmacht soldiers in genocidal violence, which brought home the 'Crimes of the Wehrmacht' committed far away. In the process it implicated far wider sections of the population in Nazi violence by indicting an institution that had hitherto retained a 'clean' image, sparking controversy and debate in public and private spheres for years.[4] It also introduced younger generations of Germans to the war, some of whom started searching for explanations for their parents' and grandparents' behaviour and exploring the extent of their complicity. This was the context for the German reception of Daniel Goldhagen's controversial book *Hitler's Willing Executioners*. In an expanded version of his Harvard doctoral thesis, Goldhagen advanced ambitious theoretical claims, seeking to root the enormity of the Holocaust in what he called a mentality of 'eliminationist antisemitism' that had allegedly persisted for centuries in Germany prior to 1945 but dramatically disappeared with the change in political structures in the Federal Republic of Germany after 1949. In dozens of public talks Goldhagen presented this to younger German generations who, as a result of decades of living within a liberal democracy (the GDR was largely ignored), had apparently left these sentiments behind. The work was heavily criticized by historians, but Goldhagen's easily digestible, highly readable, but historically unsustainable analysis, combined with the 'absolution' he offered his audiences, found widespread support among the German public.[5] This book remains a bestseller to popular audiences. But with the passage of generations and an increasingly diverse population in Germany, where a growing percentage no longer has any family links to the Nazi period, an ever-receding past has become emotionally less salient, while among professionals education for the future is seen as increasingly important.[6] Issues around perpetration and complicity, as well as the roles of wider society, are increasingly being addressed in different educational contexts, including museums.

In this extraordinarily rich and diverse wider context, why did we develop our own exhibition? Our project grew in part out of the growing realization that no amount of Holocaust representation and remembrance will be adequate if empathy with victims is situated within a wider narrative that focuses primarily on key policymakers or groups of perpetrators where individuals remain relatively anonymous, effectively hidden behind the uniforms of their organizations. In many instances it seemed almost as if portrayals of the Holocaust, particularly at sites of former atrocities where a primary consideration was remembrance of those who had suffered, was running at odds with historiographical developments. Prominent use of perpetrator sources, particularly in tracing policy developments, had been predominant in much of Western historical scholarship in the latter half of the twentieth century. The noted Holocaust historian Raul Hilberg, for example, was insistent on the importance of 'the documents' as a means of, in a sense, ensuring that perpetrators were convicted on their own evidence.[7] But with the 'era of the survivor' from the late 1970s onwards, this seemed less acceptable in historical texts as well as in sites of memory. Saul Friedländer's work was specifically intended to re-introduce victim and survivor voices to counterbalance the perpetrator-driven policy narratives – although in his work such extracts serve largely to punctuate a narrative that is still a somewhat conventional policy-driven story.[8] But alongside the ever-greater emphasis on incorporating victim voices or the perspectives of the persecuted, the historiographical context was broadening further: the rise of social history and the history of everyday life from the 1970s and 1980s was followed in subsequent decades by the 'cultural turn', and growing interest in the extent of involvement of 'ordinary' people, the possibilities of resistance and the expansion of new fields of 'perpetrator research' from the 1990s – all of which continue to flourish today.[9]

Yet exhibitions have by and large not fully reflected these debates and trends in increasingly international scholarly discussions. Displays about the Holocaust may evoke a sense of infinite sadness through empathy with victims of persecution, particularly when individuals who were persecuted can be visualized through photographs, their lives imagined through selected documents or objects or when vivid accounts of personal experiences are conveyed through survivor testimonies. However, without a better understanding of those who were doing the persecuting, it is hard to move beyond feelings of sympathy and grief. Similarly, profiles of individual rescuers often seem to highlight the significance of particular personalities – further strengthened by Yad Vashem's criteria for bestowing the title of 'Righteous among the Nations' on individuals – rather than exploring the less readily accessible questions around the conditions under which survival, rescue and resistance might be more or less feasible. While key perpetrators and policy developments are necessarily highlighted, the visitor to many Holocaust exhibitions may perhaps leave emotionally exhausted, enthusiastic about individuals having the courage to 'stand up to evil', and with a powerful sense of emotional identification with the victim position. Yet the visitor may have gained little clarity about how such violence could be perpetrated on such a scale – and more particularly, what the conditions for perpetration and the character and extent of complicity might be.

One temporary exhibition that does attempt to address these questions is 'Some Were Neighbors: Choice, Human Behavior, and the Holocaust', developed by and first shown at the United States Holocaust Memorial Museum (USHMM) and now also available online and as a travelling exhibition. Notable for its European dimension, this exhibition engages with the 'dependence' of higher-level 'perpetrators on countless others for the execution of Nazi racial policies'. It considers the 'motives and pressures' on 'ordinary people' that 'influenced individual choices to act', becoming complicit or choosing alternatives.[10] Its biographical approach and foregrounding of individual choices and motives is grounded in Holocaust scholarship emerging since the 1990s. While it effectively conveys what happened, where and who did it – important prerequisites that are still sorely needed when considering empirical studies that suggest pupils lack subject knowledge in precisely these areas – the questions of how and why it was possible, and what are its legacies, are not as yet adequately addressed.[11]

This relates directly to the question of whose voices are heard, and whose world views we are invited to enter – beyond the obvious focus on antisemitic ideology and imagery. Survivor testimony is of course crucial to conveying subjective experiences of persecution, and can not only provide a (spurious) sense of having some form of direct access to the past 'as it really was', but also offer valuable correctives to the cover-ups and deception of those responsible. But there are significant drawbacks to overuse of such testimony without adequate contextualization. For example, we have to remember that victims can only speak from a restricted perspective: exposed directly to violence, they can generally only 'see' the immediate perpetrators, those in close contact; and while they may have heard the names or know the roles of more prominent individuals, they do not necessarily have privileged insights into the wider system making perpetration possible. They cannot generally, for example, see the bureaucrats and civilian enablers behind the scenes; and while they may harbour suspicions at a local level, they may not know the identities of people who engaged in denunciation or profited from their distress. The testimonies of survivors, speaking or writing at a distance of months, years or even decades, will inevitably be coloured by later contexts of communication and knowledge. There is a history to 'memory' narratives which cannot always be brought explicitly to the attention of exhibition visitors watching brief video clips or reading short texts selected to convey an element of 'authentic' experiences and emotions.

Even while recognizing the limited consideration of perpetration and complicity, it is not easy to integrate lower-level 'perpetrator voices' into public exhibitions or educational materials. There are self-evident risks: the use of sources seeming to justify or legitimate violence needs careful contextualization and critical discussion to ensure that the perspectives of those who became complicit or actively involved in acts of perpetration are conveyed with an appropriate degree of critical distance while yet conveying effectively their motivations for involvement. Understanding and empathy through immersive exposure in alien world views are critical–historical tools, but these are not synonymous with condoning such views.

Similarly, there are significant issues to be confronted around the use of graphic images, which are hugely important to historical understanding and interpretation. Increasingly, curators are sensitive to questions around representation. This was directly problematized in an exhibition titled 'The Eye as Witness', developed by researchers and curators at the University of Nottingham and the National Holocaust Centre and Museum in Laxton, and shown in a variety of venues including the Jewish Museum London. Using images of the suppression of the 1943 Warsaw Ghetto Uprising, taken from a perpetrator perspective for the report produced by SS General Jürgen Stroop for Heinrich Himmler, the exhibition claims that 'Virtual Reality allows us to step into a famous Nazi photo, to explore what is not seen, and to critically examine the role of the official propaganda photographer'.[12] Visitors put on a headset that allows them to 'enter' the picture, walk around and explore the scene from different angles. While explicitly intended to stimulate critical thinking about the perspective from which the past is seen, the immersive experience nevertheless implies that Virtual Reality can give us a sense of 'what it was really like'. Yet inadequate documentary contextualization of how the virtual reality scene was itself constructed, not just from the 'perpetrator perspective' but also from that of the researchers, may actually detract from the process of critical thinking about modes of historical reconstruction from the available evidence: why was the decision taken to depict the scene around as so bare, so free of dead bodies or debris? What might the noise, the smell, the clamour have been like? Does 'respect' for the victims really require their portrayal in this particular way? An analysis of other photographs in the Stroop Report, as well as related documents, may suggest quite different ways of imagining the surrounding scene than the silent, eerily empty spaces of this particular version. Yet through their immersion, visitors may be left with the strong impression that they have witnessed 'how it really was'. Even if curators and educators do their best to stimulate critical discussion, the exhibition privileges vicarious experience over analysis concerning what differentiates historical documentation from fiction or, as we increasingly see in current social media, fakery. It implicitly sustains the notion that, with appropriate resources and technology, one can 'step into' the reality that a photo represents, even despite the researchers' explicit awareness that a photo is necessarily already a mediation of that reality from a particular perspective and for a specific purpose. The immersive experience thus blurs the boundaries between history and fiction, rather than reflecting on the significance of this blurring. Moreover, pointing out 'Photos taken by victims [. . .] tell a different story',[13] while highlighting the variety of perspectives at the time (in this case using the somewhat reductive dichotomy of 'perpetrators' and 'victims') does not adequately raise to attention the 'third' set of perspectives, those of contemporary researchers and viewers today. Our creative imagination is also at work while trying to reconstruct and engage with the past.

Graphic images have, of course, to be viewed critically. Visual imagery that survives from a period of radical repression can easily serve to replicate the view of the perpetrators, even when they are ultimately defeated, as in the case of Nazism. Often selective images taken by perpetrators come to dominate our visual imagination and hence to some extent interpretations of the Nazi period. This is a particular problem for those tempted to take propaganda imagery as a representation of 'what it was really like'. It is also a problem if images are designed specifically to sustain, for example, antisemitic stereotypes. Such images cannot go uncommented. Yet if students are exposed to them and learn how to interpret them they can be equipped with appropriate critical–historical skills. More rarely, images taken by victims survive, such as photos of camps and ghettos that were taken clandestinely and preserved by burying in sealed containers and dug up again after the war. Images important to survivors are vital to complement the perpetrator perspectives.

We are conscious of and acknowledge the challenges around using graphic images in educational settings in a constructive manner while being mindful of different age groups or individual circumstances of pupils. IHRA provides guidelines for educators, stressing the need for 'a sensitive approach and careful thought as to what constitutes appropriate material' while noting that graphic images, including those created by perpetrators, 'can be useful educational resources, provided that the context is made explicit. Educators should constantly question their use of sources and ask themselves what educational outcomes are served by using particular materials'.[14] While we agree with this, we are concerned about restrictive interpretations of these guidelines amid wider trends in education that seek to avoid engaging with graphic images or even prohibit using them.[15] We encountered such a case during a CPD event jointly organized with the Holocaust Educational Trust (HET), during which we discussed the latest research on perpetration and complicity and our approach to these issues in our exhibition, while Villa ten Hompel and Yad Vashem presented their pedagogic strategies. HET's selective interpretation of IHRA guidelines prevented us from sharing carefully prepared educational resources developed around a number of graphic images that we present in the exhibition. The educational charity referred to selected extracts from the IHRA's guidelines: 'The Holocaust can be taught effectively without using graphic photographs or film footage'. And: 'Using graphic images with the intent to shock and horrify is degrading to the victims and can reinforce stereotypes of Jews as victims. Images can also be insensitive to the sensibilities of learners in the room regarding human trauma or modesty'.

We came to fundamentally disagree with HET's approach for the following reasons. First, they risk effectively denying students the opportunity to explore key sources and learn how to think critically about them. For example, an image of German soldiers standing with cameras and photographing the public hanging of 'partisans' succinctly makes the point that atrocities were witnessed, and that photographs were sent home for development and discussion among family and friends; a single image can reinforce student engagement with questions around 'what Germans knew' as well as soldiers' experiences and attitudes. Secondly, educators generally do not use graphic images 'with the intent to shock and horrify' – and if they do, this is something that should be addressed on an individual basis, as with any other pedagogical issue; it is not a sufficient reason to try to teach the Holocaust without use of such images. Third, images do not necessarily 'reinforce stereotypes of Jews as victims' but can rather be used for just the opposite purpose. The well-known image of women in their underwear huddling together on the Šķēde beach near the Latvian coastal town of Liepāja, just prior to being killed in December 1941, can, for example, be used to demonstrate several very important issues: how perpetrators were seeking to portray the shooting as carried out not by Germans but by local auxiliaries; the ways in which a Jewish survivor, David Zivcon, managed successfully to smuggle out the negatives from the place where he was working and have them developed, a form of risky resistance; and the rescue efforts of a local couple, Roberts and Johanna Sedul, who helped Zivcon and others, and thus also the images, to survive.

HET's concern with the sensibilities of learners and the traumatic potential of images is laudable, but cannot lead to the blanket conclusion that all graphic images that may indeed, given the subject matter, 'shock and horrify', are inappropriate. It is not the image itself, but how it is selected and used in the classroom, that matters. We do not wish to take away from students the opportunity for critical study, reflection and deeper learning, as well as the chance to develop a visual imagination of such a key period in history.[16] Moreover, the use of photographs in a properly framed context is a potent way to push back against the narrative that the perpetrators sought to create with their pictures. The Holocaust was a modern phenomenon, and the handheld camera was at the time a relatively new invention, the use of which was actively encouraged by the Nazi regime. A true product of its time, the handheld camera thus helped not only to document but also to exacerbate discrimination against Jews and other minorities. The nuances listed by IHRA are, in effect, the 'negative' – to use a photographic term – of the reasons why perpetrators took pictures: they *were* meant to shock, to re-victimize and to dull the senses of their audiences. It should be noted that German propagandists had no qualms depicting gruesome imagery, even of their own men, to further their agenda. Pictorial reports of the September 1939 'Bromberg massacre' of ethnic Germans by Poles provided a validation for the German invasion of Poland; widespread publication of the Katyn massacre in 1943 helped create a rift in the Allied alliance; and the images of women raped and tortured by the Red Army in the final year of the war were designed to persuade Germans to fight to the bitter end. A measured use of these pictures, as well as those taken of persecuted and murdered victims of genocidal violence, can help to reframe the narrative that was so consistently and deliberately distorted by the selective use of photographs. So while we were prevented from showing some images in a public presentation organized by the HET, we nevertheless included them in the exhibition, and also discussed this issue explicitly in one of our short films.[17]

We would like to provide a brief overview of the exhibition's sections – an overview which cannot, of course, in any way replicate the exhibition itself with its fuller texts, images, films and accompanying materials.

The exhibition

Combining overviews and case studies, 'Compromised Identities? Entanglement in Collective Violence' explores how people became complicit in the Nazi system, and how their experiences were represented both at the time and after 1945, whether in their own words, in trials and media responses, or in works of film and literature. The exhibition's innovative content was designed to stimulate critical discussion and facilitate understanding of complex issues. It includes subtitled excerpts from audiovisual testimonies from the perpetrator side, with selections taken from *Final Account: Third Reich Testimonies*. Additional materials were sourced from photo collections, ego-documents, other documents, literature and newspapers. The accompanying case study materials pose wider questions about individual responsibility in systems of state-sponsored collective violence, and reflect on recent and present-day conflicts, making the exhibition relevant beyond the Third Reich and the Holocaust. The digital exhibition also includes an interactive map mapping the exhibition's case studies and films across the continent; selected objects and images; an 'explore further' section with extended excerpts from sources and questions for discussion; a section including the entire film collection; and the project blog. The colourful modernist shard-like exhibition graphics were designed by DesignMap. The digital exhibition was built by Surface Impression.

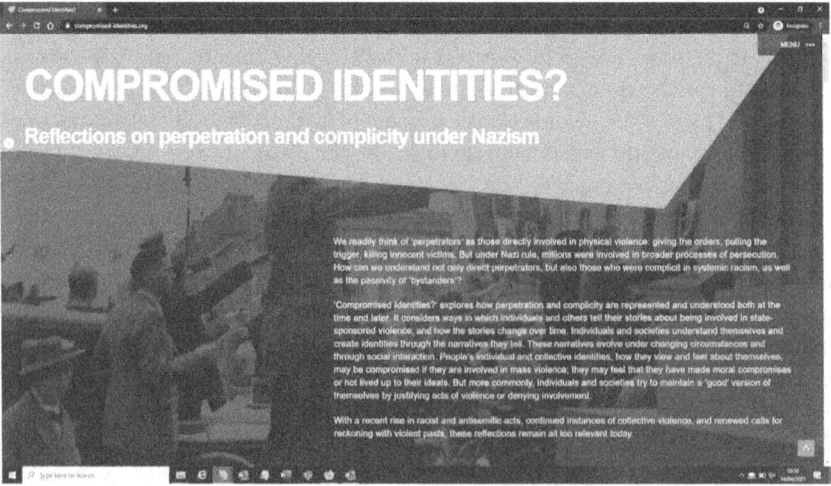

In addition, the team created three types of short films – thirty-six in total – in conjunction with Graham Riach. Some explore key issues, such as 'motives and belonging', 'denunciation' or 'ageing perpetrators', through discussion; others focus on significant topics, actors, places and events, such as 'Euthanasia Murders' or 'Kristallnacht, 1938', presented on location in Austria, Germany and Lithuania; and others explore self-representational strategies of 'Third Reich' contemporaries, discussing excerpts from interviews conducted by filmmaker Luke Holland and archived as *Final Account: Third Reich Testimonies*, excerpts from Claude Landsmann's *Shoah* outtakes and from other oral histories, including interviews by Wendy Lower held at the USHMM.[18] The films, embedded in the exhibition throughout, provide a novel, meta-level access to the exhibition and its aims, providing historical and contextual information, exploring abstract themes, reflecting on key issues and suggesting ways to interpret perpetration and complicity beyond simplistic, emotive or reductive narratives. They constitute an innovative and sensitive approach to presenting accounts from the side of the persecutors to educators, scholars and the wider public. Despite increasing emphasis in the field of Holocaust Studies on ordinary men and women, the voices of those once implicated in a system of state-ordained and -sanctioned collective violence are still largely absent from pedagogic practice. By juxtaposing interview excerpts with their discussion by the project team, we contextualized the interviews, highlighted a range of important issues, debated possible interpretations and pointed to common patterns in narrative interviews and how these are approached by scholars.

Across eight main sections, the exhibition explores how perpetration and complicity have been represented and understood both at the time and later. It considers ways in which individuals and others tell their stories about being involved in state-sponsored violence, and how the stories change over time. Individuals and societies understand themselves and create identities through the narratives they tell, their narratives evolving under changing circumstances and through social interaction. People's individual and collective identities, how they view and feel about themselves, may be compromised if they are involved in mass violence; they may feel that they have made moral compromises or not lived up to their ideals. But more commonly, individuals and societies try to maintain a 'good' version of themselves by justifying acts of violence or denying involvement. Only a flavour of the eight substantive sections can be given here.

[1] Compromised identities?

The exhibition opens by posing the questions that underpin it. How do individuals talk about their involvement in state-sponsored violence, at the time and later, and how do historians and creative writers represent them? How far do people's behaviours and attitudes compromise who they are? And what compromises do states and societies make during and after such violence? It continues by summarizing the death toll caused by Germans and their collaborators, before considering those responsible: key individuals in positions of power, direct perpetrators, those who made killings possible and the millions who sustained the wider Nazi system. The section explores ways in which people got involved in Nazi crimes, such as through denunciation, industrial exploitation of slave labour or benefitting from 'free' dentistry provided by concentration camp inmates. A map points to the involvement of several German and Austrian men and women, and how they fared after 1945 in the three successor states (East and West Germany, Austria). In response to the opening questions, we argue that 'despite widespread moral condemnation, few individuals or professional and social groups felt their behaviour undermined their own identity as decent people'.

[2] Creating a Hostile environment

Here we explore the responses of 'ordinary Germans' to Nazism before the war, in the context of foreign policy successes, full employment and youth engagement, but also the sense of resignation among people opposed to Nazism and the state-sponsored violence of Kristallnacht. The section highlights the 're-segregation' of German society, pointing to the ways in which 'non-Aryan' Germans were progressively excluded from the Nazi 'national community'. This occurred with the acquiescence and complicity of many compatriots who later had to balance positive memories of their youth with later knowledge of atrocities and post-war changes in values. This happened in part through learning the language and practice of racism, with examples including a librarian ordered to refuse serving a Jewish reader, and the widespread lack of open opposition to Kristallnacht. We raise the question: 'Is conformity evidence of ideological conviction, compliance born of fear, or self-serving complicity with a human face?'

[3] Mobilization for mass murder

This section focuses on the period 1939–45, when organized mass murder was an integral part of the Nazi vision for a German-dominated Europe. Murder encompassed 'Euthanasia', the systematic mass murder of up to six million Jews, between 250,000 and half a million Roma and Sinti ('Gypsies'), 'partisans', Slavs and Russian POWs. The brutal, public killing of Jews at Lietukis Garage in Kaunas, instigated by German Einsatzgruppe A, executed by Lithuanian activists, and observed by crowds of onlookers, highlights how the extermination of Jews in Europe could only be put into practice with the complicity or collaboration of many non-Germans. Perpetrators framed their violence as crucial to German national interests, an essential part of the war effort, or even simply as 'work'. But involvement in violence also took less direct forms, such as by Nazi ghetto administrators or the countless Germans who watched former neighbours being deported east while benefitting from their departure. How can we explain this explosion of violence? We have to understand the broader conditions under which ordinary people could facilitate or become involved in mass murder. Key factors include the role of initiators; the capacity to organize and mobilize activists, resources and additional forces; the passivity or inaction of wider 'bystander' communities; and the context of armed conflicts and/or dictatorship.

[4] Perpetration and complicity on the eastern front

Operation Barbarossa marked the beginning of the 'war of annihilation' and the mass extermination of Jews, carried out by dedicated killing squads, police battalions, local auxiliaries and frequently aided by regular army troops. The scale of wartime atrocities turned genocide into a pan-European phenomenon that implicated people across the continent. Attempts by states, institutions and individuals to represent the past as acceptable were affected by radically different conditions in eastern and western Europe both during and after the war. The section explores the involvement of 'brutalized' regular troops in the killings of alleged and actual partisans, the starvation of local populations through scorched earth policies or the use of local people as human minesweepers. After the war, German and Austrian veterans portrayed themselves as having served in a 'clean army', barely involved in genocidal policies. Other countries have also had difficulties in confronting past involvement in Nazi atrocities. In Lithuania and Latvia, the notion of 'double genocide' is often used to celebrate former anti-communists as national heroes, while ignoring the role they played in slaughtering Jews.

[5] 'Decency', duty and strategies of self-defence

Moving towards the post-war period, this section addresses the fact that not everyone who was involved in persecution and killing was necessarily antisemitic or a convinced Nazi. There was generally a committed core, a wider group that conformed for a variety of reasons, and those who were uncomfortable or opposed. Some people were both murderers and rescuers, or perpetrators in one context and victims in another. At the time, some thought that mass killing was morally and legally justifiable, necessary for defence or for the greater 'good' of the German people. However, common motives included career advancement, a sense of duty and desire for material benefits. Peer pressure and community spirit helped many to go along with killings. After 1945, the legal and moral environment changed and mass murder was condemned. Many of those involved defended and justified their behaviour, while others repudiated Nazism but denied their own involvement. Some even denied that any crimes had been committed. Few addressed their past more head-on. They all have in common that they tried to continue thinking of themselves as 'good' or 'decent' people.

Very few showed remorse or accepted responsibility.

[6] Where have all the Nazis gone?

This section addresses the question of how perpetrators and those complicit with Nazism navigated their Nazi past after 1945. Some top Nazis escaped, or were executed or imprisoned after the war. But the majority of former Nazis were rehabilitated. From April 1945 onwards, most German civilians began to deny any knowledge of atrocities. The new post-war states officially denounced Nazism, but made compromises. West Germany acknowledged responsibility but amnestied former Nazis at the expense of justice. East Germany, the self-proclaimed 'anti-fascist state', absolved itself of responsibility, but effected radical social transformation by political oppression. Austria adopted the convenient label of having been 'Hitler's first victim' and barely confronted Nazi legacies. Fictional representations of 'Nazis in disguise' challenge the idea that there is a recognizable perpetrator identity. People are not always what they seem, and even the most unlikely citizen may once have been involved in mass murder. Individuals can move in and out of perpetration without feeling they have compromised their identity.

[7] Has justice been done?

In response to this question we point to the failures of justice in the courtroom which were accompanied by resistance on the part of governments, organizations and individuals to acknowledge accountability, award compensation to victims or engage in restitution of property. The section compares the three successor states' records of who was brought to trial and when, and the levels of sentencing, revealing stark differences between West Germany, the GDR and Austria. In West Germany, many lawyers had served in the Third Reich and were sympathetic to defendants. The criminal law definition of murder in terms of individual motives also affected trial outcomes. Where there was little or no witness testimony, perpetrators were more easily able to get away with murder. Austrian Holocaust survivor Simon Wiesenthal worked tirelessly from the late 1940s to the mid-1980s to bring Nazi perpetrators to justice. However, institutions often refused to cooperate with him, many people were opposed to the trials and the ruling parties wanted to win over former Nazis as voters. Austrian investigations into Nazi perpetrators were hampered by a lack of commitment by politicians and their electorates, many of whom were implicated in the Nazi past. The GDR, self-designated as an 'anti-fascist state', nonetheless reintegrated and rehabilitated former Nazis. But once on trial, former Nazis were far more likely to be convicted than in West Germany, and the sentences were more severe.

[8] Why does it still matter?

Here we consider how state-sponsored violence entails the participation and complicity of many institutions, professions and individuals. Many people feel impotent to stand up for those being victimized, and many feel indifferent to persecution that does not affect them personally, especially if they benefit from it, directly or indirectly. Some justify violence in pursuit of national goals. Later in their lives, most people involved in state-condoned violence construct narratives that minimize their own responsibility and maintain their view of themselves as decent human beings. Institutions, companies and professions may resist acknowledging responsibility or refuse to pay compensation. Some do reflect more critically on their actions and seek to learn from these experiences. This section points to the challenge of representing violence and perpetration, the arguments for giving perpetrators a voice, the crucial role of fiction for thinking about questions of empathy and response, and the significance of oral histories at different life stages. We conclude that it is vital to continue to analyse perpetration and complicity under National Socialism in order to understand the conditions in which people were mobilized to act, and the ways in which they subsequently evaded justice and sought to deny, justify or reinterpret their past. These issues remain relevant today and we cite the examples of the genocidal violence against the Muslim Rohingya minority, the storming of the US Capitol in 2021, the UK Windrush scandal of 2018 and Viktor Orbán taking steps to undermine the rule of law in Hungary. We argue that a strong framework of democratic institutions and respect for laws upholding human rights is essential, although we recognize that even in democracies, public opinion can easily be manipulated and laws can discriminate against particular groups.

Constraints and compromises

Conceptually, the exhibition had to convey key information along a chronological timeline before being able to explore more complex issues, yet do so within the tight word limits advised by our exhibition consultancy (DesignMap). There were three major considerations and constraints that we had to negotiate. The first consideration was the emphasis placed by the UK funding body, the Arts and Humanities Research Council (AHRC), on the importance of research having a wider societal impact beyond academia. It is expected that researchers will not only communicate their research to non-academic audiences through public engagement or 'knowledge exchange' activities, but also that the research will have some form of demonstrable impact that can be measured quantitively and qualitatively. Our exhibition was therefore based on our own research projects and included mechanisms to garner feedback. The second constraint was the need for immediate intelligibility. We sought to make the exhibition accessible to as broad a non-academic audience as possible, meaning that our target audiences would have highly variable levels of prior knowledge and understanding of National Socialism, the Second World War and the Holocaust. This combined brief meant that the exhibition not only had to be rooted in original research but at the same time had to include enough descriptive context for that research to be intelligible to a lay public. We therefore tried to focus on using accessible language, restricting all discussion to short text pieces and limiting the overall amount of text per panel. Similarly, in relation to the films, discussion had to be reduced from about 30 minutes to 3–5 minutes. This proved our greatest intellectual challenge. The final constraint was financial. The exhibition had to be as appealing as possible, with visitors used to high standards of audiovisual presentation, but on a limited budget.

Some of the constraints we originally faced were considerably alleviated by benefitting from an increased budget, and, paradoxically, by the onset of the Coronavirus pandemic from spring 2020. The travelling exhibition we had originally planned grew from a simple and portable construction into an expansive, sustainable powder-coated steel and wood composition before being trimmed to accommodate smaller venues and our restricted budget. Ultimately, this was replaced with a web-based exhibition as the pandemic hit and, for future educational use, a scaled back pop-up banner version.

The digital exhibition changed the dynamics, removing visitors' ability to move through the space, engage with others or take part in guided tours or attend talks. Yet it also afforded huge opportunities that a physical, travelling exhibition could not have delivered: greatly enhanced possibilities for international engagement, especially of educators; the possibility of embedding multimedia in a way that physical media stations or sound showers could not have delivered; the ability to edit and amend; and the facility to include further resources for research and personal study. The turn from physical to digital required a new approach to design, organization and presentation, including additional content, and necessitating the services of a web design consultancy (Surface Impression) that could build the website in less than three months within our budget, enabled by further funding from the Pears Family Charitable Foundation. This additional funding was key for enhancing the scope of the exhibition and the number of films we could make. It reinforces the extent to which the widespread understanding of historical (and contemporary) events depends on the narratives or projects that receive funding, whether from government or philanthropic sources.

This also became evident when searching for images for the exhibition that did not simply replicate the standard images of perpetrators. Images in the public realm or those that do not require high copyright payments are often those that are already well known and reinforce the general understanding of perpetrators as particular high-level individuals and certain sorts of Nazis represented somewhat anonymously by their uniforms. The price tag of some images held by commercial archives made their inclusion impossible within our budgetary constraints and required a more selective approach. Restrictions placed on the use of images by some public archives also limited the level of promotion on social media.

Responses and reflections

We elicited responses to the exhibition through a survey on the website, prompting visitors to 'have their say', while also receiving informal feedback from colleagues. For an initial soft launch, our invited audience and survey respondents worked for educational or commemorative charities, in Secondary Education and in Higher Education. Following the public launch, the survey has been open to anyone, although responses have largely continued to be submitted by those who are involved in education in some form. Responses have been overwhelmingly positive. Most respondents said that they gained new knowledge from the project, and those who did not either worked for Holocaust commemoration organizations, or else were Higher Education specialists on the Holocaust. This was not uniform, as the majority of HE respondents and community or NGO workers still said they gained new information. Those who gained new knowledge praised the level of detail, and seemed particularly interested in the reactions of 'ordinary people' to the violence and antisemitism of the Nazis. They seemed to enjoy the micro-level detail of individuals' relationships to collective processes, and the greater detail on individuals who would otherwise have been part of an anonymous mass. There was also a positive response to the post-war and contemporary focuses in the website, both for the value of covering areas often not included, and enabling visitors to use historical perspectives to examine current events.

Many found the videos created by the project team to be the most engaging facet of the exhibition, and approved of the format of interweaving testimonies from individuals with critical discussions of their accounts. There were also several respondents who felt that that the videos offered valuable insights into how to interrogate perpetrator testimonies, with some reporting that it increased their confidence in using such materials. Others commented that the exhibition challenged their preconceptions about the topic, enabling them to develop a more nuanced viewpoint which they hoped to incorporate in their own practice, particularly those undertaking academic research on facets of the Holocaust. The interactive maps were commended for showing shifting national borders and important sites where atrocities occurred. Overall, respondents to the survey said that they found the website accessible and challenging, in ways that developed and deepened their own knowledge. They hoped to use this both in their teaching and research practice, and to encourage other Holocaust educators to develop a richer understanding of a complicated series of issues. The website's interactivity and the videos can lend themselves to a classroom setting, particularly for post-16 secondary school learning and in undergraduate courses. The level of detail offered in case studies provided unknown information, while the framing of the source materials is an exemplary model of the interrogation of a series of sources that many are not confident in using.

Of particular interest is the fact that every education professional who took the survey indicated that they would use this website in their working lives, demonstrating the pedagogic merits of the exhibition and the underlying research. While some felt that the level of language and ideas used, and the graphic imagery involved, precluded its use for the younger students that they teach, they noted that it could play a valuable role in teacher training. We had discussed at length the issue of whether to include graphic images in the exhibition and the embedded films (one of which addresses this issue head-on).[19] This feedback confirmed the merits of presenting images, including graphic ones, taken by perpetrators, if properly contextualized.[20]

Two very interesting responses to the exhibition have drawn attention to the position of the researchers and our overall methodological approach. One academic visitor noted that in the films using excerpts from oral history interviews, we come across as distanced and morally superior to the Third Reich contemporaries we discuss. While this visitor commended the films as informative and engaging, she also felt discomfort at how the analysis of interview excerpts and interviewees implied distance. She would have welcomed an acknowledgement that we are not so different from them, and that we, as humans, also strive to present ourselves in a good light. In our case, of course, this relates to our position as academics whose authoritative voices are supposed to carry greater weight than those of the contemporaries on whom we were commenting. We share this critic's view, and her important comment points to the ways in which researchers may seek to position themselves 'neutrally' or in ways that are politically or morally acceptable within their own context. There is no doubt that the constraints of accessibility and brevity contributed to this impression. In the process of editing the films to a manageable length, we retained primarily bold statements of interpretation, while much of the nuance in our original conversation was cut for the sake of a shorter, more coherent and watchable film. We aimed, though, to include more complex points in some of the other films, such as 'Representing Violence' or 'Ageing Perpetrators'. Yet this visitor's feedback also suggests that our exhibition fulfilled one of its key aims: bringing into view 'ordinary' actors, raising questions, and inviting reflection, not only on the past, but also on ourselves and the present.

Nevertheless, in his contribution to this volume, Stephan Jaeger too raises concerns about the distance that he sees is maintained by the 'Compromised Identities?'

exhibition. He argues: 'Whereas an almost exclusively cognitive and analytically designed exhibition like *Compromised Identities?* can document grey zones, visitors are allowed to stay passive at a safe distance'. He goes on to assert: 'As we have seen through the concepts of empathy, experientiality and agonism, an affective component is needed to challenge the visitor's own subject-position'.[21] While it is clear that all contemporary audiences are by definition 'at a safe distance' chronologically from events that took place more than seventy-five years ago, for those closely affected traumatic experiences and their consequences can remain all too present. It is not necessarily the case that 'an affective component is needed to challenge the visitor's own subject-position'. The Holocaust is intrinsically a highly emotive topic, and what Jaeger calls our 'almost exclusively cognitive and analytically designed exhibition' seeks to contribute to clarity of thinking about some of the most controversial aspects, including degrees of complicity and the conditions for involvement in perpetration. Indeed, in the initial planning stages for the exhibition, we discussed the possibility of a more interactive, experiential approach, such as using role or activity cards (along lines initially used in the USHMM's permanent exhibition) or offering different routes through the exhibition based on individual choices. Ultimately we decided against these approaches. We concluded first that they risked over-simplifying the complex circumstances we wanted to explore, and secondly that the vicarious thrill and 'gamebook experience' seemed inappropriate in the context of the exhibition's focus. As educators appealing to a wide and diverse audience, we felt it important to highlight key points while also raising open questions; and by concluding with some contemporary examples, we draw out the relevance for issues that people are grappling with today.

Thus, while the exhibition overall takes a more 'distant' and generally cognitive approach, we sought to encourage reflection by asking questions, integrating literary perspectives, offering a meta-discussion of the exhibition in our films and by linking the exhibition to more recent and current issues. This contrasts with the recently re-opened permanent Holocaust exhibition at London's Imperial War Museum (IWM) that takes an ostensibly distanced yet highly emotive approach, and that insists on remaining strictly within the period, using only contemporary sources. The IWM exhibition's representation of perpetration and complicity is largely limited to: Hitler and his inner circle; SS perpetrators; and select war criminals on the stand at the International Military Tribunal in Nuremberg or other significant and well-known early post-war trials. The fact that the exhibition devotes significant space to the *Volksgemeinschaft* indicates an increasing consensus on the need to consider the roles of the wider population. Integrating this issue into the wider purview of war and genocide remains a challenge. At the IWM, the topic remains linked to the pre-war years and is as such effectively siloed. More lowly actors, the extensive role of the Wehrmacht and the complexities of the wider European dimension and involvement of a wide range of non-Germans in making the Holocaust possible, under differing circumstances according to areas and stages of the war, are proportionately under-emphasized. While the IWM exhibition is immensely well resourced and includes many striking features, the overall narrative may leave the visitor with a great deal of factual knowledge alongside empathy and emotional discomfort around the fates of victims, but less by way of an overall interpretive framework for understanding patterns of perpetration and complicity.²² How to balance different aspects as part of an exhibition aiming to give a comprehensive view of the Holocaust continues to pose a challenge given significant constraints set by competing demands and ideas, audience expectations, historiographical complexity and practical feasibility. More specialized or temporary exhibitions that focus on only one aspect, event or location, or set of issues do not avoid these issues altogether but certainly have an advantage; it may even be time to consider the future of museum exhibitions attempting to provide a 'master narrative' that will inevitably fall short of their original ambitions yet remain in place for decades.

Ultimately, we chose to rely on the capacity of visitors to our site to engage actively with the exhibition by using both their intellect and their imagination to explore and respond to the intrinsically emotive materials and still significant questions we raised. The material is offered to stimulate further study and reflection. And this is, we believe, what is most urgently needed today. We turn, finally, to reflect on the wider theoretical implications of our approach.

Notes

1 The exhibition was curated by Stephanie Bird, Mary Fulbrook, Stefanie Rauch, Christoph Thonfeld and Bastiaan Willems. Available at https://compromised-identities.org/.
2 For example Stephan Jaeger, 'Empathetic Challenges: Representing and Performing Compromised and Uncompromised Identities in Contemporary Second-World-War and Holocaust Exhibitions', Ch. 16 in this volume. See also Susanne Luhmann, 'Managing Perpetrator Affect: The Female Guard Exhibition at Ravensbrück', in *Perpetrating Selves: Doing Violence, Performing Identity*, ed. Clare Bielby and Jeffrey Stevenson Murer (London: Palgrave Macmillan, 2018), 247–69; Sarah Kleinmann, 'Exhibiting Ordinary Men and Women – The Representation of National Socialist Perpetrators in Memorials', in *War and Memorials: The Second World War and Beyond*, ed. Frank Jacob and Kenneth Pearl (Paderborn: Ferdinand Schöningh, 2019), 19–37.
3 See further: Mary Fulbrook, *Reckonings: Legacies of Nazi Persecution and the Quest for Justice* (Oxford: Oxford University Press, 2018), Ch. 19, 'Oblivion and Memorialization', 483–517; Mary Fulbrook, 'Complicity and the Holocaust in Eastern Europe', *Jewish Historical Studies* 53 (2021): 115–35; Martin Winstone, *The Holocaust Sites of Europe* (London: I. B. Tauris, 2010).
4 See for example: Hannes Heer, *Vom Verschwinden der Täter: Der Vernichtungskrieg fand statt, aber keiner war dabei* (Berlin: Aufbau-Verlag, 2004); Hamburger Institut für Sozialforschung (ed.), *Eine Ausstellung und ihre Folgen: zur Rezeption der Ausstellung 'Vernichtungskrieg. Verbrechen der Wehrmacht 1941 bis 1944'* (Hamburg: Hamburger Edition, 1999); Hannes Heer, '20 Jahre Wehrmachtsausstellung: Thesen, Debatten, Folgen. Ein persönlicher Blick', in '*So war der deutsche Landser . . .' Das populäre Bild der Wehrmacht*, ed. Jens Westemeier (Paderborn: Ferdinand Schöningh, 2019), 79–100.
5 Daniel Jonah Goldhagen, *Hitler's Willing Executioners: Ordinary Germans and the Holocaust* (New York: A. Knopf, 1996). On the debate, see for example Bernhard

Rieger, '"Daniel in the Lion's Den?" The German Debate about Goldhagen's *Hitler's Willing Executioners*', *History Workshop Journal* 43 (1997): 226–33; Lars Rensmann, 'Holocaust Memory and Mass Media in Contemporary Germany: Reflections on the Goldhagen Debate', *Patterns of Prejudice* 33, no. 1 (1999): 59–76.

6 Indeed, as the recent controversy surrounding Achille Mbembe and Dirk Moses has shown, other historic and present injustices are increasingly taking centre stage, with the German post-war consensus being challenged and re-negotiated once again. Cf. the article by Dirk Moses on what he called the 'German catechism' and responses to it available at: https://newfascismsyllabus.com/category/opinions/the-catechism-debate/ (Accessed 3 May 2022).

7 Raul Hilberg, *The Destruction of the European Jews*, 3rd ed. (New Haven and London: Yale University Press, 2003; orig. 1961).

8 Saul Friedländer, *Nazi Germany and the Jews*, vol. 1, *The Years of Persecution, 1933–1939* (London: HarperCollins, 1998); and *Nazi Germany and the Jews, Vol. 2, The Years of Extermination. 1933–45* (New York: HarperCollins, 2007). For discussion, see for example Alon Confino, 'Narrative Form and Historical Sensation: On Saul Friedländer's *The Years of Extermination*', *History and Theory* 48, no. 3 (2009): 199–219.

9 The implications of these developments for our theoretical approach are discussed further in the concluding chapter which follows.

10 United States Holocaust Memorial Museum, 'Some Were Neighbors'. https://somewereneighbors.ushmm.org/#/exhibitions. The exhibition opened in 2015. Online exhibition available at https://www.ushmm.org/information/exhibitions/traveling-exhibitions/some-were-neighbors (Accessed 28 April 2022).

11 See for example Stuart Foster, Alice Pettigrew, Andy Pearce, Rebecca Hale, Adrian Burgess, Paul Salmons and Ruth-Anne Lenga, *What do Students Know and Understand about the Holocaust? Evidence from English Secondary Schools* (London: UCL Institute of Education, 2016). https://holocausteducation.org.uk/wp-content/uploads/What-do-students-know-and-understand-about-the-Holocaust-2nd-Ed.pdf (Accessed 28 April 2022); Andreas Geike, 'Die Verankerung nationalsozialistischer Gewaltverbrechen im Unterricht: Dargelegt anhand der Rahmenlehrpläne der Länder', *Gedenkstättenrundbrief* 177 (2015): 26–33. Geike observes a trend in German history curricula, with teaching aims about National Socialism, war and genocide having shifted from subject knowledge towards 'competencies'.

12 'The Eye as Witness'. https://witness.holocaust.org.uk/exhibition (Accessed 17 August 2022).

13 Ibid.

14 International Holocaust Remembrance Alliance (IHRA), *Recommendations for Teaching and Learning about the Holocaust* (2015), 28. https://www.holocaustremembrance.com/sites/default/files/inline-files/IHRA-Recommendations-Teaching-and-Learning-about-Holocaust.pdf (Accessed 2 May 2022).

15 Paradoxically, this comes at a time when research is increasingly turning to analyse photographs as key historical sources. See for example Wendy Lower, *The Ravine: A Family, a Photograph, a Holocaust Massacre Revealed* (London: Head of Zeus, 2021) and Janina Struk, *Photographing the Holocaust: Interpretations of the Evidence* (London: Routledge, 2005).

16 On the debates surrounding the use of Holocaust pictures in a classroom setting, see Ruth-Anne Lenga, 'Seeing Things Differently: The Use of Atrocity Images in Teaching about the Holocaust', in *Holocaust Education: Contemporary Challenges*

and Controversies, ed. Stuart Foster, Andy Pearce, and Alice Pettigrew (London: UCL Press, 2020), 195–220.
17 'Representing Violence'. https://compromised-identities.org/film-collection/.
18 For access to the archival collection, see https://www.ucl.ac.uk/library/collections/ucl-digital-collections/browse-collections/final-account-third-reich-testimonies or watch this recording https://www.youtube.com/watch?v=lYZqe-ZoEVU (Accessed 2 May 2022).
19 'Representing Violence'. https://compromised-identities.org/film-collection/ (Accessed 28 April 2022).
20 See also the discussion above.
21 Jaeger, 'Empathetic Challenges', Ch. 16 above.
22 See also the accompanying catalogue to the IWM exhibition: James Bulgin, *The Holocaust* (London: IWM, 2021).

18

Conclusion

Stephanie Bird, Mary Fulbrook, Stefanie Rauch and Bastiaan Willems

In Varlam Shalamov's story 'The Red Cross', the narrator wonders how the escort guard, who has often killed prisoners in the Kolyma camp, will talk about his job: 'what is he going to tell the girl he marries about his work in the Far North? Will he tell her about using his rifle butt to hit starving old men who could no longer walk'?[1] What this volume has demonstrated is that whatever the escort guard tells his wife or any other audience, his narrative, like those of most involved in perpetration, will conform to a positive view of himself. Perpetrators of direct violence, as well as those who are complicit with it, fashion their narratives in response to the context in which they recount it and the discourses available for them to most effectively retain a positive image of themselves. Well-established discourses include references to duty, obeying orders, fear of punishment, having no choice under dictatorship, ignorance, individual powerlessness and 'war is war'. Clearly, such exculpatory discourses may disguise motives that have become totally unacceptable in later moral contexts, such as ideological antisemitism and a belief in the racial hierarchy of peoples. But more commonly such explanations, even if justifiable in part or whole, nevertheless coexist with or veil a range of motivations for active participation in a violent regime that are more mundane: job satisfaction, new opportunities, individual fulfilment, career progression, better income, institutional loyalty or looking after the interests of one's family, for example. These reasons, often considered laudable in nonviolent societies, or societies that perceive themselves as such, seem abhorrent when the cost is systematic persecution and mass murder. This complicates how we analyse both involvement at the time and later responses – including our own critical and moral evaluations. The approach we have set out bridges disciplinary, temporal and geographic boundaries.

Our approach sits within a wider context of debates around questions of structure and the extent and limits of individual agency, as well as the historical constitution of the individual subject and self-perceptions. The complex interplay between historical representations and personal narratives affect notions of responsibility, or even culpability. In the German context, the narratives that individuals, institutions and professional bodies have used to speak of their involvement in or complicity with National Socialist violence have varied over time. They have both influenced and been influenced by the changing interpretative frameworks developed by historians, sociologists and psychologists among others. Germans already started to assert ignorance of the Jewish genocide in 1945, pointing to the culpability of Hitler, elite Nazis and the terror they imposed. In this rendering of events, most Germans could be styled as victims, a view that received a degree of credibility from the West German historiographical focus during the 1950s and 1960s on significant Nazis at the top of a repressive totalitarian pyramid of power. There was in many quarters a version of great man history, with a focus on the agency of key individuals and institutions such as the SS, and, particularly in military-related narratives, an emphasis on the supposed decency of soldiers.[2]

Even as the historiography of Nazi Germany became more sophisticated, the Holocaust remained largely out of sight in the first three decades after the war. It was indeed often marginalized by West German historians as 'Jewish' history, carried out by survivors or those connected with victims who were deemed insufficiently 'objective' to be taken seriously. Magisterial scholarly overviews of the Nazi dictatorship, emphasizing the significance of Hitler's antisemitism and the structures of power in what was conceived as a 'totalitarian' state, condemned the dictatorship but failed adequately to expand the horizon to the extermination of European Jews.[3] Analyses were shaped by ostensibly 'impartial' senior West German historians, whose own entanglement in Nazism was addressed only in the late 1990s.[4] In the GDR, historians were constrained by theories of fascism that emphasized the role of monopoly capitalism and imperialism, and effectively removed agency from the workers and peasants who were variously manipulated or blinded by the dominant forces.[5] Among minority left-wing intellectual circles in the Anglo-American sphere, the relative loss of agency was compounded in neo-Marxist structuralist approaches, or tangled up in the inescapable webs of 'false consciousness' and 'hegemonic ideologies' of neo-Marxists of a more voluntarist bent.

Agency never disappeared in the wider popular imagination: it simply remained limited to the few evil men at the top. There was a continuing fascination with Hitler and his supposed nearly magical capacity to ensnare and captivate innocent Germans, whose will was appropriated and entirely absorbed into his, effectively absolving them of any responsibility while blinded in this way. In popular perceptions, the central role of Hitler was further buttressed during the so-called 'Hitler-wave' by numerous films and trade publications in the 1970s, while the figure of 'the perpetrator' as a deviant figure was consolidated and reinforced by the fascination with the psychopathology of powerful Nazis.

Yet all this was increasingly at odds with wider developments in social history and the history of everyday life from the 1970s, with shifts of historiographical emphasis in understanding National Socialism. Since the 1960s, a focus on 'Hitler's social revolution', and on the significance of class, had become influential for analysing wider social support for the Nazi party on the one hand, and its ruthless persecution of communist and socialist opponents on the other.[6] Social and economic structures assumed much greater importance, with a renewed interest also in the pre-war analyses of fascism and modernity. Notions of culpability for Nazism started to broaden, albeit along class lines, with the lower-middle classes coming in for particular criticism, alongside a politically tinged search for traces of resistance among the subjugated working classes. Religion was highlighted in relation to Catholics, whose commitment to the Centre Party supposedly made them more 'resistant' to the lures of Nazism. Yet societal history left little room for culture and mentalities.

Even the debates in the 1980s between 'intentionalists', who reiterated the key role of Hitler's intentions, and 'structuralists' or 'functionalists', in seeking to explain the Holocaust did not significantly broaden the location of agency: the intentionalists retained the primary focus on the key men at the top of a totalitarian pyramid, while the functionalists explored the significance of a 'polycratic' system where individual agency seemed at risk of disappearing behind the more abstract notion of 'cumulative radicalisation'. These remained largely debates among specialists, with little popular resonance (it could be said that on occasion the early proponents of the functionalist side were well-nigh unintelligible to lay audiences). Meanwhile historical apologetics and refusal to acknowledge popular complicity were evident in the so-called 'historians' controversy' (*Historikerstreit*) in West Germany (1986–7), as conservatives sought to reawaken a sense of German national pride by suggesting that the evils of Stalinism were both prior to and in some way also causative of Nazism as a pre-emptive, self-defensive (and hence implicitly justifiable) response.[7] In this debate it is notable that some historians on the right echoed popular discourses from the time, prioritizing empathy with soldiers battling against Bolshevism on the Eastern Front over the prolongation of suffering in the concentration camps.[8]

All this began to change with the passage of generations. A near consensus has emerged incorporating the significance of Hitler within a structure now generally viewed as polycratic, with recent research exploring the dynamism of interactions between local and regional initiatives and central directives, and restoring agency to multiple different arenas and actors. At the same time, from the 1980s research into widespread accommodation (*Anpassung*) in everyday life served also to challenge earlier class-based analyses. Analyses of popular opinion began to demonstrate the complexities of people's often partial, self-interested and largely pragmatic responses to Nazism, and the significance of indifference to the fates of 'others'.[9] Research pointing to the centrality of race to the reorganization of German society[10] effectively broadened the scope of who could be considered complicit with Nazi crimes. These analyses dramatically widened the scope of culpability, a shift that was further radicalized during the 1990s. Not only were perpetrators of extreme violence now seen as 'ordinary men', but 'ordinary Germans' could be seen as potential perpetrators, as complicit or as beneficiaries, even if they were not ideologically antisemitic.[11] The Wehrmacht exhibition, which reflected research findings that had been well known among historians for years, seemed to be an eye-opener for many lay visitors.[12] But yet again, the views of historians did not necessarily map neatly onto popular responses.

It is apparent that controversies over interpretations of the Nazi past were also highly sensitive and contentious matters in the later present, touching as they did on the raw nerves of self-representations and perceptions of others in the family and community. This was the case even as historiographical approaches shifted again with the so-called 'cultural turn'. The research into the '*Volksgemeinschaft*' from the 2000s onwards pointed towards the ways in which racist ideology co-existed with a future vision of commonality and opportunity for members of the national community. The fact that individuals, as well as groups and professions, variously opted to take advantage of the opportunities offered by the regime for their own purposes, or 'self-empowerment', once again brought people's agency and choices into the foreground.[13] And increasingly it became clear that it was not only men who were implicated: a growing focus on questions of gender began to complicate earlier controversies over women's subjection under Nazism as well as more active complicity and involvement in Nazi occupation policies and even genocide.[14] Perhaps one of the most significant shifts in recent decades has been the growing internationalization of historical debates in the wake of major geopolitical developments, increased mobility, technological advancements and scholarly trends towards transnational and comparative studies. The focus of 'perpetrator research' has expanded massively beyond a parochial focus on 'the Germans', with growing interest in patterns of collaboration across Europe, while a concern with broader comparisons has brought debates over colonialism and genocides elsewhere to the fore.[15]

These broad historiographical developments, often overlapping or differing in emphasis or returning to and reinvigorating previous research, have different implications for understanding perpetration and complicity. The relationship of structure and agency is key, as is the conceptualization of the individual and identity that informs them. The summary of general historiographical trends suggests an initial focus on individual agency (which has proved persistent, particularly in popular approaches to Nazis), but generally agency limited to a powerful elite or a few significant opponents of the regime (such as the mostly conservative July Plotters); through a subsequent shift to primarily structural explanations in which the individual's causal role in events is minimized; to an emergent re-animation of the notion of agency, now distributed more broadly across the population. The understanding of what constitutes structure and agency has shifted. Theories of totalitarianism, themselves politically informed by Cold War politics, have been partially displaced by inquiries into the nature of dictatorship, be that a polycratic regime or a 'consensual dictatorship'. The significance of the state structure has been complicated by studies of institutions, state or non-state, and the structures of groups and their dynamics, within which individuals situate themselves and derive a sense of agency. The notion of agency has also developed and remains contested. Initially placed in a zero-sum relationship to structure, where agency is diminished in direct proportion to the power of the state structures, it has increasingly been understood to be more relational, with individuals making decisions informed by often competing senses of belonging (to family, locality, religious community, professional group, class, for example). Furthermore, apparent choices may disguise the extent to which an individual's sense of self and agency is constructed through social processes and discourse, where, for example, modes of collective participation are affirmed as manifestations of individual agency.

So where might this book be situated in relation to contemporary developments? With broader relevance beyond the German context, asking the question about compromised identities as a heuristic starting point offers an analytical framework that encompasses three crucial dimensions. First, it facilitates exploration of the relationships between subjective perceptions, emotions, sense of individual and collective identity, and wider social and structural circumstances; how people are inevitably shaped by the societies within which they make their lives, and which, in turn, affect their perceptions and interpretations of the violence that may be escalating all around them. Second, it emphasizes the importance of people's perceptions of themselves and their actions over time and how these changing perceptions influence the ways in which violence and its consequences are understood. The shifting comprehension of perpetration and complicity is in constant tension with the desire to maintain a stable, positive narrative of self, be that individual or collective. Third, the question extends to those, including the researcher, who inhabit a position that aspires to be and/or can appear to be distant from violence, be that temporal or geographical. This position too brings with it the aspiration to be uncompromised, personally and professionally, which influences how questions are framed or indeed which questions are shied away from.

Thinking about compromised identities in this way reinforces the importance of moving away from the term 'perpetrator', which assigns a unitary identity, to understanding 'perpetration'. 'Perpetration' better reflects the complexity of inflicting harm: the fact that most individuals perpetrate violence under specific conditions and then return to 'normal' life; the fact that an individual may be many more things than just a perpetrator, even a victim in another situation; the fact that there is no one type of person who is a perpetrator. To use 'perpetration' also better reflects the narratives of those who have themselves perpetrated violence. They do not recognize themselves as perpetrators and to label them as such can hinder an analysis of their self-representation and concurrently reinforce the 'tacit agreement' that helps position others as innocent, or, in the case of historians and critics, as impartial.[16]. Nevertheless, by retaining identity as a central analytic term, the book emphasizes the ways in which the desire for positive and coherent identity narratives contribute to the mobilization of individuals for mass violence, the ways in which involvement is understood or denied at the time and later, and how those narratives are interpreted and represented in the present. To this extent, agency remains an important term, precisely because it invokes the realm of moral responsibility, as those who defend themselves against charges of perpetration and complicity well know when they seek to underplay their scope for action. This is no naïve invocation, however, that would disregard the critiques of the sovereign rational moral subject made from all angles, including from within philosophy, psychoanalysis, evolutionary psychology, sociology and more recently by feminist posthumanists. It is, rather, to insist on the importance of actions, individual and collective, as well as responsibility for the consequences of actions, and not to re-introduce static subject positions (the implicated subject, the complicit subject) out of renewed concern with structure.

Our approach, then, is in and of itself part of a wider development in which the locus of power and action has been increasingly dispersed, and within which we seek to rescue rather than jettison agency and identity as they relate to wider structures and situational factors. Recognizing the entanglement, implication or complicity of large sections of society in a system of state-sponsored, collective violence persisting over a long period of time raises questions about the capacity for choice – let alone meaningful choice – amid existing and emerging structures and systems of sociopolitical stratification. Rather than consider everyone as virtually equally culpable, complicit or 'implicated', we propose teasing out crucial distinctions and the fluidity of positioning along an ever-shifting spectrum of involvement. What this analytic framework does not do is affirm a distinct and intelligible link between identity, self-awareness, moral culpability and responsibility. Feeling compromised or refusing to feel compromised in one's identity, individual or collective, is no indication of people's willingness to be active or complicit in perpetrating violence or of how they will respond to their involvement. The juxtaposition of the victim of violence whose sense of identity has been utterly undermined and compromised with those whose self-regard has barely been touched by involvement in collective violence, is an injustice that continues to play out in many situations. So continuing to ask questions about how situational dynamics interact with personal value systems, how inner conceptions of the good self interrelate with outer constraints and pressures, remains vital, even if links between identity and (moral) responsibility at all levels remain as malleable as the narratives being scrutinized and newly fashioned.

If the final invocation to continue to ask questions feels like a repeat of so many other conclusions, then so it is. But this does not undermine its importance, even if there is something Sisyphus-like about it. As Imre Kertész's narrator says at the conclusion of *Fiasco*: 'One must imagine Sisyphus happy, the tale runs. Most assuredly.' For, he goes on, 'in the end [the stone] wears down'.[17]

Notes

1 Varlam Shalamov, *Kolyma Stories*, trans. Donald Rayfield (New York: New York Review Books, 2018), 176.
2 Noted already by critical historians outside Germany; cf. for example Gerald Reitlinger, *The SS. Alibi of a Nation 1922–1945* (London: Arms and Armour Press, 1981; orig. 1956).
3 Cf. for example K. D. Bracher, *The German Dictatorship: The Origins, Structure and Consequences of National Socialism* (New York, Praeger, 1970; orig. 1969).
4 See for example Rüdiger Hols and Konrad Jarausch (eds), *Versäumte Fragen: Deutsche Historiker im Schatten des Nationalsozialismus* (Munich: DVA, 2000).
5 Discussed in further detail in Mary Fulbrook, *German National Identity after the Holocaust* (Cambridge: Polity Press, 1999), where additional references may be found.
6 The seminal text exploring the disjuncture between 'ideology' and 'social reality' in the Nazi Germany was David Schoenbaum, *Hitler's Social Revolution* (London: Weidenfeld and Nicolson, 1967; orig. 1966); for subsequent developments, see for example the influential work of Tim Mason, *Social Policy in the Third Reich: The Working Class and the 'National Community'* (New York: Berg, 1993; orig. German 1977).
7 See contributions reprinted in Peter Baldwin (ed.), *Reworking the Past. Hitler, the Holocaust and the Historians' Dispute* (Boston: Beacon Press, 1990).
8 Andreas Hillgruber, *Zweierlei Untergang: Die Zerschlagung des Deutschen Reiches und das Ende des europäischen Judentums* (Berlin: Siedler, 1986).
9 The work of British historian Ian Kershaw was pioneering in this area; see particularly Ian Kershaw, *Popular Opinion and Political Dissent in the Third Reich. Bavaria, 1933–45* (Oxford: Oxford University Press, 1983); and Ian Kershaw, *The 'Hitler Myth'. Image and Reality in the Third Reich* (Oxford: Oxford University Press, 1987). So too was the work of Israeli historian David Bankier, *The Germans and the Final Solution. Public*

Opinion under Nazism (Oxford: Blackwell, 1992), indicating the growing significance of international exchanges for German historiography at this time.

10 Michael Burleigh and Wolfgang Wippermann, *The Racial State: Germany 1933–1945* (Cambridge: Cambridge University Press, 1991).

11 Contrast Christopher Browning's pioneering *Ordinary Men* (London: Harper Perennial, 1998) with Daniel J. Goldhagen's *Hitler's Willing Executioners: Ordinary Germans and the Holocaust* (New York: Alfred A. Knopf 1996).

12 See also chapters 8 and 17 in this volume.

13 Michael Wildt, *Volksgemeinschaft als Selbstermächtigung: Gewalt gegen Juden in der Deutsch Provinz, 1919–1939* (Hamburg: Hamburger Edition, 2007). The title of the English version does not quite capture this: *Hitler's Volksgemeinschaft and the Dynamics of Racial Exclusion. Violence against Jews in Provincial Germany, 1919–1939* (New York: Berghahn, 2012; trans. Bernard Heise).

14 Approaches in this field have developed from the pioneering work on women in Nazi Germany by Jill Stephenson, through the controversies among feminist historians unleashed by, for example, Claudia Koonz, to recent work on women in the occupied territories by Elizabeth Harvey, Wendy Lower, and others.

15 See for example Devin O. Pendas, Mark Roseman, and Richard F. Wetzell (eds), *Beyond the Racial State: Rethinking Nazi Germany* (Cambridge: Cambridge University Press, 2017).

16 Imre Kertész, *Fiasco*, trans. Tim Wilkinson (New York: Melville, 2011 [1988]), 305.

17 Ibid., 361.

Index

accomplices   8–11, 45, 47, 53–61, 67, 166, 189–91
agency   1, 2, 10, 159, 166, 219, 271–4
aliyah   134
Allende, Salvador   213
allies   5, 159, 162, 174
ambivalence   2, 26, 40, 53–6, 62, 147, 168
Amsterdam   222
Anderson, Kjell   5
antisemitism   4, 36, 44, 46, 71, 72, 74, 89, 92, 131, 253, 261, 271–2
apartheid   2, 56
Arab-Israeli War   134
Arendt, Hannah   2, 3, 55, 222
Argentina   205–16
Argentina, Dirty War   205, 215
Aryan   4, 36, 40, 41, 44, 45, 71, 101, 107, 108, 152, 161, 260
Austria   44, 100, 107, 240 1, 252, 260–2
  as "First victim of the Nazis"   5
  Austrian media   173–83
  Austrian perpetrators   105, 113–15, 119, 123–4
auxiliaries   35, 86, 87, 90, 91, 261

Bacchae   61
Balkans   122
Baranovichi   91, 92
Bauman, Zygmund   14, 219–31
  Modernity and the Holocaust   219–24, 227, 231–2
Becker, August   225
Belarus   11, 85–94, 101–6
Benbassa, Esther   133
beneficiaries   192
Beneš, Evard   57, 58
Berger, Karl Friedrich   28
Berlin   105, 116, 178, 221, 245, 251–2
Black Panthers   214
Bobruisk   94
Bolivia   214

Bomba, Abraham   224, 231
Borisov   85
Breaking the Silence   129–32, 137–9
Breithaupt, Fritz   24
Brooks, Peter   32
Browning, Christopher   146, 223, 224
brutalization   118
Budapest   207–8
Budapest Rescue and Aid Committee   219, 226
Buenos Aires   207, 210–12
bureaucracy   2, 46, 62, 67, 220–1, 225, 255
bystanders   9, 10, 35–9, 68–75, 86, 160, 166–7
  "Innocent bystander"   15, 35, 40, 44
bystanding   9–11, 38, 44, 67–75, 260
  Bystander effect   71
  Bystander society   44, 47, 71

camps
  Auschwitz   28–9, 57, 74, 104, 153, 221, 229
  Auschwitz trial (Frankfurt)   177
  Bergen Belsen   28
  Buchenwald   251–2
  Chełmno   223–5, 251
  extermination camps   175
  Janowska concentration camp   25
  Majdanek   28, 104, 180
  Maly Trostenets   105
  Mauthausen   252
  Neuengamme   28, 252
  Operation Reinhardt   174–9
  Ravensbrück   252
  Sachsenhausen   251
  Salaspils   251
  Sobibor   178
  Stutthof   30, 104
  Theresienstadt   57
  Treblinka   175–81, 221, 224, 231, 252
  Treblinka trial (Düsseldorf)   177

Westerbork 242
Caracciola-Delbrück, Günther 164
Castro, Fidel 214
CDU 181
Channel Islands 244
Chayut, Noam 130–40
Chayut, Noam, *The Girl Who Stole My Holocaust* 130–2, 137
Chicago 214
Chile 13, 14, 187–97, 213
   Appeals Court 188–91, 194
   Civil claims 187, 189, 192–3
   Coup 193
   Criminal code 189
   Direccion de Inteligencia Nacional 189
   Junta 194
   National College of Journalists 194
   Naval Museum 194
   Supreme Court 188, 190, 195
   Treasury 192
cinema 105
Cleveland 214
Clingman, Stephen 2, 3
coercion 8, 70, 152
Coesfeld (Westphalia) 161
cognitive dissonance 6, 10, 39, 44, 73, 131, 138
Cold War 5, 12, 47, 72, 86, 207, 222, 251, 273
collaboration 57, 87, 92, 191, 227–9, 238–45, 273
   in eastern Europe 46, 87, 206
   in Vichy France 2
collaborators 35, 42, 57, 72, 147, 197, 237–42, 259
   in Belarus 85–9
collective
   farms (kolkhoz) 91, 105
   guilt 3, 36
   violence 1, 4, 8, 15–16, 24, 37–44, 47, 258–9, 274–5
communism 36, 40, 47, 92, 152, 209, 215, 216
   anti-Communism 208–16, 261
   communist resisters 251, 271
   post-communism 47, 59
communities 5–7, 42–3, 58, 75, 90–1, 123, 159–69

blood-community (*Blutsgemeinschaft*) 151–2
communities of empathy 41, 46, 48
community aliens 148, 215
immigrant communities 74
Jewish communities 67–8, 88, 90, 215, 222
National Community (*Volksgemeinschaft*) 4–8, 36, 40–6, 68–72, 99–101, 150–2, 159–69, 260
religious communities 39, 273
compliance 10, 39–48, 68, 260
complicity 1–16, 35–9, 42–8, 55, 219–20, 250–62
   in Belarus 86–94
   in Chile 190
   etymologic roots 2
   in Hungary 205–6, 216
   in literature 21–3, 31–2, 52–4, 57, 61–2, 129–32, 137–9
   and Nazi law 147–50, 155
   notion of complicity 8, 9, 219–20
   portrayed in museums 235–48
compromise 3, 4, 7, 13, 14, 21, 22, 39
concentration camps 134, 165
conformity 5, 10, 35–48, 101, 160, 163, 169, 260–1, 270
consent 35, 70
cooperation 219
Córdoba (Argentina) 205, 210, 214
Council of the Evangelical Church of Germany 174
courts 3, 12–15, 28–31, 115, 123, 159–60, 166–9, 174–82, 187–97
   courtrooms 175–7, 182–3, 262
   German Federal Supreme Court 177, 179
   Inter-American Court of Human Rights (IACtHR) 194
   International Criminal Tribunal for the former Yugoslavia 189
   -martial 13
   summary courts 159–69
Croatia 115
culpability 2, 13–14, 36, 48, 56, 131, 137, 178, 182, 226, 270–2, 275
Czechoslovakia 57, 58, 118

DAF (Deutsche Arbeitsfront)   69
decolonization   214
defeatism   13
dehumanization   90, 116–18, 153, 220–1
denazification   54, 252
Denemarkova, Radka   9, 57, 58, 61
Denemarková, Radka, *Money from Hitler*   9, 52, 57
Denmark   36
denunciations   43, 92, 163, 255, 259
deportation   36, 45–6, 70, 99–100, 105, 108, 210, 221, 227–30, 241–4
Derrida, Jacques   2
Dey, Bruno   30
dictatorship   3, 5, 8–14, 38, 40, 43, 166, 194–6, 260, 270, 273
   Chile   181–3, 187–90
   consensual dictatorship   8, 36, 273
   positive memories of   208, 211, 214–15
disappearances   187, 190
Dopolavoro   100
Dresden   246
Dutch East Company (NOC)   102–3

East Germany (GDR)   74, 251, 253, 260, 262, 271
East Prussia   163
Eastwood, James   136, 139
Egof, David   85, 87, 91
Eichmann, Adolf   173, 181, 226
Einsatzgruppen   35, 44, 90, 260
Einsatzgruppen, Einsatzgruppen trial (Ulm)   177
Émigrés   205–6, 211–13
emotion   1, 14, 22–32, 44–8, 56, 72, 101, 176–8, 253–5
   in the IDF   133–40
   in museums   236–8, 245–8, 266
empathy   10, 23, 24, 56, 236, 241–2
Engelhardt, Eugen von   85
Europe   10, 54–5, 205, 208, 211–16, 238, 260–1
   Central   52, 86, 211, 251
   Eastern   36, 42, 45–7, 52, 57, 62, 69, 72, 85, 94, 102–6, 251
   European-Christian civilisation   12

Holocaust   as European phenomenon   48, 67–9
   Nazi-dominated Europe   35–6, 45–6, 103–6, 134
   WESTERN Europe   36, 46, 104–6, 207, 251
Evian conference   232

Fábryová, Eliška   57
Facilitation   11, 24, 42, 45–7, 191, 210, 219, 250
fascism   12, 59, 95, 100, 205–11, 216, 238, 271
fear   23, 35–6, 59, 99, 136, 163, 260, 270
   as motive to commit violence   7, 39, 153–4, 159, 181, 245, 270
Fiala, Ferenc   207, 215
Flintenweiber ('rifle wenches')   113
forgiveness   9, 24, 25, 27–31
Fraenkel, Ernst   148
France   36, 118, 251
Franz, Kurt   177
Freud, Sigmund   62, 213
Friedländer, Saul   68–9, 253

Gandhi   214
gassings   40, 105, 153, 221–2, 231
gas vans   105, 219–25
gays   145, 161
Gdańsk   239, 242
Gelsenkirchen   165
gender   99, 100, 104, 113
genocide   2, 35–6, 71–5, 107, 158, 250, 261–2
   incitement to genocide   92
   and Israeli identity   133
   and modernity   215, 219–25, 229–32
Gerlach, Christian   53, 162
Germanization   45, 46, 103, 109
Gestapo   21, 47, 178
Ghetto   69, 92, 99, 105–7, 136, 222, 227–8
   Warsaw Ghetto Uprising   255
Ghettoization   46
Gleichschaltung (Coordination)   54
Goebbels, Joseph   44, 102, 116
Goethe, Johann Wolfgang von   164
Goldhagen, Daniel   253
graphic images   256–7

Great War 208
Gröning, Oskar 30
Grossman, David 23
guilt 2–3, 6, 22–4, 29, 58, 139–40, 166, 179–80
    collective 3, 55
Guilt, Gradations of guilt 36
Gutman, Yifat 129

Haganah 134
Hamburg 99, 104, 107, 108
Hebron 130
Hechtsheim 167
Heer, Hannes 123–4, 160
Heuser, Georg 178
Hilberg, Raul 10, 36, 69, 90, 221–2, 243
Himmler, Heinrich 45, 166, 255
    Flag Order 167
Historikerstreit 272
Hitler, Adolf 7, 26–8, 40, 118, 145, 151, 212, 252, 261, 271
HJ (Hitler Youth) 69, 116, 167
Holland, Luke 259
    Final Account 258
Holocaust 2, 12, 145–54, 206, 219, 235–7, 250–67
    in Belarus 86–94, 99–109
    European Holocaust Research Infrastructure (EHRI) 251
    final solution of the Jewish question 45, 88, 92, 94, 252
    Holocaust by bullets 45, 86, 100, 104
    Holocaust Educational Trust (HET) 256–8
    Holocaust historiography 2, 35, 67–75
    Holocaust Memorial Day Trust 250
    International Holocaust Remembrance Alliance (IHRA) 251, 256
    and Israel 132–9
    'Normality' 221
    Yom Hashoah, Holocaust Memorial Day 133–4
home front 165
Horthy, Miklós 208
human rights violations 187, 194
humiliation 38, 44, 117, 122, 138, 240
Hungary 205–13, 219, 227, 229, 262
    Arrow Cross 207, 209, 215

National Press Chamber 207, 210
Racial defenders' (fajvédők) 208
Supreme Court (*Kúria*) 209

identity 3, 4, 21, 29, 47, 70, 131, 275
ideology 146, 152
implication 1, 3, 12–13, 45, 70, 73–4, 109, 166, 241, 245, 252–3, 259–62, 273–4
IMT (International Military Tribunal, Nuremberg) 148–9, 166, 175, 181, 188
    crimes against humanity 166
    crimes against peace 166
    Nuremberg Trials Memorial 252
    war crimes 166
indifference 4, 28, 41–2, 47–8, 68, 220, 262, 272
International Auschwitz Committee 31
Israel 129–31, 135–9
    Knesset 130
    West Bank 131, 135
    Yom Hazikaron, Memorial Day 134, 137
Israeli Defense Force (IDF) 129–30, 135–9

Jankélévitch, Vladimer 22, 24, 25, 27, 31, 32
Jedwabne 89, 240
Jehova's Witnesses 7
Jelinek, Elfriede 9, 52, 57, 59–62
Jelinek, Elfriede, *Rechnitz (Der Würgeengel)* 52, 57–61
Jerusalem 131
Jews 7–12, 35–8, 44, 118, 153–4, 165, 215, 219–24, 240–5, 257–60
    in Belarus 85–94, 99, 101, 104–8
    Hausjuden (Domestic Jews) 103
    historiography of persecution 67–75, 134
    Judenräte 225–8
    survival chances. 46, 73
journalists 12, 25, 176–7, 180–1, 194, 205–13
judges 151, 160–3, 166, 169, 176–7, 191
Judt, Tony 72
Just, Willy 14, 223–4, 230
justice 12, 26, 28, 29, 31, 149

"Victor's Justice" 173
transitional justice 193–5
justifications 1, 6–12, 45–8, 57–62, 136,
 152–4, 259–62
 ideological justification 24
 of individual acts of violence 113–20,
  124
 justificatory discourses 52–7
 self-justification 36, 42
Justiz und NS-Verbrechen 164

Kasztner, Rezsö 14, 219, 226–31
Kaunas 260
Kertész, Imre 32, 275
Kertész, Imre, *Fiasco* 32
Kesserű, Zsuzsánna Haynalné 210
KGB 87, 88, 94
King, Martin Luther 214
Knittel, Susanne 54
Kolosváry-Borcsa, Mihály 207
Königsberg 163–4
Kor, Eva Moses 30
Kraft durch Freude (KdF, Strength through
 Joy) 99–109
Kremer, Johann Paul 153
Kretschmer, Karl 153–4
Kristallnacht 44, 45, 245, 260
Kube, Anita 103
Kube, Wilhelm 91, 102, 103
Kühl, Stefan 4
Kühne, Thomas 100, 116

Laabs, Gustav 224
Lake Naroch 85, 86
Landau, Felix 153–4
language 9, 23–4, 43, 53–9, 70, 92, 138,
 154, 161, 188, 206, 210–13, 224,
 260, 263, 265
Lanzmann, Claude 14, 219–31
 The Four Sisters 221, 232
Latvia 251, 261
Laval, Pierre 242
Lavigne, Michael 28
 Not Me 28–30
Law 12–15, 40–1, 55, 69, 145–52,
 187–97, 262–3
 common law 152
 criminal law 187
 Enabling Act 145, 148

International law 187–8, 192
legal officials 148
lex praevia 188
Nazi law 145–55
nulla poena sine lege 166
Nuremberg laws 41, 148, 210
perversion of 12, 13, 145
Reichstag Fire Decree 145, 148
Roman law 151
rule of law 151
lawyers 145, 177
Lévi, Primo 54
liability 3, 8, 13, 60, 187–93, 196–7
Liepāja 257
Lithuania 36, 85, 88, 227, 251, 261
Littell, Jonathan 22
 The Kindly Ones 22
Łódź 222
looting 44, 106
Loth, Peter 30
Lower, Wendy 100, 259
Lukashenko, Alexander 88
Luzoro, Juan 190

magazines 173–5
 Bridgehead (Hídfő) 207, 215
 Chronicle (Krónika) 207, 210
 Der Spiegel 30, 31, 175, 180, 183
 Hungarian Path (Magyarok útja) 207,
  211
 We Are Alone (Egyedül
  Vagyunk) 210
Mao Zedong 27
Marxism 12, 211–13
mass
 murder 6–7, 11, 35, 45–6, 85, 90, 92,
  175–82, 219–25, 260–1
 violence 52–4, 56, 59, 60, 109, 193
massacre 62, 85, 91, 191
 Bromberg massacre 257
 Katyn massacre 257
May, Heinrich 225
media 13, 173–82
melodrama 9, 22, 31–32
memoirs 88
memory 25–8, 53–4, 72–5, 131–6, 139,
 177, 179, 215, 231, 255
 agonistic memory 236–9, 247
 antagonistic memory 238–9

collective memory 53, 59, 133, 161, 239–40
memory activism 129–31, 138–40
memory studies 206
nationalized Holocaust memory 133–4
perpetrator memory 205–6, 215–16
sites of memory 251, 253
Menasse, Eva 61
Dunkelblum 61
Mengele, Josef 30
Miami 214
Milotay, István 209
Minsk 6, 85, 92–4, 99–109, 178
Mittelstand 163
modernity 14, 55, 219–32, 271
Mogilev 93
morality 39, 114, 151–3, 230\
immorality 149
moral judgement 4, 53, 56, 121
Munich 164, 207
museums 235–47, 250
Bundeswehr Military History Museum, Dresden 243, 246
Compromised Identities? 240–1
Curators 235
'Eagle's Nest' 252
Imperial War Museum 251
Jewish Museum, London 255
Mémorial de Caen (Memorial Museum Caen) 240–2
Muzeum II Wojny Światowej (MIIWŚ, Museum of the Second World War) 239–45
National Holocaust Centre and Museum, Laxton 255
Representing complicity 235–6
Schöneweide Forced Labour Documentation Centre 252
'Some Were Neighbors' 254
Topography of Terror 245, 252
United States Holocaust Memorial Museum (USHMM) 245, 251, 254
University of Huddersfield Holocaust Exhibition and Learning Centre 251, 266
Verzetsmuseum (Dutch Resistance Museum) 239, 242
Villa ten Hompel 252, 256
Visitors 235–7, 242
Wannsee villa 252
Yad Vashem 251, 256
Mussert, Anton 242
Mussolini, Benito 208

Nakba 129, 131
Nederlandse Unie (Netherlands Union) 239
neighbours 75
Some were Neighbors 75
Netherlands 36, 73, 239, 242, 244
newspapers 173–6
Daily Mail 31
Die Welt 31
Die ZEIT 31, 173, 178–82
El Mercurio 194
Frankfurter Allgemeine Zeitung 175–80
Frankfurter Neue Presse 182
Frankfurter Rundschau 179
Hamburger Morgenpost 31
The Hungarian (Magyarság) 205–9, 213
Israeli newspapers 177
La Segunda 194
Le Monde 25
New York Times 139
Rheinische Post 176
Süddeutsche Zeitung 31
The Times of Israel 31
NKVD 85
NSB 239, 242
NSDAP 47, 102, 115, 151–2, 174
Gauleiter 102, 162
Kreisleiter 161, 163
Ortsgruppenleiter 164
party officials 162–3

obedience 14, 181, 220, 230–2
occupation 6, 10–11, 52, 57–9, 69–73, 85–94, 99–106, 120, 206–10, 238–45
Palestinian Occupied Territories 129–39
Oláh, György 12, 205–16
receives Order of the German Eagle 210
Operation Last Chance 27, 31
Organization Todt (OT) 106, 174

Orwell, George 131
Osiel, Mark 188, 192

Palestine 129, 136, 139
  occupied Palestinian Territories 129–31, 139
Palestinians 129–32, 135, 137
partisans 6, 86, 87, 99, 101, 113–21, 257, 260
Pauer-Studer, Herlinde 151–3
Peer Group pressure 35
Pekić, Borislav 21–3
Pekić, Borislav, *How to Quiet a Vampire* 21
Peron, Juan 213
perpetration 8, 14, 15, 23, 108, 113, 176, 235, 250–1, 259, 270, 274
perpetrators 1–16, 37–8, 45–8, 60–1, 134, 146–54, 187–96, 223–5, 261, 270
  age profile 22, 27–9, 163
  artists 162
  behaviour 116–22
  in Belarus 85–8, 91, 94, 100
  civilians as perpetrators 190–2
  empathizing with 22–3, 32, 56, 236–47
  historiography of 67–74, 139
  immediate perpetrators 35–8, 45
  Late-war violence 159–69
  perpetrator memory 205–6, 215–16
  perpetrator society 36–7
  persecuted perpetrator 133
  representation of perpetrators 22
  on trial 166–9, 173–83
  'uncompromising generation' 163
  as "victims" 118, 177, 225, 244
perpetrator society 36, 47
persecution 1, 67, 86, 88
Picault, Jodi, *The Storyteller* 28–30
Picoult, Jodi 28, 29, 32
Pinochet, Augusto 189
Pittsburgh 214
Podlasie region 89
Poland 36, 45, 89, 118, 134–5, 160, 225, 227, 240, 244, 257
police 45, 47, 100, 167, 261
Posen speech 45
Priluki 103

propaganda 89, 100–1, 108, 154, 161, 193–4, 207, 215, 242–3, 256
property 91–4

Radio Liberty 85
Ram, Uri 133
rape 6, 115, 134, 257
rationalization 5–6, 8, 72, 122, 176
Rauff, Walter 223–5
Red Army 60, 87, 108, 113, 114, 207
Red Cross 99, 103, 232, 270
rehabilitation 121, 178, 261–2
Reich Labour Service 42
Reich Ministry for the Occupied Eastern Territories 85
Reich Ministry of Propaganda 101
Reichsbahn 222
Reich Security Main Office (RSHA) 252
Reich Theatre Train 107
remorse 23–5, 28, 32, 130, 132, 261
Renno, Georg 182
rescuers 74, 254, 261
resistance 6, 36, 43, 47, 93, 239–45, 251, 254, 262
  encountered by German troops 119–20
  narratives of 21, 22, 36, 87
  by Palestinians 136–8
revenge 26
Riddagshausen 163
Riga 251
Rohingya 262
Roma ('gypsies') 35, 145, 161, 260
Rome–Berlin Axis 206
Römer, Felix 113
Roosevelt, Eleanor 245
Rosenberg, Heinz 106–7
Rothberg, Michael 3
Rothberg, Michael, *The Implicated Subject* 3, 38, 274
Rumbula 251
Russian Empire 89

SA (Sturmabteilung) 69
sadism 92
Salisco, Alfred 164
Sander, Mark 2
Sémelin, Jacques 53, 60
Sereny, Gitta 177
Shakespeare 101
  The Merchant of Venice 101, 108

Shalamov, Varlam   270
Shoah   14, 59, 134, 219–22, 230–2, 259
Slovenia   115
Social Identity Theory   72
solidarity   221
Sonderkommando   230
Soviet Union   86–92, 101, 106, 160, 244
spectators   165–8, 180
Srebrnik, Simon   224
SS   28–31, 69, 100–1, 105, 109, 113, 118, 136, 271
  Waffen-SS   113, 123
Stalin, Joseph   27
Stalinism   36, 272
Stangl, Franz   177–83
  Play *Commandant in Treblinka- The obedient life of Franz Stangl*   181
Stankevich, Stanislav   85, 94
Steiner, George   22, 26, 27
  The Portage to San Cristóbal of A. H.   22, 26, 27
Stepanova, Maria   52
  In Memory of Memory   52
Stollberg   161
Stolleis, Michael   148–9
Stolzfus, Nathan   7
Stone, Dan   150, 155
Stroop, Jürgen   255
Suchomel, Franz   224
summary executions   159–69
Switzerland   226

T4 'euthanasia' programme   7, 174, 180, 182, 225, 252, 259–60
teachers   162
television   174
terror   35–7, 40, 52, 60, 148, 159
  Legal terror   146
testimony   238
Theologians   177
Toronto   214
Torres, Juan José   214
torture   21–3, 70, 75, 189, 191, 214–15, 257
totalitarianism   55–7, 62, 162, 271, 273
Totschweigen (Wall of Silence)   60
tragedy   59, 60, 62, 227
trauma   7, 60, 257

trials   13, 31, 181–2
Tucholsky, Kurt   37

UCL Centre for Holocaust Education   250
Ukraine   88
United States   213
Uruguay   213

Verdeja, Ernesto   4
veterans   7, 87, 113–24, 137–9, 261
  IDF veterans   11, 129–32
Vichy France   2, 240
victimhood   133–4
victims   14, 35–8, 41–8, 60–2, 71–4, 190–6, 250, 253, 266
  cooperation with violence   54, 57, 219, 222–5
  Germans as victims   13, 160, 176–8, 183
  Jewish victims   12, 14, 86, 91–4, 133–9, 161
  social outsiders   10, 38, 145, 160–1, 165
  of summary courts   166–7
  victim narratives   7
Vienna   105, 114, 124
Vileyka   92
village elders   91
village populations   88
Vilnius (Vilna)   222, 228
Vinkovci   119
violence   1, 8, 35, 38, 44, 47, 52, 54, 62, 69, 70, 113, 146, 152, 193, 255, 259, 274
  collective violence   16, 275
  direct violence   159, 270
  gendered violence   113–24
  German-versus-German violence   160
  motivations   39, 88, 159–61, 270
  representations of   1, 6
  transgressive violence   123–4
  violence against women   11, 113–24
Volkssturm   161, 163
Vrba, Rudolf   227

Wachsmann, Nikolaus   148
war crimes   8, 25, 148, 166, 207, 238, 266
war of annihilation   120, 260
Warsaw   6, 136, 228

Wehrmacht   5, 7, 11, 35, 44, 74, 100, 101, 109, 113, 114, 116, 123, 154, 241, 246
  battle commander   167
  German High Command   165
  myth of the Clean Wehrmacht   5, 261
  exhibition   117, 123–4, 253
Weidenau   164
Welzer, Harald   4
Werwolf   167
Westermann, Edward   116
West Germany (BRD)   5, 13, 174–83, 207, 215, 246–7, 251, 260–2, 271–2
Wiesenthal, Simon   25–7, 262
  The Sunflower   25, 28, 29

Wildt, Michael   166
Wilhelmshafen   167
Windrush scandal   262
witnesses   10, 15, 31, 35–8, 46, 60–1, 104–6, 119, 124, 130, 160–1, 182–3, 222–30, 241
  witness testimony   13, 166–8, 176–9, 262
Wolfrum, Edgar   164

Yom Kippur   139
Yugoslavia   116

ZDF   31
Zembin   85
Zionism   129–37
Zweig, Arnold   37

www.ingramcontent.com/pod-product-compliance
Lightning Source LLC
Chambersburg PA
CBHW071807300426
44116CB00009B/1232